PLATINUM *garden*

Created by Maki Fujita

Volume 1

TOKYOPOP®

HAMBURG // LONDON // LOS ANGELES // TOKYO

Platinum Garden Volume 1
Created by Maki Fujita

Translation - Egan Loo
English Adaptation - Sarah Dyer
Retouch and Lettering - Erika "Skooter" Terriquez
Cover Design - Anne Marie Horne

Editor - Julie Taylor
Digital Imaging Manager - Chris Buford
Managing Editor - Lindsey Johnston
VP of Production - Ron Klamert
Publisher - Mike Kiley
Editor in Chief - Rob Tokar
President and C.O.O. - John Parker
C.E.O. and Chief Creative Officer - Stuart Levy

A  Manga

TOKYOPOP Inc.
5900 Wilshire Blvd. Suite 2000
Los Angeles, CA 90036

E-mail: info@TOKYOPOP.com
Come visit us online at www.TOKYOPOP.com

ISBN: 1-59816-361-2

First TOKYOPOP printing: June 2006
10 9 8 7 6 5 4 3 2 1
Printed in the USA

PLATINUM garden

Created by Maki Fujita

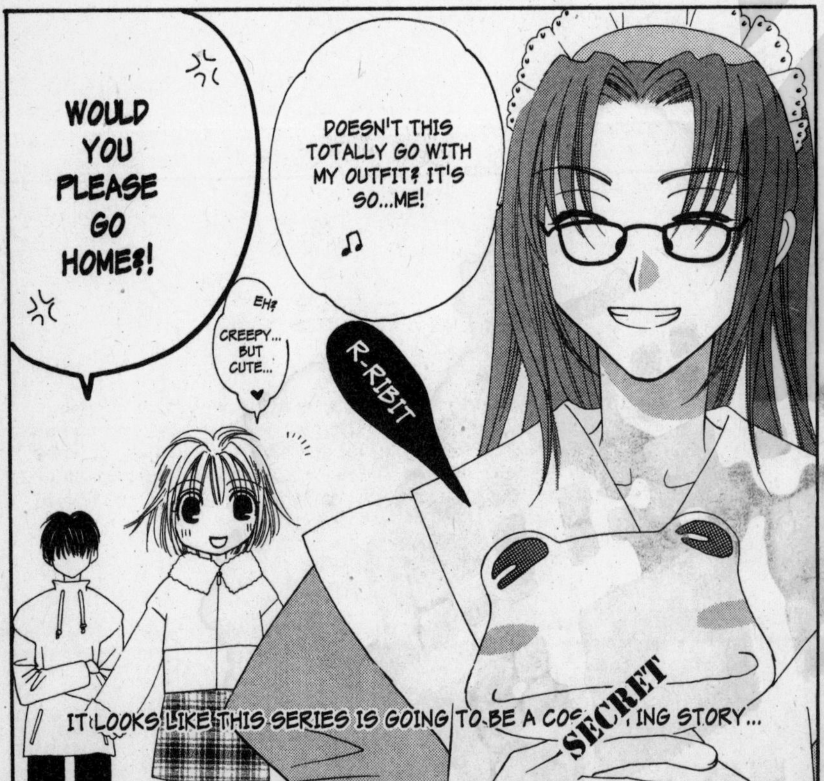
DOESN'T THIS TOTALLY GO WITH MY OUTFIT? IT'S SO...ME! ♫
R-RIBIT
WOULD YOU PLEASE GO HOME?!
EH?
CREEPY... BUT CUTE... ♥
IT LOOKS LIKE THIS SERIES IS GOING TO BE A COS ING STORY...
SECRET

PLATINUM *garden*

Volume: 1
CONTENTS

MIZUKI & KAITO

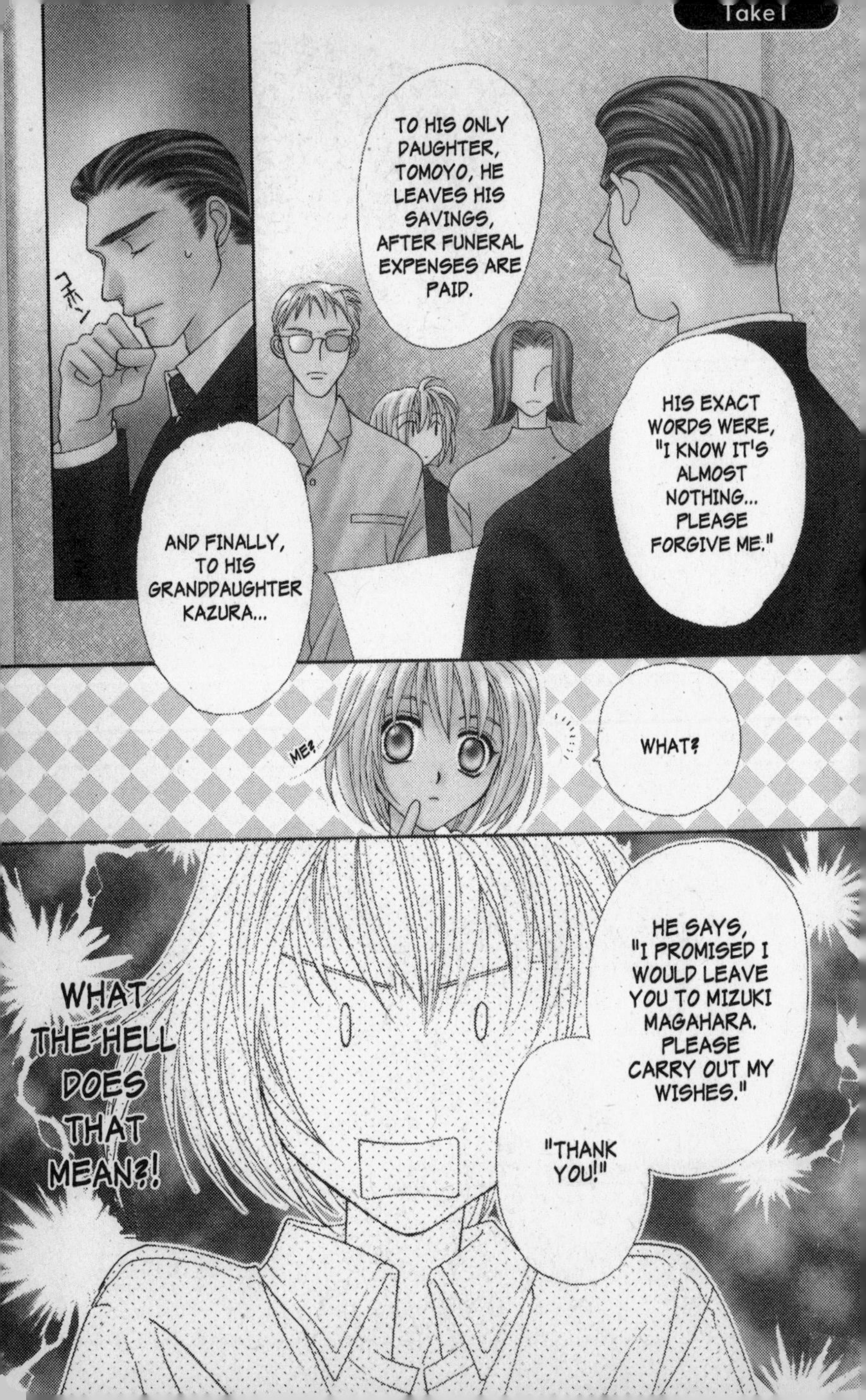
TO HIS ONLY DAUGHTER, TOMOYO, HE LEAVES HIS SAVINGS, AFTER FUNERAL EXPENSES ARE PAID.
HIS EXACT WORDS WERE, "I KNOW IT'S ALMOST NOTHING... PLEASE FORGIVE ME."
コホン
AND FINALLY, TO HIS GRANDDAUGHTER KAZURA...
WHAT?
ME?
HE SAYS, "I PROMISED I WOULD LEAVE YOU TO MIZUKI MAGAHARA. PLEASE CARRY OUT MY WISHES."
"THANK YOU!"
WHAT THE HELL DOES THAT MEAN?!

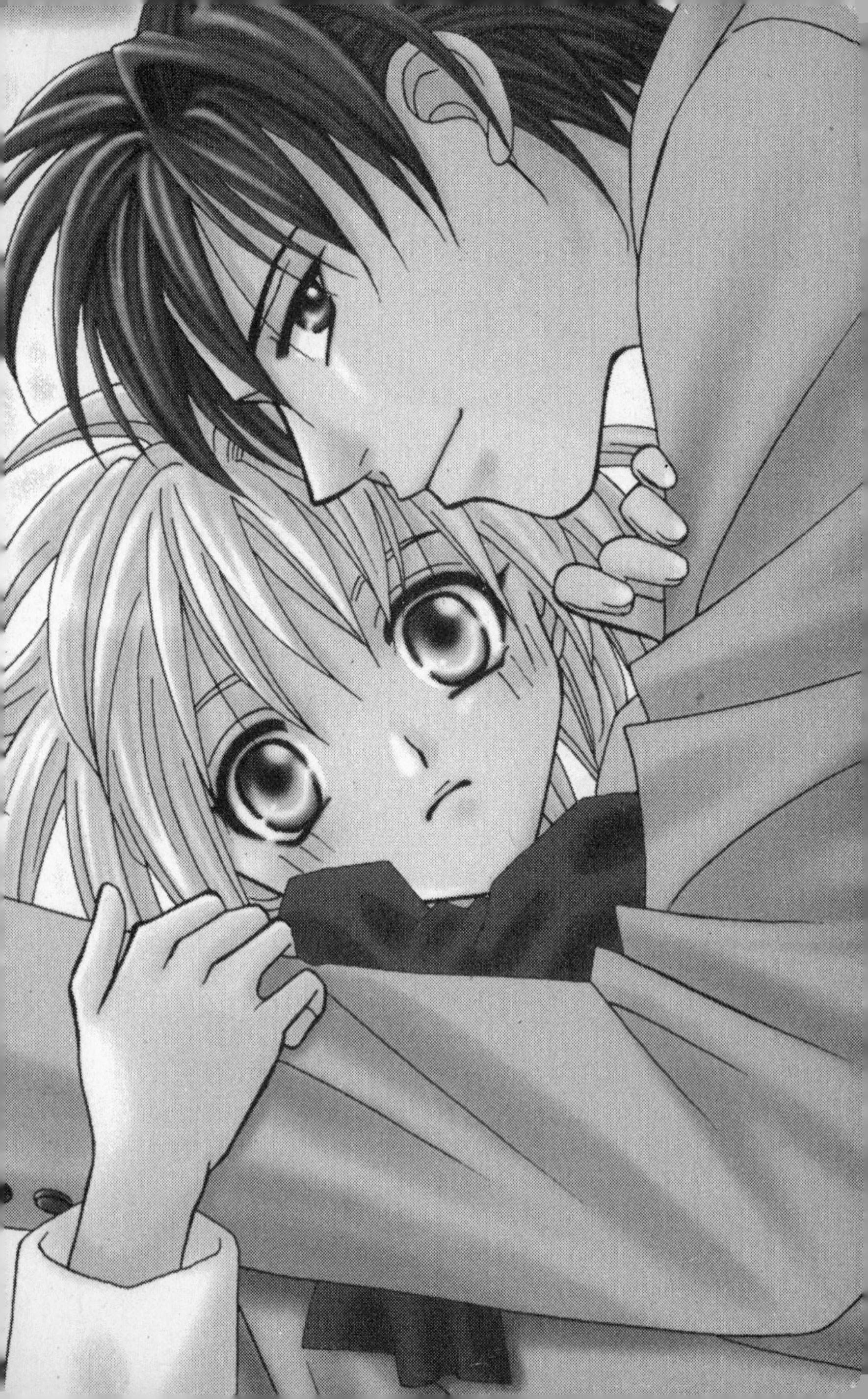

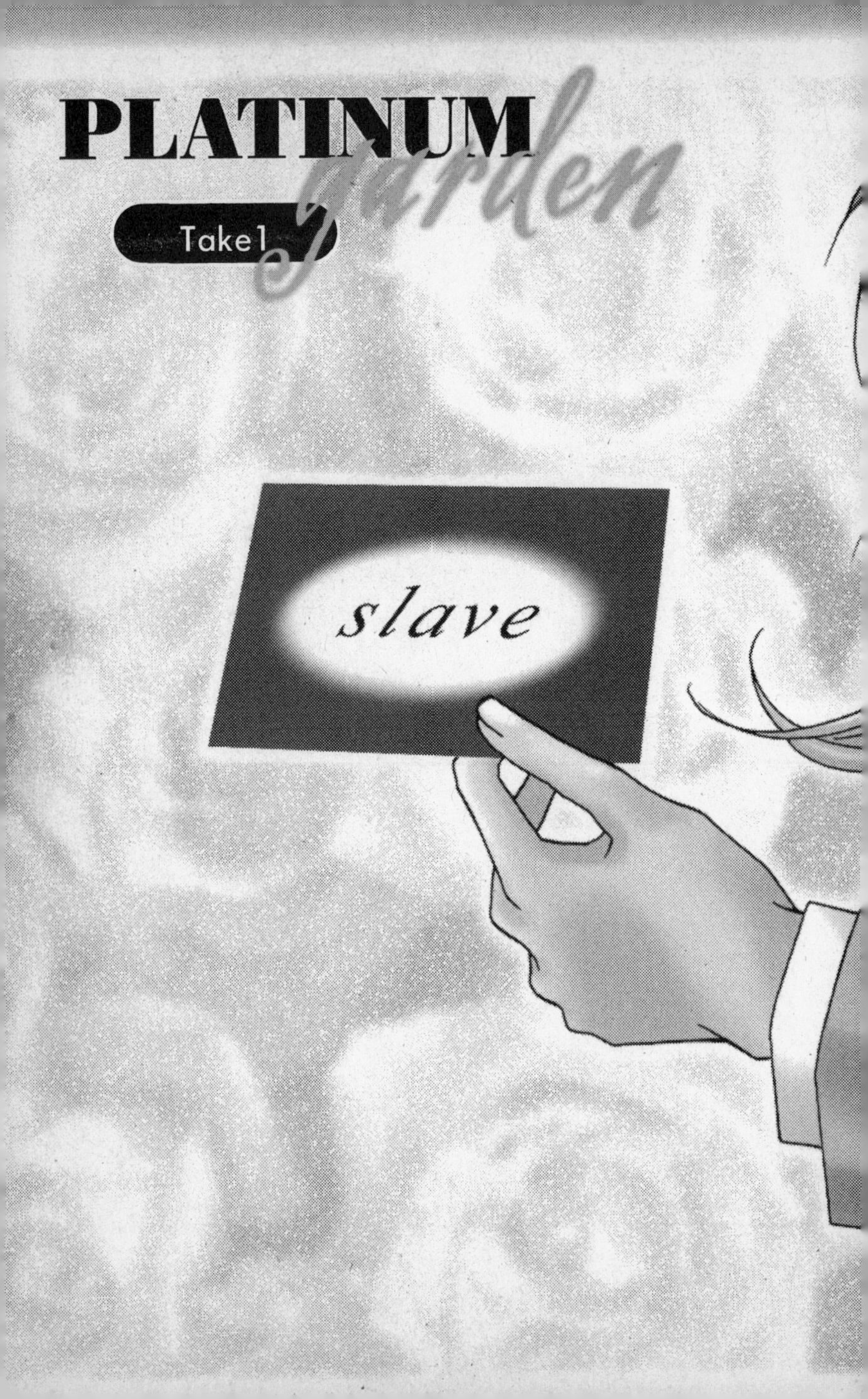
PLATINUM garden
Take 1
slave

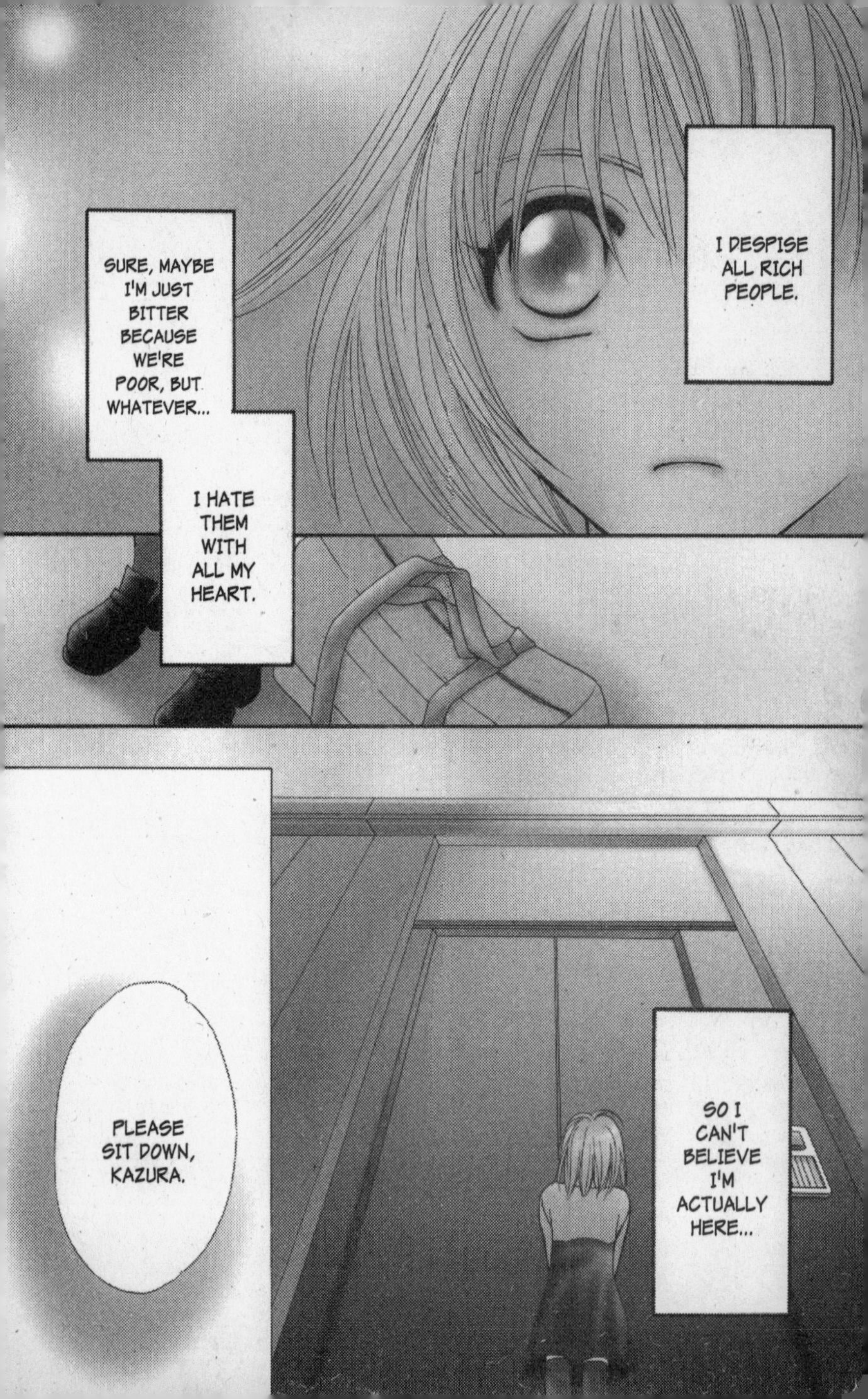
I DESPISE ALL RICH PEOPLE.
SURE, MAYBE I'M JUST BITTER BECAUSE WE'RE POOR, BUT WHATEVER...
I HATE THEM WITH ALL MY HEART.
SO I CAN'T BELIEVE I'M ACTUALLY HERE...
PLEASE SIT DOWN, KAZURA.

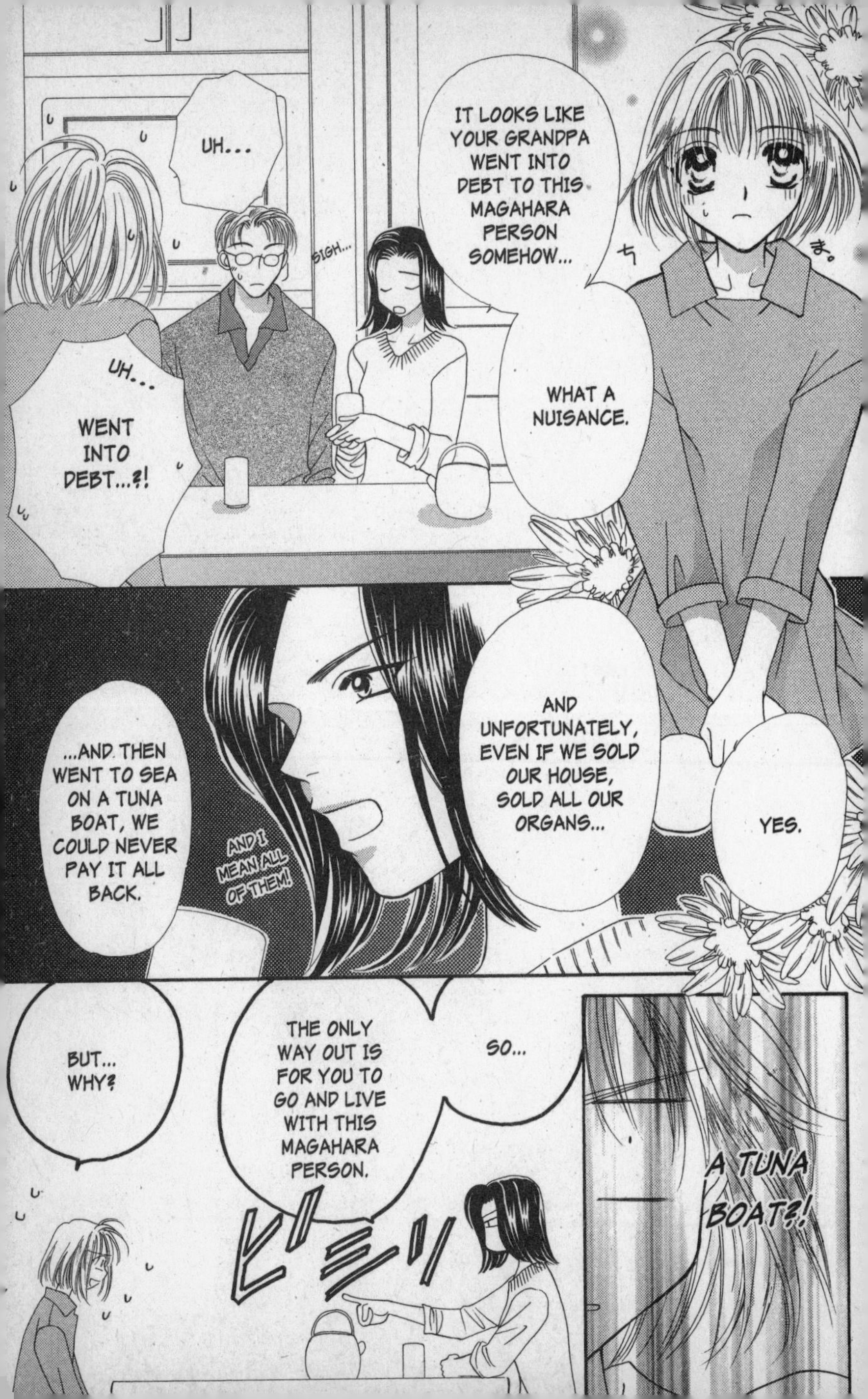
IT LOOKS LIKE YOUR GRANDPA WENT INTO DEBT TO THIS MAGAHARA PERSON SOMEHOW...
UH...
SIGH...
WHAT A NUISANCE.
UH...
WENT INTO DEBT...?!
YES.
AND UNFORTUNATELY, EVEN IF WE SOLD OUR HOUSE, SOLD ALL OUR ORGANS...
AND I MEAN ALL OF THEM!
...AND THEN WENT TO SEA ON A TUNA BOAT, WE COULD NEVER PAY IT ALL BACK.
A TUNA BOAT?!
SO...
THE ONLY WAY OUT IS FOR YOU TO GO AND LIVE WITH THIS MAGAHARA PERSON.
BUT... WHY?

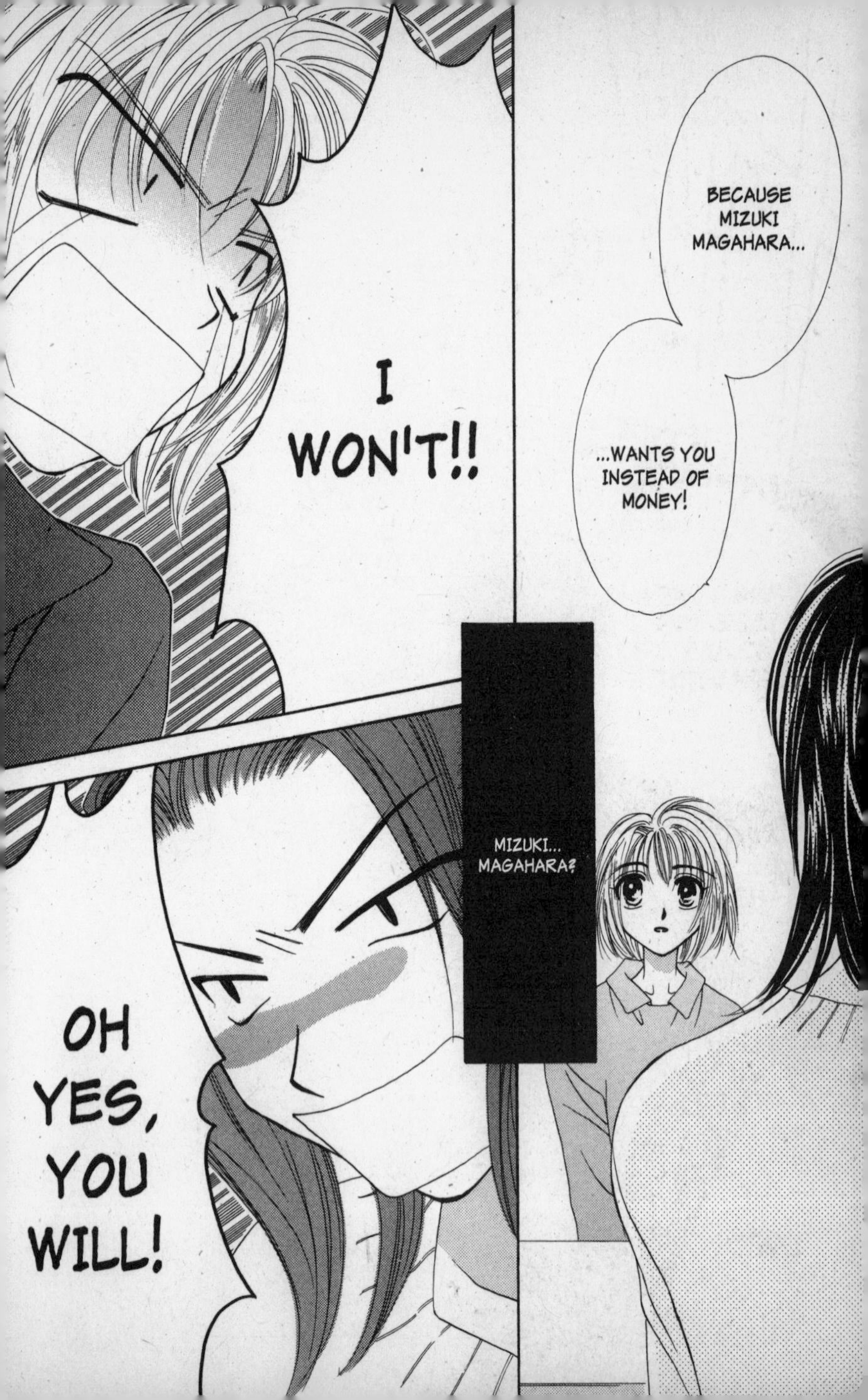
BECAUSE MIZUKI MAGAHARA...
...WANTS YOU INSTEAD OF MONEY!
I WON'T!!
MIZUKI... MAGAHARA?
OH YES, YOU WILL!

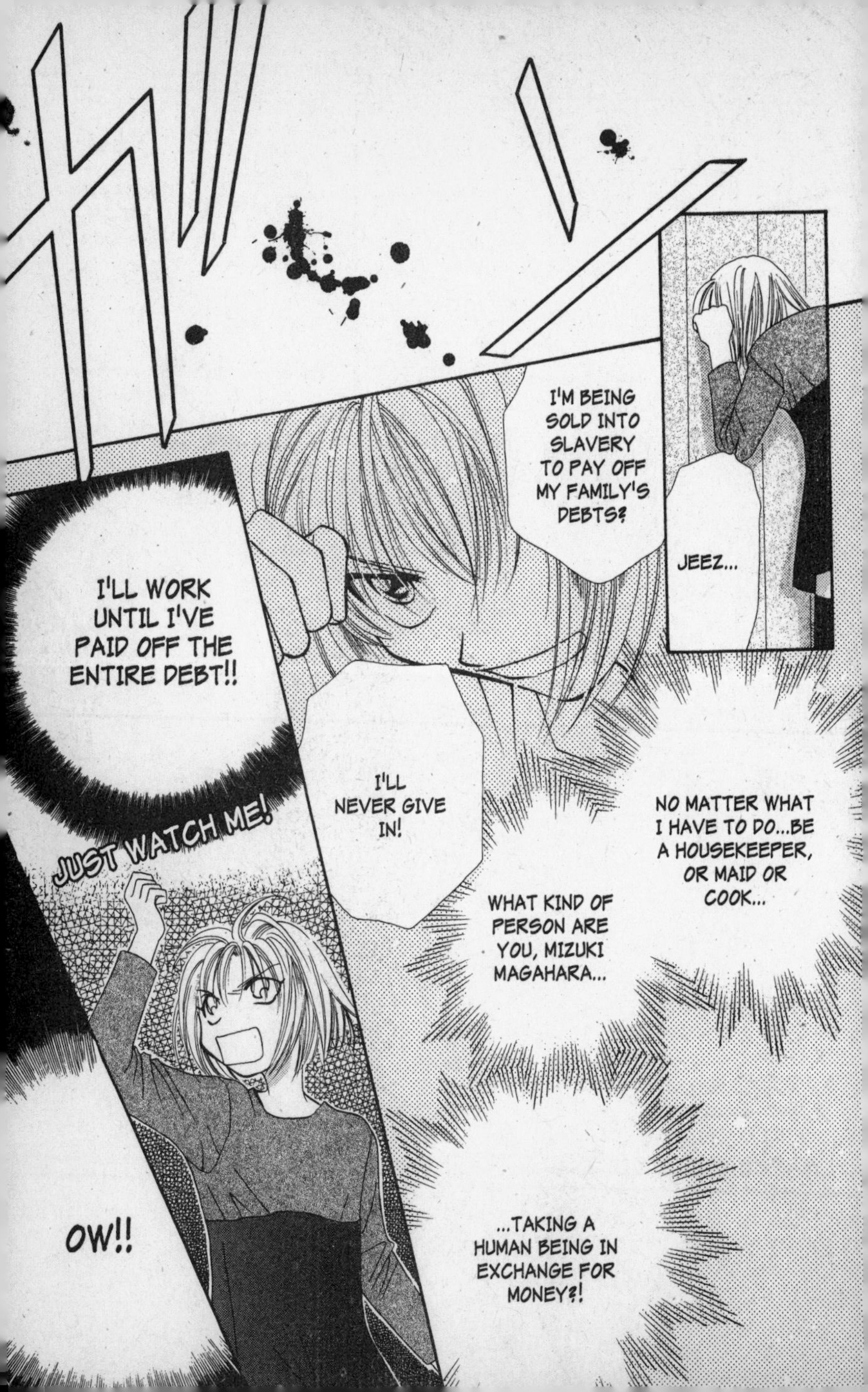
JEEZ...
I'M BEING SOLD INTO SLAVERY TO PAY OFF MY FAMILY'S DEBTS?
I'LL NEVER GIVE IN!
NO MATTER WHAT I HAVE TO DO...BE A HOUSEKEEPER, OR MAID OR COOK...
WHAT KIND OF PERSON ARE YOU, MIZUKI MAGAHARA...
...TAKING A HUMAN BEING IN EXCHANGE FOR MONEY?!
I'LL WORK UNTIL I'VE PAID OFF THE ENTIRE DEBT!!
JUST WATCH ME!
OW!!

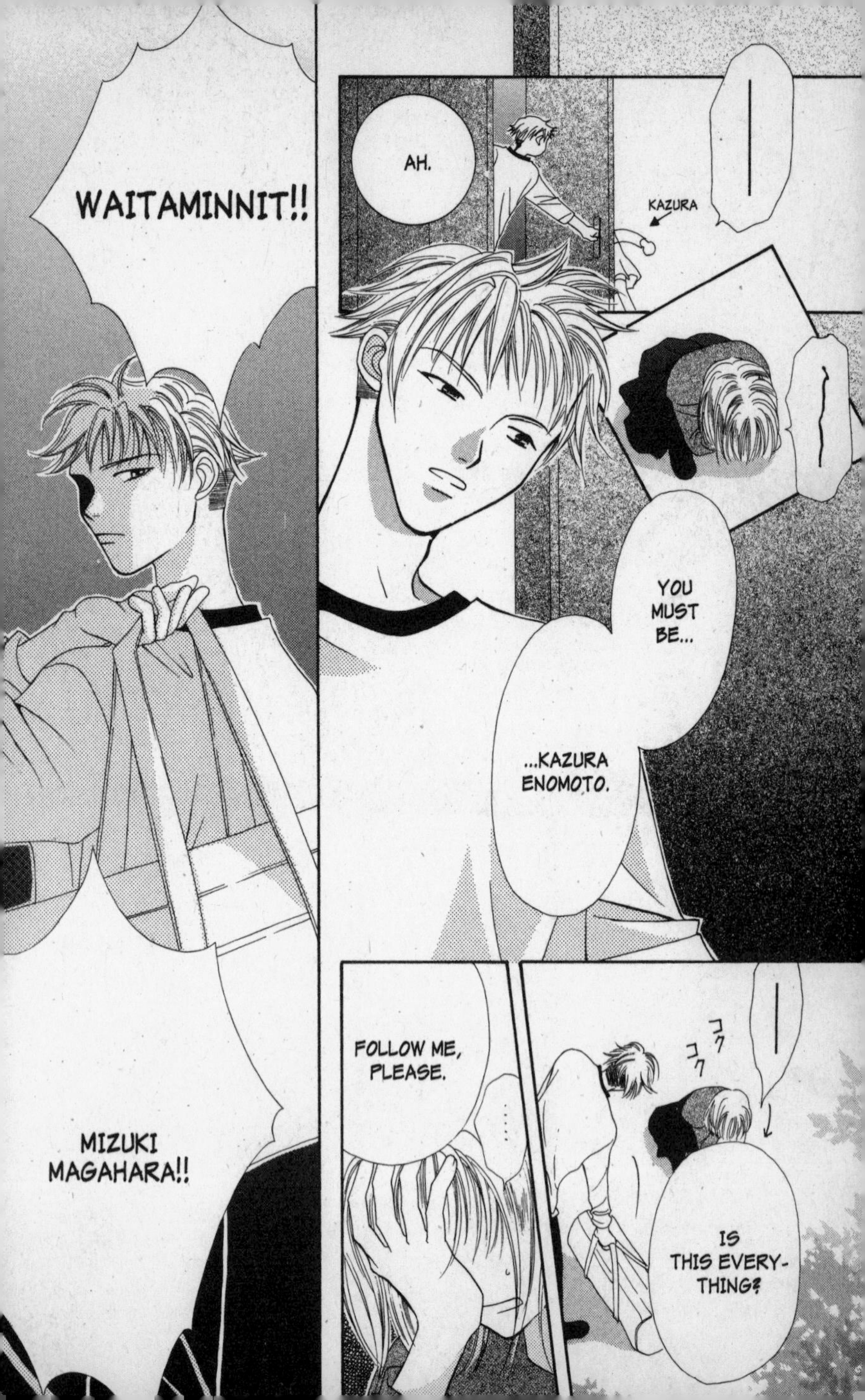
—
KAZURA
AH.
—
YOU MUST BE...
...KAZURA ENOMOTO.
—
コク
コク
IS THIS EVERYTHING?
......
FOLLOW ME, PLEASE.
WAITAMINNIT!!
MIZUKI MAGAHARA!!

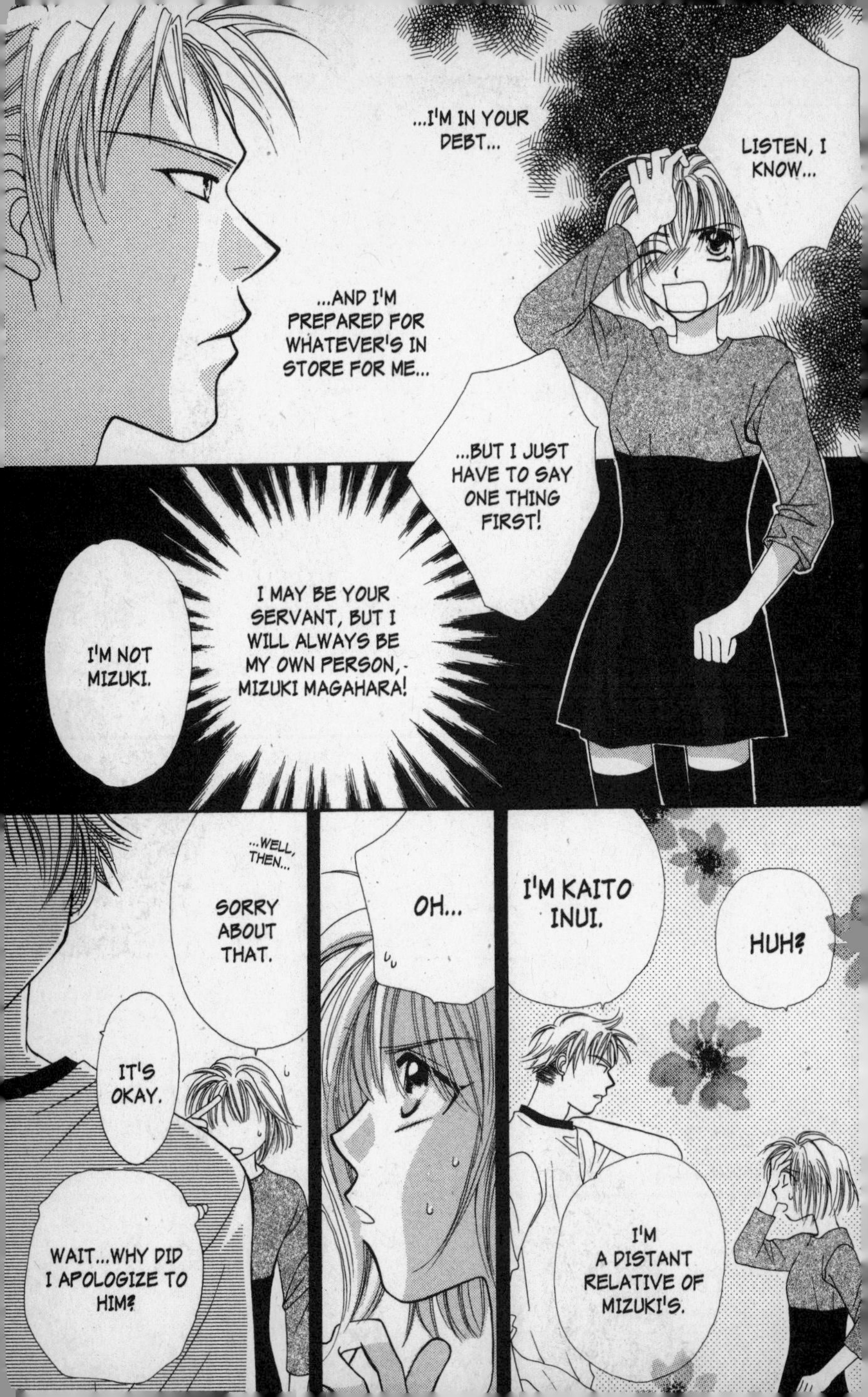
LISTEN, I KNOW...
...I'M IN YOUR DEBT...
...AND I'M PREPARED FOR WHATEVER'S IN STORE FOR ME...
...BUT I JUST HAVE TO SAY ONE THING FIRST!
I MAY BE YOUR SERVANT, BUT I WILL ALWAYS BE MY OWN PERSON, MIZUKI MAGAHARA!
I'M NOT MIZUKI.
HUH?
I'M KAITO INUI.
I'M A DISTANT RELATIVE OF MIZUKI'S.
OH...
...WELL, THEN...
SORRY ABOUT THAT.
IT'S OKAY.
WAIT...WHY DID I APOLOGIZE TO HIM?

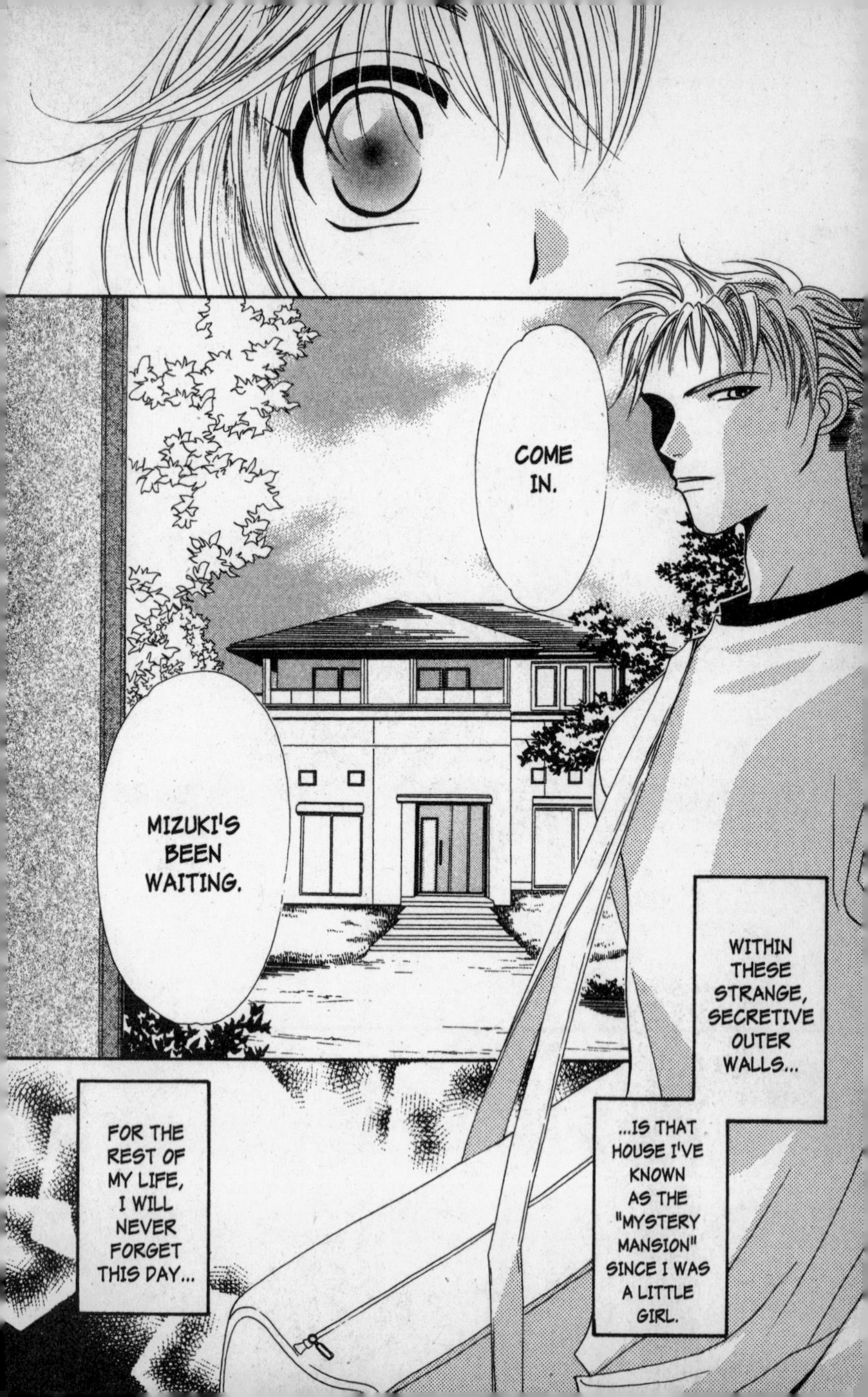
COME IN.
MIZUKI'S BEEN WAITING.
WITHIN THESE STRANGE, SECRETIVE OUTER WALLS...
...IS THAT HOUSE I'VE KNOWN AS THE "MYSTERY MANSION" SINCE I WAS A LITTLE GIRL.
FOR THE REST OF MY LIFE, I WILL NEVER FORGET THIS DAY...

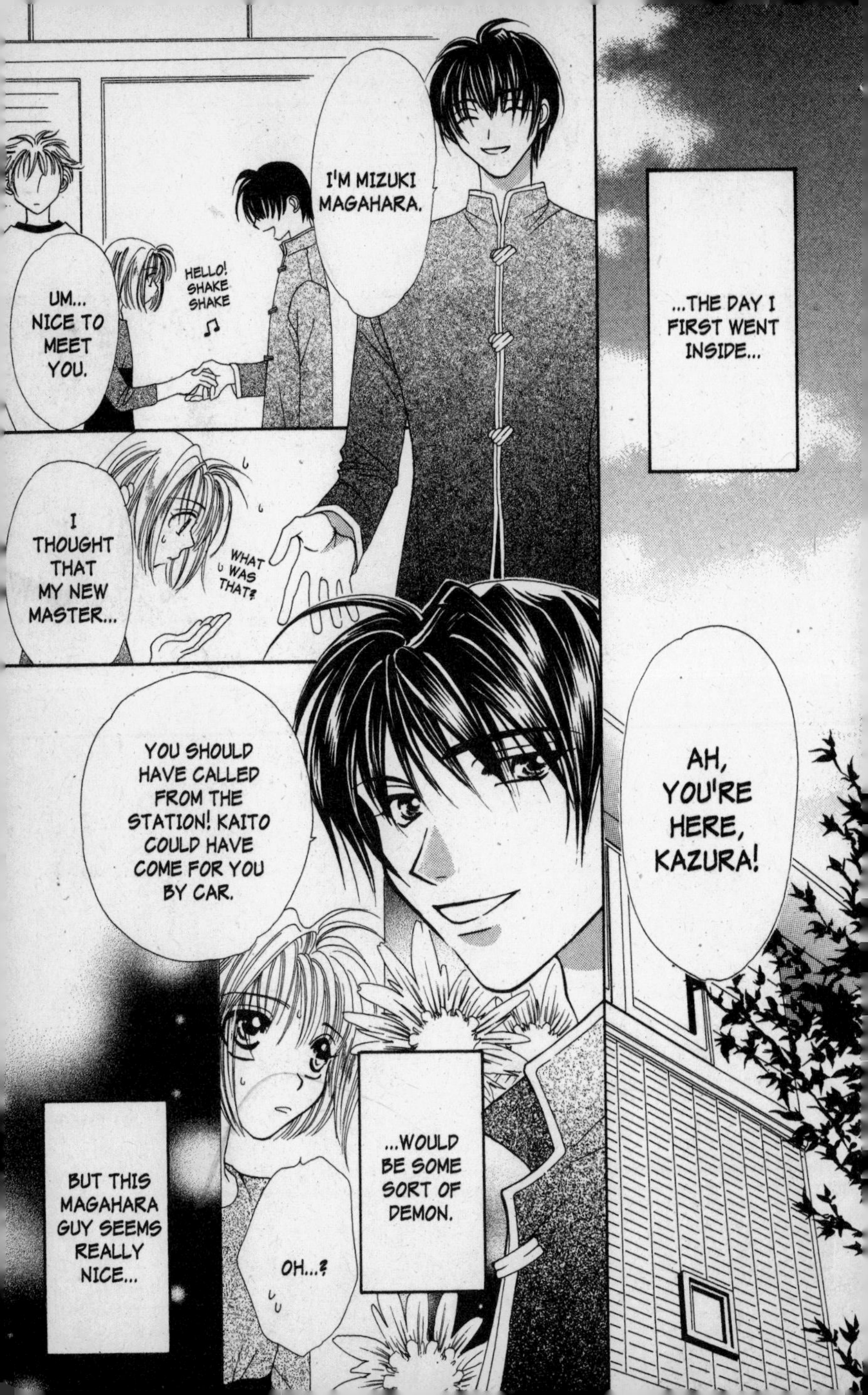
...THE DAY I FIRST WENT INSIDE...
AH, YOU'RE HERE, KAZURA!
I'M MIZUKI MAGAHARA.
HELLO! SHAKE SHAKE ♫
UM... NICE TO MEET YOU.
WHAT WAS THAT?
I THOUGHT THAT MY NEW MASTER...
YOU SHOULD HAVE CALLED FROM THE STATION! KAITO COULD HAVE COME FOR YOU BY CAR.
...WOULD BE SOME SORT OF DEMON.
OH...?
BUT THIS MAGAHARA GUY SEEMS REALLY NICE...

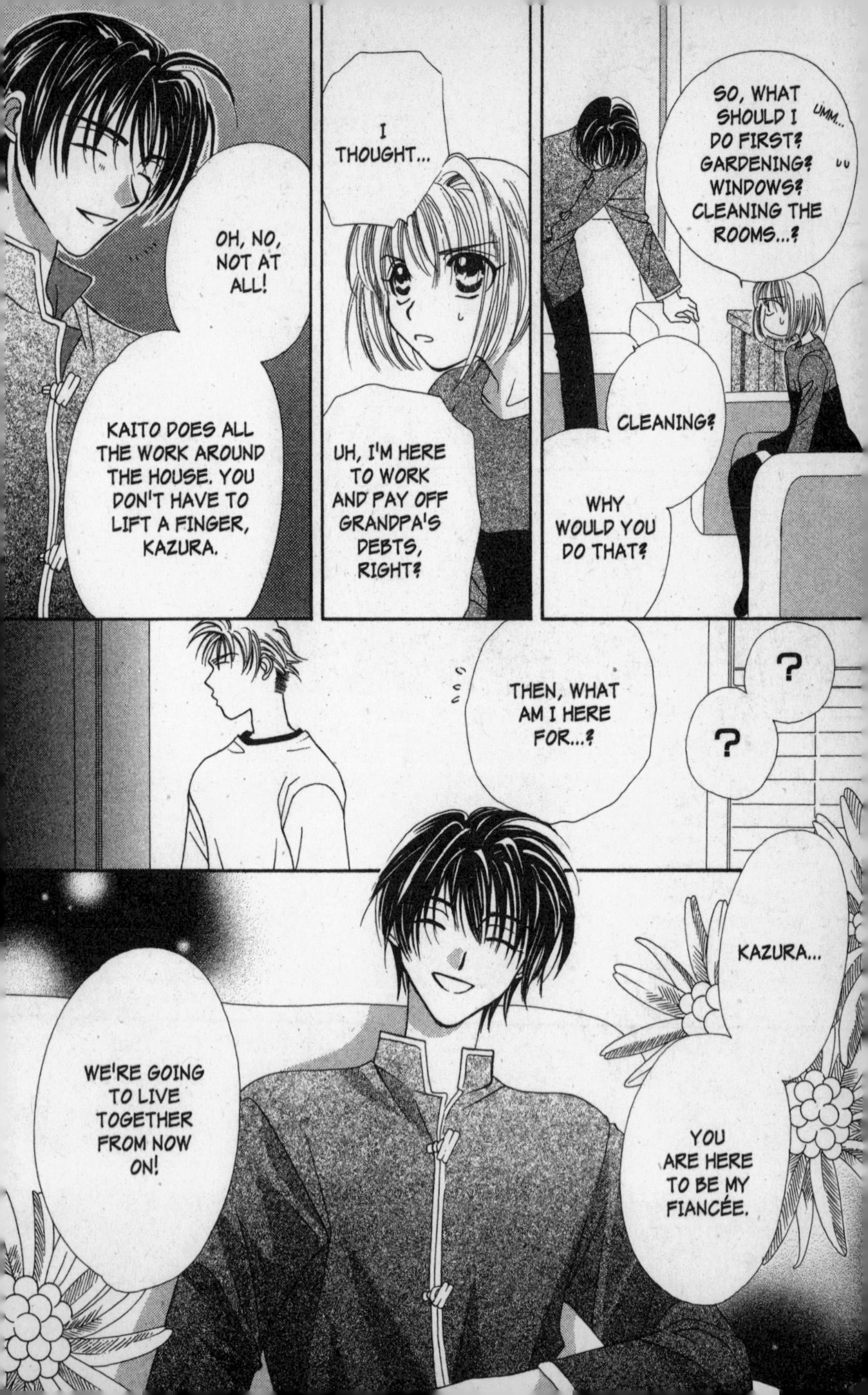
SO, WHAT SHOULD I DO FIRST? GARDENING? WINDOWS? CLEANING THE ROOMS...?
UMM...
CLEANING?
WHY WOULD YOU DO THAT?
I THOUGHT...
UH, I'M HERE TO WORK AND PAY OFF GRANDPA'S DEBTS, RIGHT?
OH, NO, NOT AT ALL!
KAITO DOES ALL THE WORK AROUND THE HOUSE. YOU DON'T HAVE TO LIFT A FINGER, KAZURA.
?
?
THEN, WHAT AM I HERE FOR...?
KAZURA...
YOU ARE HERE TO BE MY FIANCÉE.
WE'RE GOING TO LIVE TOGETHER FROM NOW ON!

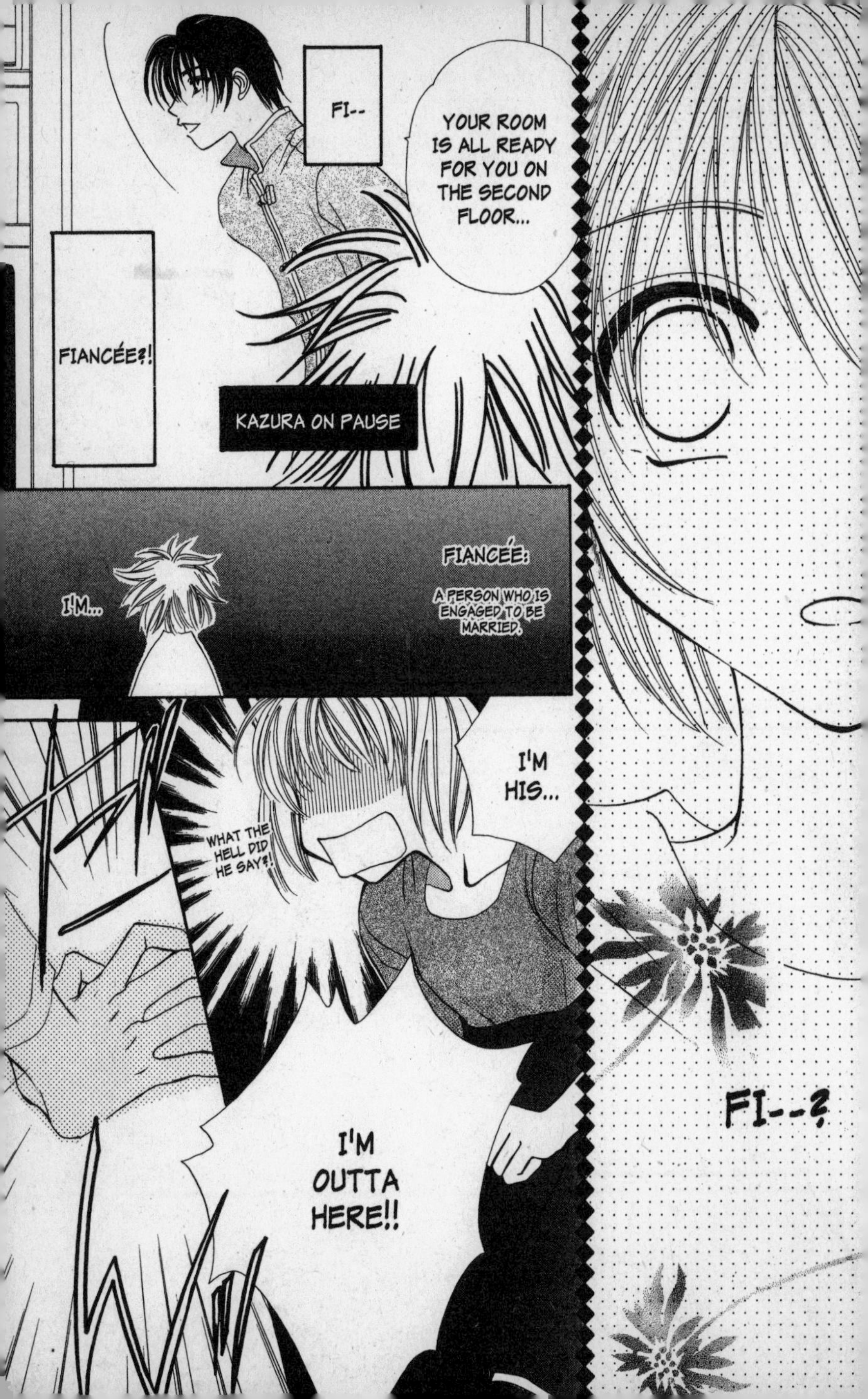
FI--?
YOUR ROOM IS ALL READY FOR YOU ON THE SECOND FLOOR...
FI--
FIANCÉE?!
KAZURA ON PAUSE
FIANCÉE:
A PERSON WHO IS ENGAGED TO BE MARRIED.
I'M...
I'M HIS...
WHAT THE HELL DID HE SAY?!
I'M OUTTA HERE!!

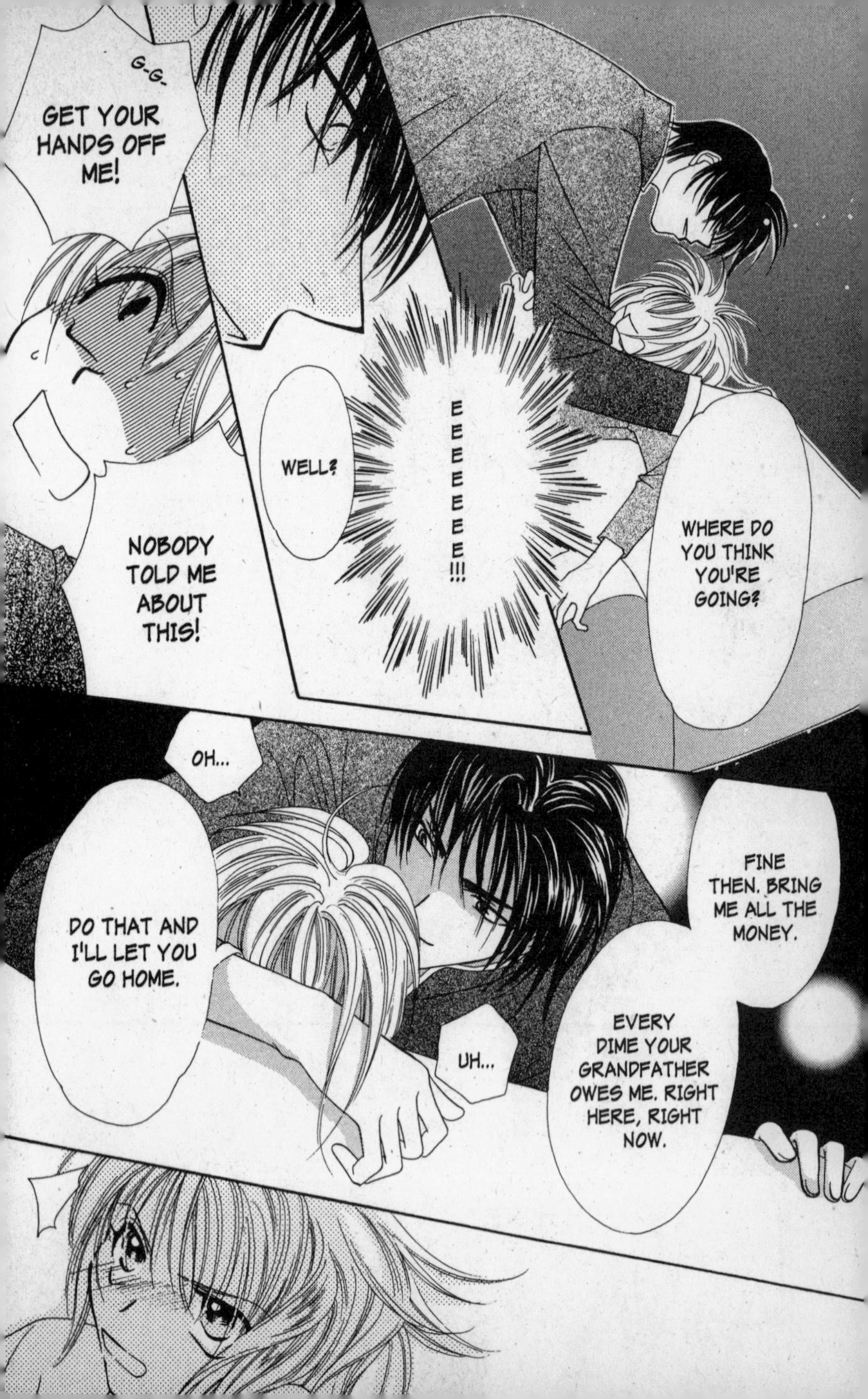

WHERE DO YOU THINK YOU'RE GOING?
EEEEEEEE!!!
WELL?
G-G-
GET YOUR HANDS OFF ME!
NOBODY TOLD ME ABOUT THIS!
FINE THEN. BRING ME ALL THE MONEY.
EVERY DIME YOUR GRANDFATHER OWES ME. RIGHT HERE, RIGHT NOW.
OH...
UH...
DO THAT AND I'LL LET YOU GO HOME.

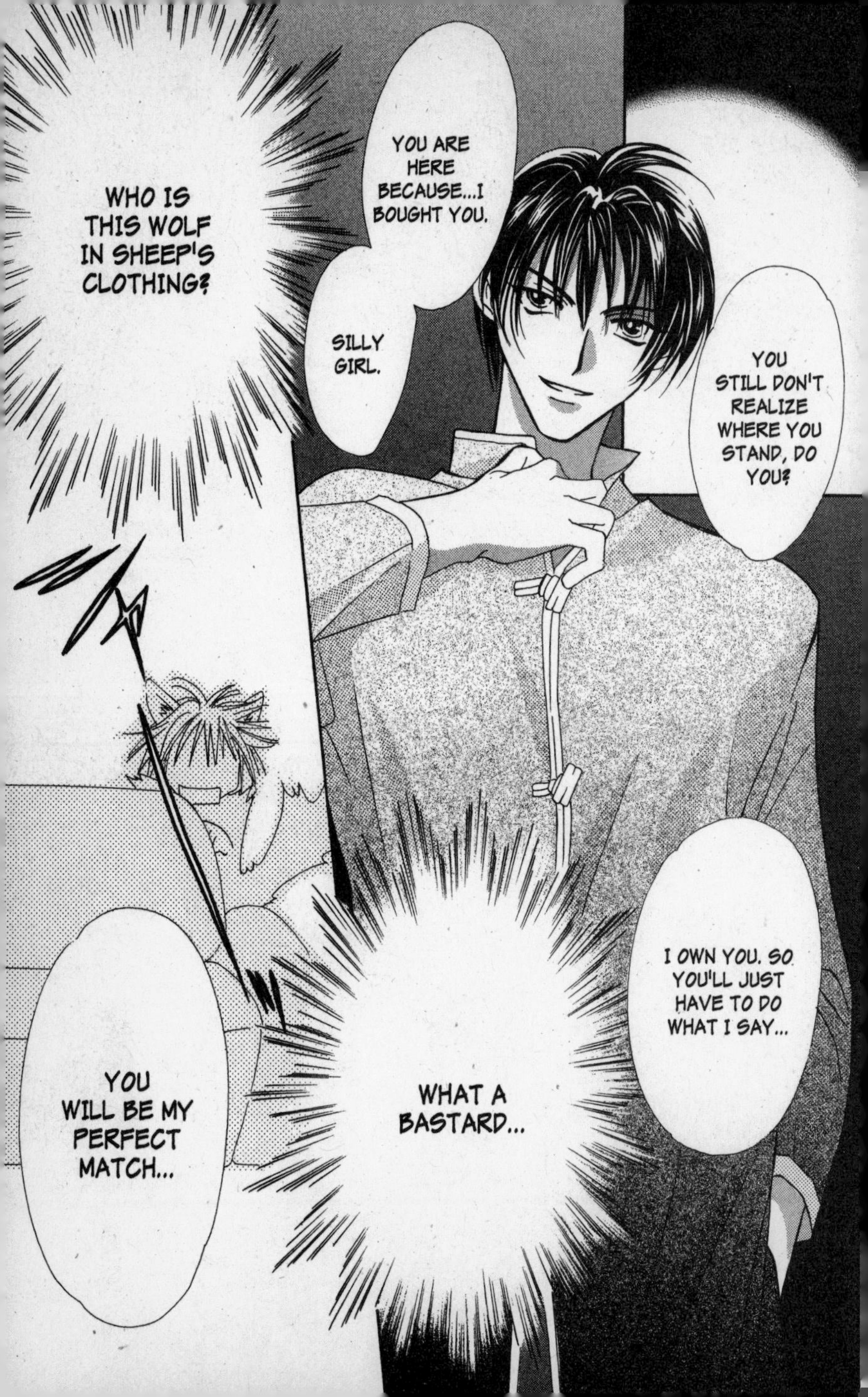
YOU STILL DON'T REALIZE WHERE YOU STAND, DO YOU?
SILLY GIRL.
YOU ARE HERE BECAUSE...I BOUGHT YOU.
I OWN YOU. SO YOU'LL JUST HAVE TO DO WHAT I SAY...
YOU WILL BE MY PERFECT MATCH...
WHO IS THIS WOLF IN SHEEP'S CLOTHING?
WHAT A BASTARD...

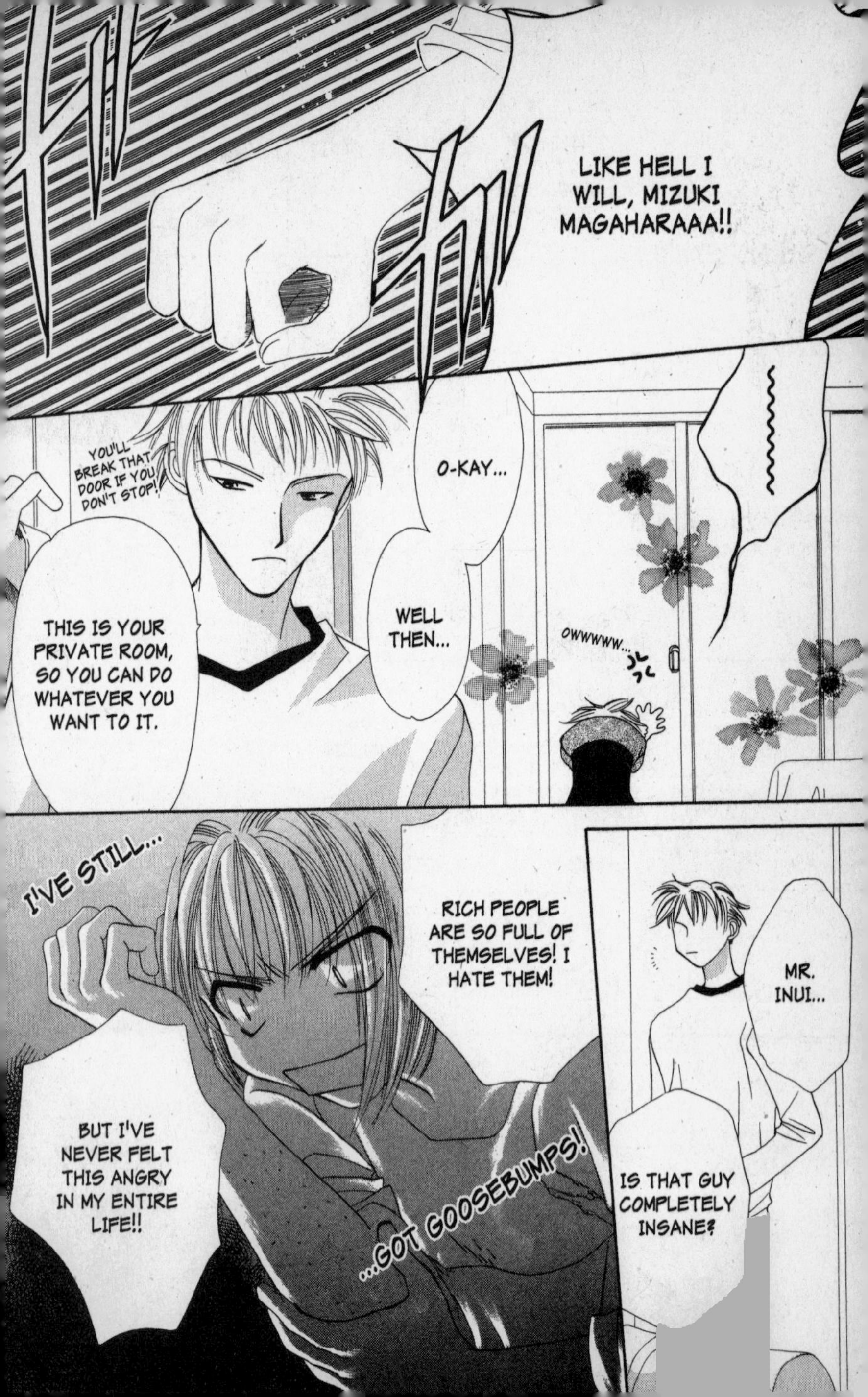
LIKE HELL I WILL, MIZUKI MAGAHARAAA!!
OWWWWW...
O-KAY...
WELL THEN...
YOU'LL BREAK THAT DOOR IF YOU DON'T STOP!
THIS IS YOUR PRIVATE ROOM, SO YOU CAN DO WHATEVER YOU WANT TO IT.
MR. INUI...
IS THAT GUY COMPLETELY INSANE?
RICH PEOPLE ARE SO FULL OF THEMSELVES! I HATE THEM!
I'VE STILL...
...GOT GOOSEBUMPS!
BUT I'VE NEVER FELT THIS ANGRY IN MY ENTIRE LIFE!!

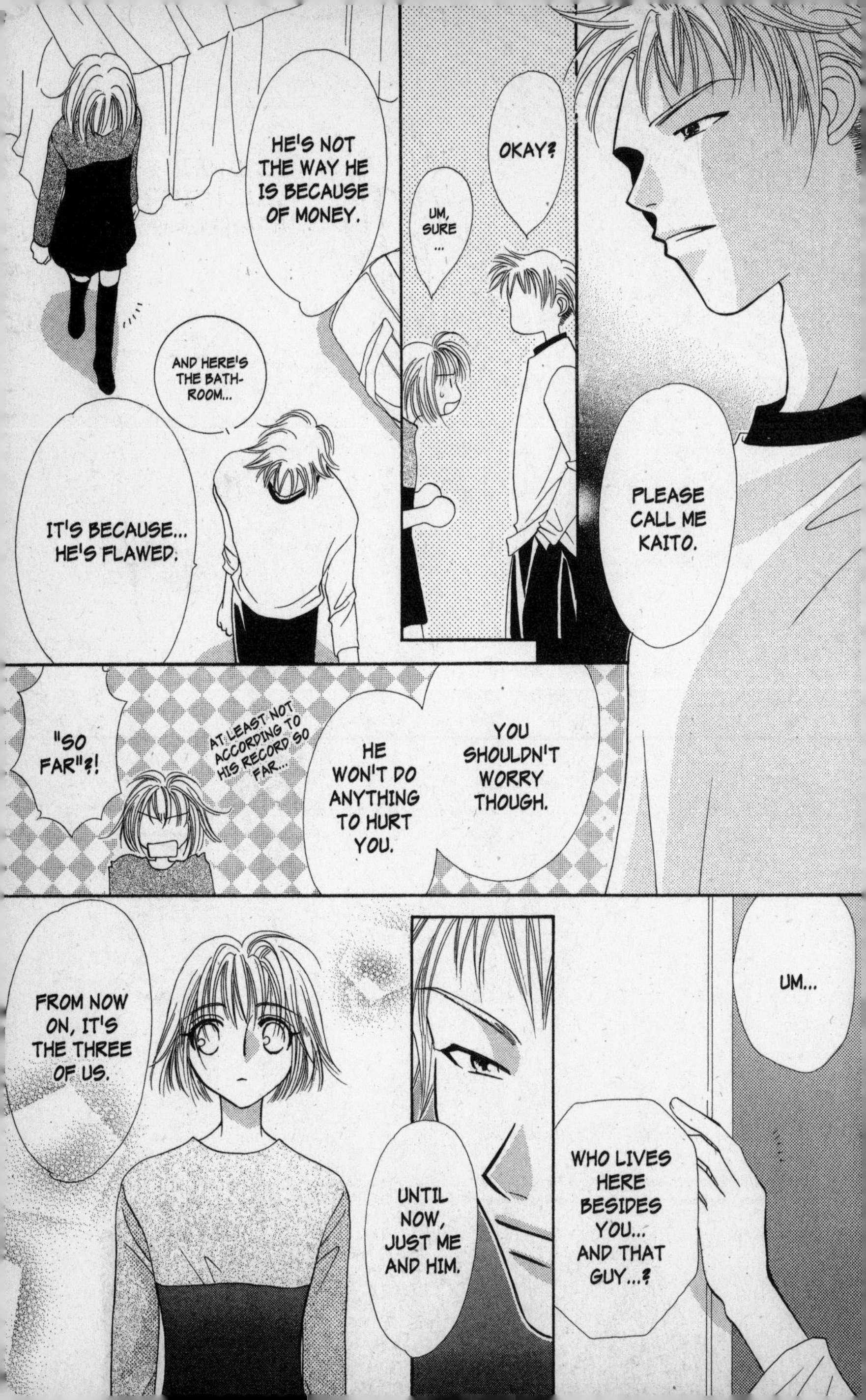
PLEASE CALL ME KAITO.
OKAY?
UM, SURE ...
HE'S NOT THE WAY HE IS BECAUSE OF MONEY.
AND HERE'S THE BATH-ROOM...
IT'S BECAUSE... HE'S FLAWED.
YOU SHOULDN'T WORRY THOUGH.
HE WON'T DO ANYTHING TO HURT YOU.
AT LEAST NOT ACCORDING TO HIS RECORD SO FAR...
"SO FAR"?!
UM...
WHO LIVES HERE BESIDES YOU... AND THAT GUY...?
UNTIL NOW, JUST ME AND HIM.
FROM NOW ON, IT'S THE THREE OF US.

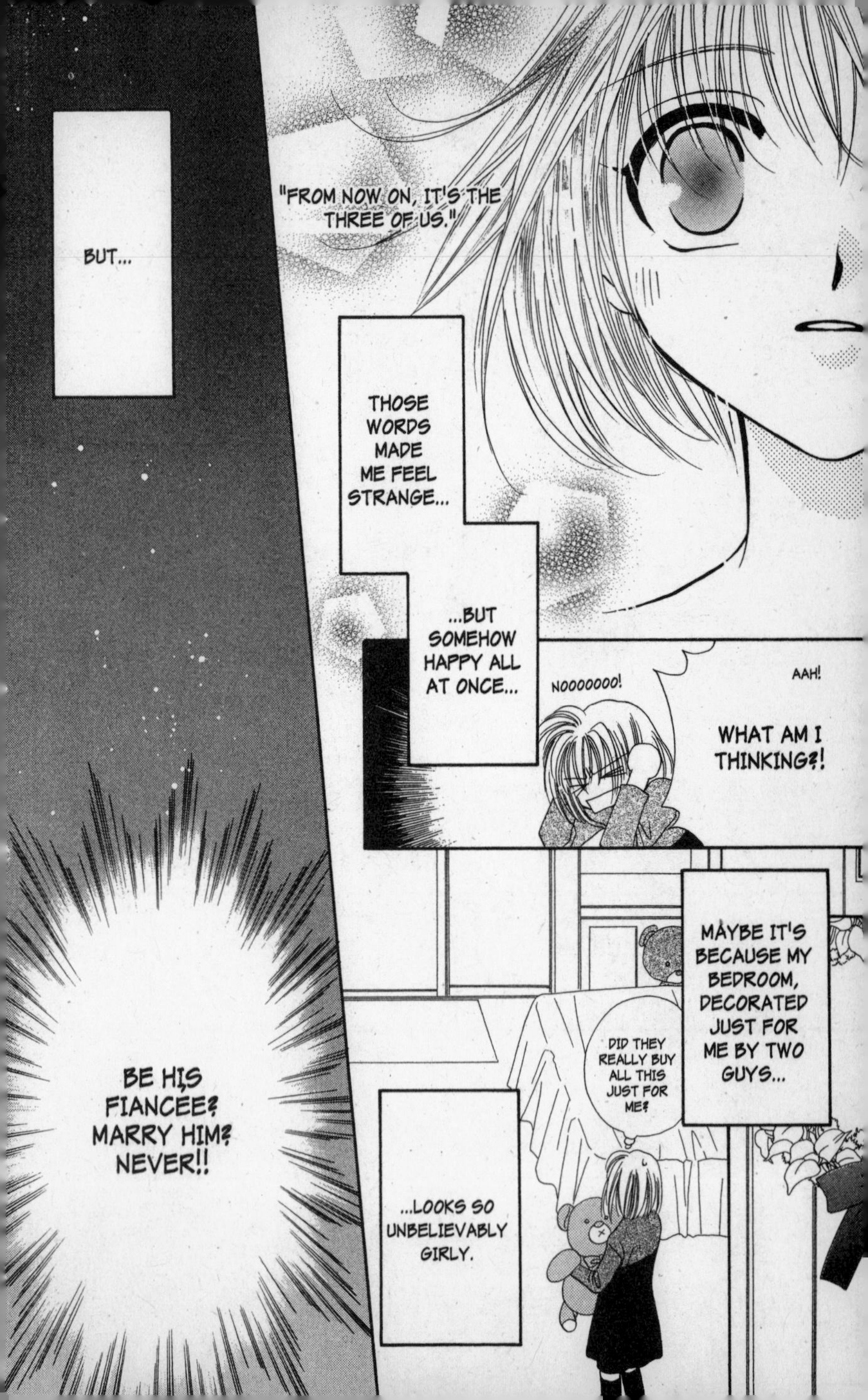

"FROM NOW ON, IT'S THE THREE OF US."
THOSE WORDS MADE ME FEEL STRANGE...
...BUT SOMEHOW HAPPY ALL AT ONCE...
AAH!
NOOOOOOO!
WHAT AM I THINKING?!
MAYBE IT'S BECAUSE MY BEDROOM, DECORATED JUST FOR ME BY TWO GUYS...
DID THEY REALLY BUY ALL THIS JUST FOR ME?
...LOOKS SO UNBELIEVABLY GIRLY.
BUT...
BE HIS FIANCEE? MARRY HIM? NEVER!!

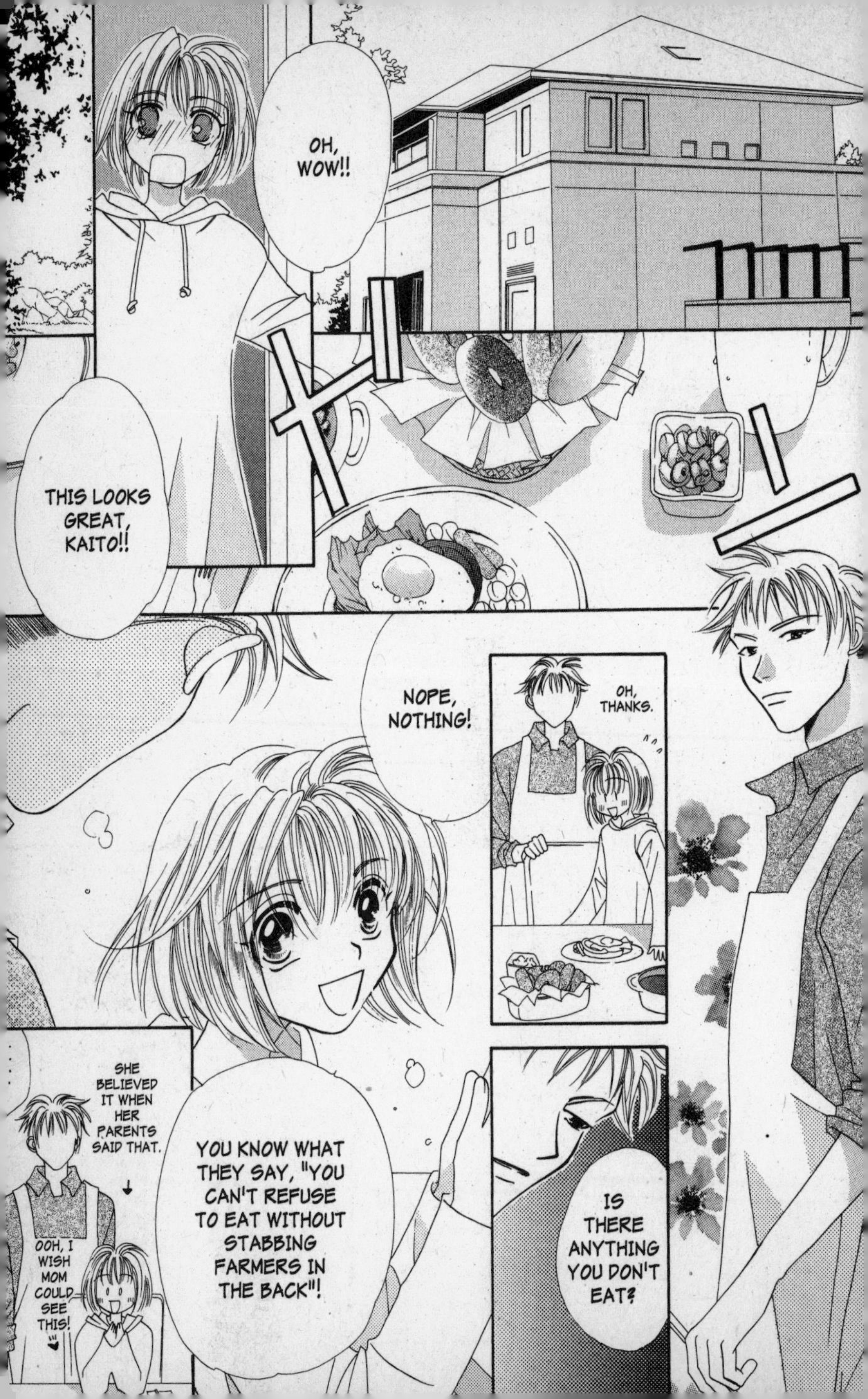
OH, WOW!!
THIS LOOKS GREAT, KAITO!!
IS THERE ANYTHING YOU DON'T EAT?
NOPE, NOTHING!
OH, THANKS.
YOU KNOW WHAT THEY SAY, "YOU CAN'T REFUSE TO EAT WITHOUT STABBING FARMERS IN THE BACK"!
SHE BELIEVED IT WHEN HER PARENTS SAID THAT.
OOH, I WISH MOM COULD SEE THIS!

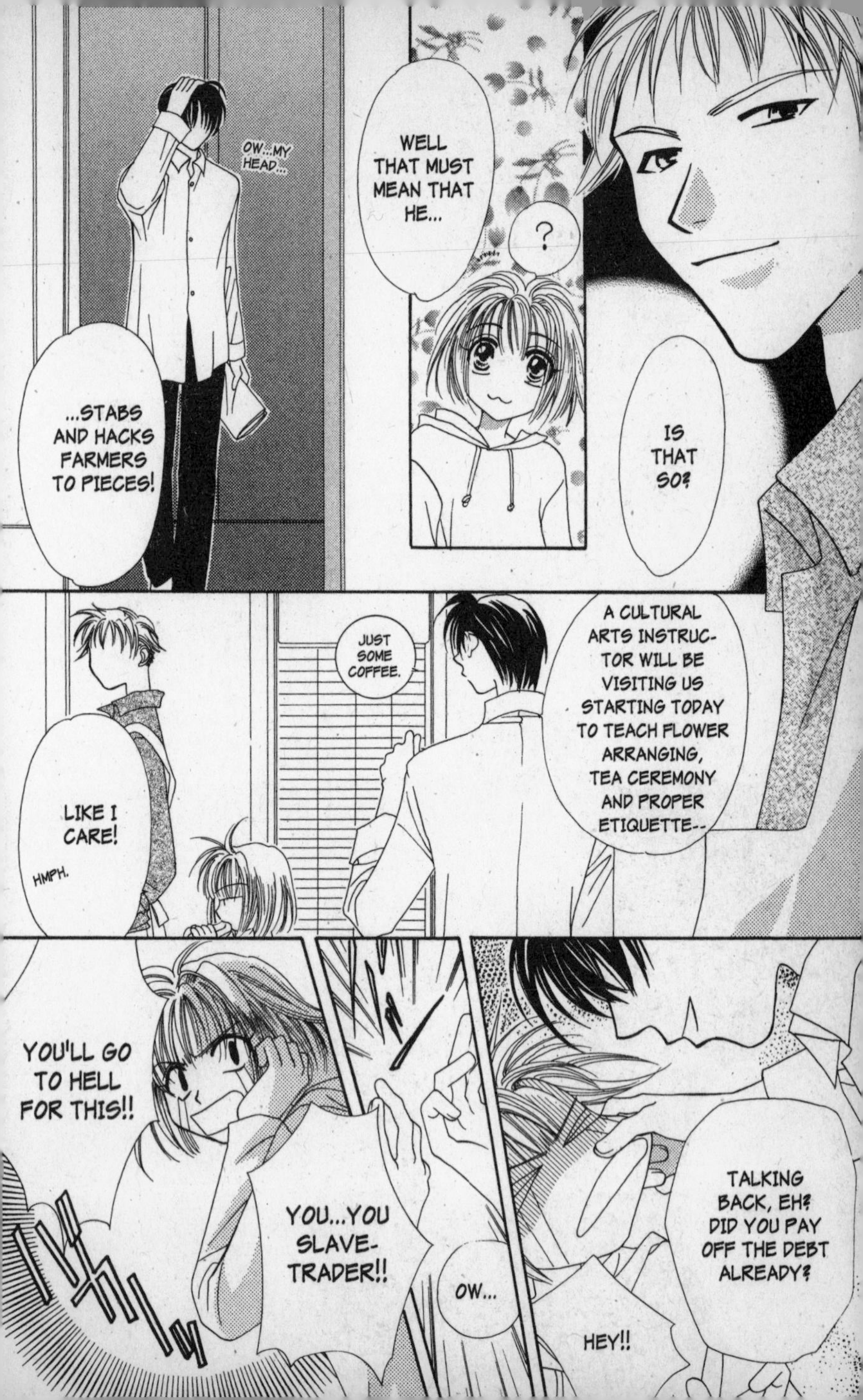
IS THAT SO?
WELL THAT MUST MEAN THAT HE...
?
OW...MY HEAD...
...STABS AND HACKS FARMERS TO PIECES!
A CULTURAL ARTS INSTRUC-TOR WILL BE VISITING US STARTING TODAY TO TEACH FLOWER ARRANGING, TEA CEREMONY AND PROPER ETIQUETTE--
JUST SOME COFFEE.
LIKE I CARE!
HMPH.
TALKING BACK, EH? DID YOU PAY OFF THE DEBT ALREADY?
HEY!!
OW...
YOU...YOU SLAVE-TRADER!!
YOU'LL GO TO HELL FOR THIS!!

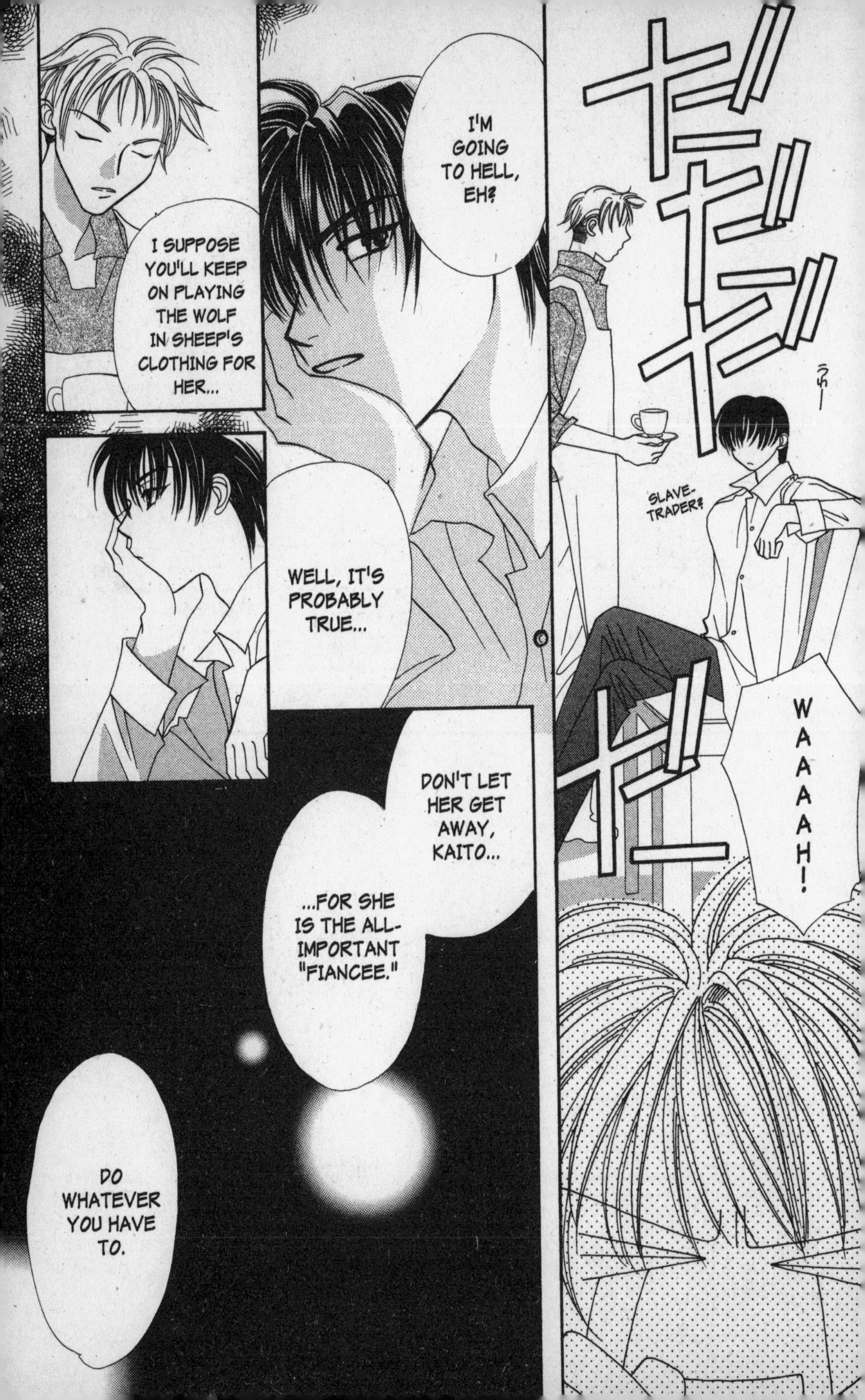
SLAVE-TRADER?
WAAAAAH!
I'M GOING TO HELL, EH?
I SUPPOSE YOU'LL KEEP ON PLAYING THE WOLF IN SHEEP'S CLOTHING FOR HER...
WELL, IT'S PROBABLY TRUE...
DON'T LET HER GET AWAY, KAITO...
...FOR SHE IS THE ALL-IMPORTANT "FIANCEE."
DO WHATEVER YOU HAVE TO.

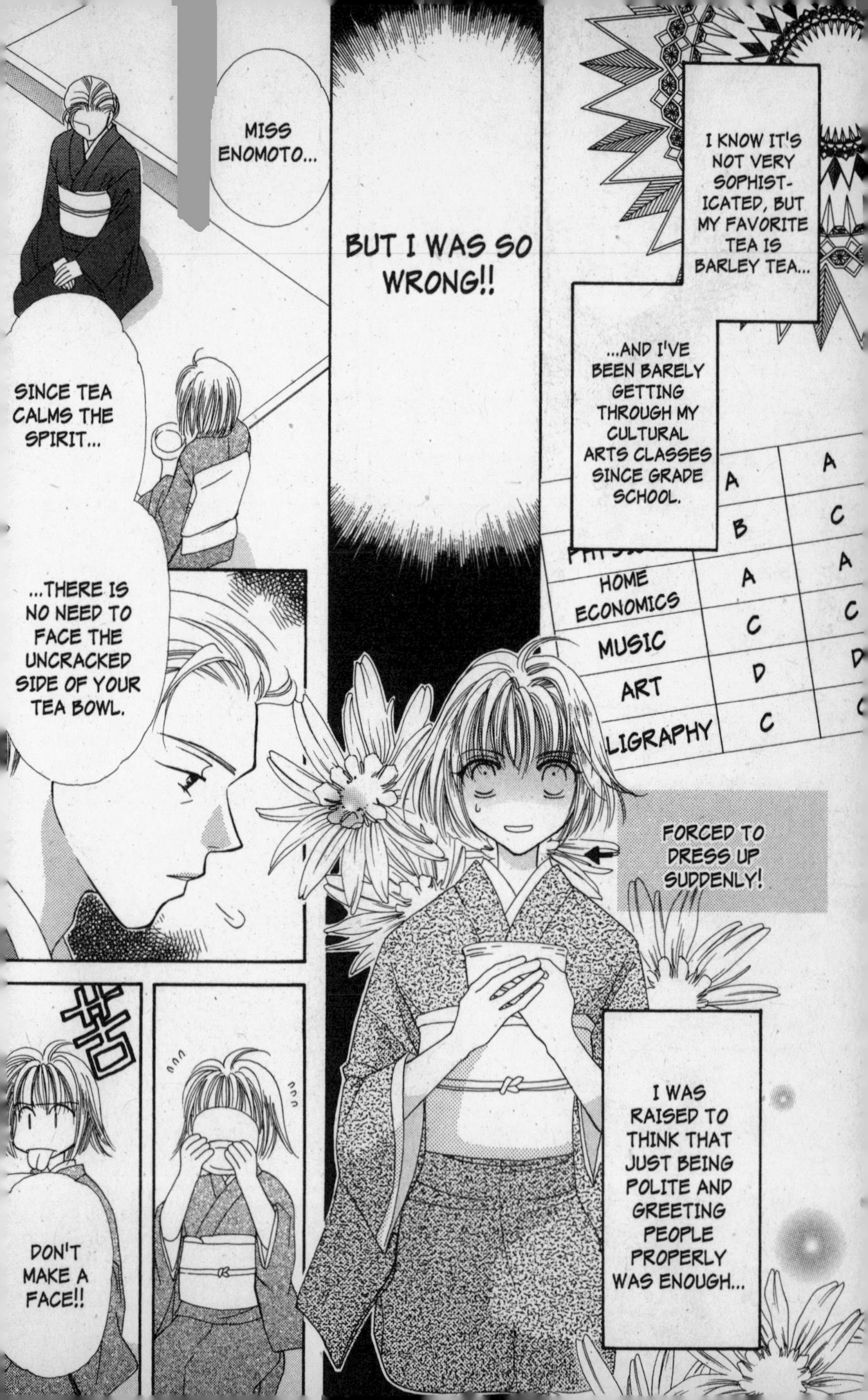

I KNOW IT'S NOT VERY SOPHIST-ICATED, BUT MY FAVORITE TEA IS BARLEY TEA...
...AND I'VE BEEN BARELY GETTING THROUGH MY CULTURAL ARTS CLASSES SINCE GRADE SCHOOL.
A A
B C
HOME ECONOMICS A A
MUSIC C C
ART D D
LIGRAPHY C
FORCED TO DRESS UP SUDDENLY!
I WAS RAISED TO THINK THAT JUST BEING POLITE AND GREETING PEOPLE PROPERLY WAS ENOUGH...
BUT I WAS SO WRONG!!
MISS ENOMOTO...
SINCE TEA CALMS THE SPIRIT...
...THERE IS NO NEED TO FACE THE UNCRACKED SIDE OF YOUR TEA BOWL.
DON'T MAKE A FACE!!

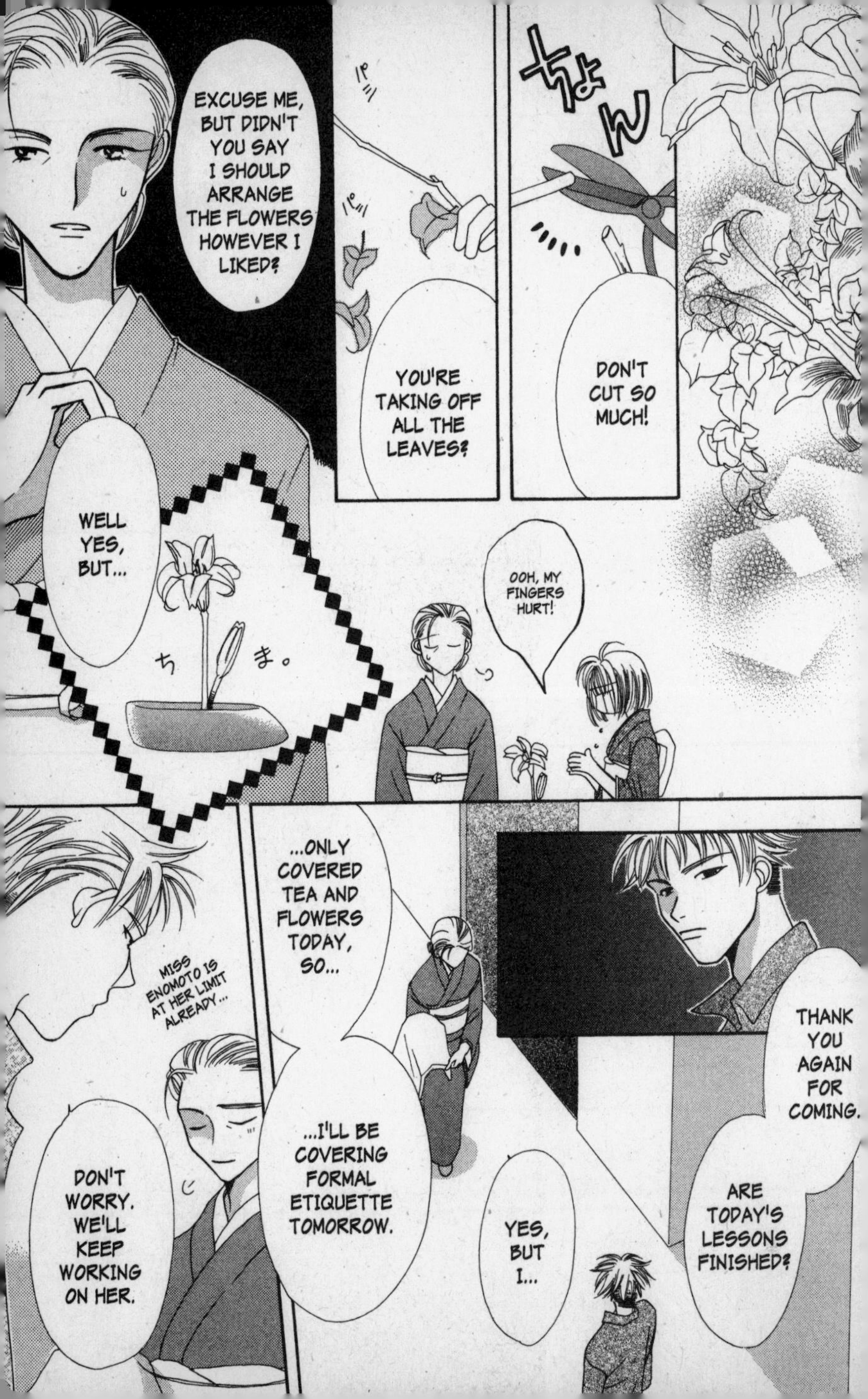
ちょん
......
DON'T CUT SO MUCH!
YOU'RE TAKING OFF ALL THE LEAVES?
OOH, MY FINGERS HURT!
EXCUSE ME, BUT DIDN'T YOU SAY I SHOULD ARRANGE THE FLOWERS HOWEVER I LIKED?
WELL YES, BUT...
ち ま。
THANK YOU AGAIN FOR COMING.
ARE TODAY'S LESSONS FINISHED?
YES, BUT I...
...ONLY COVERED TEA AND FLOWERS TODAY, SO...
...I'LL BE COVERING FORMAL ETIQUETTE TOMORROW.
MISS ENOMOTO IS AT HER LIMIT ALREADY...
DON'T WORRY. WE'LL KEEP WORKING ON HER.

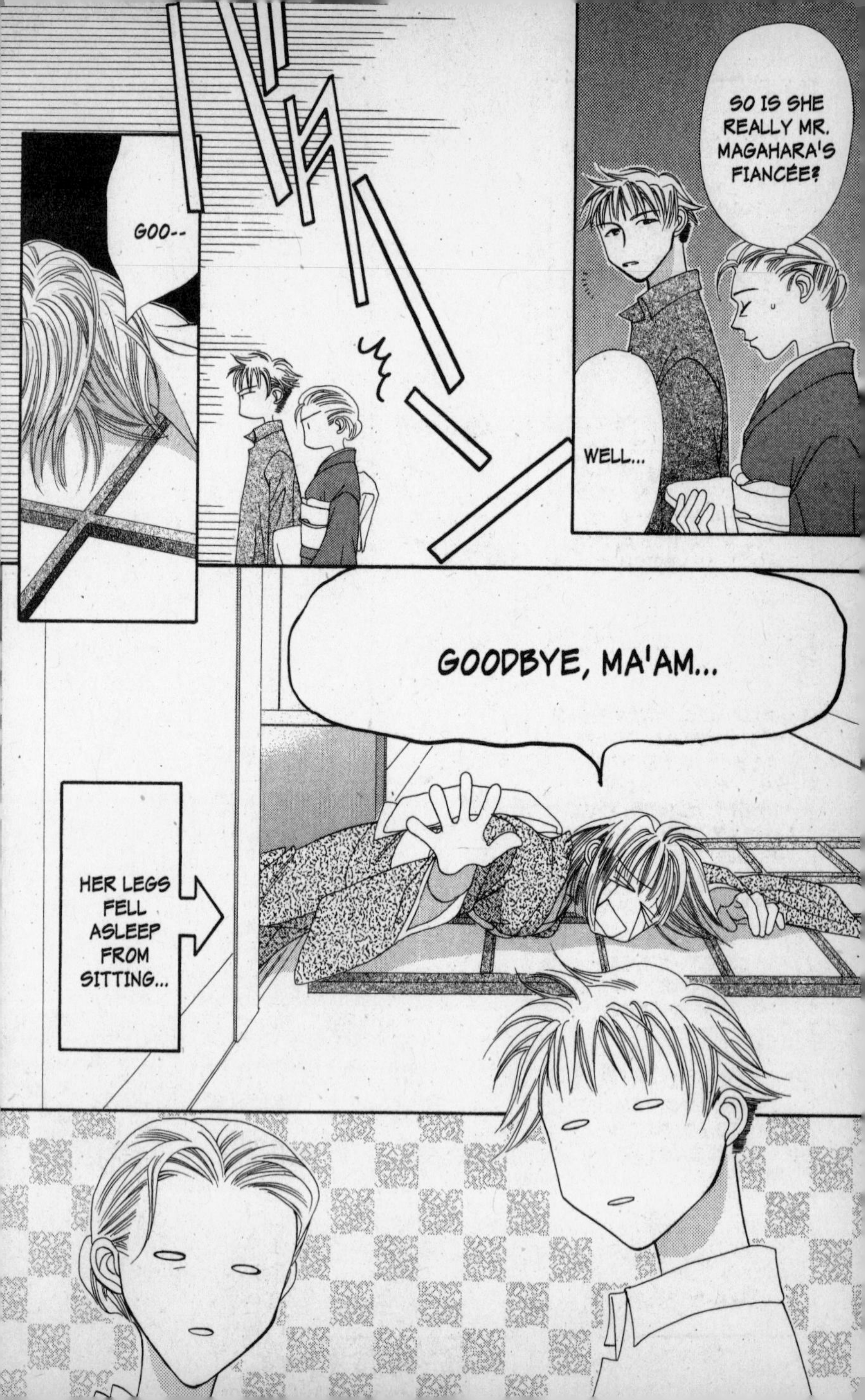
SO IS SHE REALLY MR. MAGAHARA'S FIANCÉE?
WELL...
GOO--
GOODBYE, MA'AM...
HER LEGS FELL ASLEEP FROM SITTING...

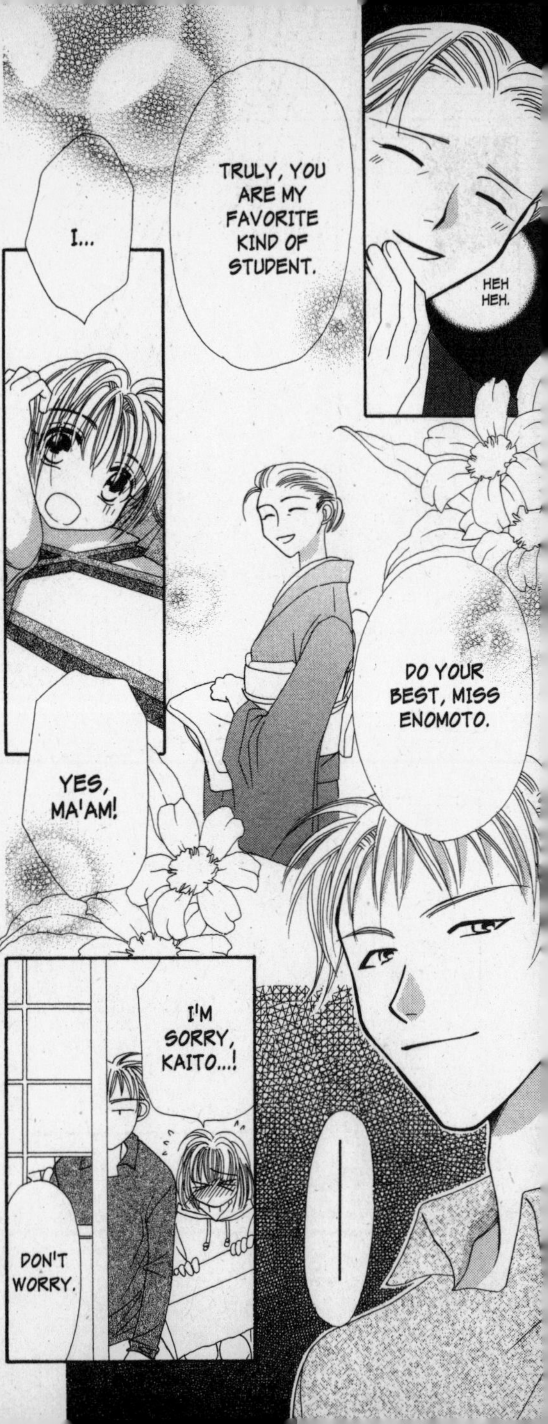
TRULY, YOU ARE MY FAVORITE KIND OF STUDENT.
HEH HEH.
I...
DO YOUR BEST, MISS ENOMOTO.
YES, MA'AM!
—
I'M SORRY, KAITO...!
DON'T WORRY.

IDIOTIC RAMBLINGS I

PLEASED TO MEET YOU! OR, IF YOU'VE READ MY STORIES BEFORE, HELLO AGAIN! THANKS FOR BUYING MY 16TH COMIC, PLATINUM GARDEN (OR "PLA-G" AS WE LIKE TO SAY)!

I HAVE TO SAY, I REALLY HAVE A DREAM JOB, DON'T I? AND THANKS TO ALL OF YOU WHO HAVE READ AND BOUGHT MY WORK (INCLUDING THIS BOOK)! THANK YOU VERY MUCH!!

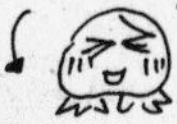

I THINK YOU'LL UNDERSTAND WHAT I'M ABOUT TO SAY WHEN YOU READ THE BOOK, BUT...IT'S ONE OF "THOSE" STORIES. WHEN I WAS WRITING IT, I KEPT THINKING..."WOW, THERE'S A LOT OF ROTTEN STUFF IN HERE!" HA HA HA!

I JUST HOPE IT DOESN'T MAKE YOU TOO UNCOMFORTABLE TO READ...

PLEASE READ IT WITH OPEN EYES AND MIND AND THINK "WAY TO GO, FUJITA" AS YOU ENJOY IT!

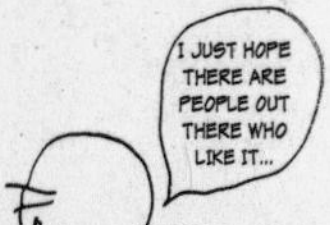
I JUST HOPE THERE ARE PEOPLE OUT THERE WHO LIKE IT...

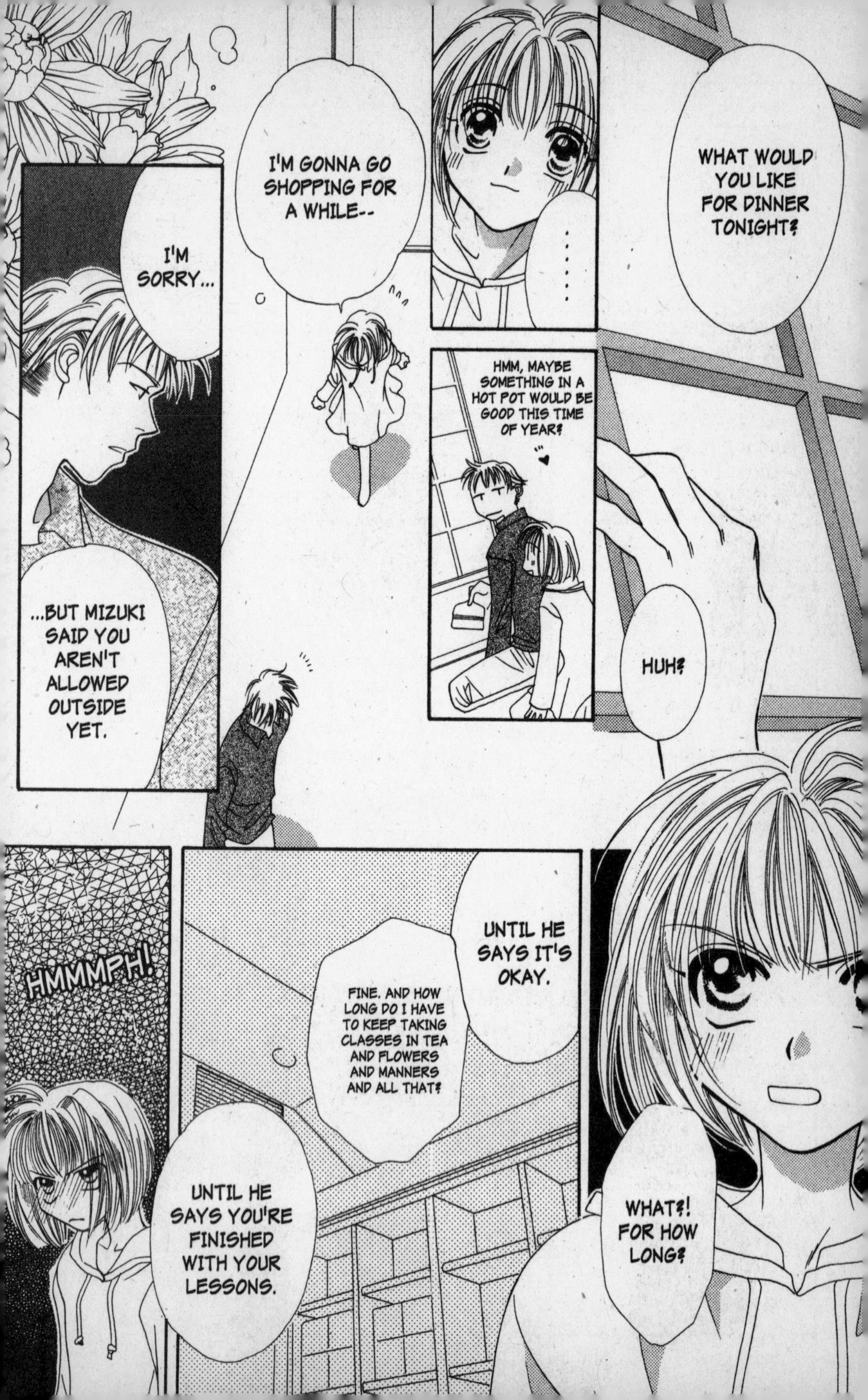
WHAT WOULD YOU LIKE FOR DINNER TONIGHT?
HUH?
.....
HMM, MAYBE SOMETHING IN A HOT POT WOULD BE GOOD THIS TIME OF YEAR?
I'M GONNA GO SHOPPING FOR A WHILE--
I'M SORRY...
...BUT MIZUKI SAID YOU AREN'T ALLOWED OUTSIDE YET.
WHAT?! FOR HOW LONG?
UNTIL HE SAYS IT'S OKAY.
FINE. AND HOW LONG DO I HAVE TO KEEP TAKING CLASSES IN TEA AND FLOWERS AND MANNERS AND ALL THAT?
UNTIL HE SAYS YOU'RE FINISHED WITH YOUR LESSONS.
HMMMPH!

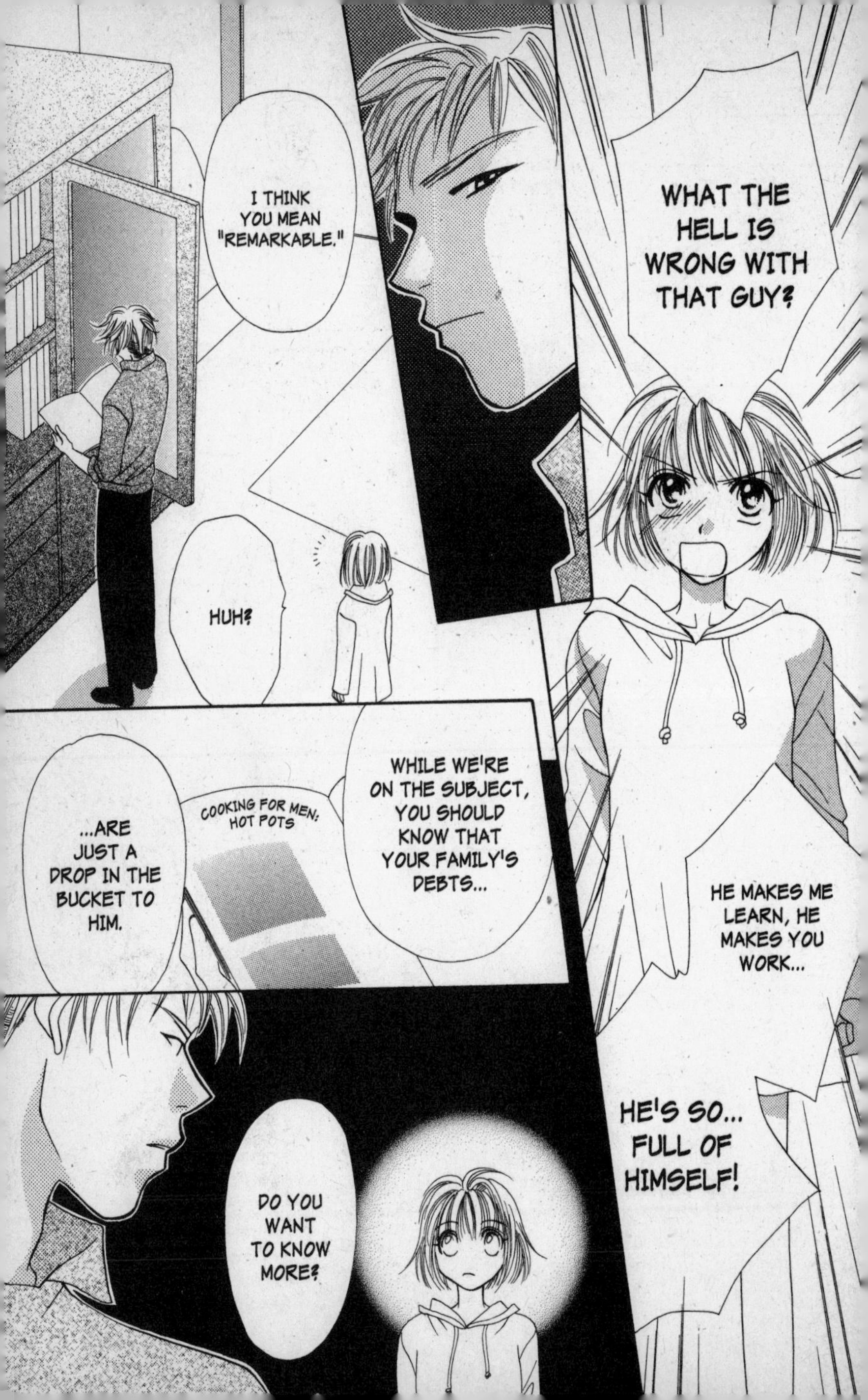
WHAT THE HELL IS WRONG WITH THAT GUY?
HE MAKES ME LEARN, HE MAKES YOU WORK...
HE'S SO... FULL OF HIMSELF!
I THINK YOU MEAN "REMARKABLE."
HUH?
WHILE WE'RE ON THE SUBJECT, YOU SHOULD KNOW THAT YOUR FAMILY'S DEBTS...
COOKING FOR MEN: HOT POTS
...ARE JUST A DROP IN THE BUCKET TO HIM.
DO YOU WANT TO KNOW MORE?

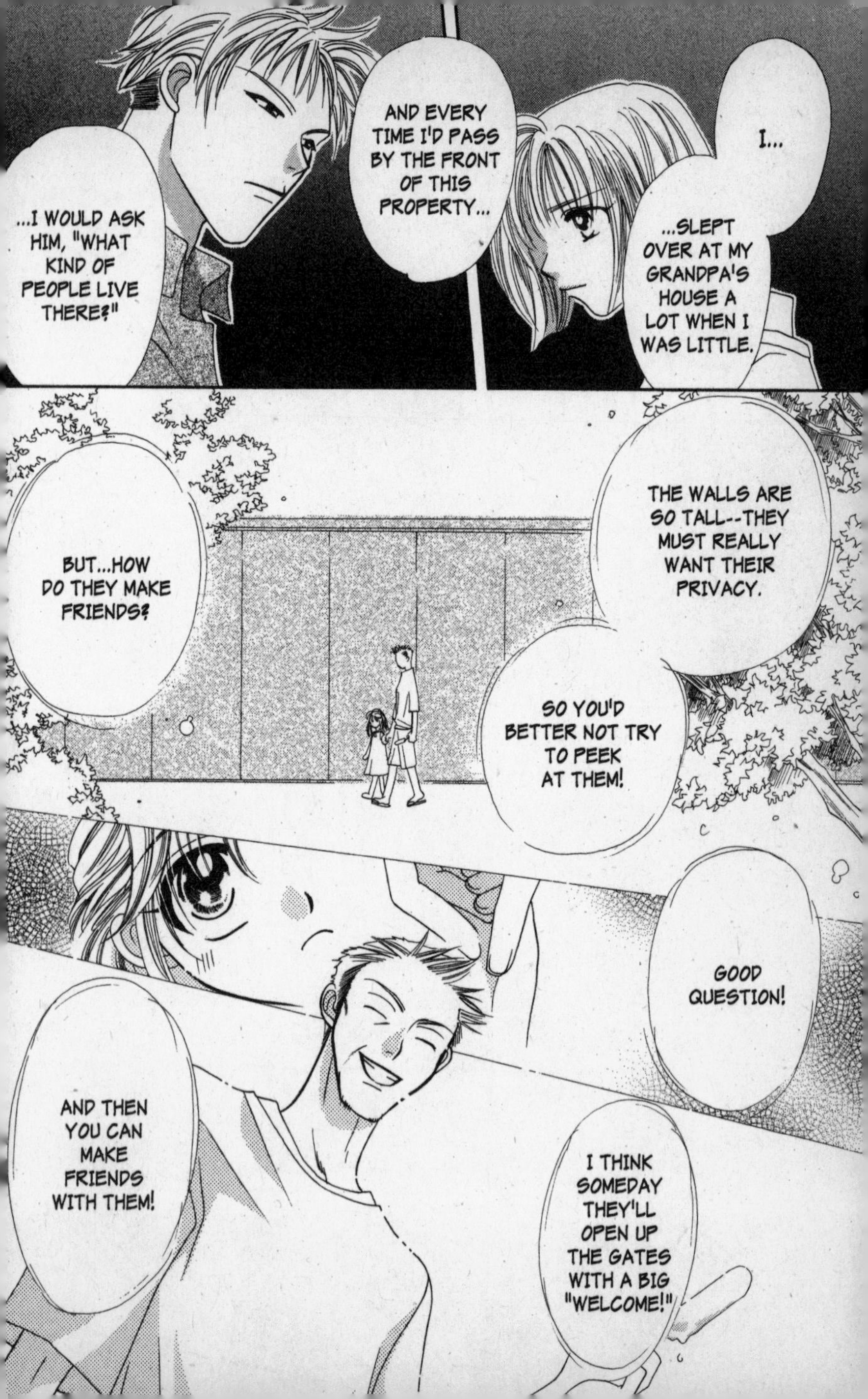
I...
...SLEPT OVER AT MY GRANDPA'S HOUSE A LOT WHEN I WAS LITTLE.
AND EVERY TIME I'D PASS BY THE FRONT OF THIS PROPERTY...
...I WOULD ASK HIM, "WHAT KIND OF PEOPLE LIVE THERE?"
THE WALLS ARE SO TALL--THEY MUST REALLY WANT THEIR PRIVACY.
SO YOU'D BETTER NOT TRY TO PEEK AT THEM!
BUT...HOW DO THEY MAKE FRIENDS?
GOOD QUESTION!
I THINK SOMEDAY THEY'LL OPEN UP THE GATES WITH A BIG "WELCOME!"
AND THEN YOU CAN MAKE FRIENDS WITH THEM!

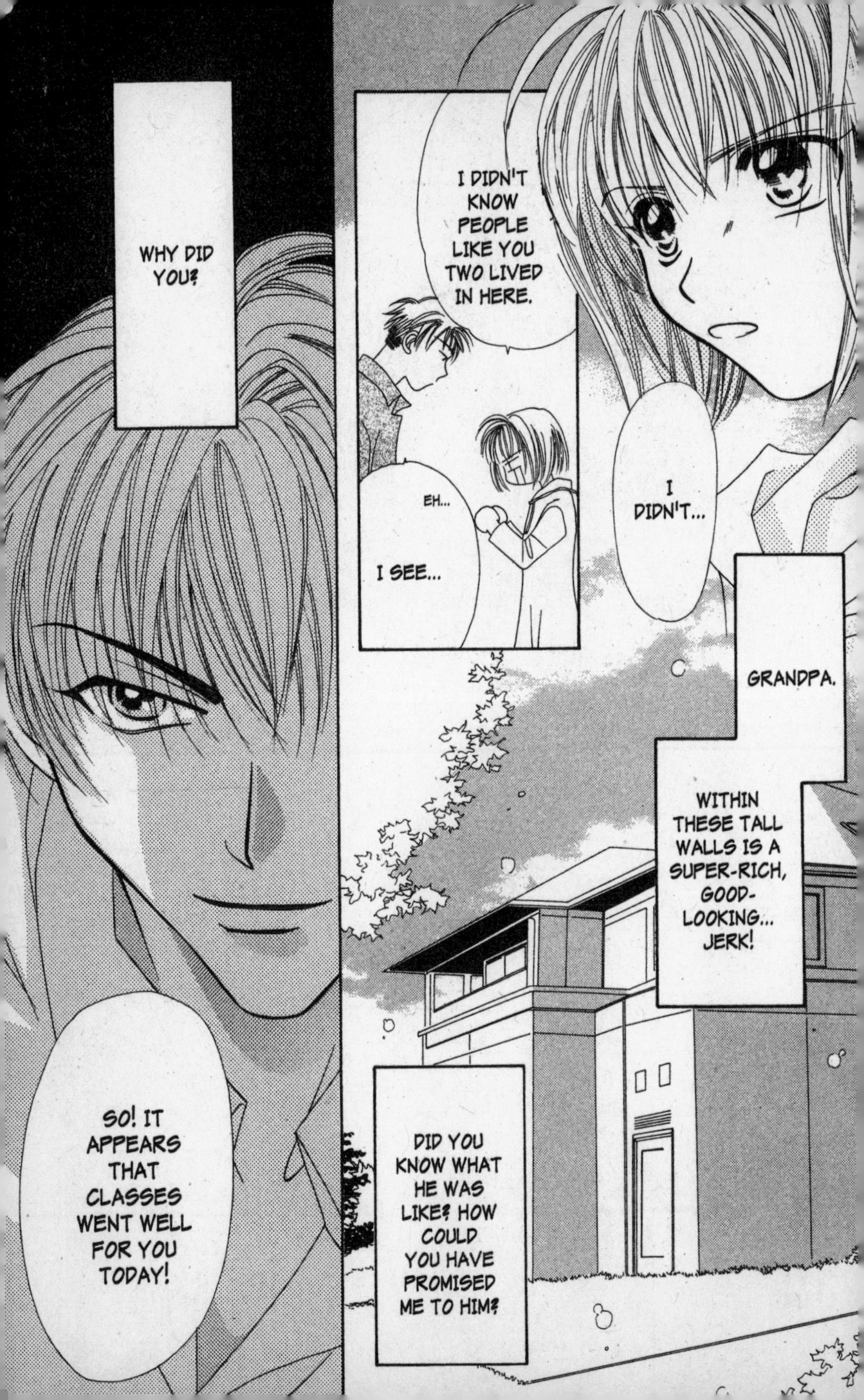
I DIDN'T KNOW PEOPLE LIKE YOU TWO LIVED IN HERE.
EH...
I SEE...
I DIDN'T...
GRANDPA.
WITHIN THESE TALL WALLS IS A SUPER-RICH, GOOD-LOOKING... JERK!
DID YOU KNOW WHAT HE WAS LIKE? HOW COULD YOU HAVE PROMISED ME TO HIM?
WHY DID YOU?
SO! IT APPEARS THAT CLASSES WENT WELL FOR YOU TODAY!

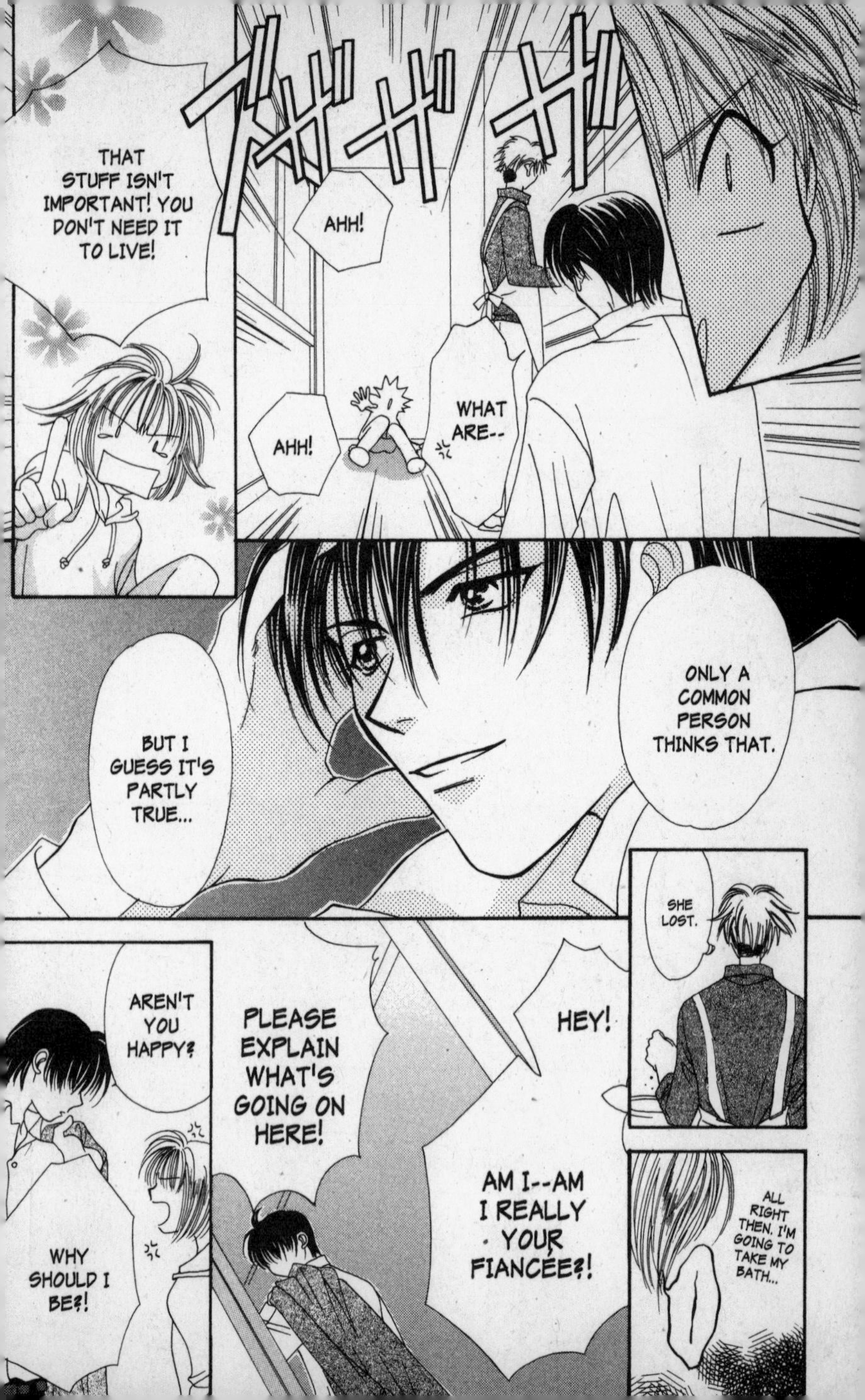
AHH!
WHAT ARE--
AHH!
THAT STUFF ISN'T IMPORTANT! YOU DON'T NEED IT TO LIVE!
ONLY A COMMON PERSON THINKS THAT.
BUT I GUESS IT'S PARTLY TRUE...
SHE LOST.
ALL RIGHT THEN. I'M GOING TO TAKE MY BATH...
HEY!
PLEASE EXPLAIN WHAT'S GOING ON HERE!
AM I--AM I REALLY YOUR FIANCÉE?!
AREN'T YOU HAPPY?
WHY SHOULD I BE?!

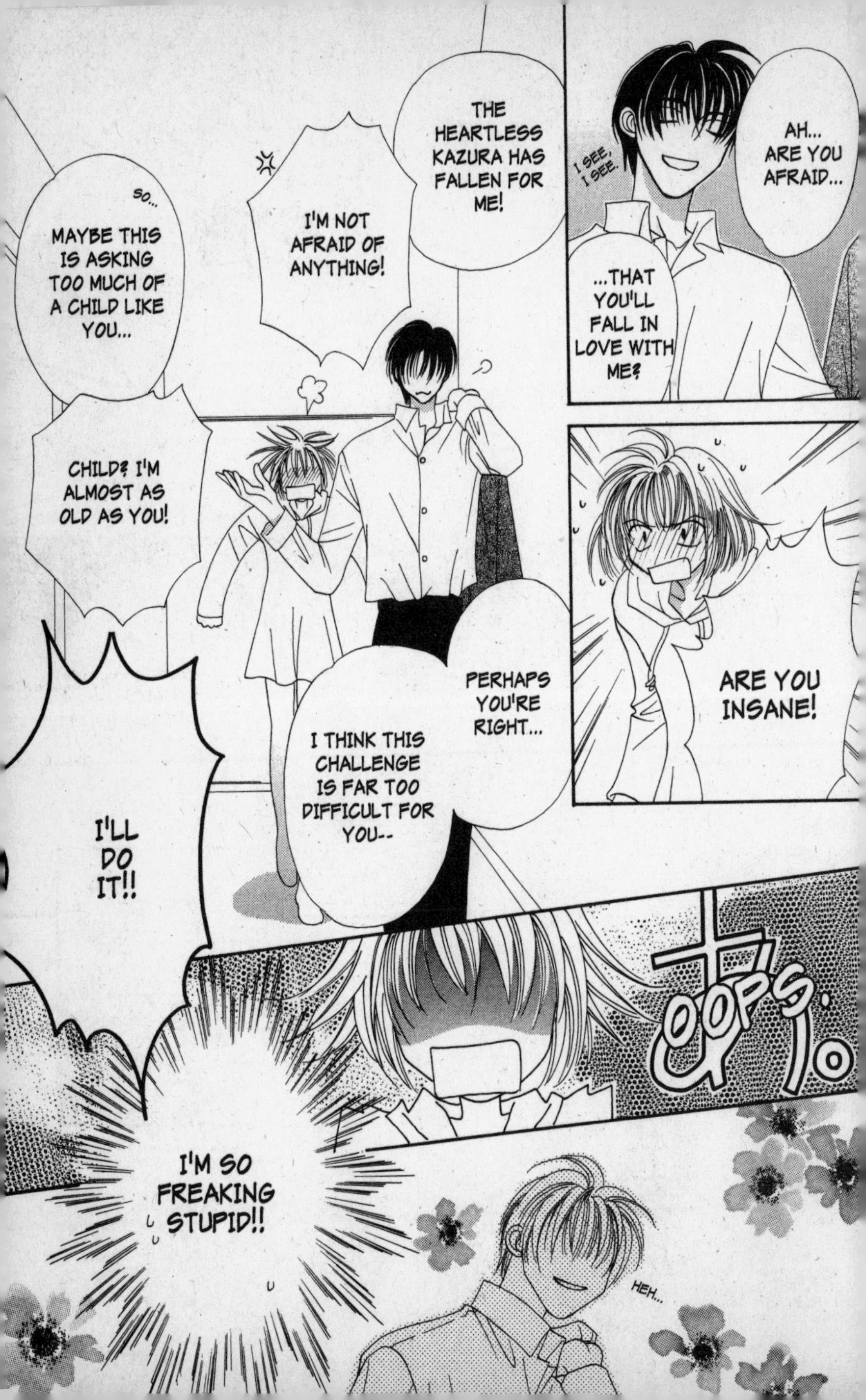
AH... ARE YOU AFRAID...
I SEE, I SEE.
...THAT YOU'LL FALL IN LOVE WITH ME?
ARE YOU INSANE!
THE HEARTLESS KAZURA HAS FALLEN FOR ME!
I'M NOT AFRAID OF ANYTHING!
SO...
MAYBE THIS IS ASKING TOO MUCH OF A CHILD LIKE YOU...
CHILD? I'M ALMOST AS OLD AS YOU!
PERHAPS YOU'RE RIGHT...
I THINK THIS CHALLENGE IS FAR TOO DIFFICULT FOR YOU--
I'LL DO IT!!
OOPS.
I'M SO FREAKING STUPID!!
HEH...

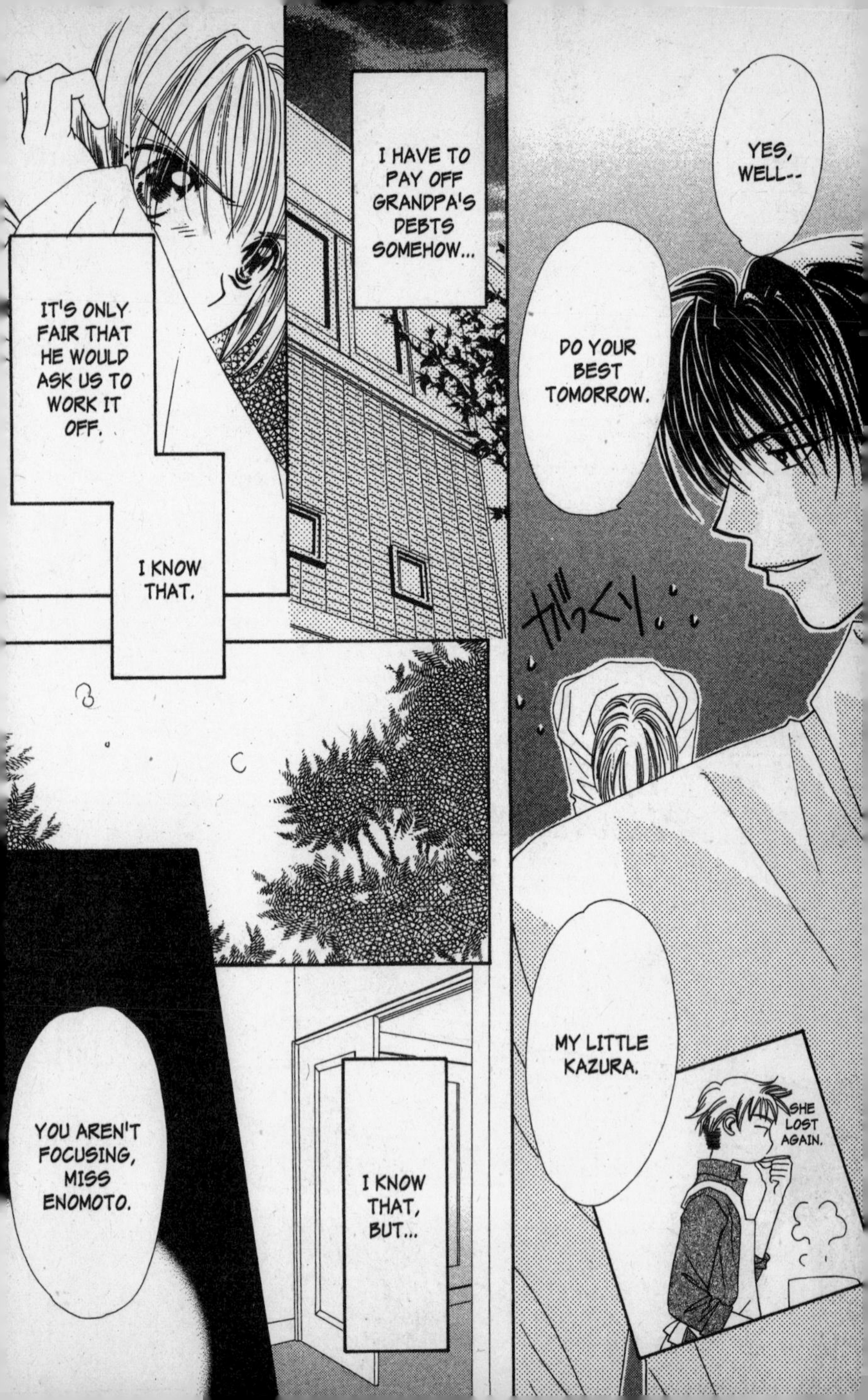
YES, WELL--
DO YOUR BEST TOMORROW.
がっくり
MY LITTLE KAZURA.
SHE LOST AGAIN.
I HAVE TO PAY OFF GRANDPA'S DEBTS SOMEHOW...
IT'S ONLY FAIR THAT HE WOULD ASK US TO WORK IT OFF.
I KNOW THAT.
I KNOW THAT, BUT...
YOU AREN'T FOCUSING, MISS ENOMOTO.

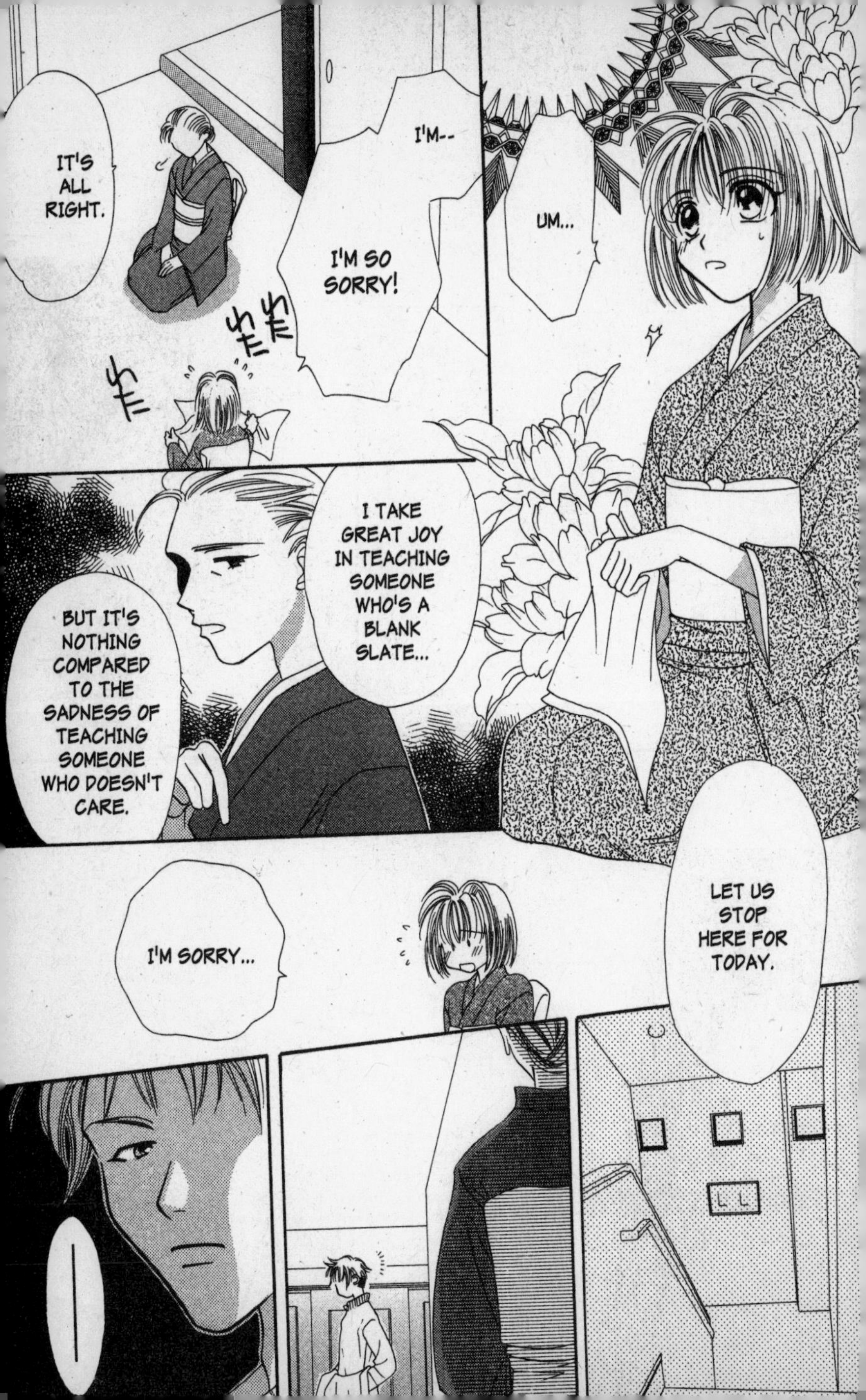
UM...
I'M--
I'M SO SORRY!
IT'S ALL RIGHT.
I TAKE GREAT JOY IN TEACHING SOMEONE WHO'S A BLANK SLATE...
BUT IT'S NOTHING COMPARED TO THE SADNESS OF TEACHING SOMEONE WHO DOESN'T CARE.
LET US STOP HERE FOR TODAY.
I'M SORRY...
—

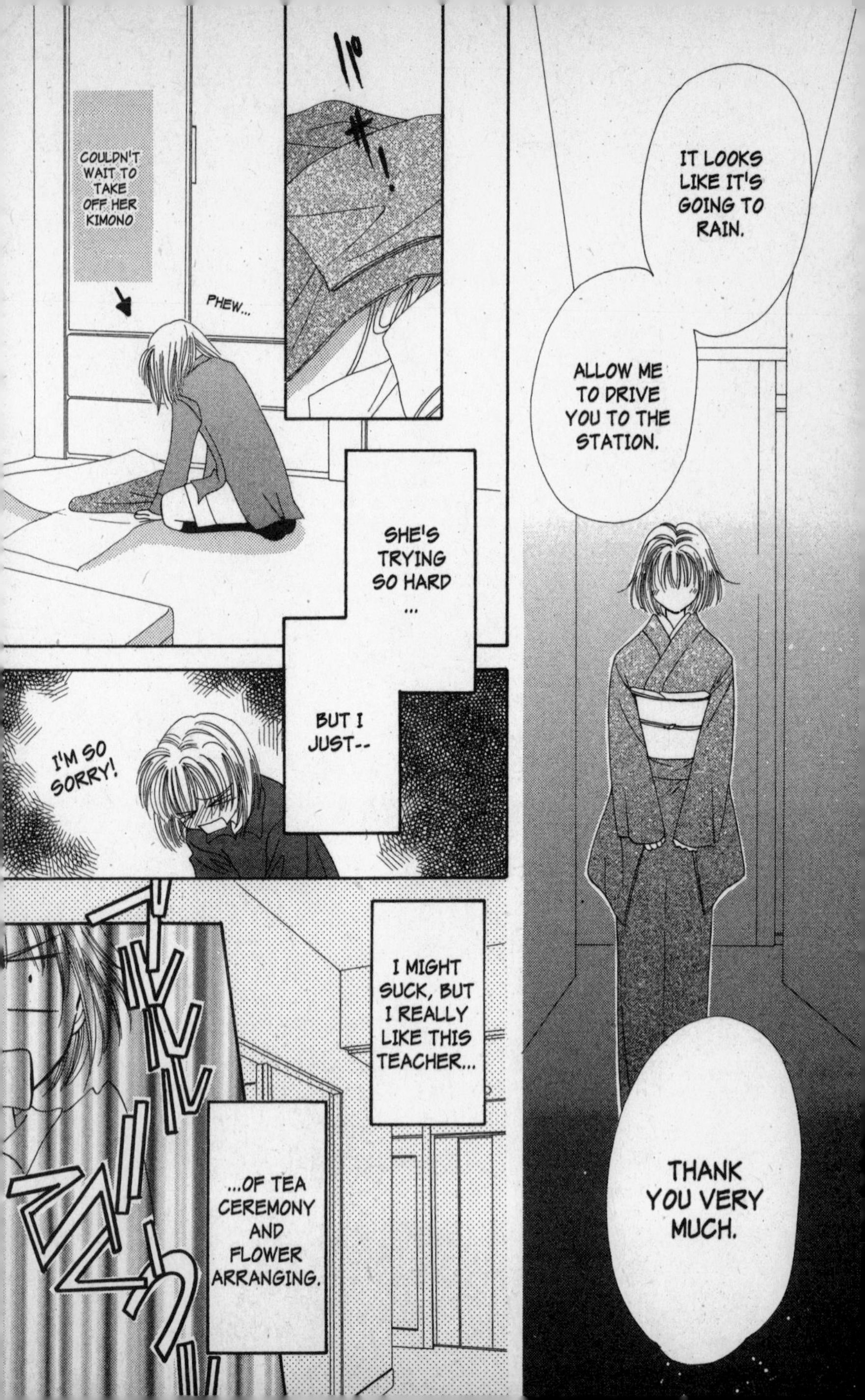
IT LOOKS LIKE IT'S GOING TO RAIN.
ALLOW ME TO DRIVE YOU TO THE STATION.
THANK YOU VERY MUCH.
COULDN'T WAIT TO TAKE OFF HER KIMONO
PHEW...
SHE'S TRYING SO HARD ...
BUT I JUST--
I'M SO SORRY!
I MIGHT SUCK, BUT I REALLY LIKE THIS TEACHER...
...OF TEA CEREMONY AND FLOWER ARRANGING.

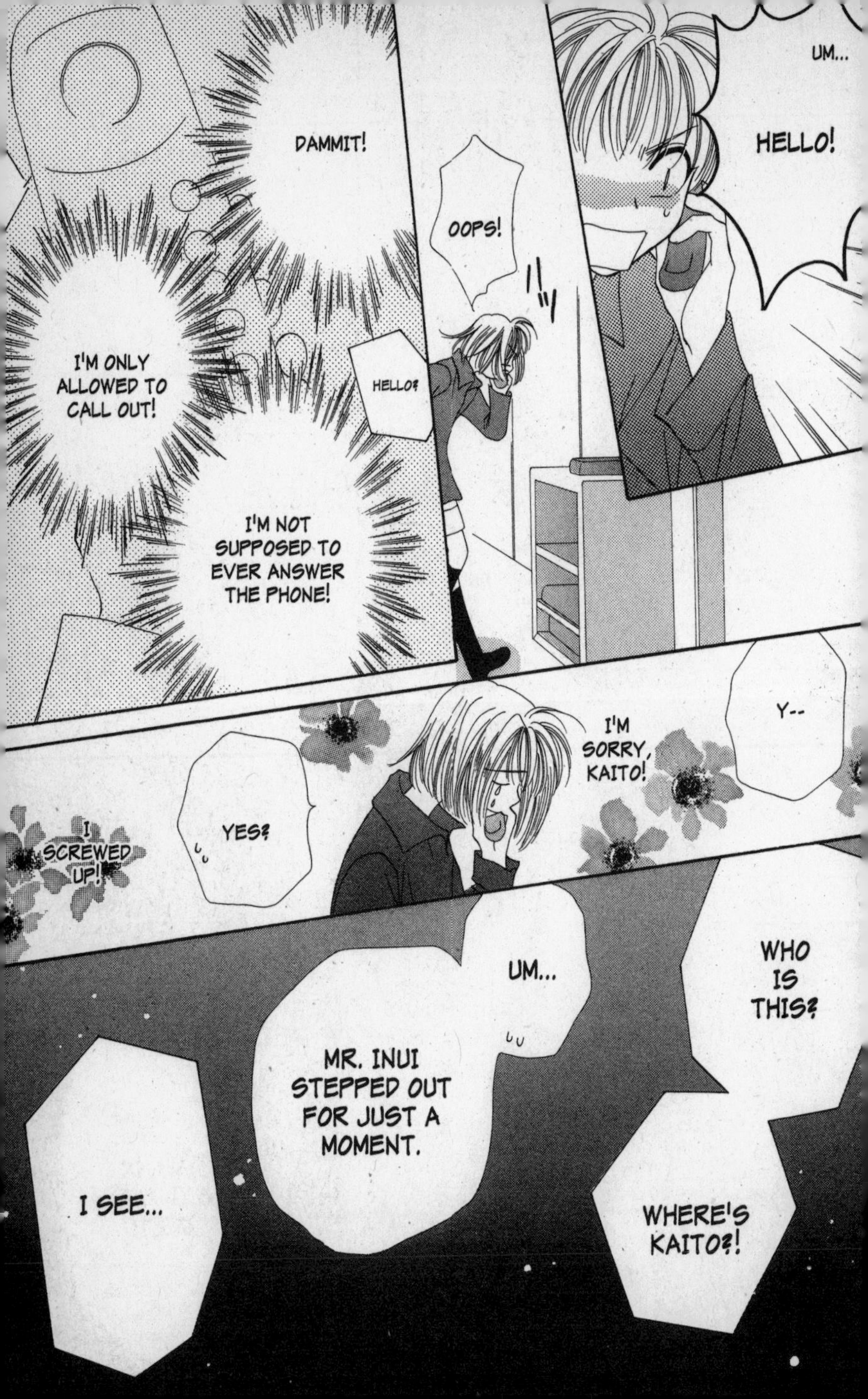
UM...
HELLO!
OOPS!
HELLO?
DAMMIT!
I'M ONLY ALLOWED TO CALL OUT!
I'M NOT SUPPOSED TO EVER ANSWER THE PHONE!
Y--
I'M SORRY, KAITO!
YES?
I SCREWED UP!
WHO IS THIS?
WHERE'S KAITO?!
UM...
MR. INUI STEPPED OUT FOR JUST A MOMENT.
I SEE...

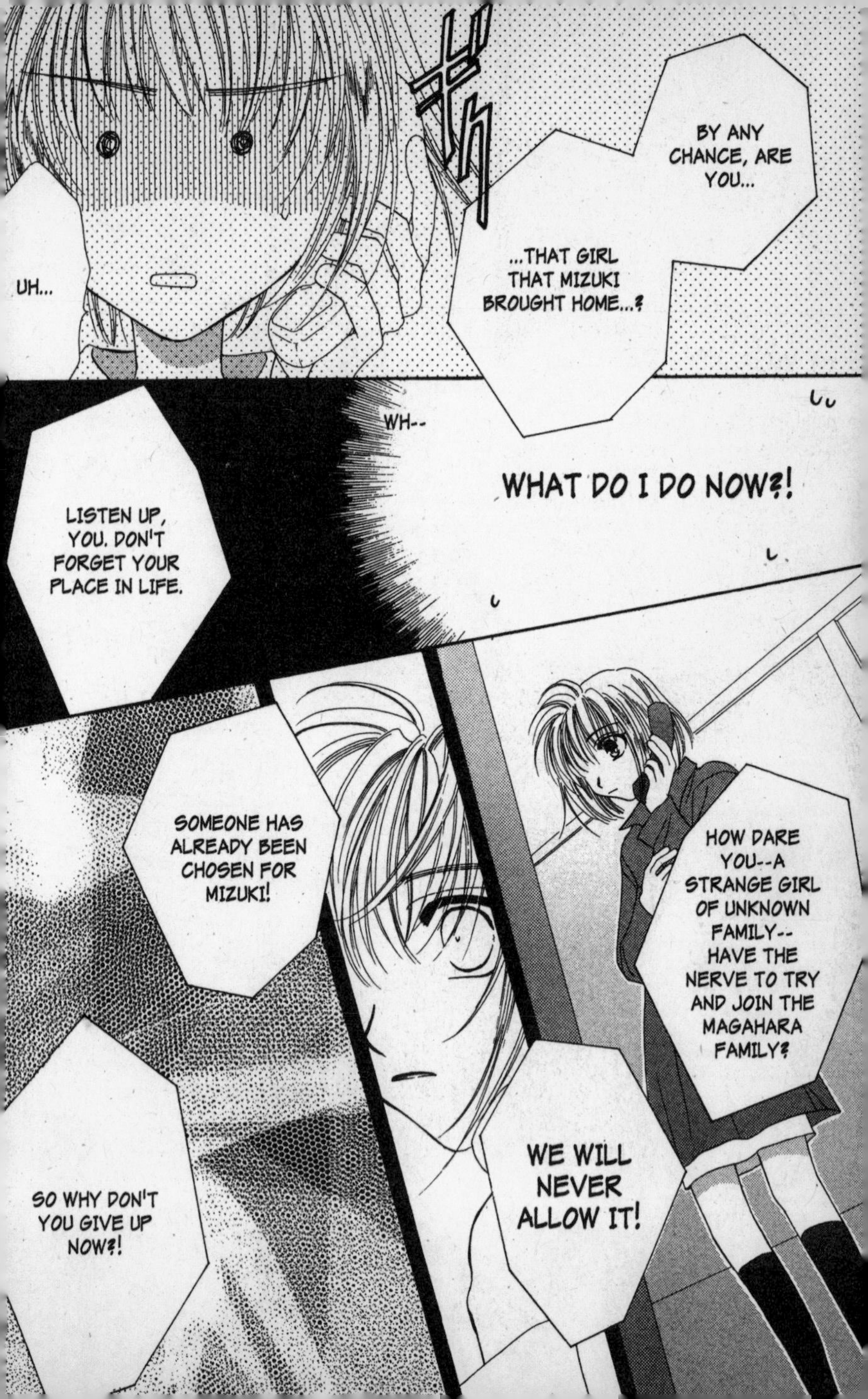
BY ANY CHANCE, ARE YOU...
...THAT GIRL THAT MIZUKI BROUGHT HOME...?
UH...
WH--
WHAT DO I DO NOW?!
LISTEN UP, YOU. DON'T FORGET YOUR PLACE IN LIFE.
HOW DARE YOU--A STRANGE GIRL OF UNKNOWN FAMILY--HAVE THE NERVE TO TRY AND JOIN THE MAGAHARA FAMILY?
WE WILL NEVER ALLOW IT!
SOMEONE HAS ALREADY BEEN CHOSEN FOR MIZUKI!
SO WHY DON'T YOU GIVE UP NOW?!

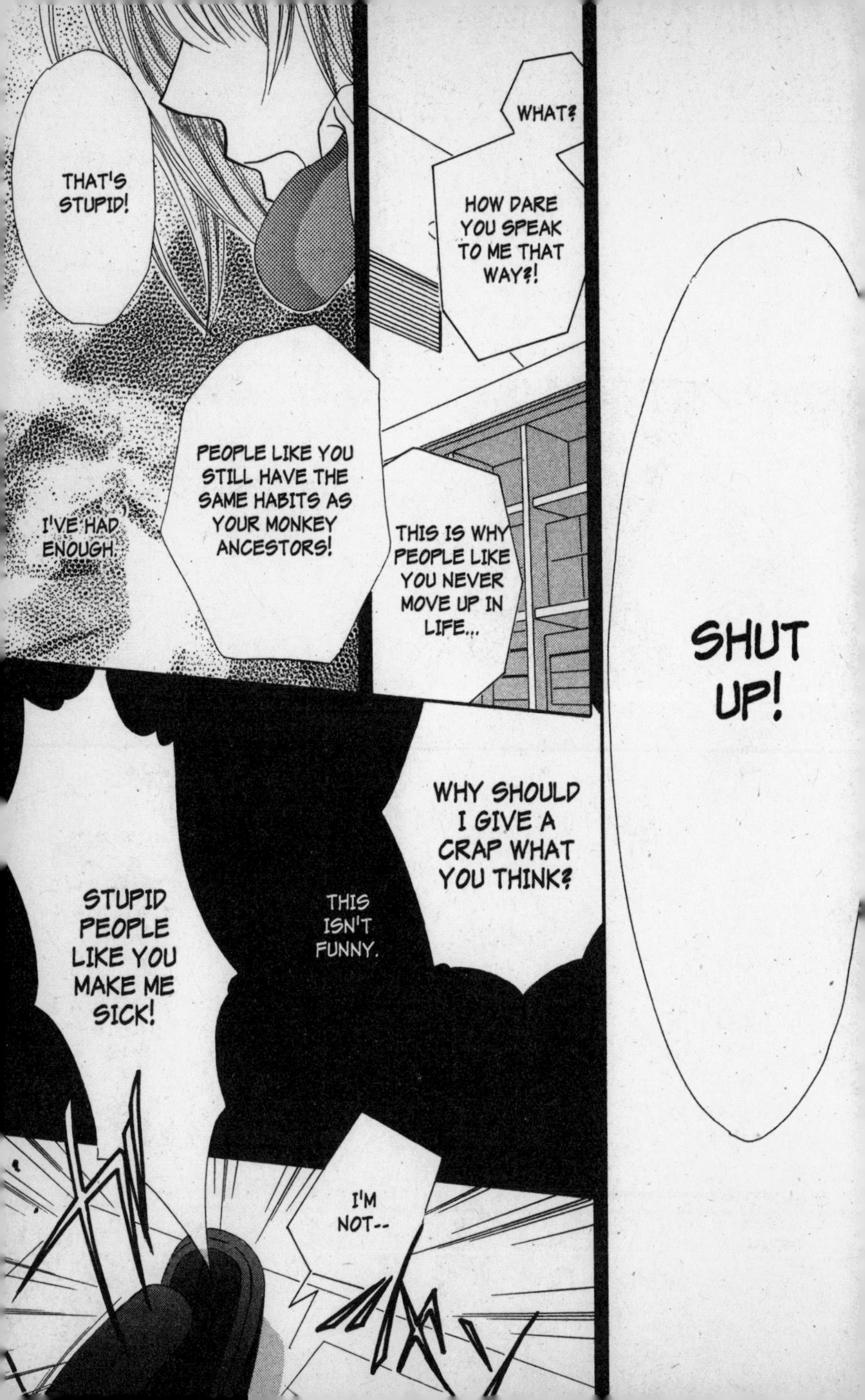
SHUT UP!
WHAT?
HOW DARE YOU SPEAK TO ME THAT WAY?!
THIS IS WHY PEOPLE LIKE YOU NEVER MOVE UP IN LIFE...
THAT'S STUPID!
PEOPLE LIKE YOU STILL HAVE THE SAME HABITS AS YOUR MONKEY ANCESTORS!
I'VE HAD ENOUGH.
WHY SHOULD I GIVE A CRAP WHAT YOU THINK?
THIS ISN'T FUNNY.
STUPID PEOPLE LIKE YOU MAKE ME SICK!
I'M NOT--

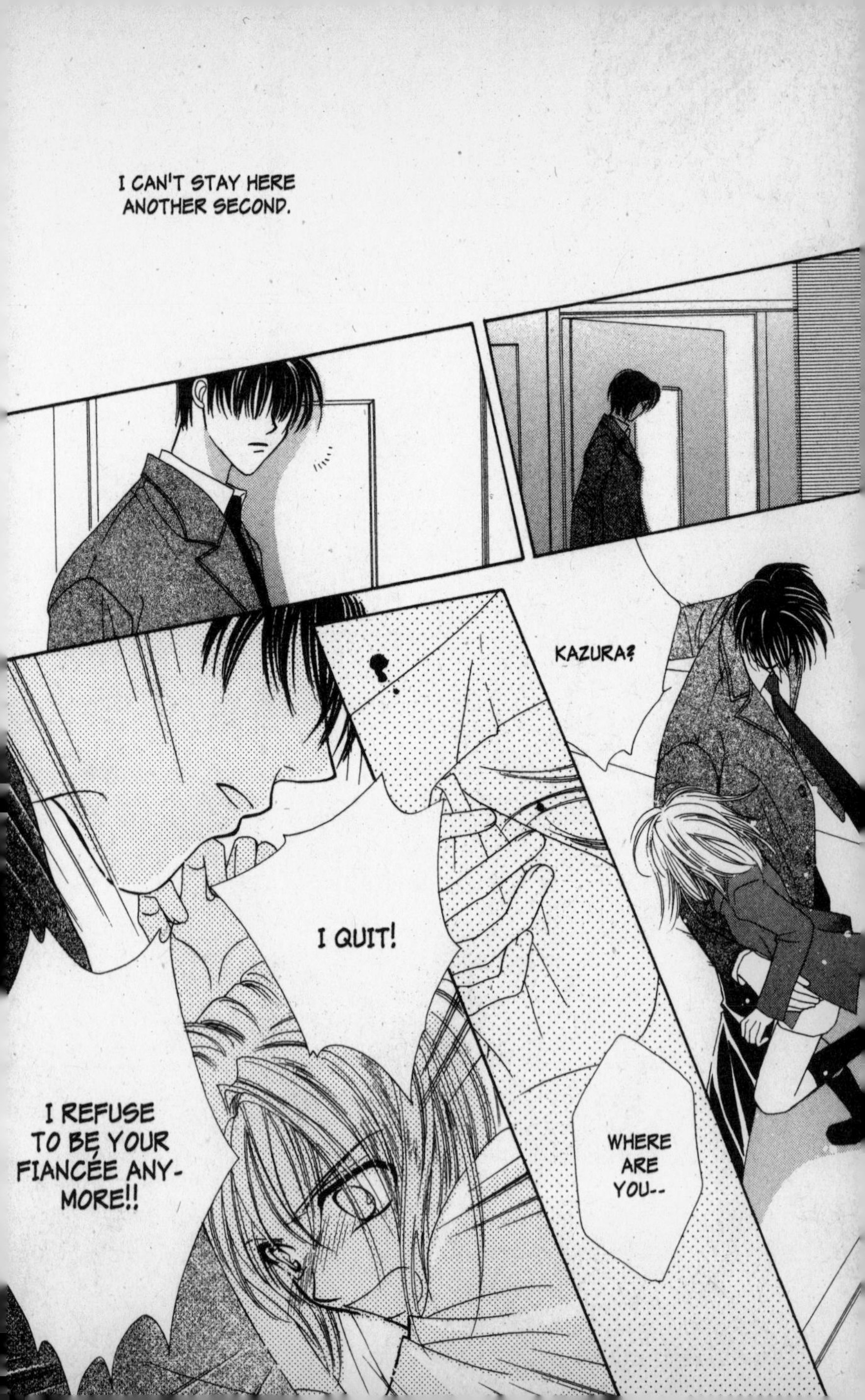
I CAN'T STAY HERE ANOTHER SECOND.
KAZURA?
WHERE ARE YOU--
I QUIT!
I REFUSE TO BE YOUR FIANCÉE ANYMORE!!

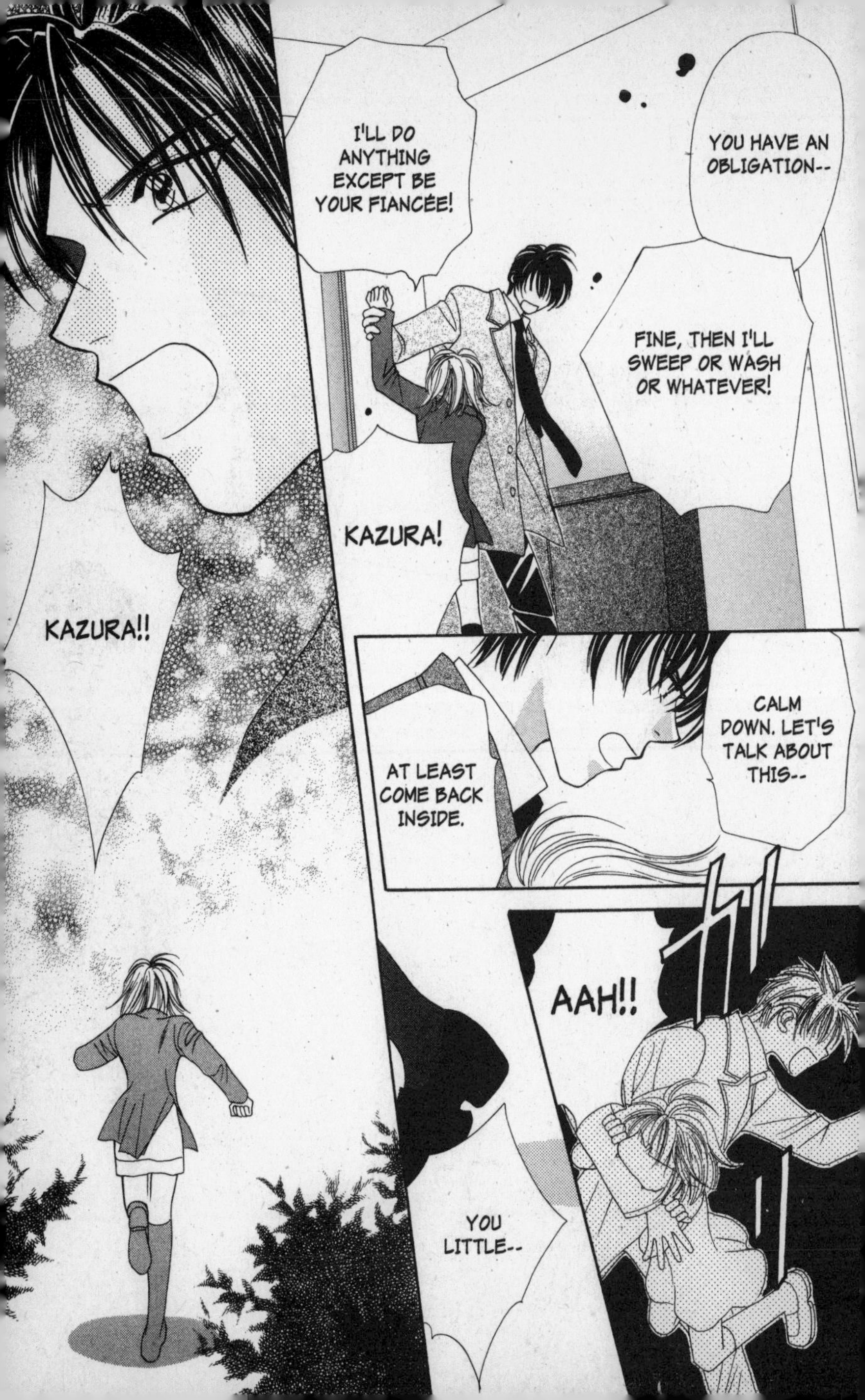
YOU HAVE AN OBLIGATION--
I'LL DO ANYTHING EXCEPT BE YOUR FIANCÉE!
FINE, THEN I'LL SWEEP OR WASH OR WHATEVER!
KAZURA!
CALM DOWN. LET'S TALK ABOUT THIS--
AT LEAST COME BACK INSIDE.
AAH!!
YOU LITTLE--
KAZURA!!

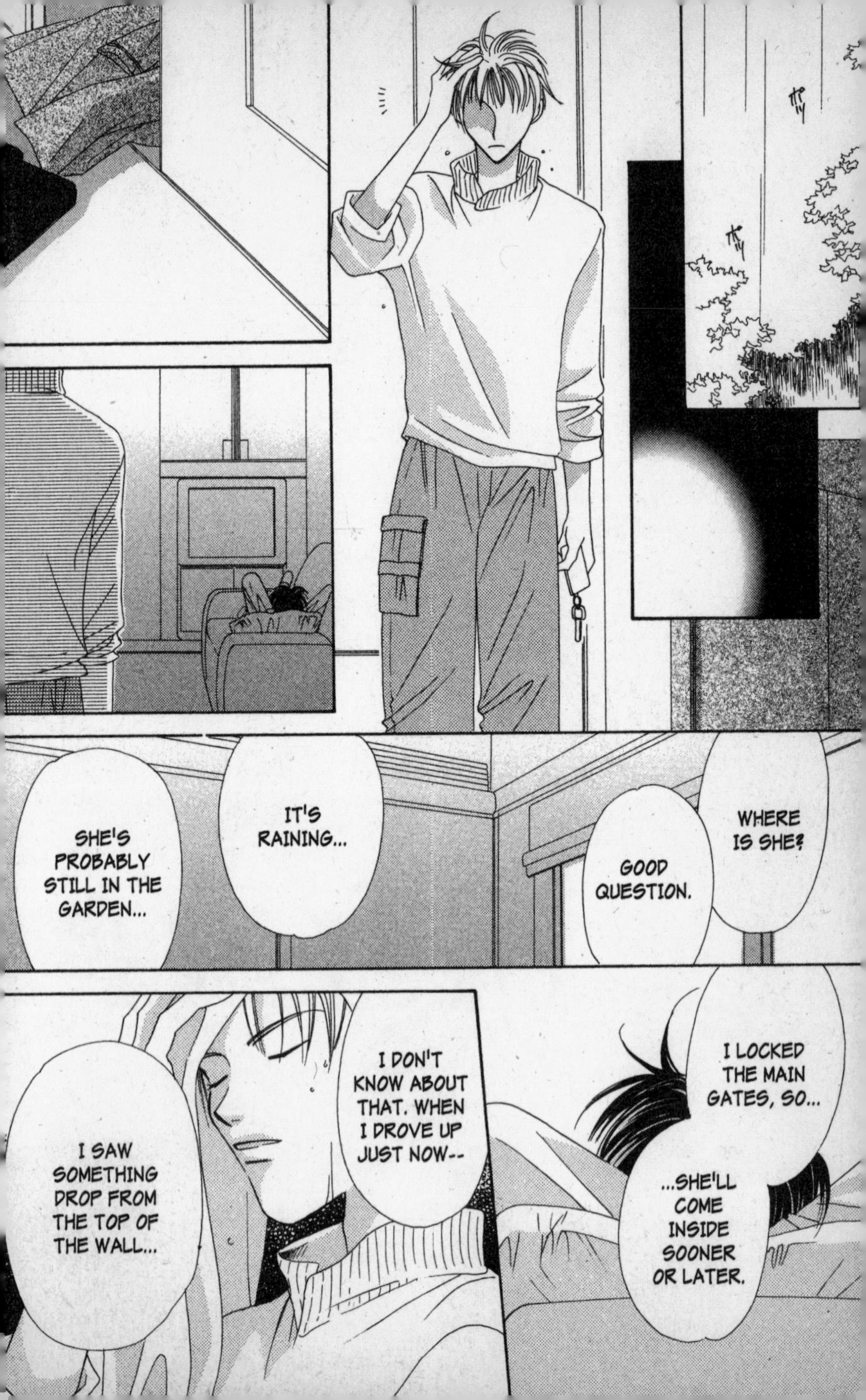
WHERE IS SHE?
GOOD QUESTION.
IT'S RAINING...
SHE'S PROBABLY STILL IN THE GARDEN...
I LOCKED THE MAIN GATES, SO...
...SHE'LL COME INSIDE SOONER OR LATER.
I DON'T KNOW ABOUT THAT. WHEN I DROVE UP JUST NOW--
I SAW SOMETHING DROP FROM THE TOP OF THE WALL...

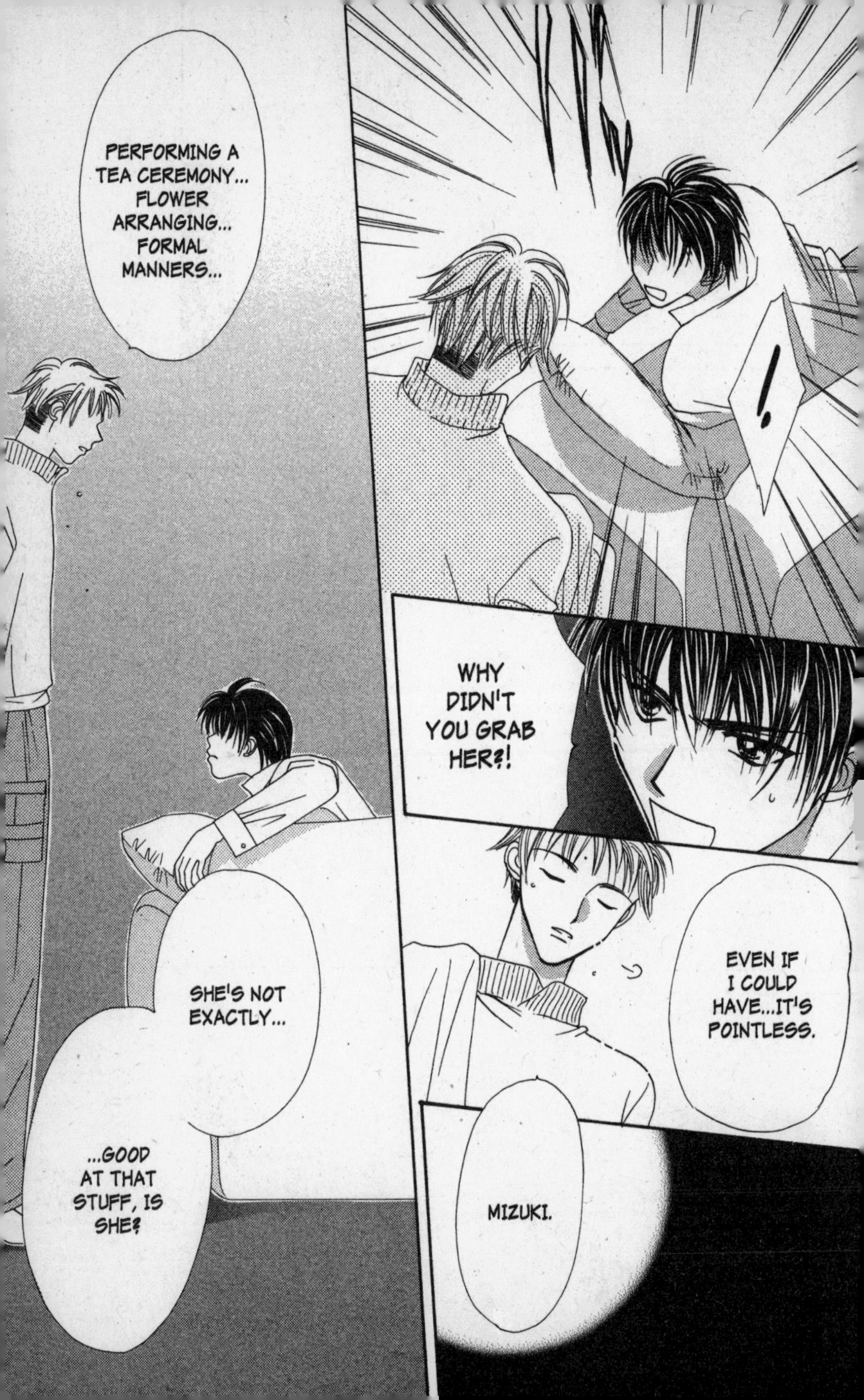
!
WHY DIDN'T YOU GRAB HER?!
EVEN IF I COULD HAVE...IT'S POINTLESS.
MIZUKI.
PERFORMING A TEA CEREMONY... FLOWER ARRANGING... FORMAL MANNERS...
SHE'S NOT EXACTLY...
...GOOD AT THAT STUFF, IS SHE?

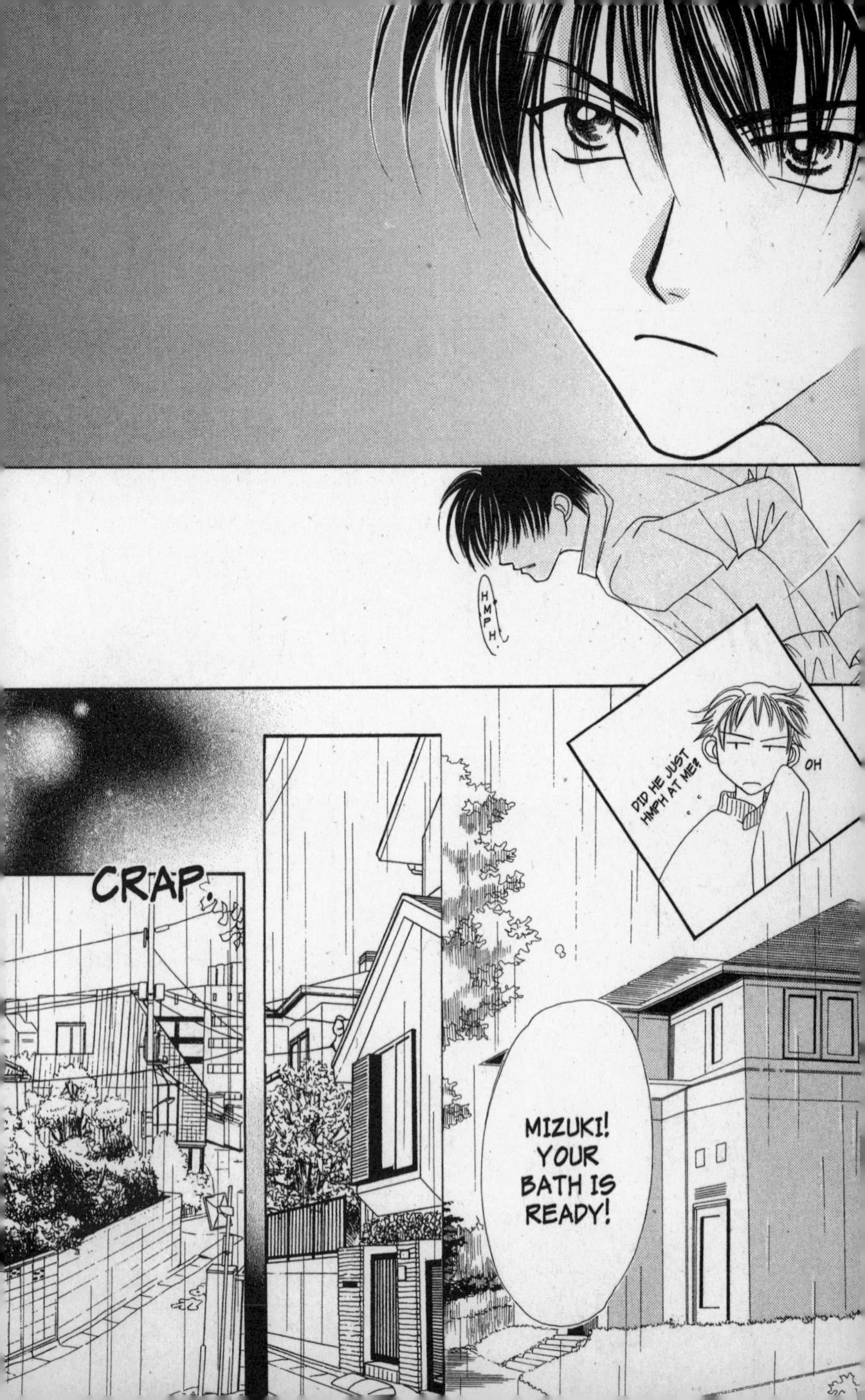
HMPH.
OH
DID HE JUST HMPH AT ME?
MIZUKI! YOUR BATH IS READY!
CRAP

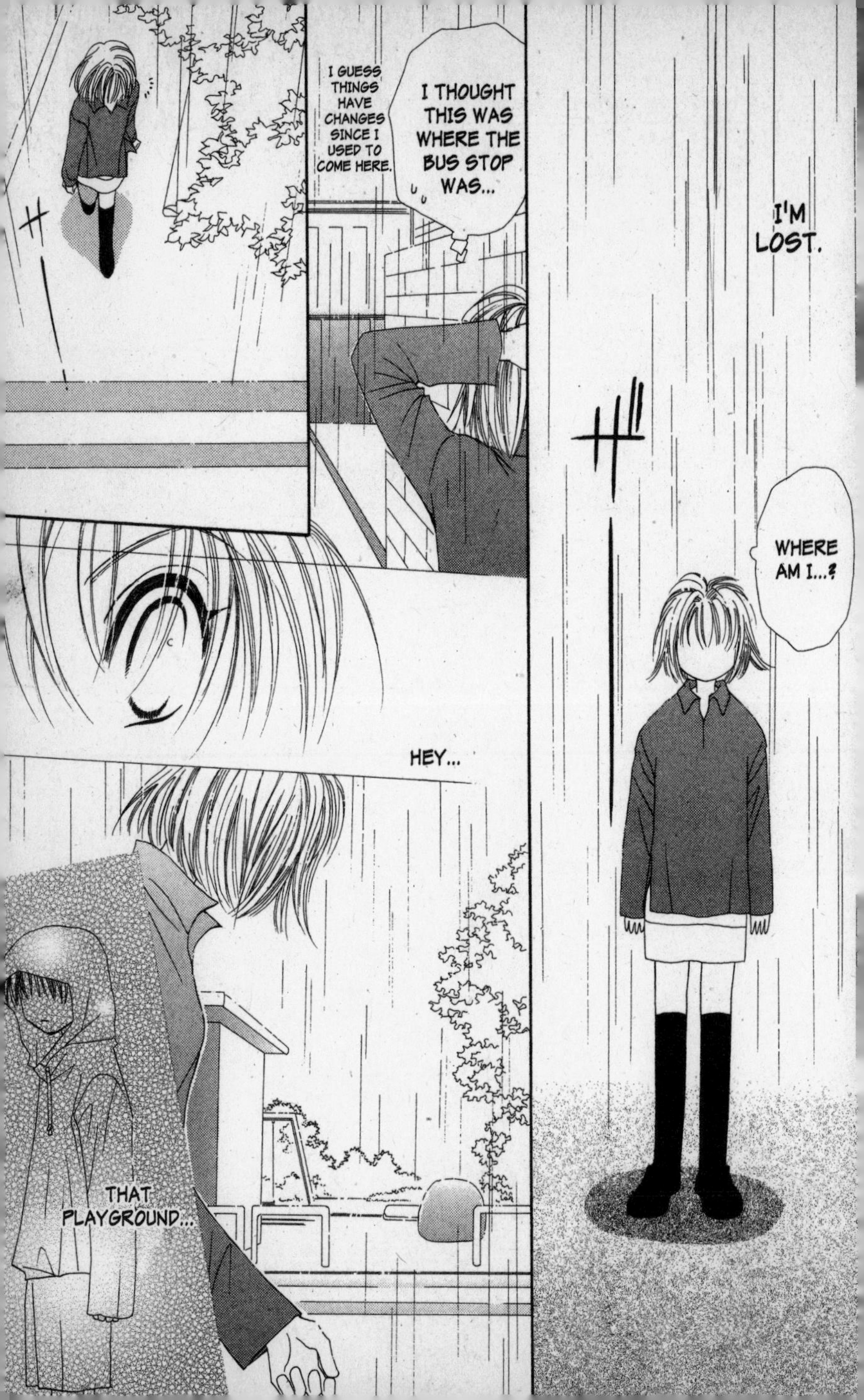
I'M LOST.
WHERE AM I...?
I THOUGHT THIS WAS WHERE THE BUS STOP WAS...
I GUESS THINGS HAVE CHANGES SINCE I USED TO COME HERE.
HEY...
THAT PLAYGROUND...

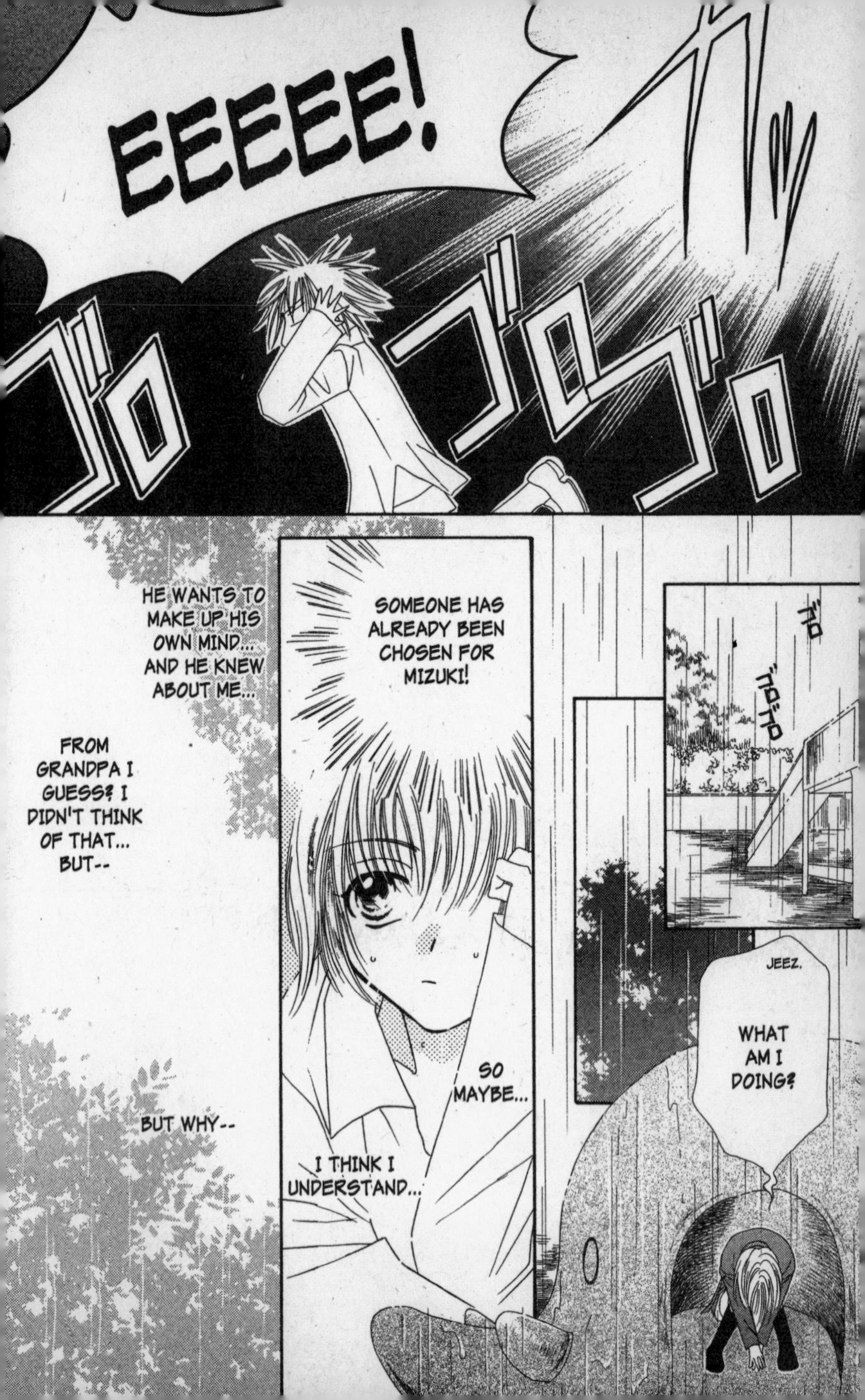
EEEEEE!
ゴロ ゴロ ゴロ
JEEZ.
WHAT AM I DOING?
SOMEONE HAS ALREADY BEEN CHOSEN FOR MIZUKI!
SO MAYBE...
I THINK I UNDERSTAND...
HE WANTS TO MAKE UP HIS OWN MIND... AND HE KNEW ABOUT ME...
FROM GRANDPA I GUESS? I DIDN'T THINK OF THAT... BUT--
BUT WHY--

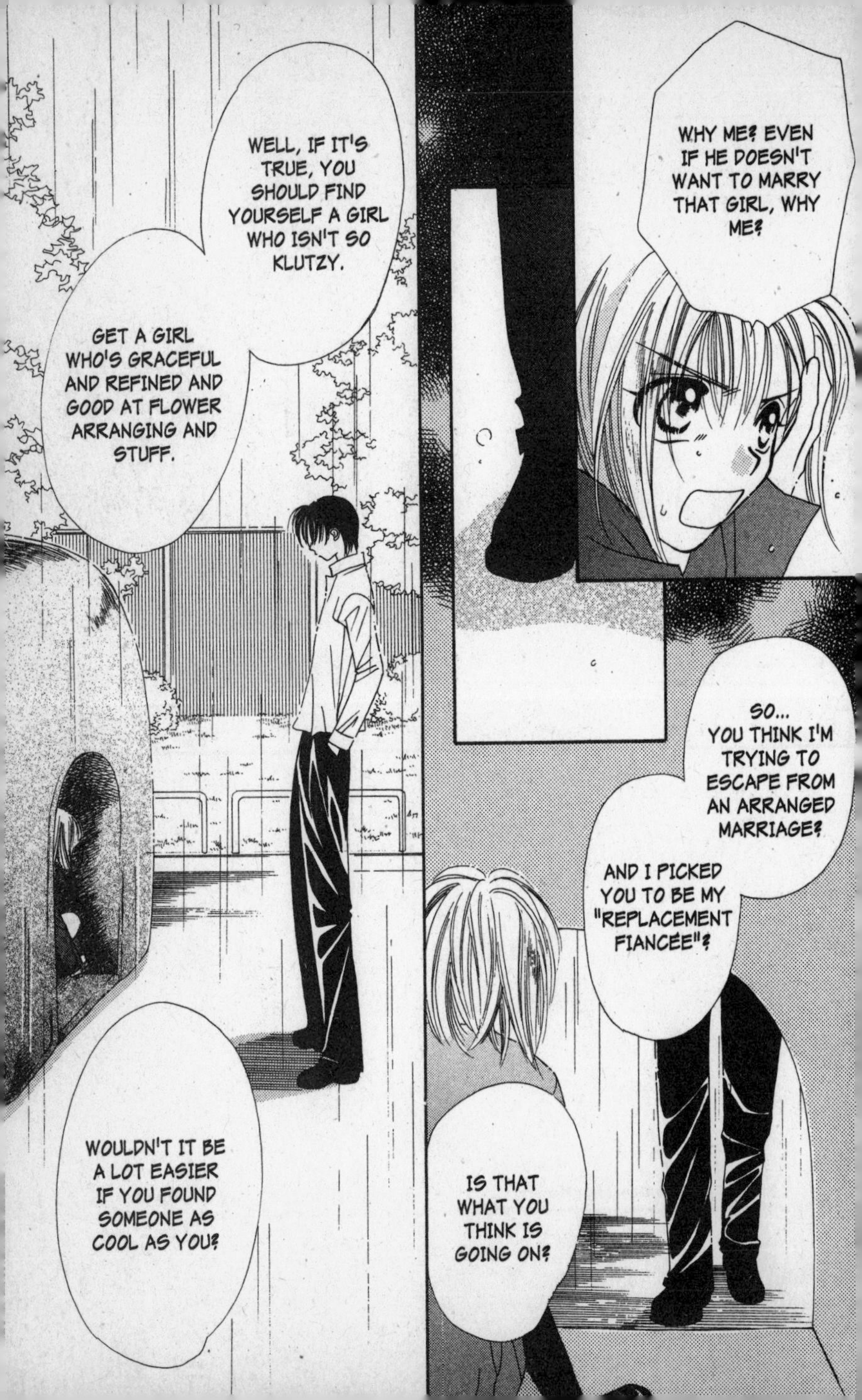
WHY ME? EVEN IF HE DOESN'T WANT TO MARRY THAT GIRL, WHY ME?
SO... YOU THINK I'M TRYING TO ESCAPE FROM AN ARRANGED MARRIAGE?
AND I PICKED YOU TO BE MY "REPLACEMENT FIANCEE"?
IS THAT WHAT YOU THINK IS GOING ON?
WELL, IF IT'S TRUE, YOU SHOULD FIND YOURSELF A GIRL WHO ISN'T SO KLUTZY.
GET A GIRL WHO'S GRACEFUL AND REFINED AND GOOD AT FLOWER ARRANGING AND STUFF.
WOULDN'T IT BE A LOT EASIER IF YOU FOUND SOMEONE AS COOL AS YOU?

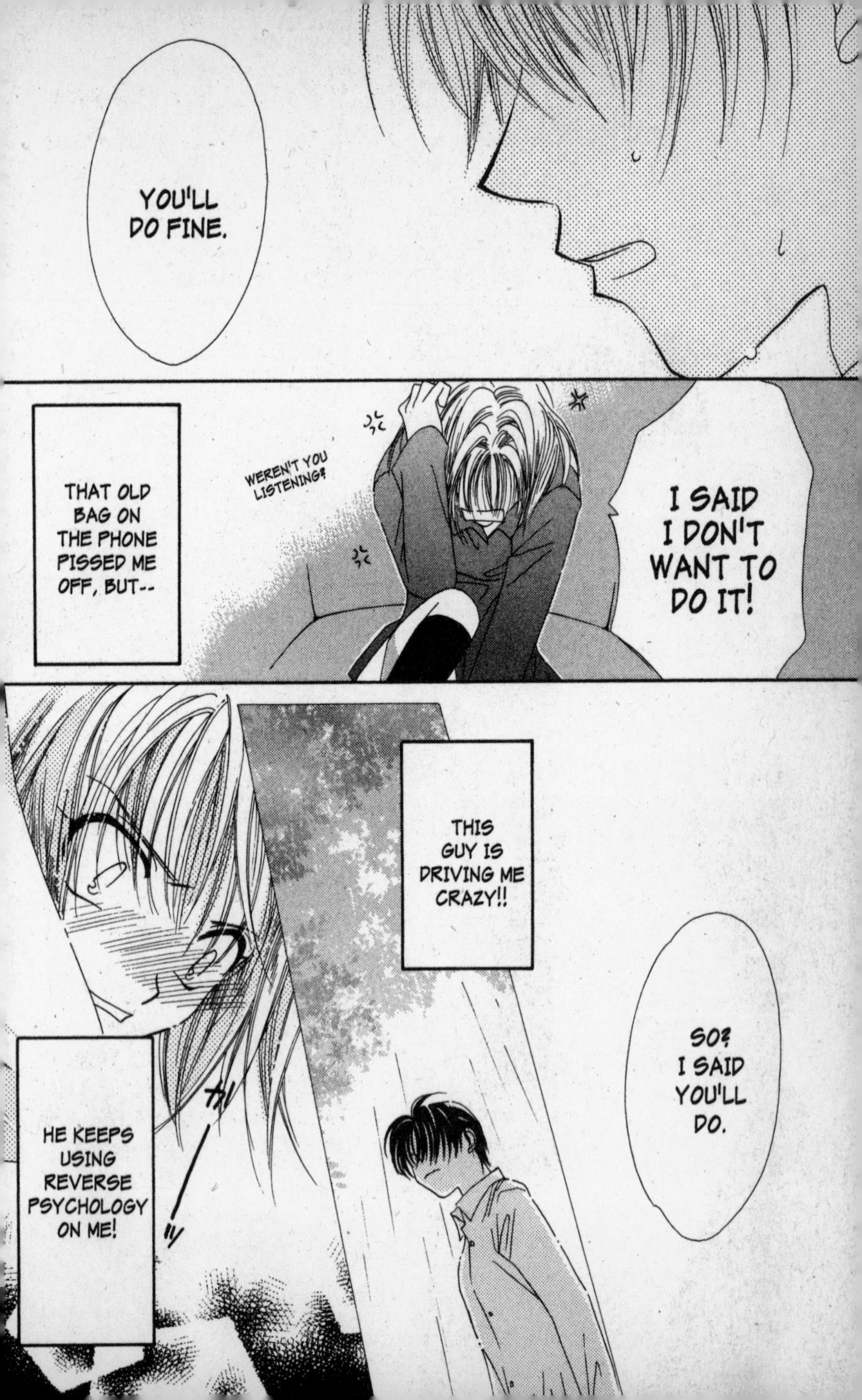
YOU'LL DO FINE.
I SAID I DON'T WANT TO DO IT!
WEREN'T YOU LISTENING?
THAT OLD BAG ON THE PHONE PISSED ME OFF, BUT--
SO? I SAID YOU'LL DO.
THIS GUY IS DRIVING ME CRAZY!!
HE KEEPS USING REVERSE PSYCHOLOGY ON ME!

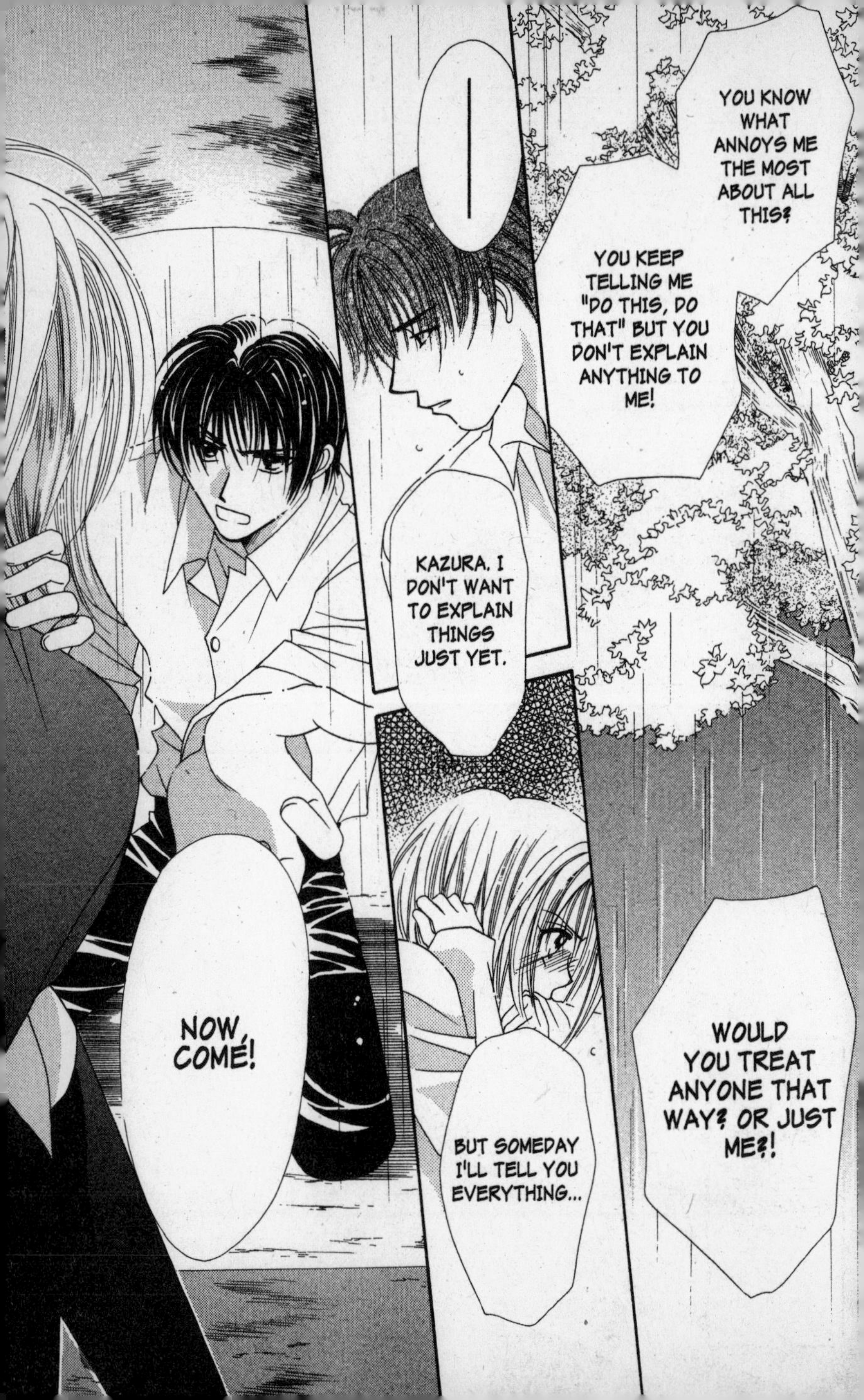

YOU KNOW WHAT ANNOYS ME THE MOST ABOUT ALL THIS?
YOU KEEP TELLING ME "DO THIS, DO THAT" BUT YOU DON'T EXPLAIN ANYTHING TO ME!
WOULD YOU TREAT ANYONE THAT WAY? OR JUST ME?!
—
KAZURA. I DON'T WANT TO EXPLAIN THINGS JUST YET.
BUT SOMEDAY I'LL TELL YOU EVERYTHING...
NOW, COME!

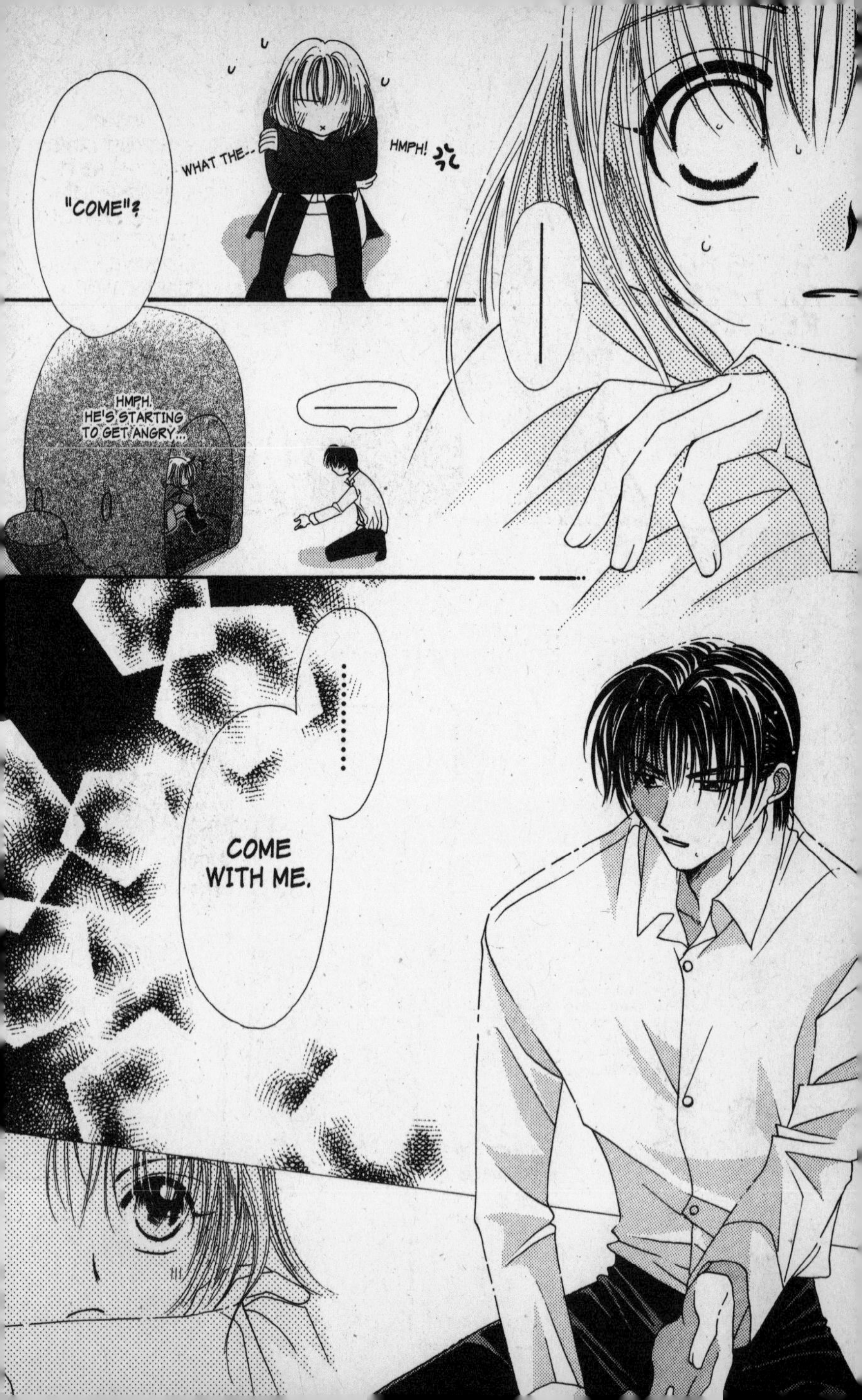
—
HMPH!
WHAT THE...
"COME"?
———
HMPH. HE'S STARTING TO GET ANGRY...
......
COME WITH ME.

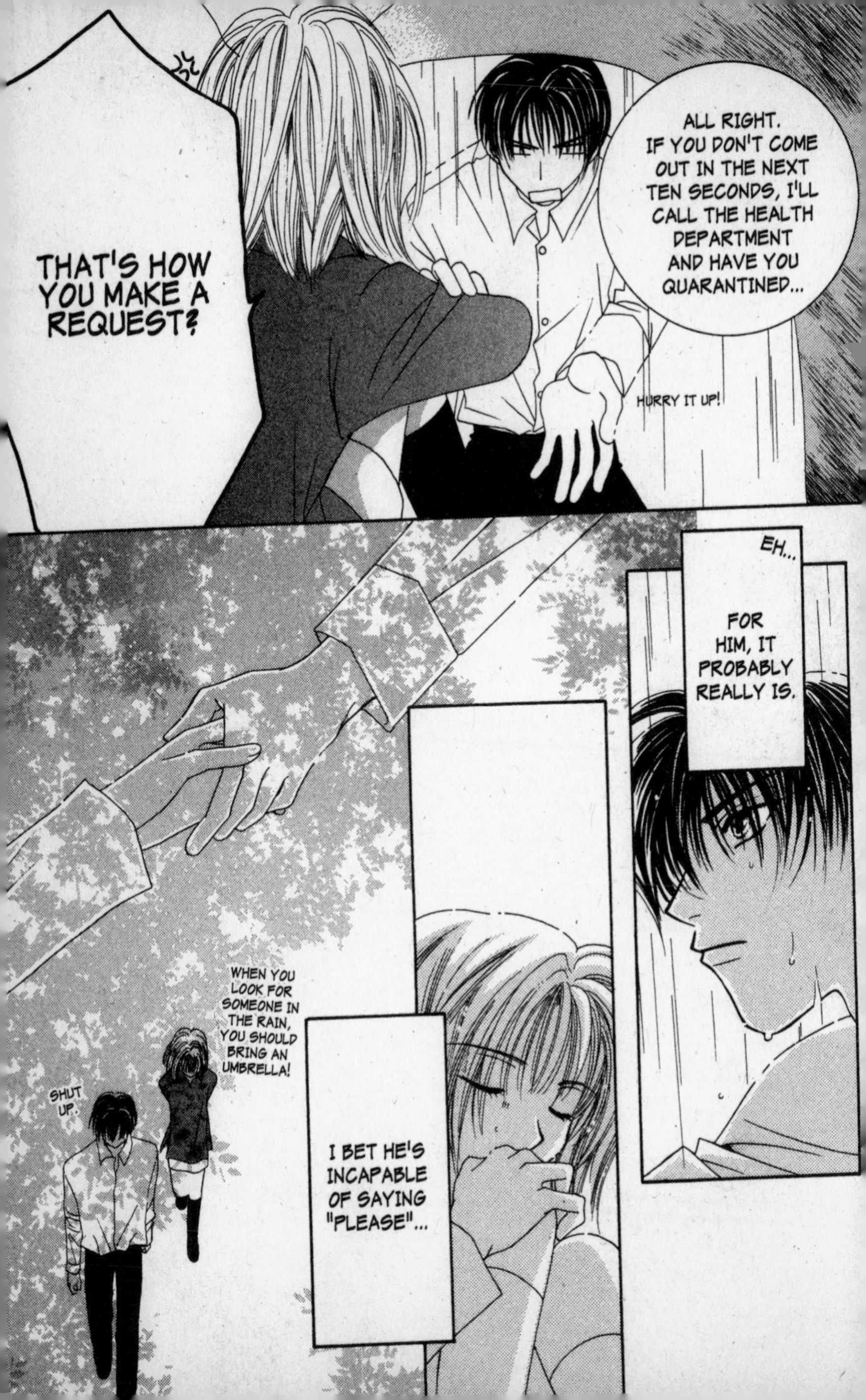
ALL RIGHT. IF YOU DON'T COME OUT IN THE NEXT TEN SECONDS, I'LL CALL THE HEALTH DEPARTMENT AND HAVE YOU QUARANTINED...
HURRY IT UP!
THAT'S HOW YOU MAKE A REQUEST?
EH...
FOR HIM, IT PROBABLY REALLY IS.
I BET HE'S INCAPABLE OF SAYING "PLEASE"...
WHEN YOU LOOK FOR SOMEONE IN THE RAIN, YOU SHOULD BRING AN UMBRELLA!
SHUT UP.

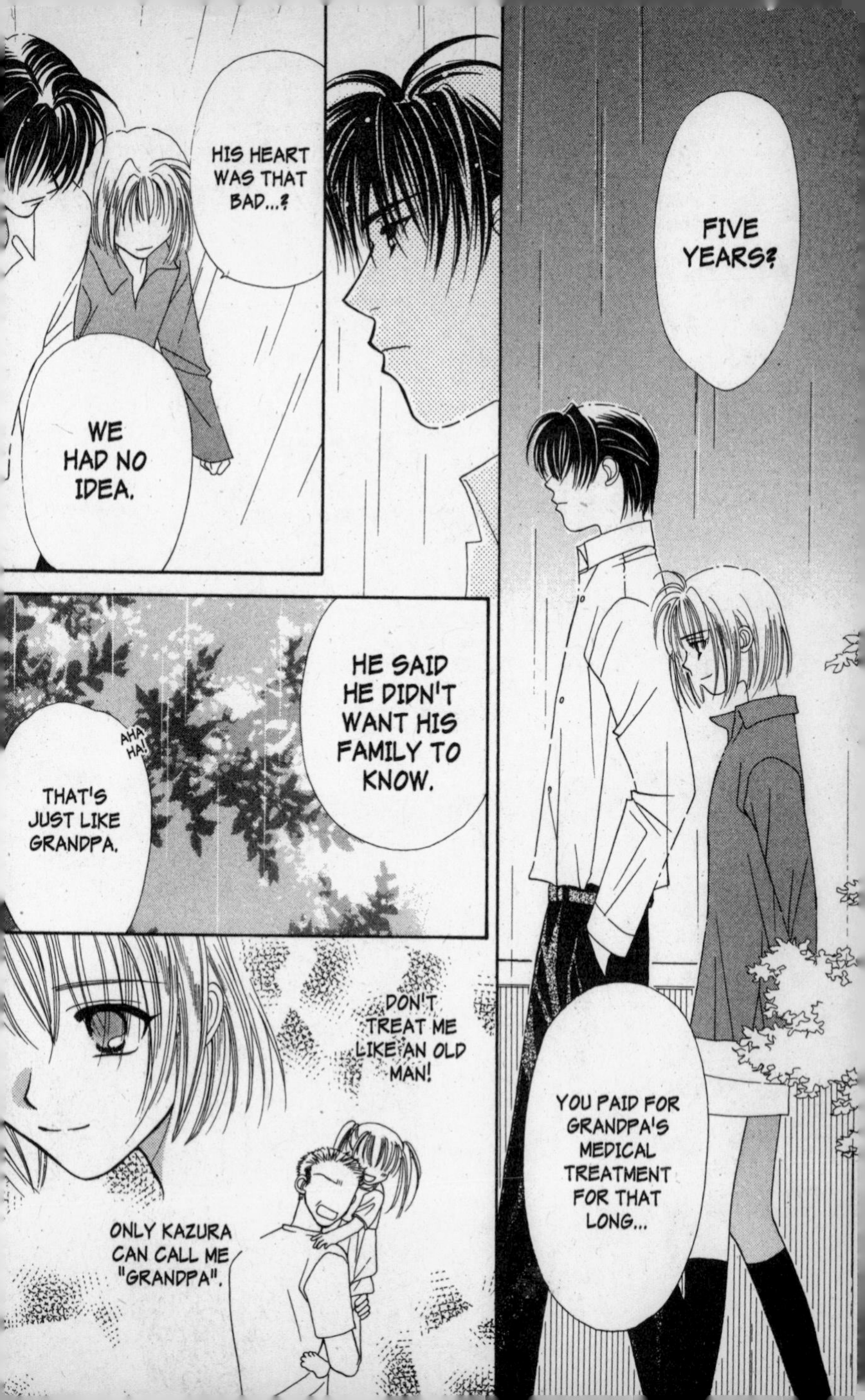
FIVE YEARS?
YOU PAID FOR GRANDPA'S MEDICAL TREATMENT FOR THAT LONG...
HIS HEART WAS THAT BAD...?
WE HAD NO IDEA.
HE SAID HE DIDN'T WANT HIS FAMILY TO KNOW.
AHA HA!
THAT'S JUST LIKE GRANDPA.
DON'T TREAT ME LIKE AN OLD MAN!
ONLY KAZURA CAN CALL ME "GRANDPA".

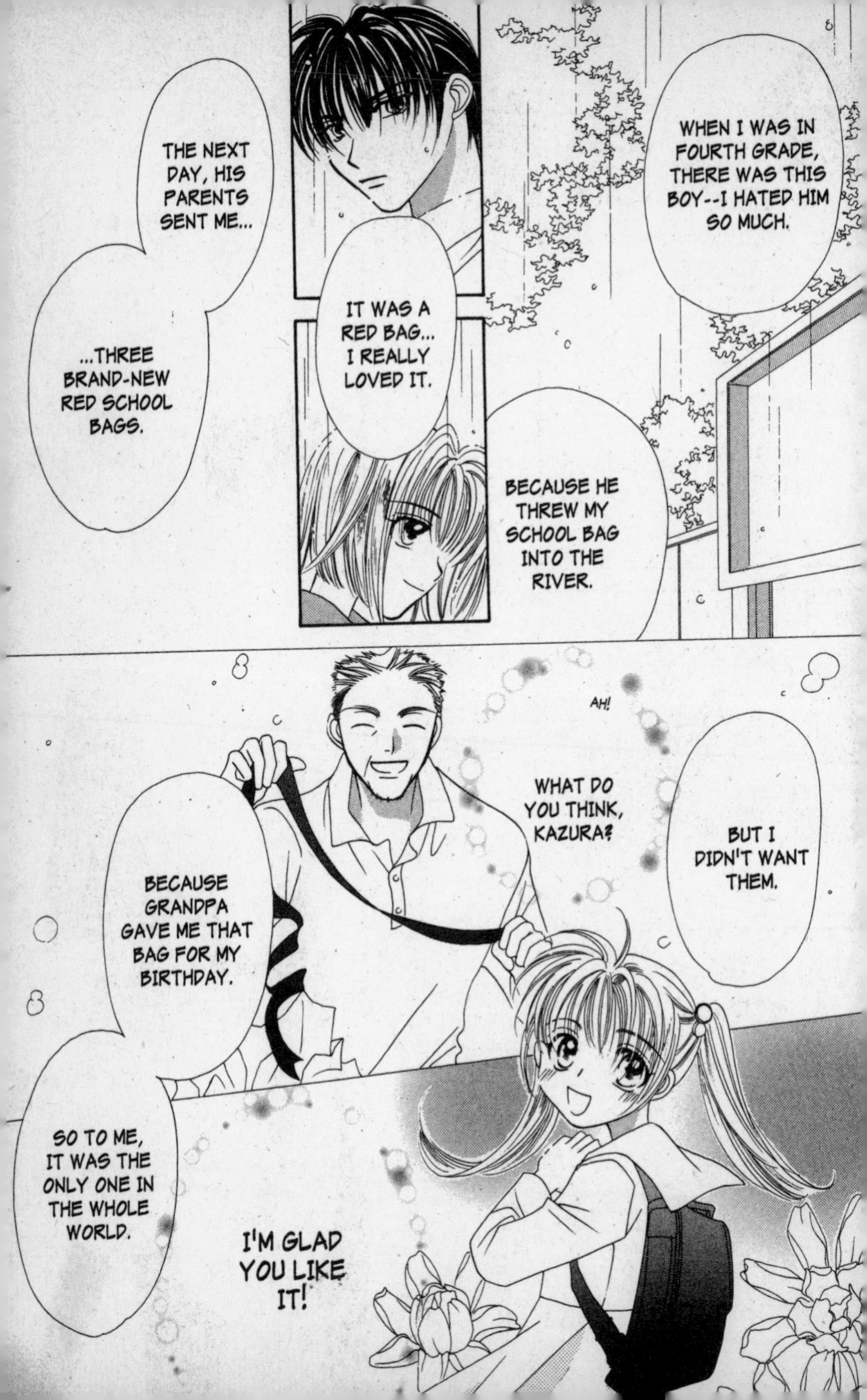
WHEN I WAS IN FOURTH GRADE, THERE WAS THIS BOY--I HATED HIM SO MUCH.
BECAUSE HE THREW MY SCHOOL BAG INTO THE RIVER.
IT WAS A RED BAG... I REALLY LOVED IT.
THE NEXT DAY, HIS PARENTS SENT ME...
...THREE BRAND-NEW RED SCHOOL BAGS.
BUT I DIDN'T WANT THEM.
AH!
WHAT DO YOU THINK, KAZURA?
BECAUSE GRANDPA GAVE ME THAT BAG FOR MY BIRTHDAY.
I'M GLAD YOU LIKE IT!
SO TO ME, IT WAS THE ONLY ONE IN THE WHOLE WORLD.

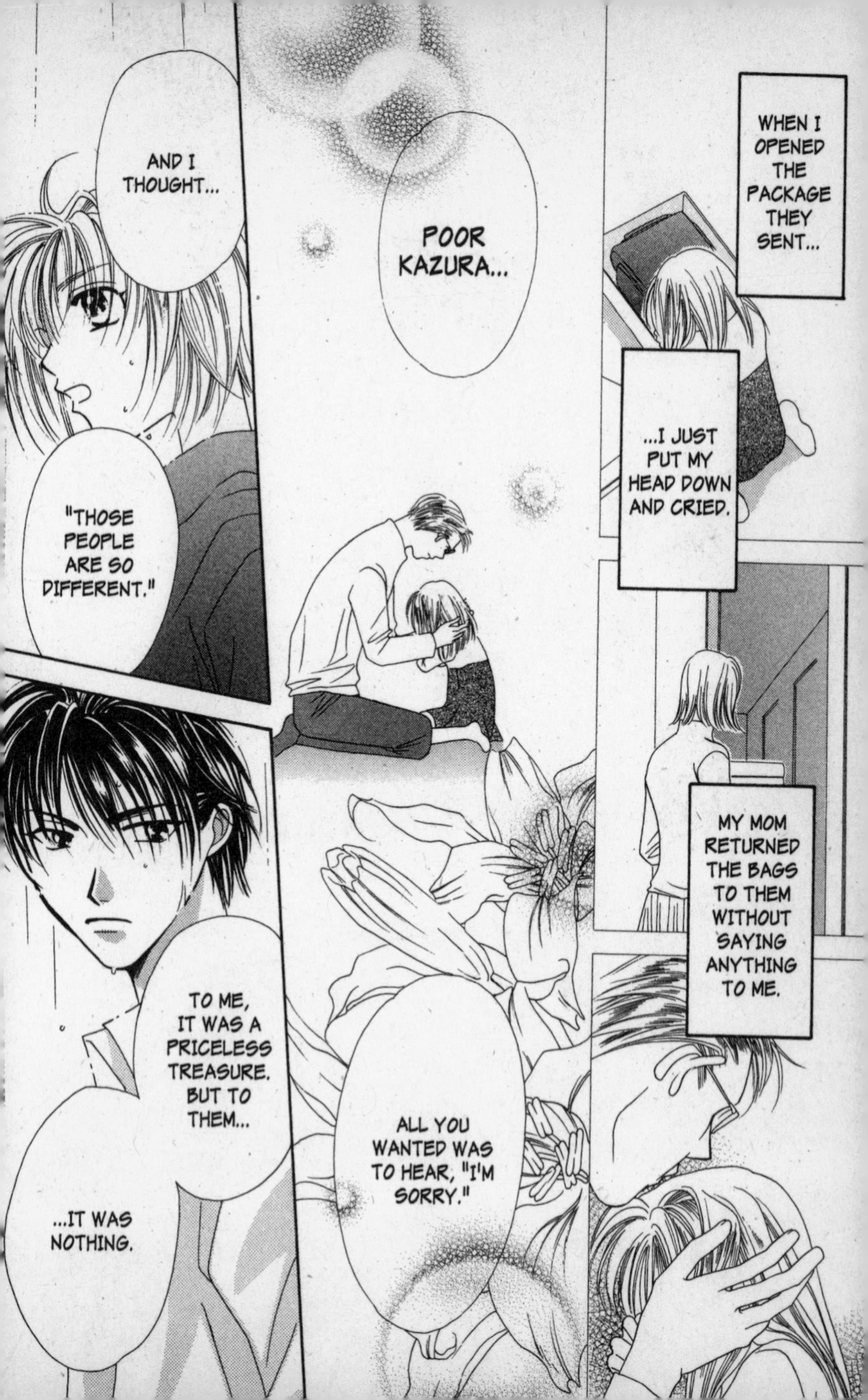
WHEN I OPENED THE PACKAGE THEY SENT...
...I JUST PUT MY HEAD DOWN AND CRIED.
MY MOM RETURNED THE BAGS TO THEM WITHOUT SAYING ANYTHING TO ME.
POOR KAZURA...
ALL YOU WANTED WAS TO HEAR, "I'M SORRY."
AND I THOUGHT...
"THOSE PEOPLE ARE SO DIFFERENT."
TO ME, IT WAS A PRICELESS TREASURE. BUT TO THEM...
...IT WAS NOTHING.

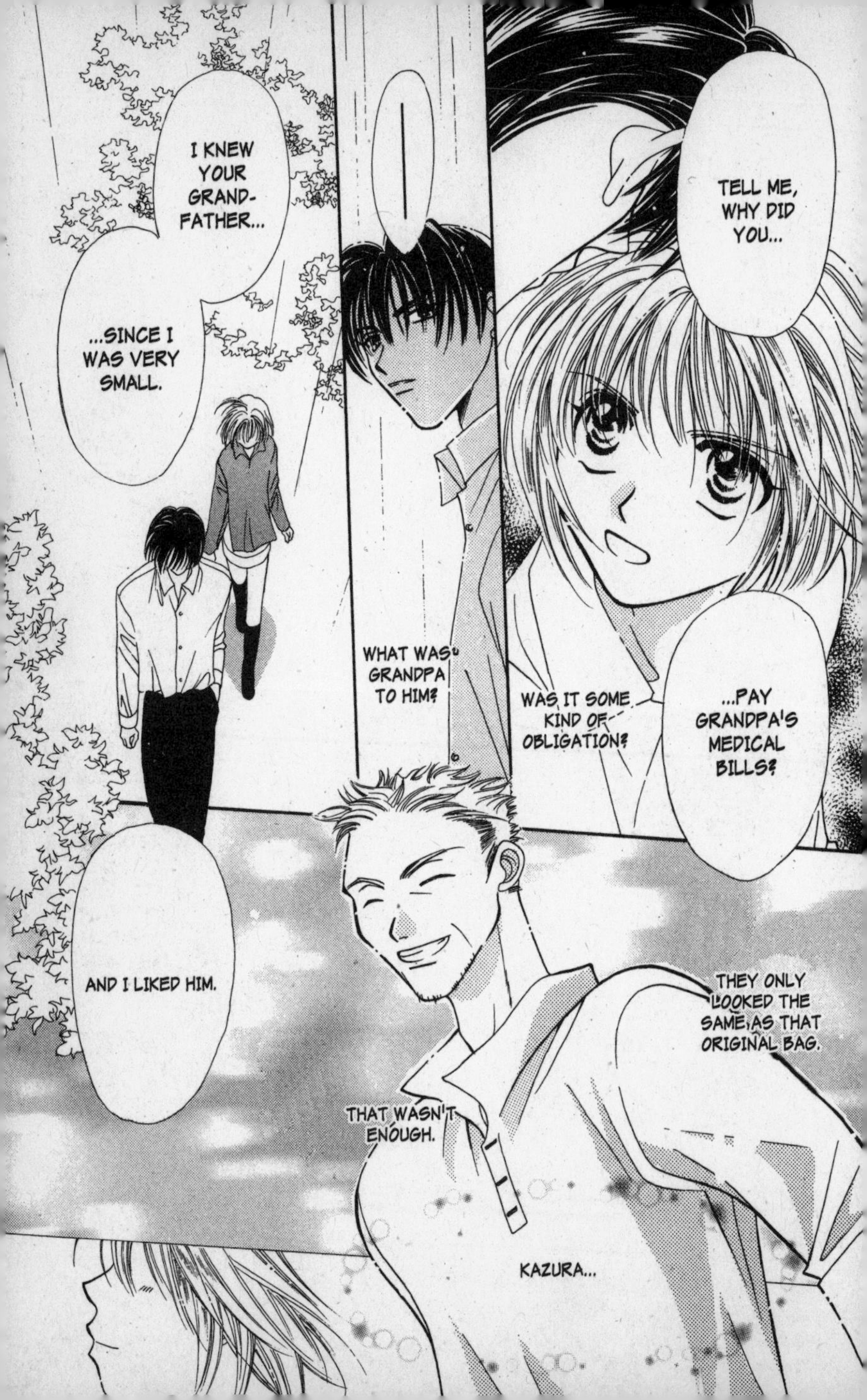
TELL ME, WHY DID YOU...
...PAY GRANDPA'S MEDICAL BILLS?
WAS IT SOME KIND OF OBLIGATION?
!
WHAT WAS GRANDPA TO HIM?
I KNEW YOUR GRAND-FATHER...
...SINCE I WAS VERY SMALL.
AND I LIKED HIM.
THEY ONLY LOOKED THE SAME AS THAT ORIGINAL BAG.
THAT WASN'T ENOUGH.
KAZURA...

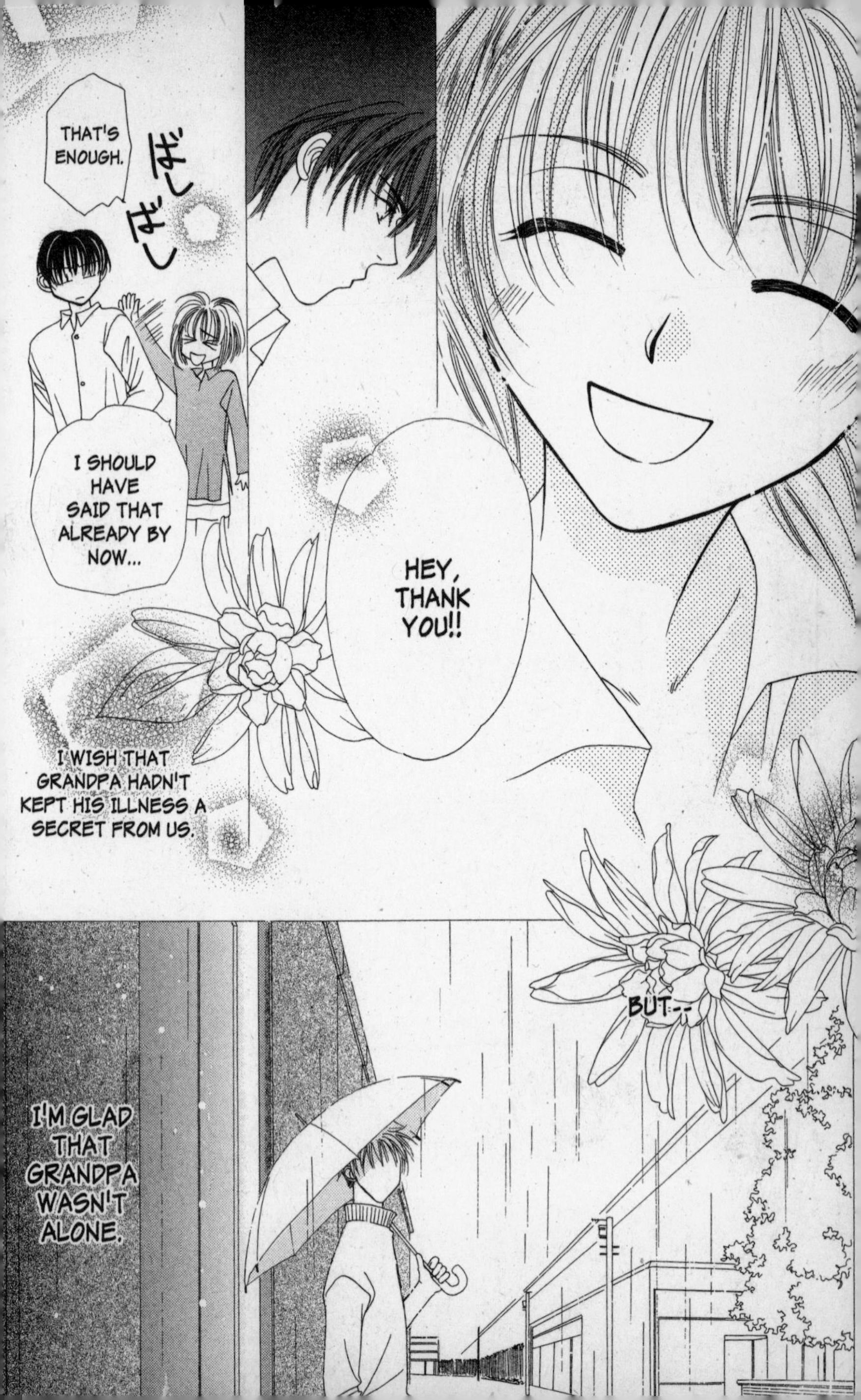
HEY, THANK YOU!!
THAT'S ENOUGH.
ばしばし
I SHOULD HAVE SAID THAT ALREADY BY NOW...
I WISH THAT GRANDPA HADN'T KEPT HIS ILLNESS A SECRET FROM US.
BUT--
I'M GLAD THAT GRANDPA WASN'T ALONE.

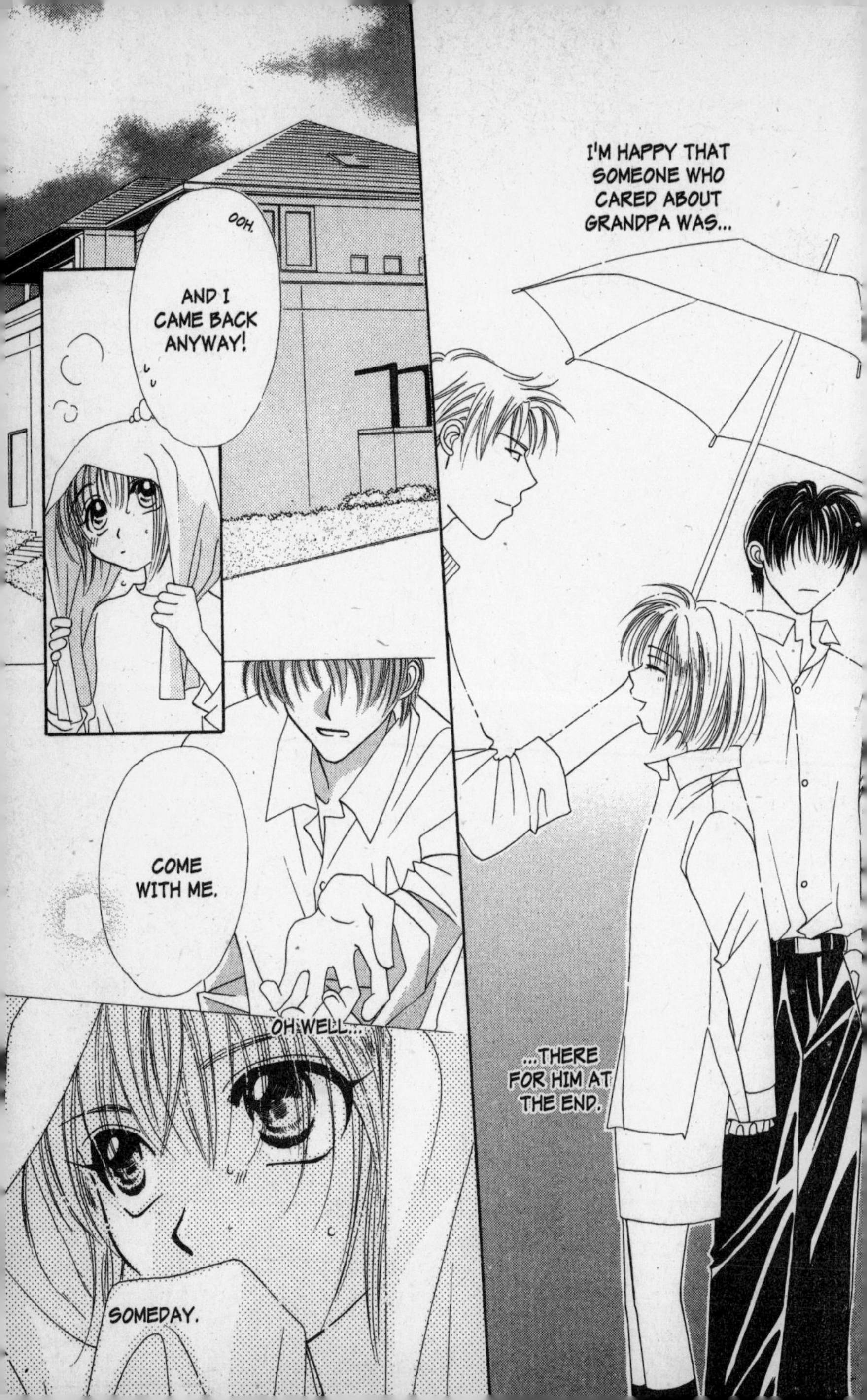
I'M HAPPY THAT SOMEONE WHO CARED ABOUT GRANDPA WAS...
...THERE FOR HIM AT THE END.
OOH.
AND I CAME BACK ANYWAY!
COME WITH ME.
OH WELL...
SOMEDAY.

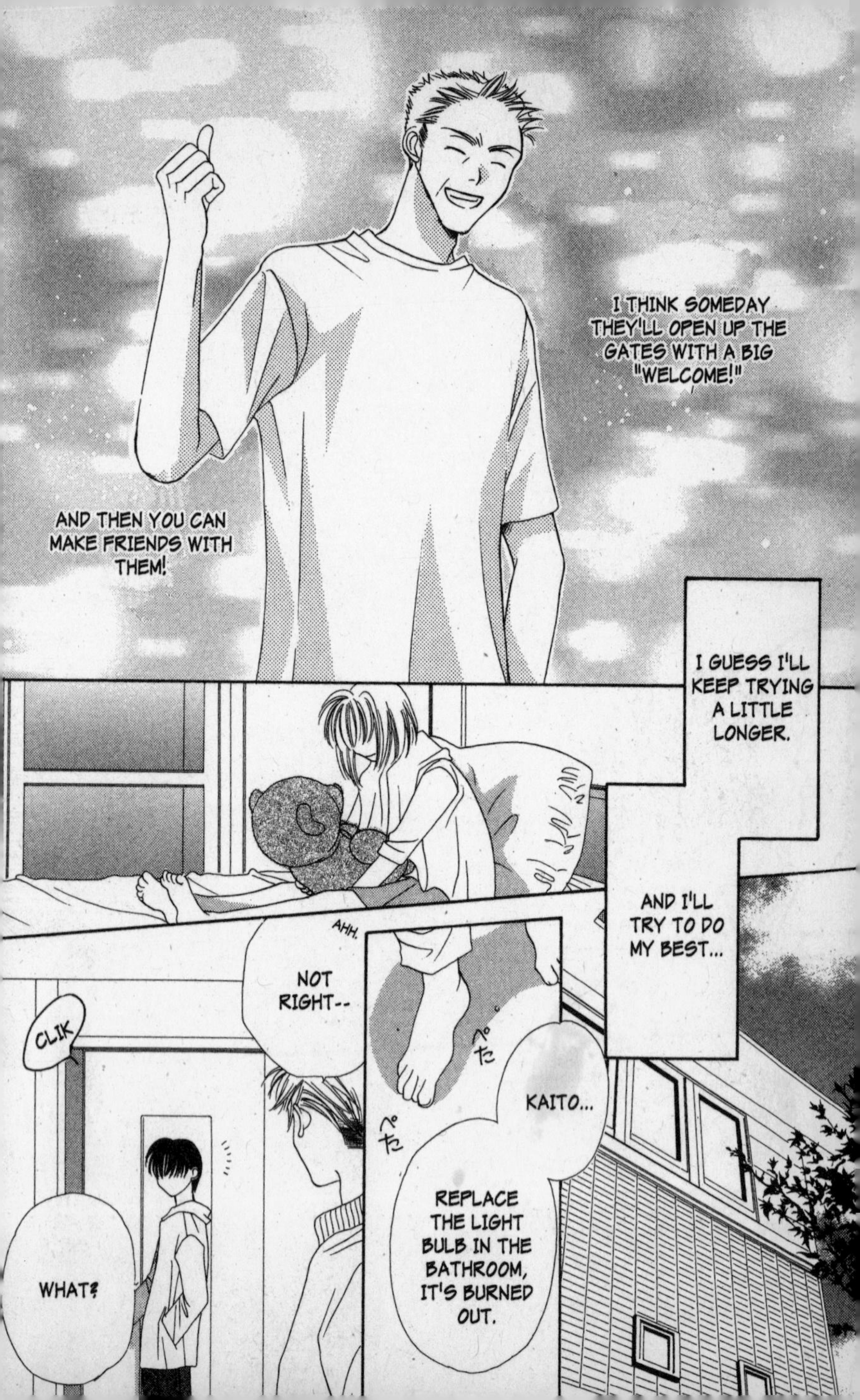
I THINK SOMEDAY THEY'LL OPEN UP THE GATES WITH A BIG "WELCOME!"
AND THEN YOU CAN MAKE FRIENDS WITH THEM!
I GUESS I'LL KEEP TRYING A LITTLE LONGER.
AND I'LL TRY TO DO MY BEST...
ぺた
ぺた
KAITO...
REPLACE THE LIGHT BULB IN THE BATHROOM, IT'S BURNED OUT.
AHH.
NOT RIGHT--
CLIK
WHAT?

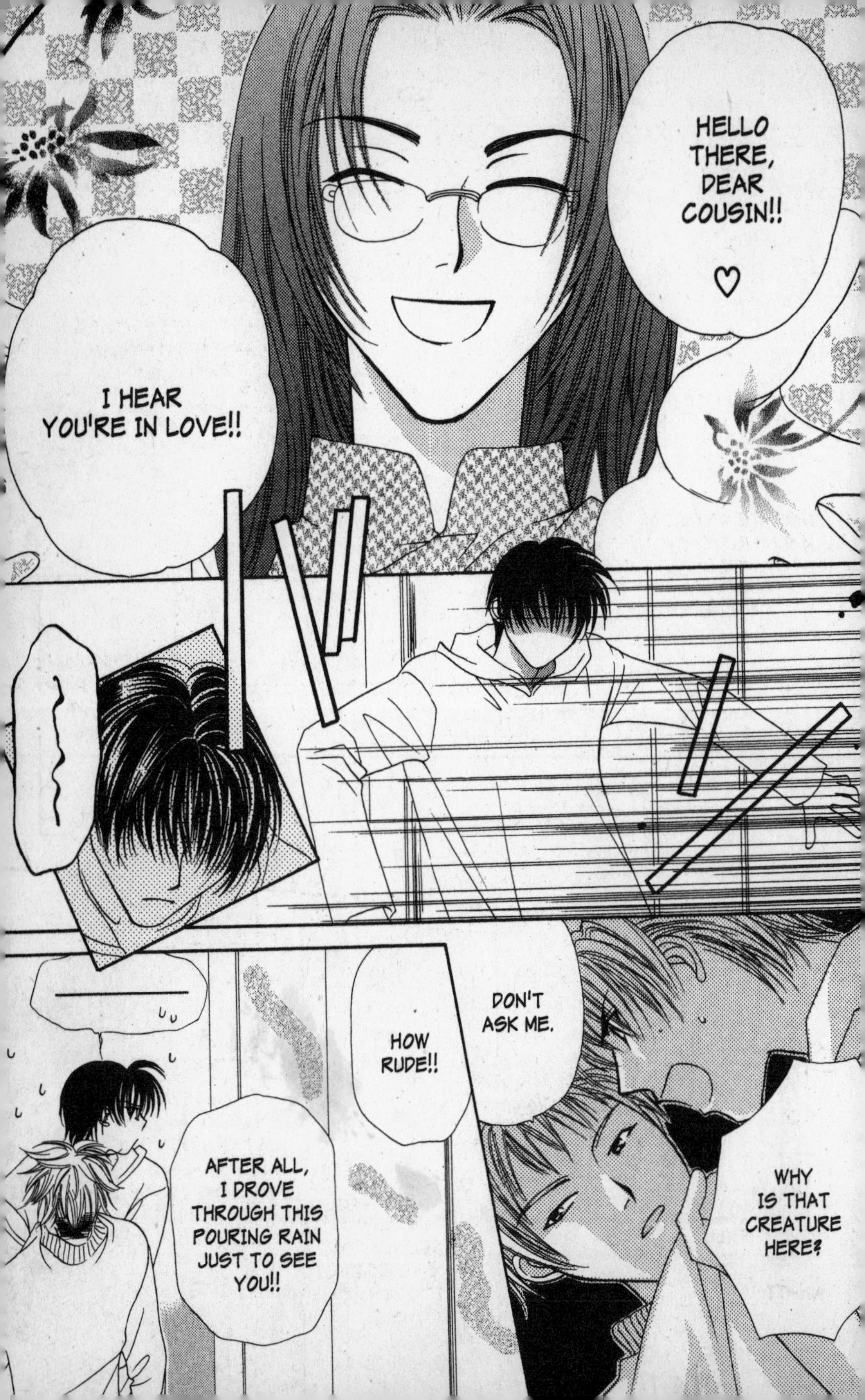
HELLO THERE, DEAR COUSIN!! ♡
I HEAR YOU'RE IN LOVE!!
WHY IS THAT CREATURE HERE?
DON'T ASK ME.
HOW RUDE!!
AFTER ALL, I DROVE THROUGH THIS POURING RAIN JUST TO SEE YOU!!
——

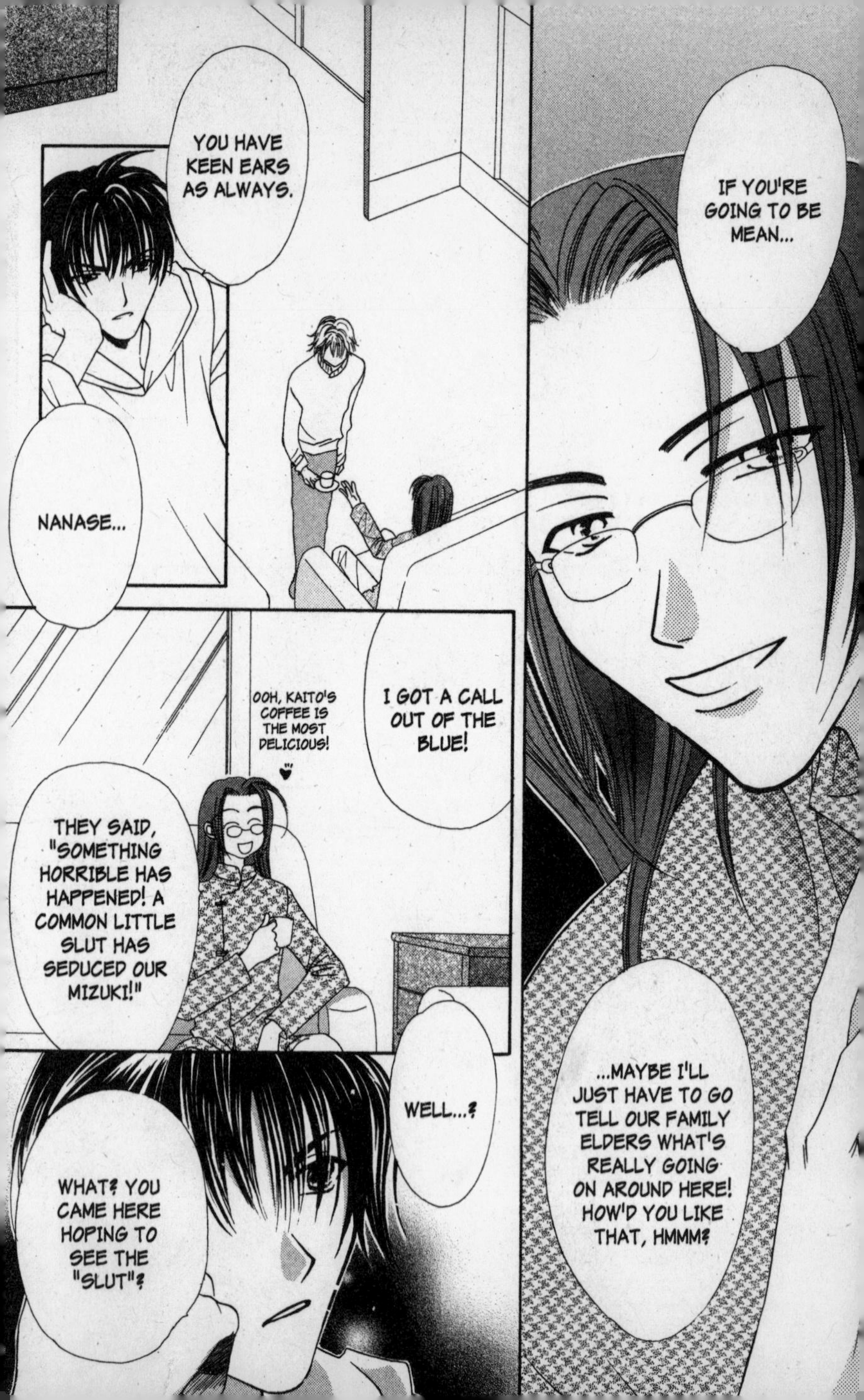
YOU HAVE KEEN EARS AS ALWAYS.
NANASE...
OOH, KAITO'S COFFEE IS THE MOST DELICIOUS!
I GOT A CALL OUT OF THE BLUE!
THEY SAID, "SOMETHING HORRIBLE HAS HAPPENED! A COMMON LITTLE SLUT HAS SEDUCED OUR MIZUKI!"
WELL...?
WHAT? YOU CAME HERE HOPING TO SEE THE "SLUT"?
IF YOU'RE GOING TO BE MEAN...
...MAYBE I'LL JUST HAVE TO GO TELL OUR FAMILY ELDERS WHAT'S REALLY GOING ON AROUND HERE! HOW'D YOU LIKE THAT, HMMM?

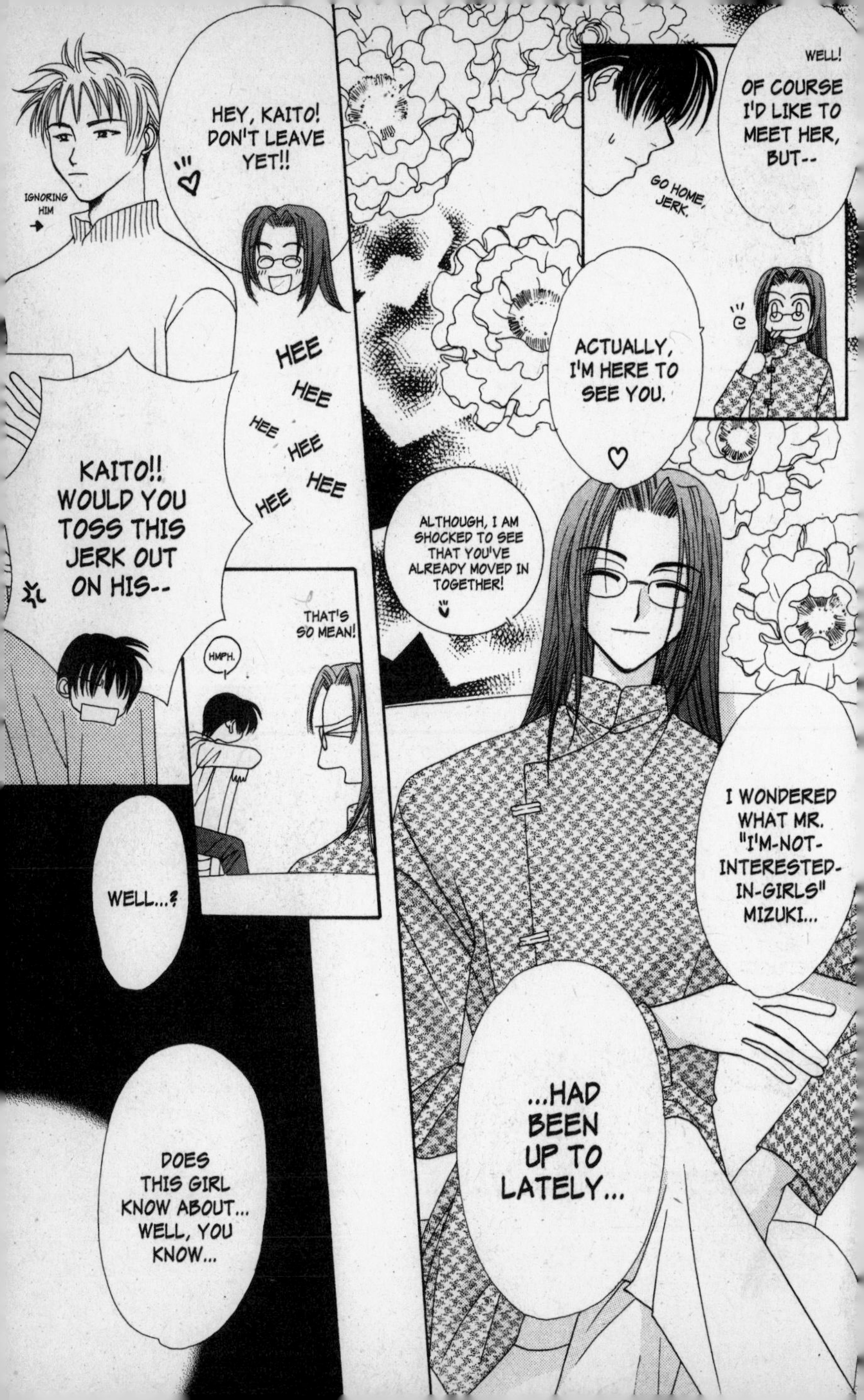
WELL!
OF COURSE I'D LIKE TO MEET HER, BUT--
GO HOME, JERK.
ACTUALLY, I'M HERE TO SEE YOU.
ALTHOUGH, I AM SHOCKED TO SEE THAT YOU'VE ALREADY MOVED IN TOGETHER!
I WONDERED WHAT MR. "I'M-NOT-INTERESTED-IN-GIRLS" MIZUKI...
...HAD BEEN UP TO LATELY...
IGNORING HIM
HEY, KAITO! DON'T LEAVE YET!!
HEE HEE HEE HEE HEE HEE
KAITO!! WOULD YOU TOSS THIS JERK OUT ON HIS--
THAT'S SO MEAN!
HMPH.
WELL...?
DOES THIS GIRL KNOW ABOUT... WELL, YOU KNOW...

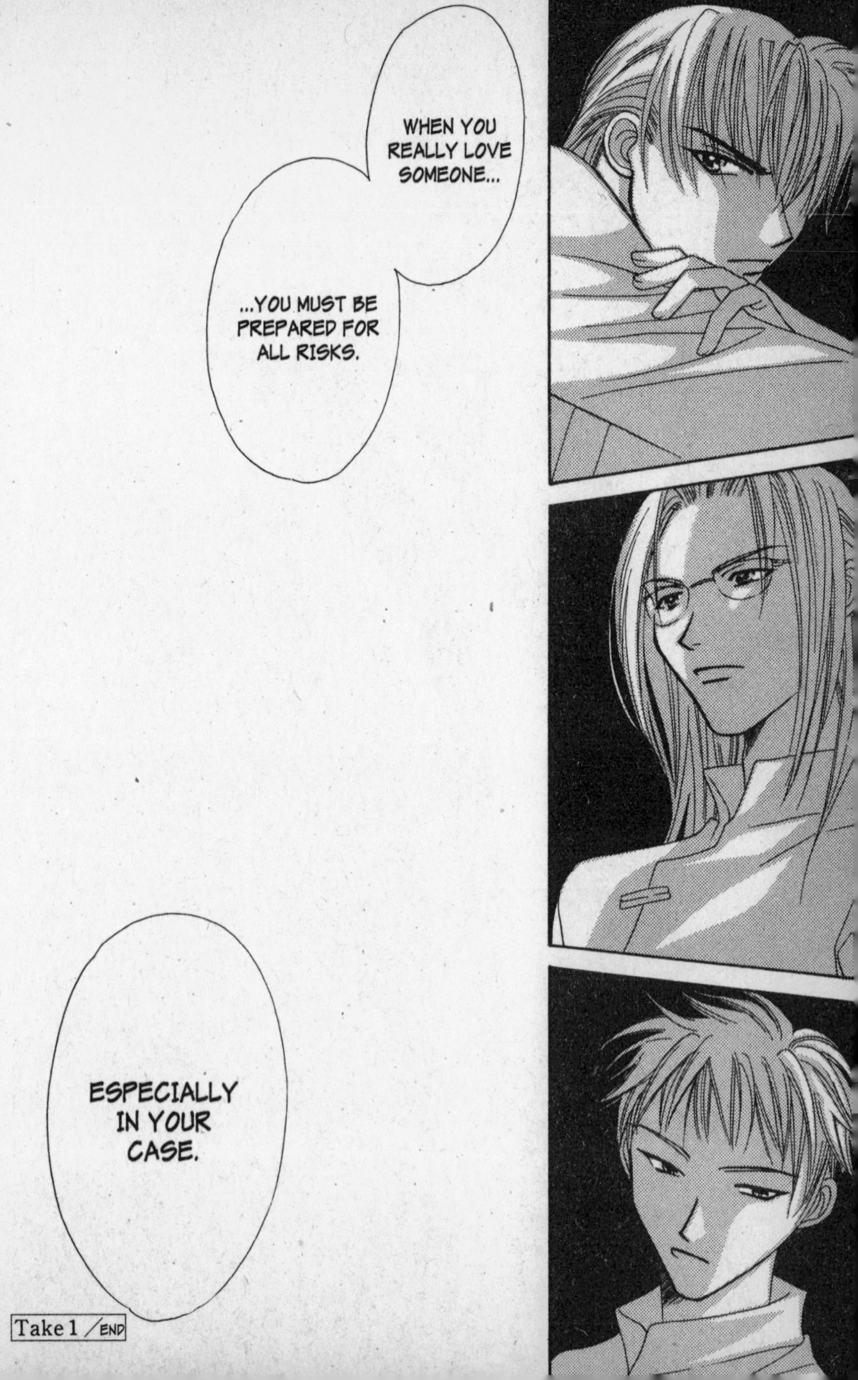
WHEN YOU REALLY LOVE SOMEONE...
...YOU MUST BE PREPARED FOR ALL RISKS.
ESPECIALLY IN YOUR CASE.
Take 1 / END

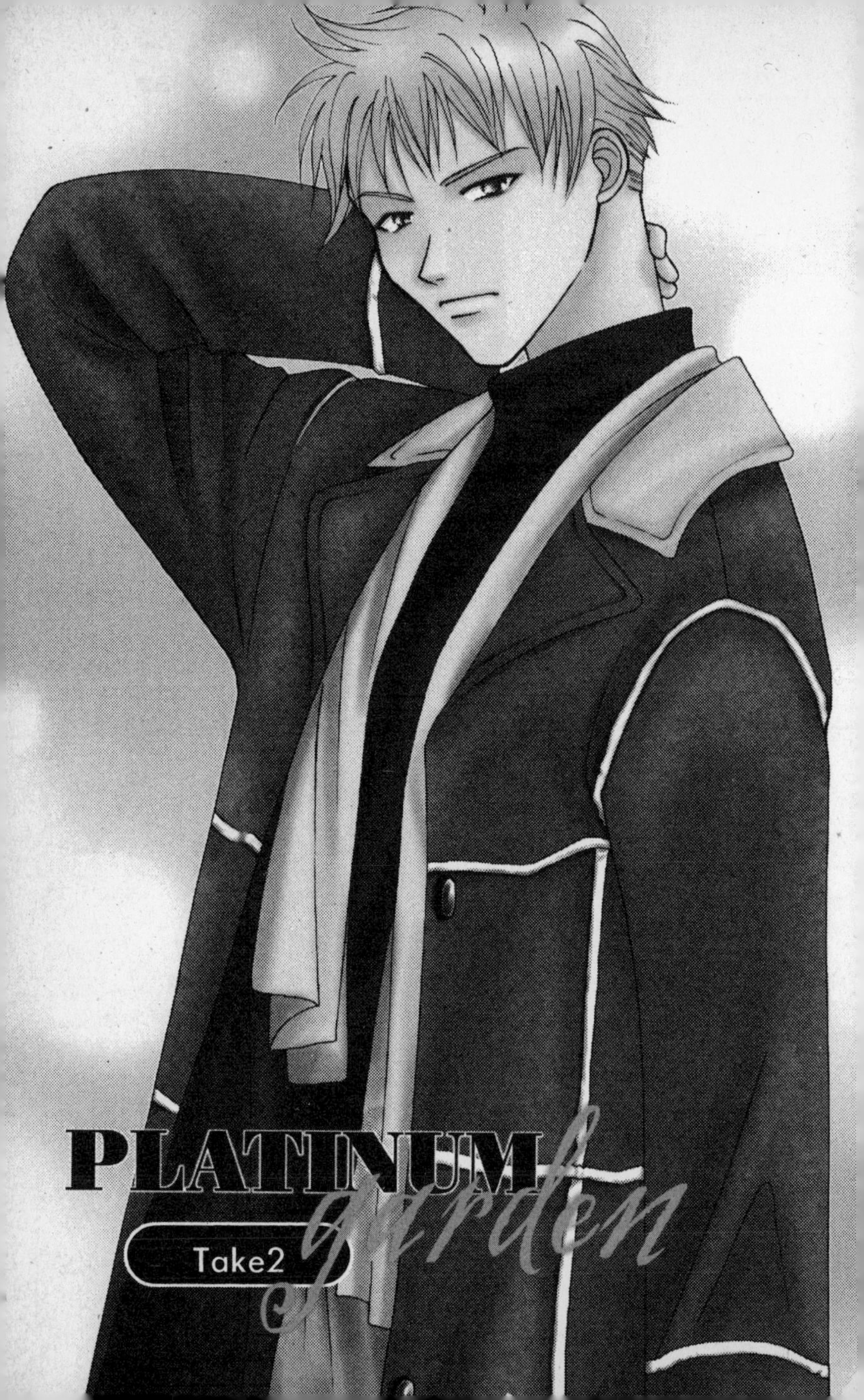
PLATINUM garden
Take2

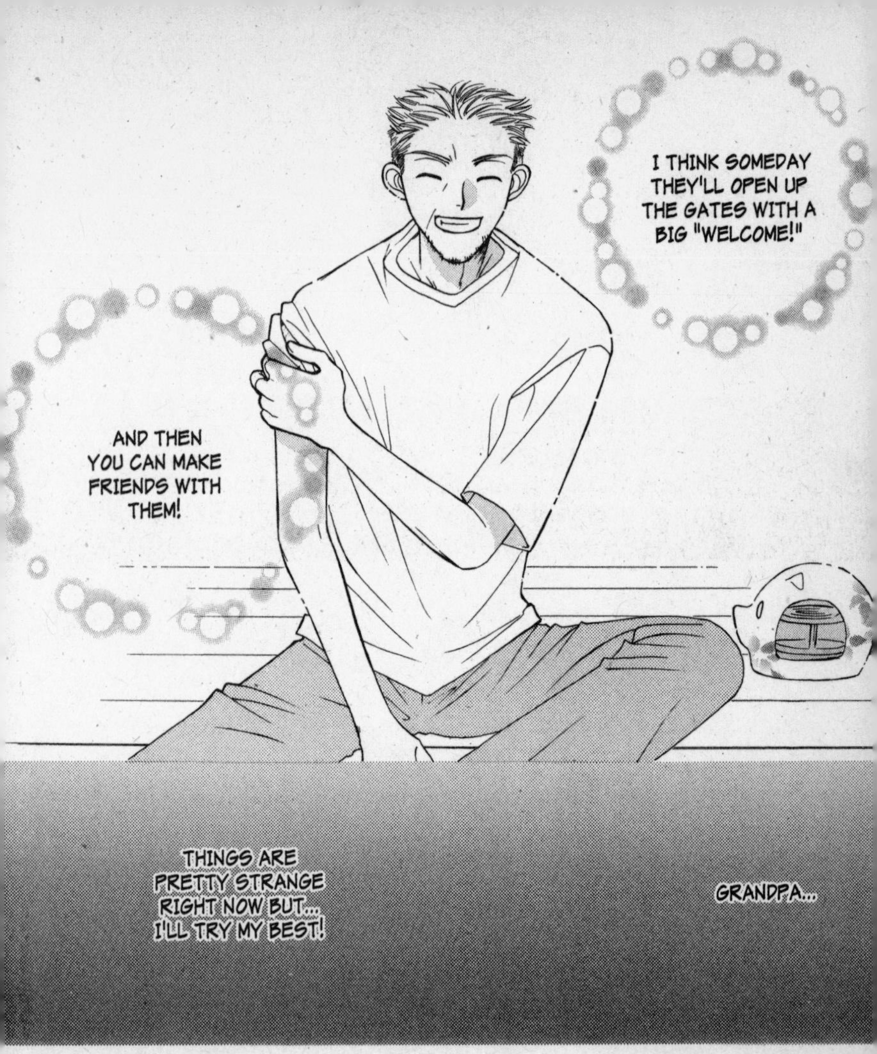
I THINK SOMEDAY THEY'LL OPEN UP THE GATES WITH A BIG "WELCOME!"
AND THEN YOU CAN MAKE FRIENDS WITH THEM!
GRANDPA...
THINGS ARE PRETTY STRANGE RIGHT NOW BUT... I'LL TRY MY BEST!

I'M ADDICTED TO MONSTER MOVIES!
I'VE BEEN SENDING "GODZILLA LOVE!"
FAXES TO ALL MY FRIENDS --
MOTHRA FLIES BY, GAMERA ROARS.
IF YOU HAVEN'T WATCHED THESE MOVIES YET,
WHAT ARE YOU WAITING FOR?

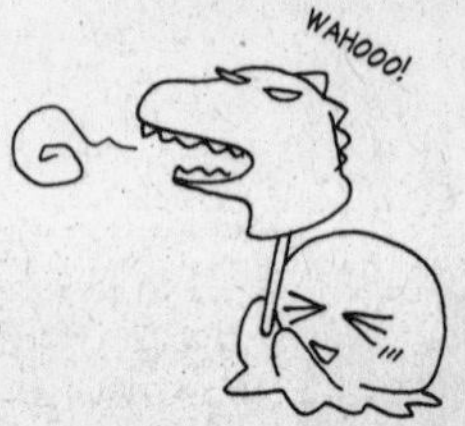
WAHOOO!

FUJITA'S WINTER, 2001

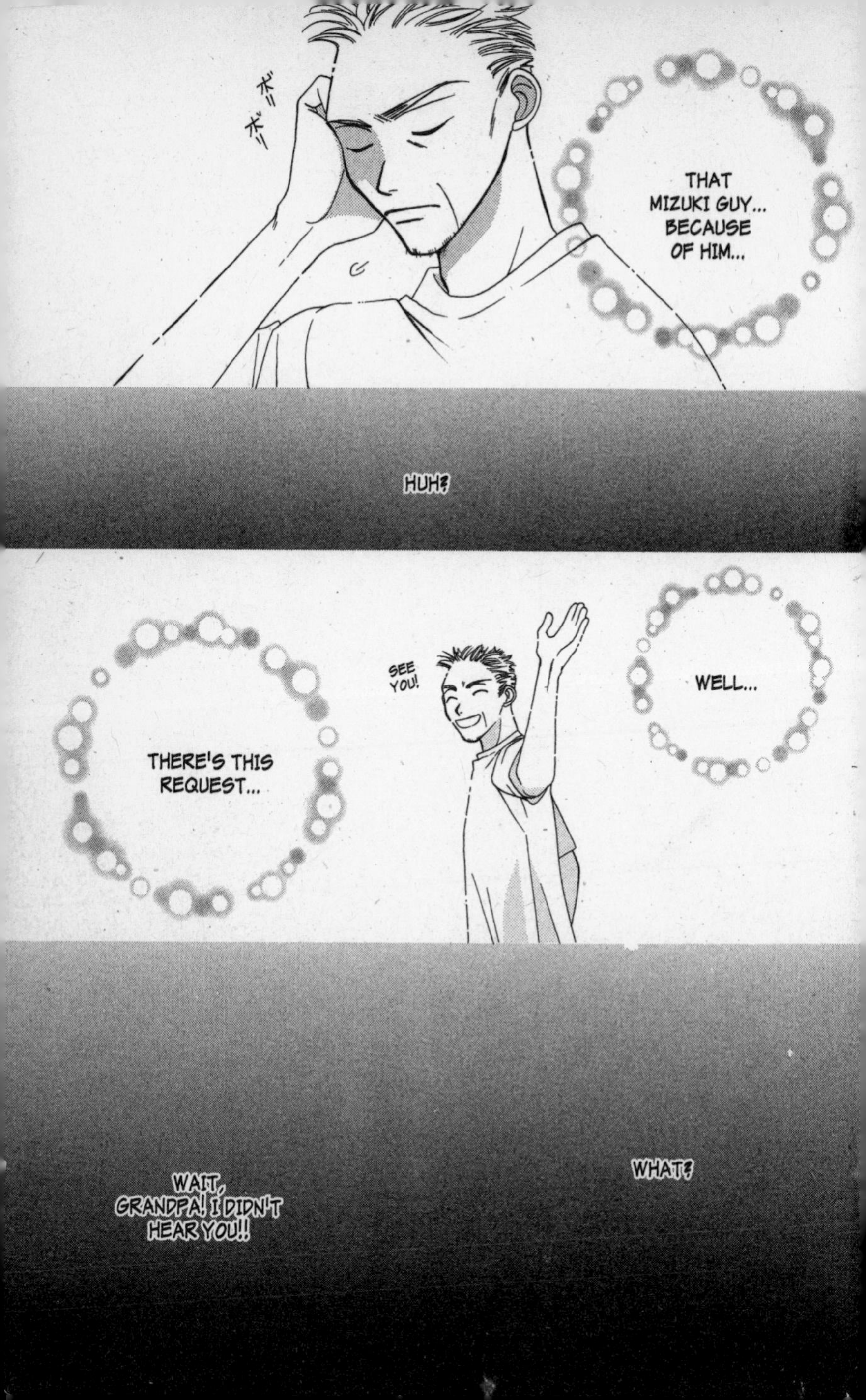
THAT MIZUKI GUY... BECAUSE OF HIM...
ボリボリ
HUH?
WELL...
SEE YOU!
THERE'S THIS REQUEST...
WHAT?
WAIT, GRANDPA! I DIDN'T HEAR YOU!!

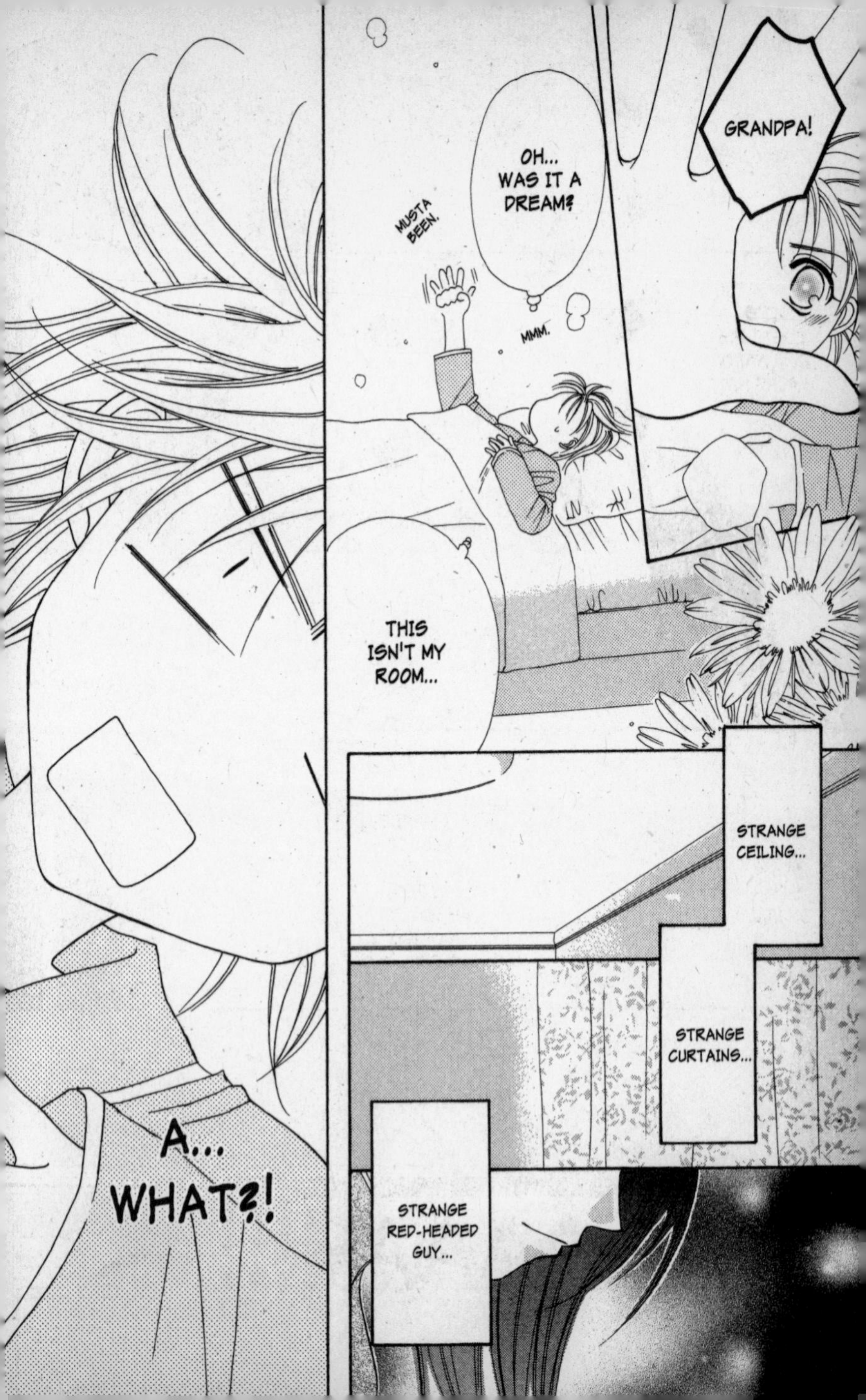
GRANDPA!
OH... WAS IT A DREAM?
MUSTA BEEN.
MMM.
THIS ISN'T MY ROOM...
STRANGE CEILING...
STRANGE CURTAINS...
STRANGE RED-HEADED GUY...
A... WHAT?!

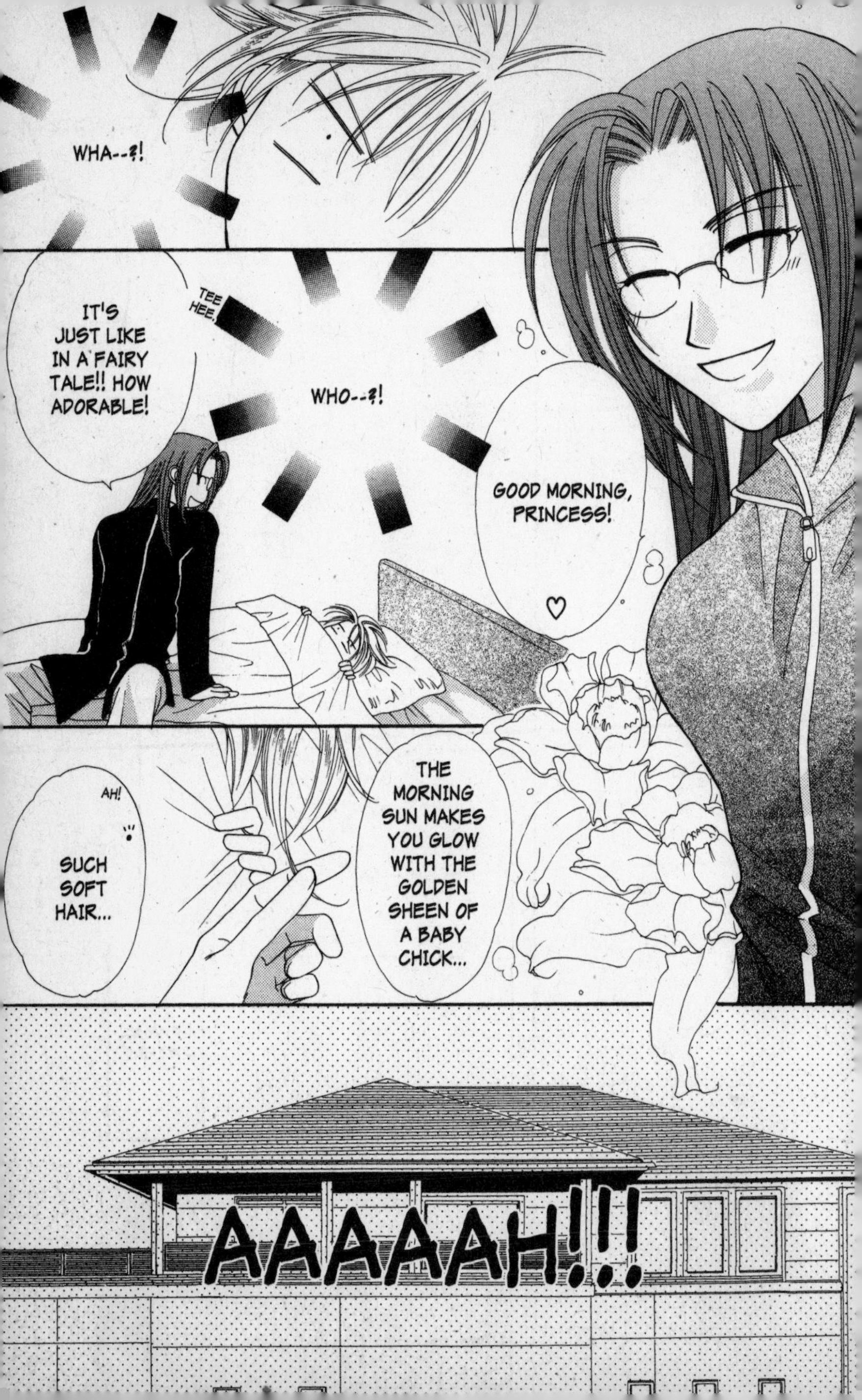
GOOD MORNING, PRINCESS!
WHA--?!
TEE HEE,
IT'S JUST LIKE IN A FAIRY TALE!! HOW ADORABLE!
WHO--?!
THE MORNING SUN MAKES YOU GLOW WITH THE GOLDEN SHEEN OF A BABY CHICK...
AH!
SUCH SOFT HAIR...
AAAAAH!!!

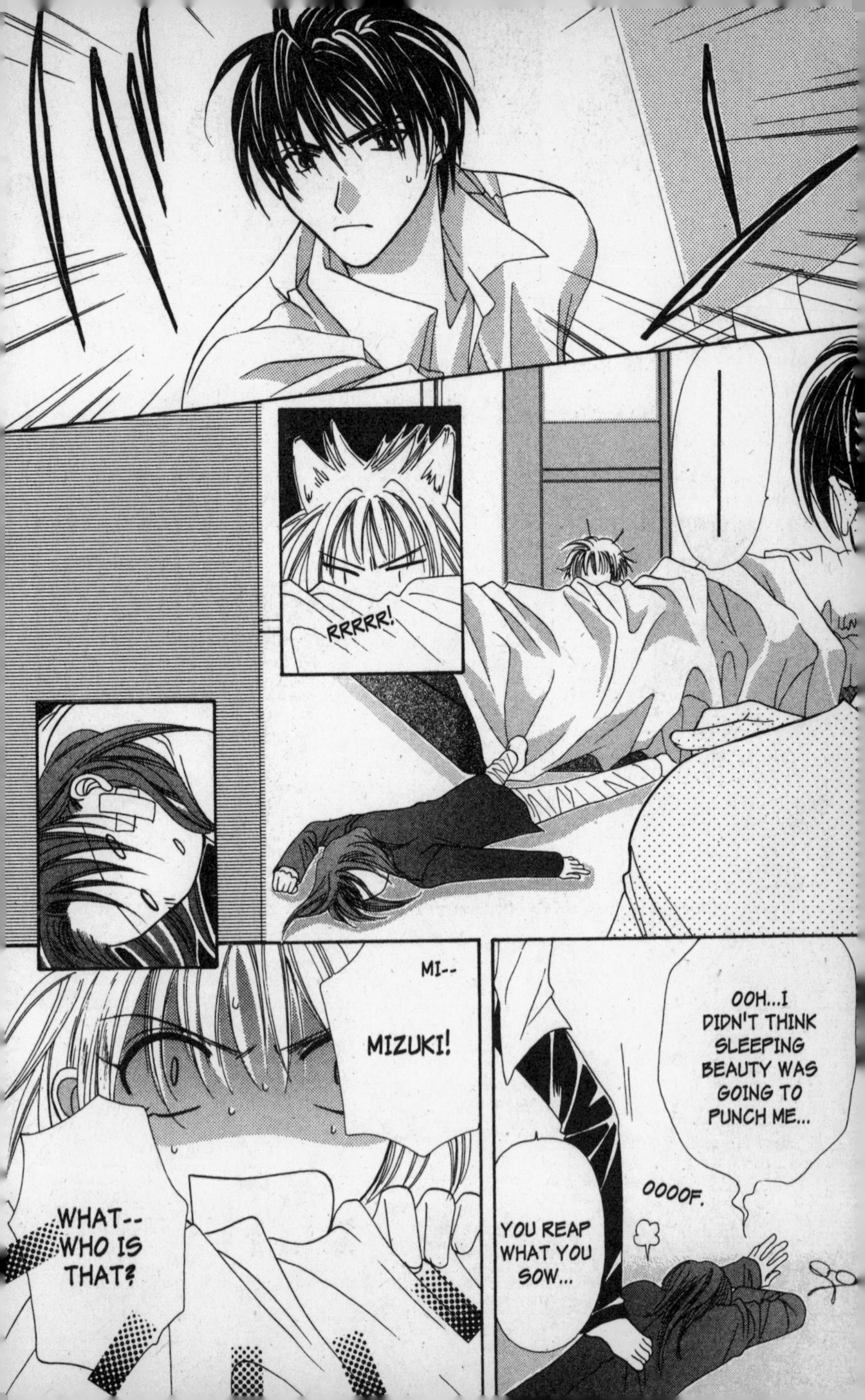
RRRRR!
OOH...I DIDN'T THINK SLEEPING BEAUTY WAS GOING TO PUNCH ME...
OOOOF.
YOU REAP WHAT YOU SOW...
MI--
MIZUKI!
WHAT-- WHO IS THAT?

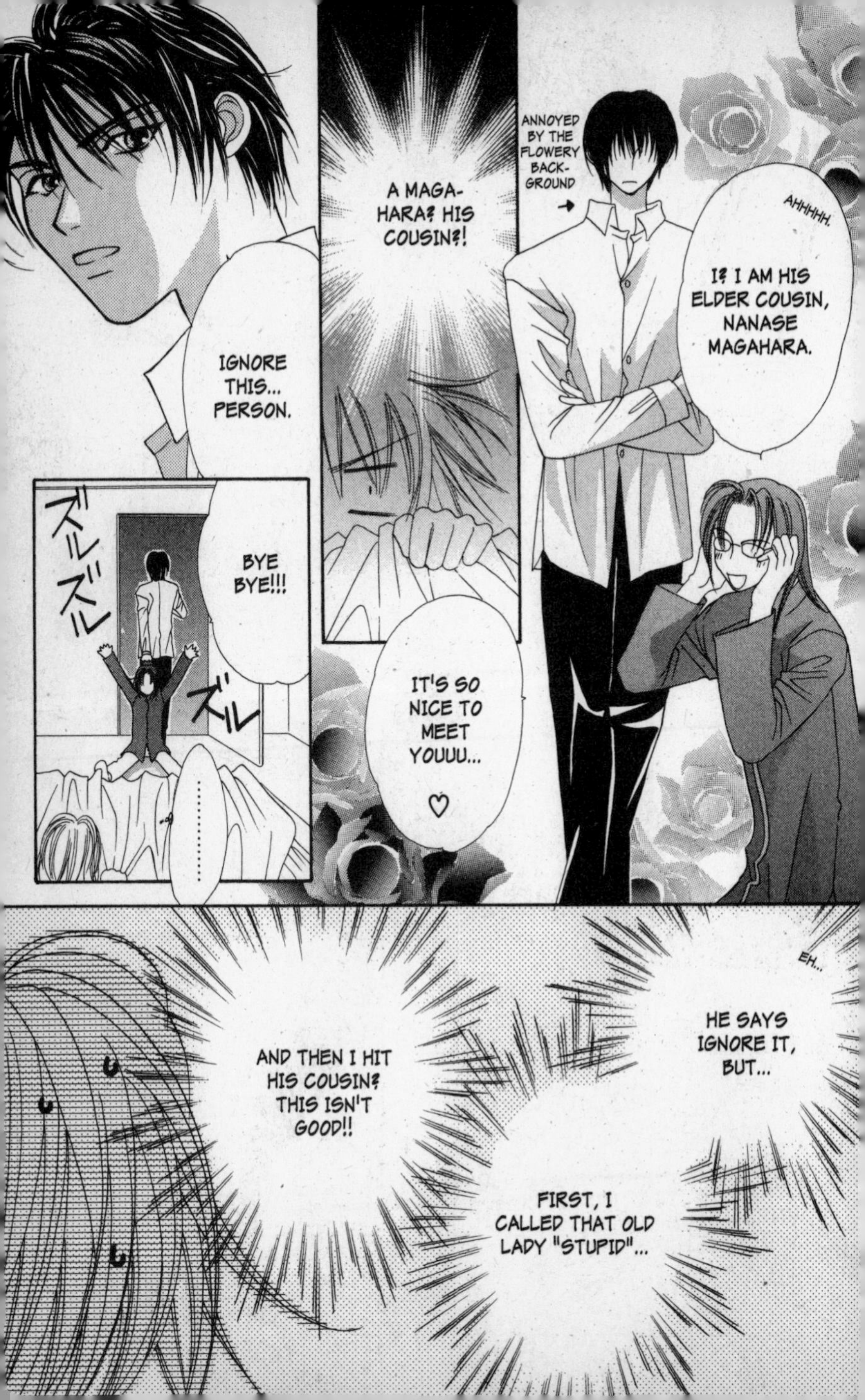
AHHHHH.
I? I AM HIS ELDER COUSIN, NANASE MAGAHARA.
ANNOYED BY THE FLOWERY BACK-GROUND
IT'S SO NICE TO MEET YOUUU... ♡
A MAGA-HARA? HIS COUSIN?!
IGNORE THIS... PERSON.
BYE BYE!!!
ズルズル
ズル
......
EH...
HE SAYS IGNORE IT, BUT...
FIRST, I CALLED THAT OLD LADY "STUPID"...
AND THEN I HIT HIS COUSIN? THIS ISN'T GOOD!!

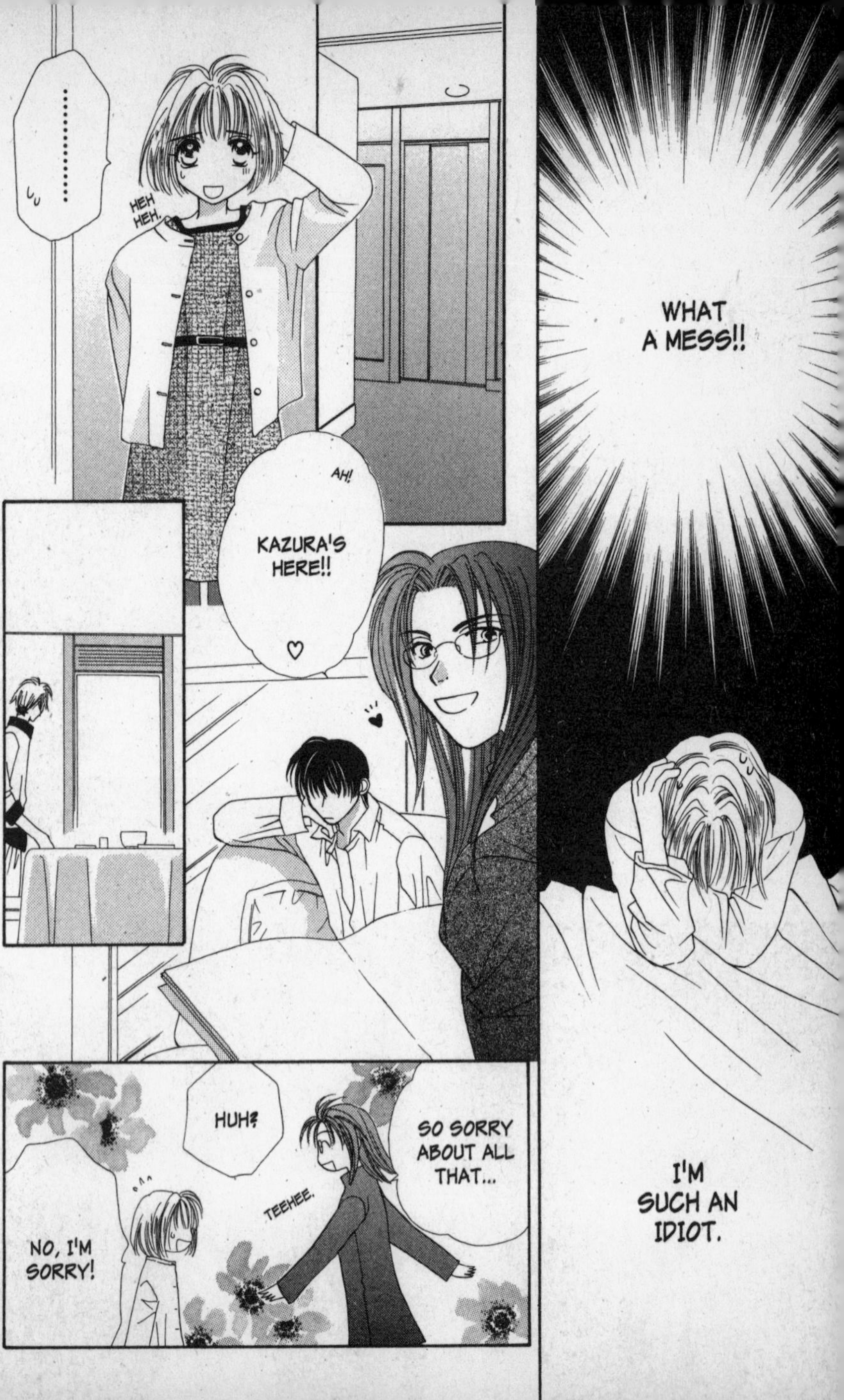
WHAT A MESS!!
I'M SUCH AN IDIOT.
......
HEH HEH.
AH!
KAZURA'S HERE!! ♡
SO SORRY ABOUT ALL THAT...
TEEHEE.
HUH?
NO, I'M SORRY!

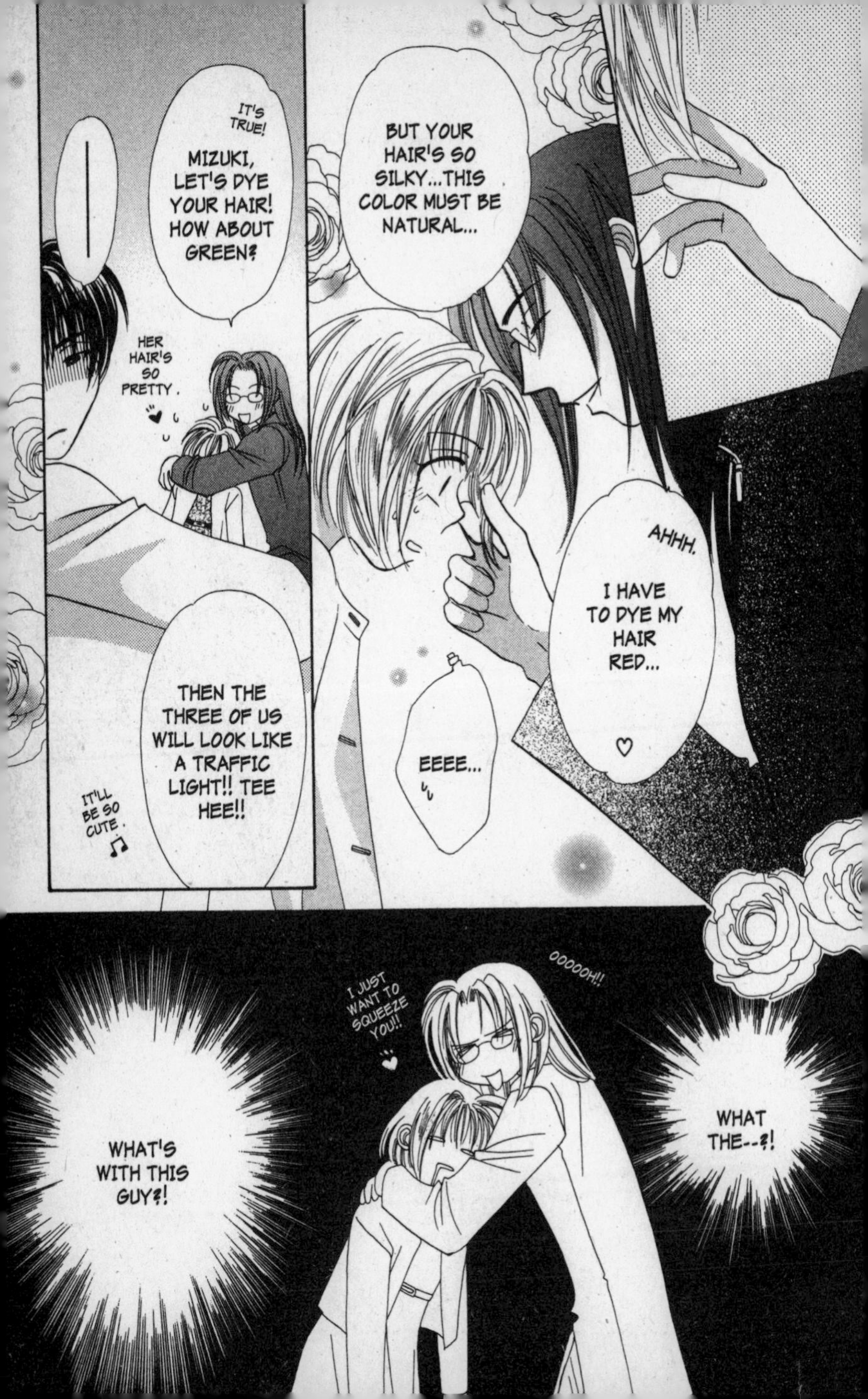

BUT YOUR HAIR'S SO SILKY...THIS COLOR MUST BE NATURAL...
AHHH. I HAVE TO DYE MY HAIR RED... ♡
EEEE...
IT'S TRUE!
MIZUKI, LET'S DYE YOUR HAIR! HOW ABOUT GREEN?
HER HAIR'S SO PRETTY.
THEN THE THREE OF US WILL LOOK LIKE A TRAFFIC LIGHT!! TEE HEE!!
IT'LL BE SO CUTE. ♪
OOOOOH!!
I JUST WANT TO SQUEEZE YOU!!
WHAT THE--?!
WHAT'S WITH THIS GUY?!

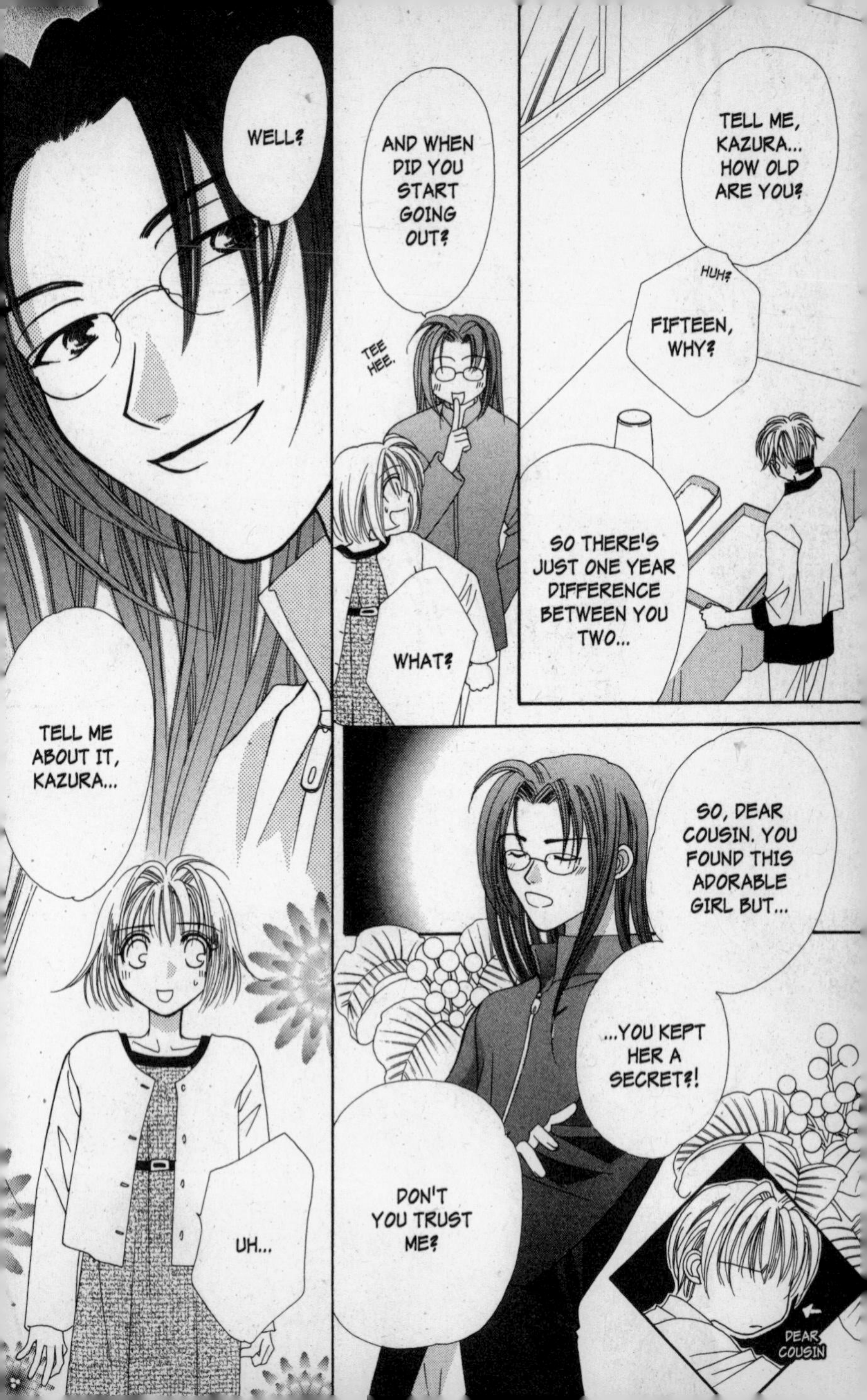
TELL ME, KAZURA... HOW OLD ARE YOU?
HUH?
FIFTEEN, WHY?
SO THERE'S JUST ONE YEAR DIFFERENCE BETWEEN YOU TWO...
AND WHEN DID YOU START GOING OUT?
TEE HEE.
WHAT?
SO, DEAR COUSIN. YOU FOUND THIS ADORABLE GIRL BUT...
...YOU KEPT HER A SECRET?!
DON'T YOU TRUST ME?
DEAR COUSIN
WELL?
TELL ME ABOUT IT, KAZURA...
UH...

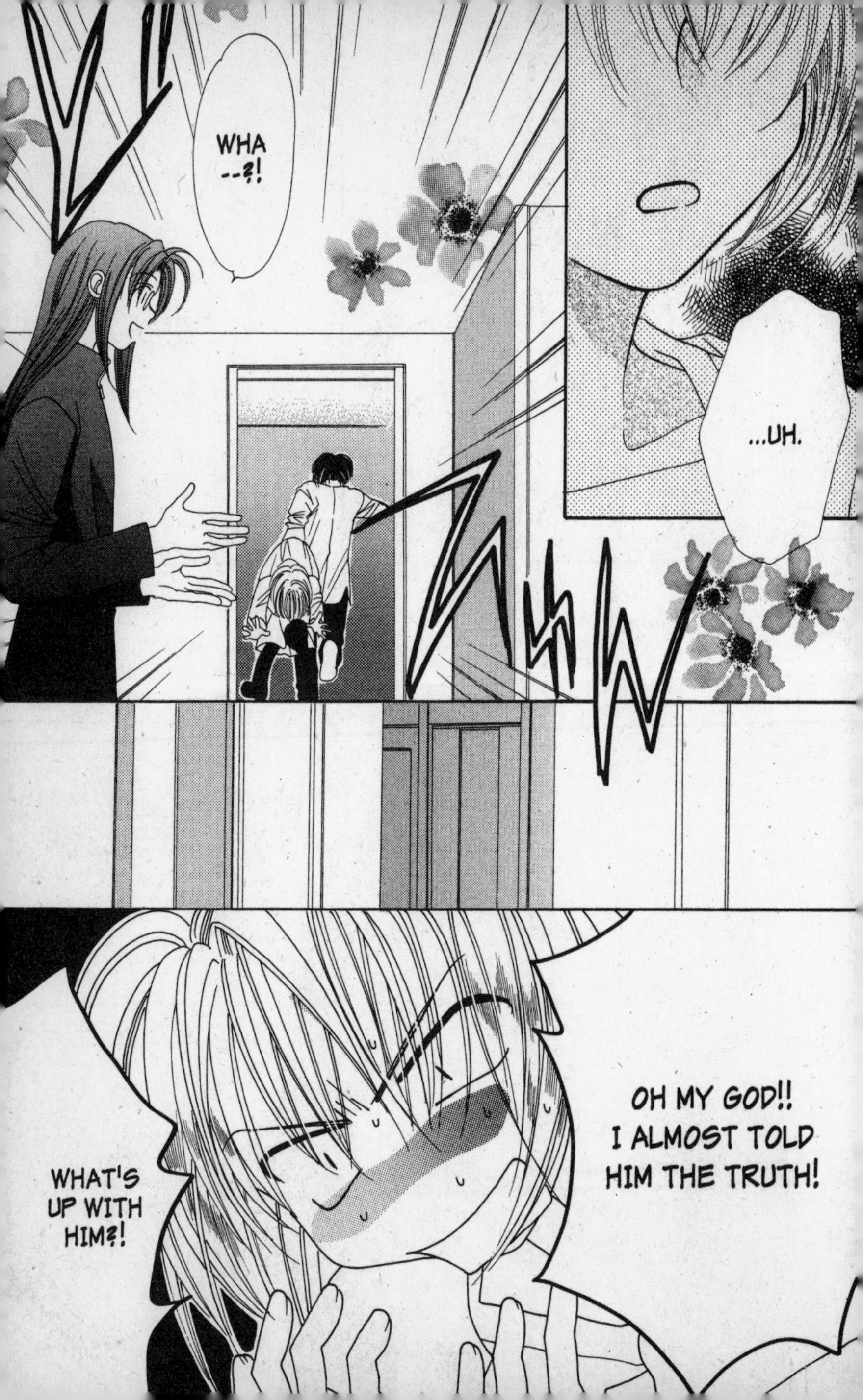
...UH.
WHA --?!
OH MY GOD!! I ALMOST TOLD HIM THE TRUTH!
WHAT'S UP WITH HIM?!

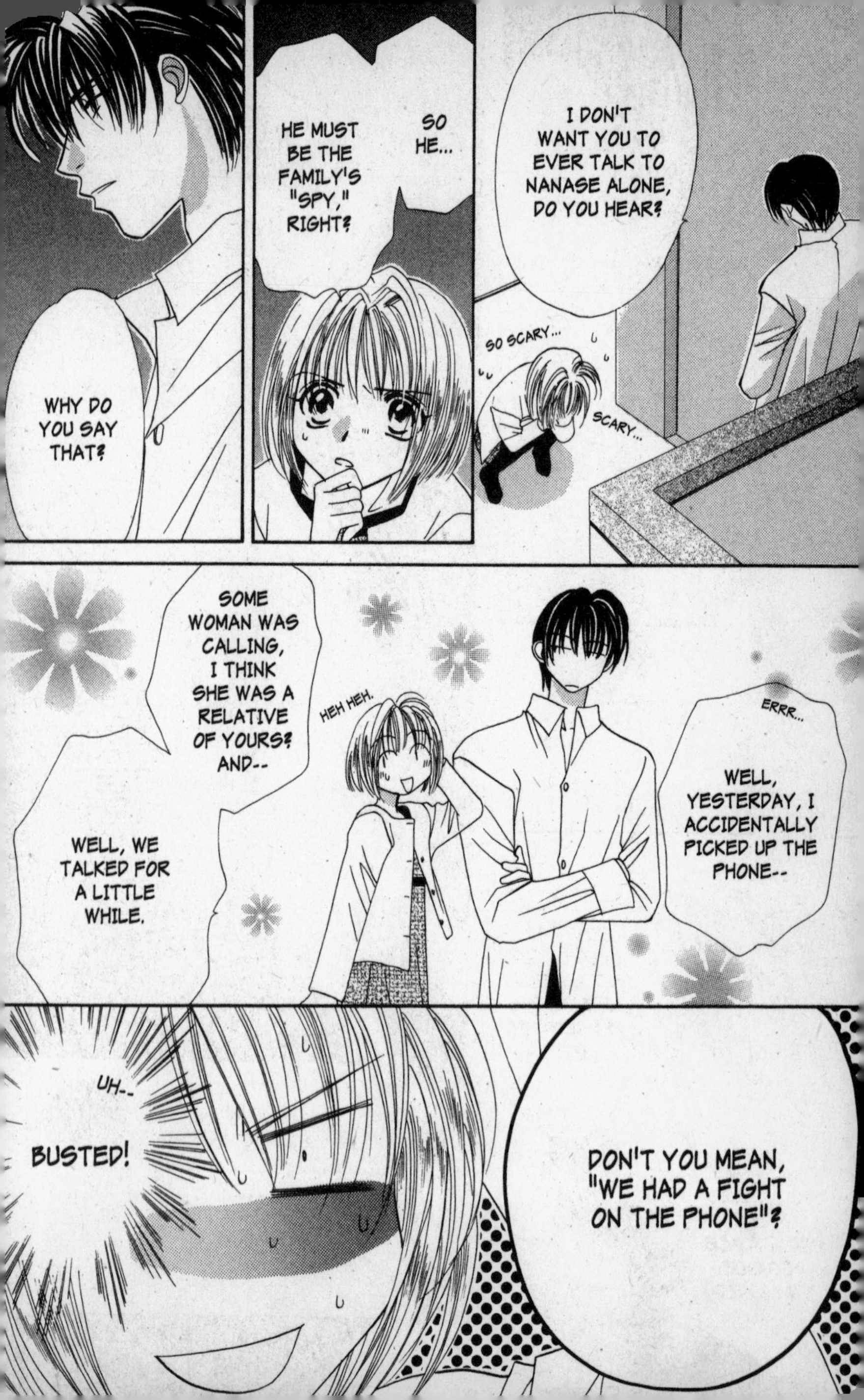
I DON'T WANT YOU TO EVER TALK TO NANASE ALONE, DO YOU HEAR?
SO SCARY...
SCARY...
SO HE...
HE MUST BE THE FAMILY'S "SPY," RIGHT?
WHY DO YOU SAY THAT?
ERRR...
WELL, YESTERDAY, I ACCIDENTALLY PICKED UP THE PHONE--
HEH HEH.
SOME WOMAN WAS CALLING, I THINK SHE WAS A RELATIVE OF YOURS? AND--
WELL, WE TALKED FOR A LITTLE WHILE.
DON'T YOU MEAN, "WE HAD A FIGHT ON THE PHONE"?
UH--
BUSTED!

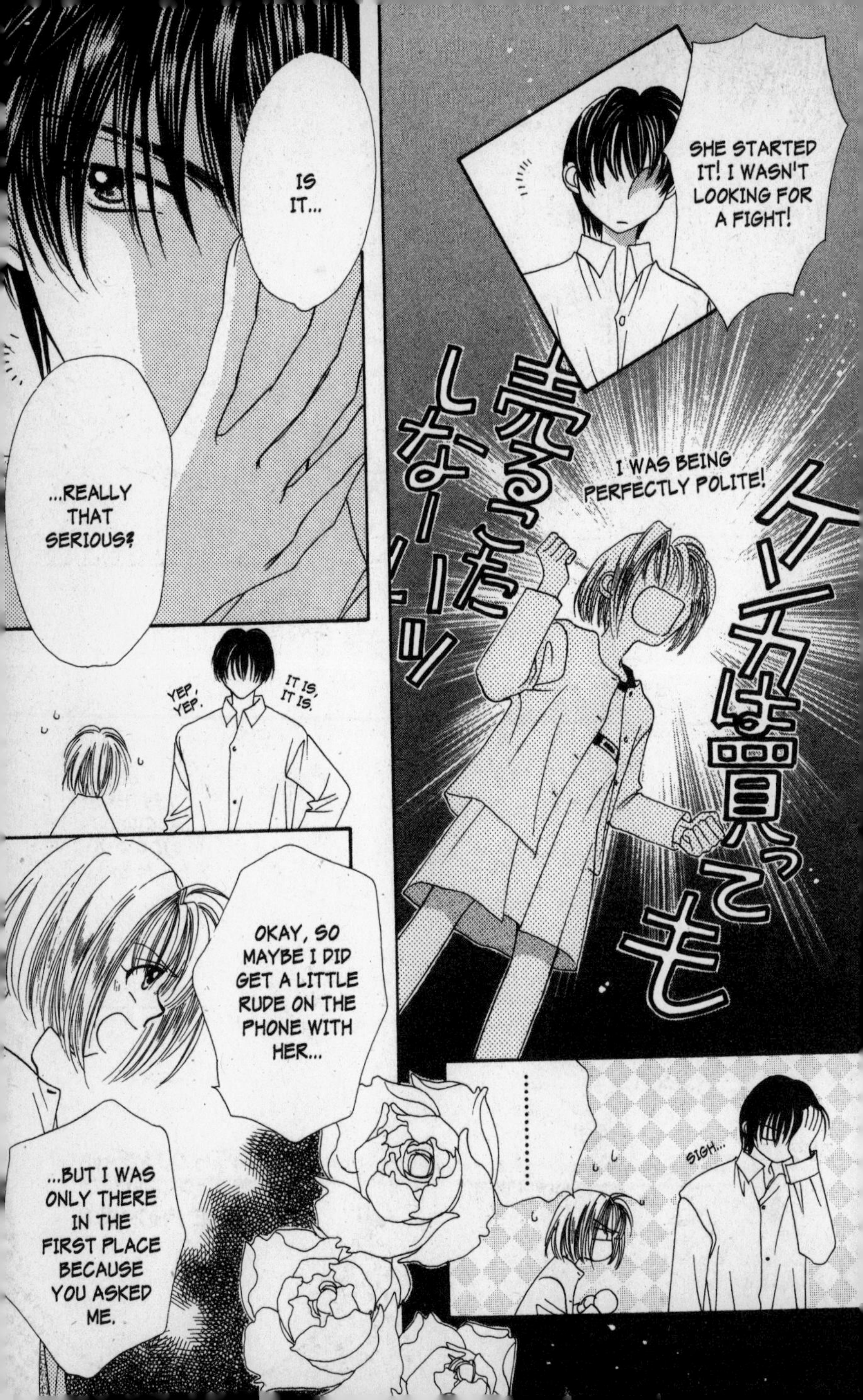
SHE STARTED IT! I WASN'T LOOKING FOR A FIGHT!
ケンカは買っても
売るったりしなーいッ
I WAS BEING PERFECTLY POLITE!
IS IT...
...REALLY THAT SERIOUS?
IT IS, IT IS.
YEP, YEP.
......
SIGH...
OKAY, SO MAYBE I DID GET A LITTLE RUDE ON THE PHONE WITH HER...
...BUT I WAS ONLY THERE IN THE FIRST PLACE BECAUSE YOU ASKED ME.

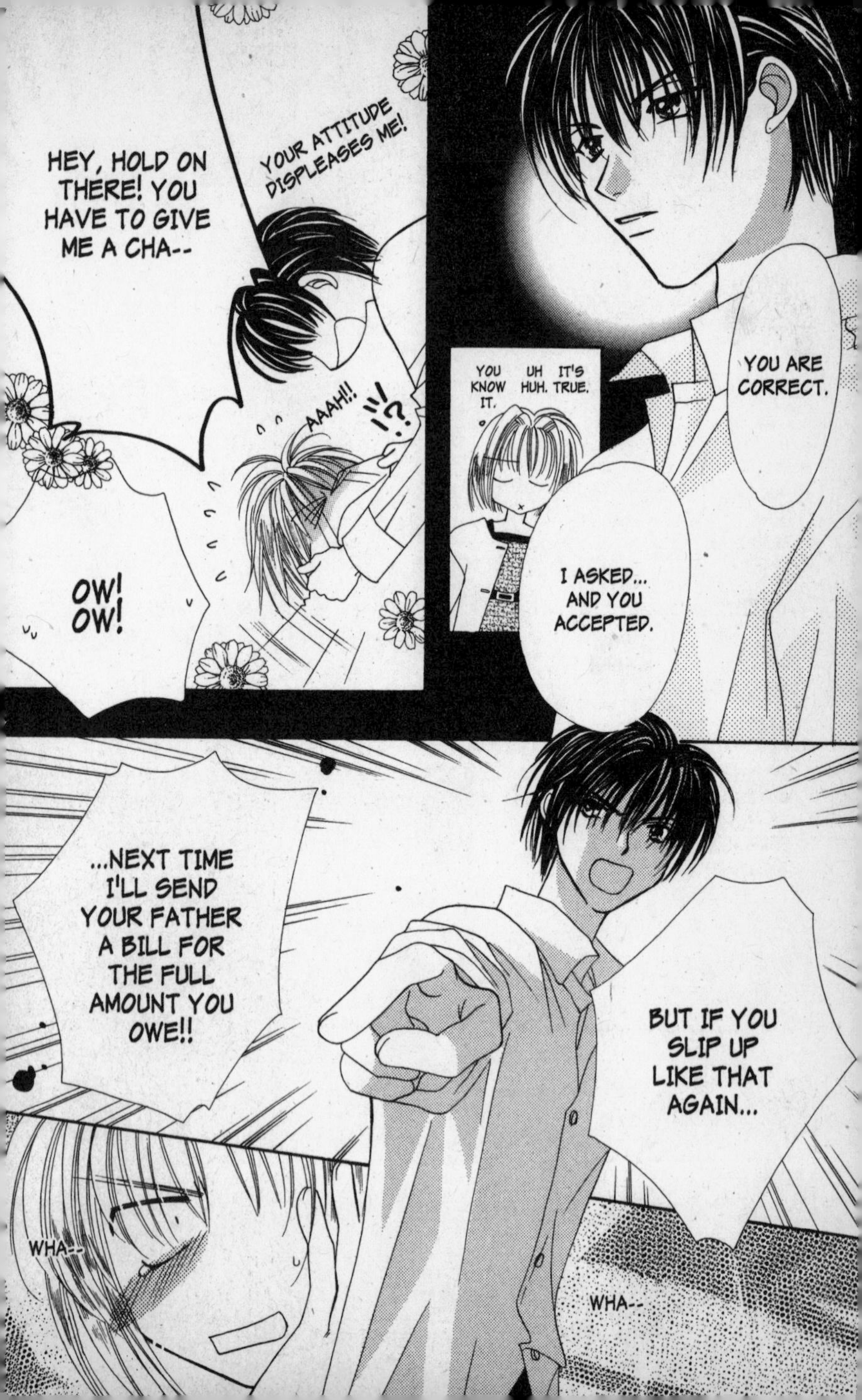
YOU ARE CORRECT.
I ASKED... AND YOU ACCEPTED.
IT'S TRUE.
UH HUH.
YOU KNOW IT.
YOUR ATTITUDE DISPLEASES ME!
HEY, HOLD ON THERE! YOU HAVE TO GIVE ME A CHA--
!?
AAAH!!
OW! OW!
BUT IF YOU SLIP UP LIKE THAT AGAIN...
...NEXT TIME I'LL SEND YOUR FATHER A BILL FOR THE FULL AMOUNT YOU OWE!!
WHA--
WHA--

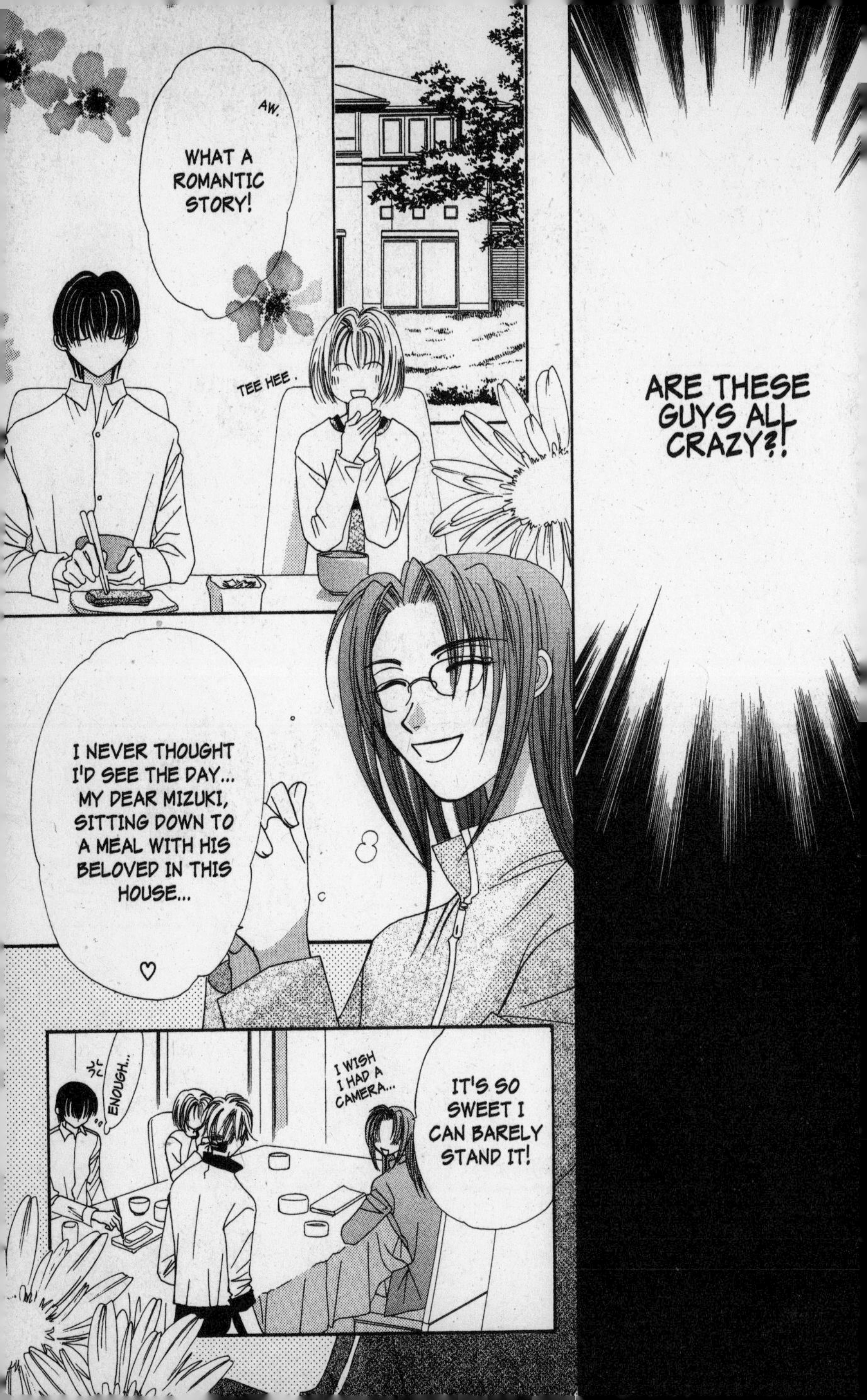
ARE THESE GUYS ALL CRAZY?!
AW.
WHAT A ROMANTIC STORY!
TEE HEE.
I NEVER THOUGHT I'D SEE THE DAY... MY DEAR MIZUKI, SITTING DOWN TO A MEAL WITH HIS BELOVED IN THIS HOUSE... ♡
IT'S SO SWEET I CAN BARELY STAND IT!
I WISH I HAD A CAMERA...
ENOUGH...

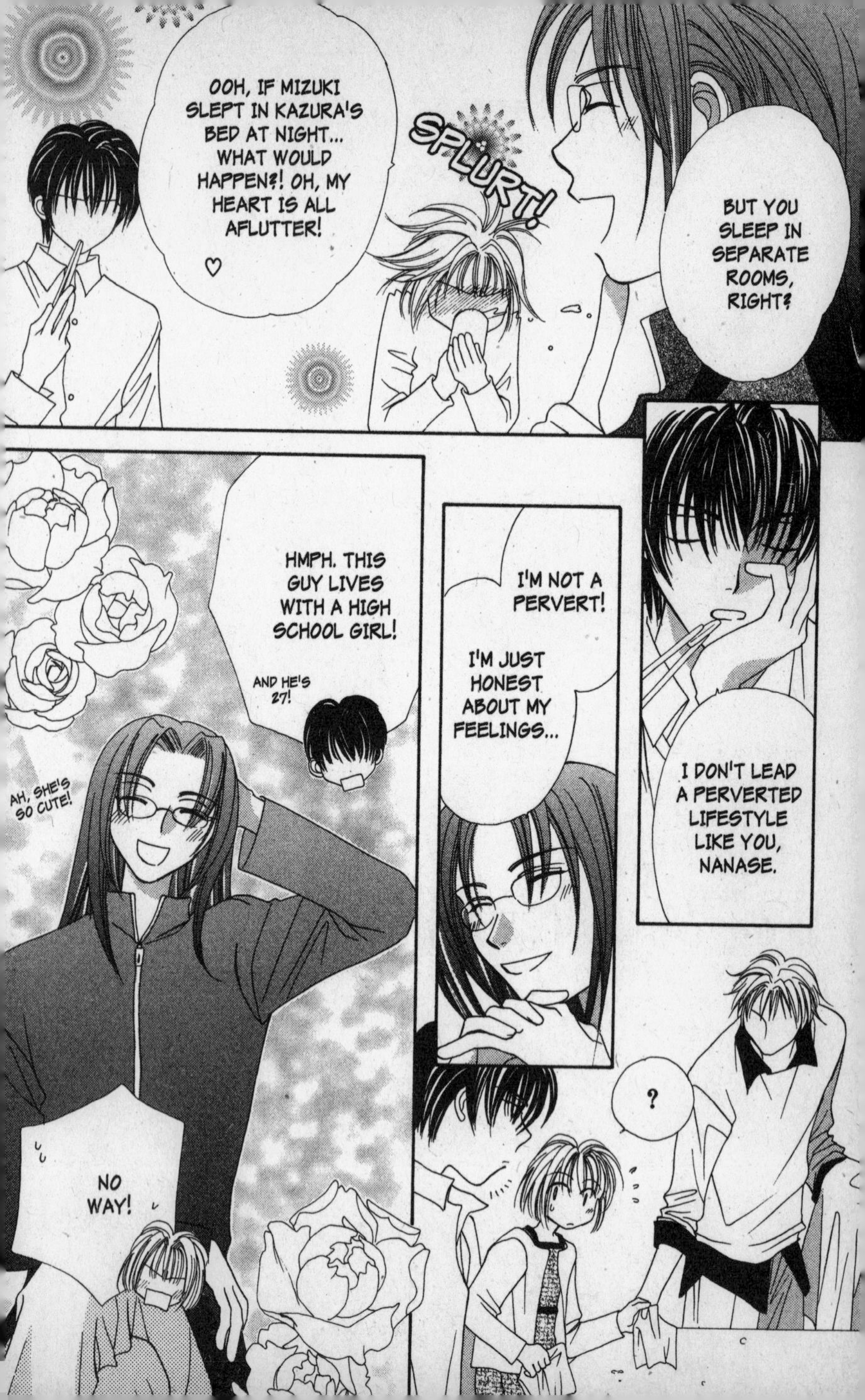
OOH, IF MIZUKI SLEPT IN KAZURA'S BED AT NIGHT... WHAT WOULD HAPPEN?! OH, MY HEART IS ALL AFLUTTER! ♡
SPLURT!
BUT YOU SLEEP IN SEPARATE ROOMS, RIGHT?
I DON'T LEAD A PERVERTED LIFESTYLE LIKE YOU, NANASE.
I'M NOT A PERVERT!
I'M JUST HONEST ABOUT MY FEELINGS...
HMPH. THIS GUY LIVES WITH A HIGH SCHOOL GIRL!
AND HE'S 27!
AH, SHE'S SO CUTE!
NO WAY!
?

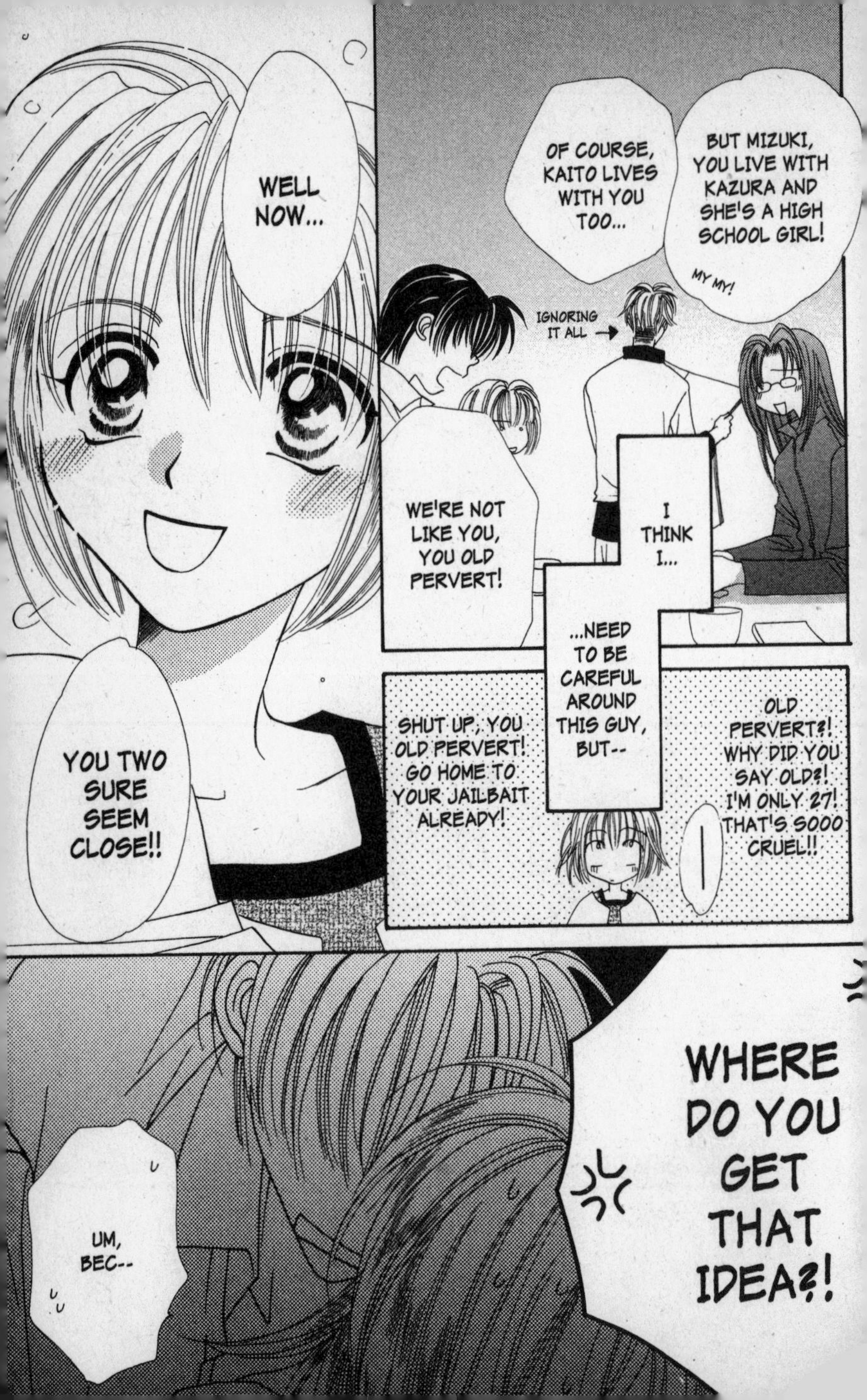
BUT MIZUKI, YOU LIVE WITH KAZURA AND SHE'S A HIGH SCHOOL GIRL!
MY MY!
OF COURSE, KAITO LIVES WITH YOU TOO...
IGNORING IT ALL
I THINK I...
WE'RE NOT LIKE YOU, YOU OLD PERVERT!
...NEED TO BE CAREFUL AROUND THIS GUY, BUT--
OLD PERVERT?! WHY DID YOU SAY OLD?! I'M ONLY 27! THAT'S SOOO CRUEL!!
SHUT UP, YOU OLD PERVERT! GO HOME TO YOUR JAILBAIT ALREADY!
WELL NOW...
YOU TWO SURE SEEM CLOSE!!
WHERE DO YOU GET THAT IDEA?!
UM, BEC--

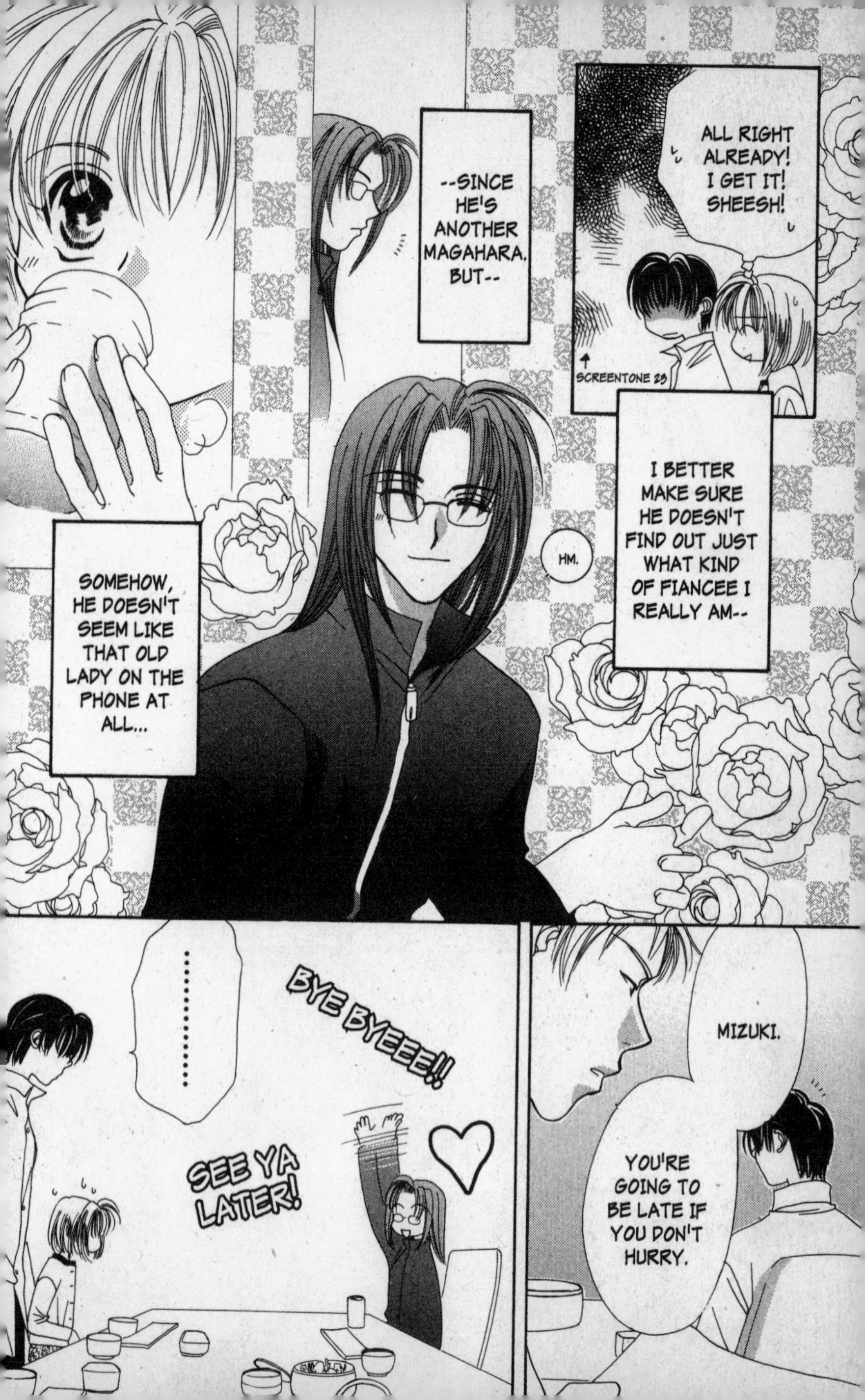
ALL RIGHT ALREADY! I GET IT! SHEESH!
SCREENTONE 23
--SINCE HE'S ANOTHER MAGAHARA, BUT--
I BETTER MAKE SURE HE DOESN'T FIND OUT JUST WHAT KIND OF FIANCEE I REALLY AM--
HM.
SOMEHOW, HE DOESN'T SEEM LIKE THAT OLD LADY ON THE PHONE AT ALL...
MIZUKI.
YOU'RE GOING TO BE LATE IF YOU DON'T HURRY.
BYE BYEEE!!
....
SEE YA LATER!

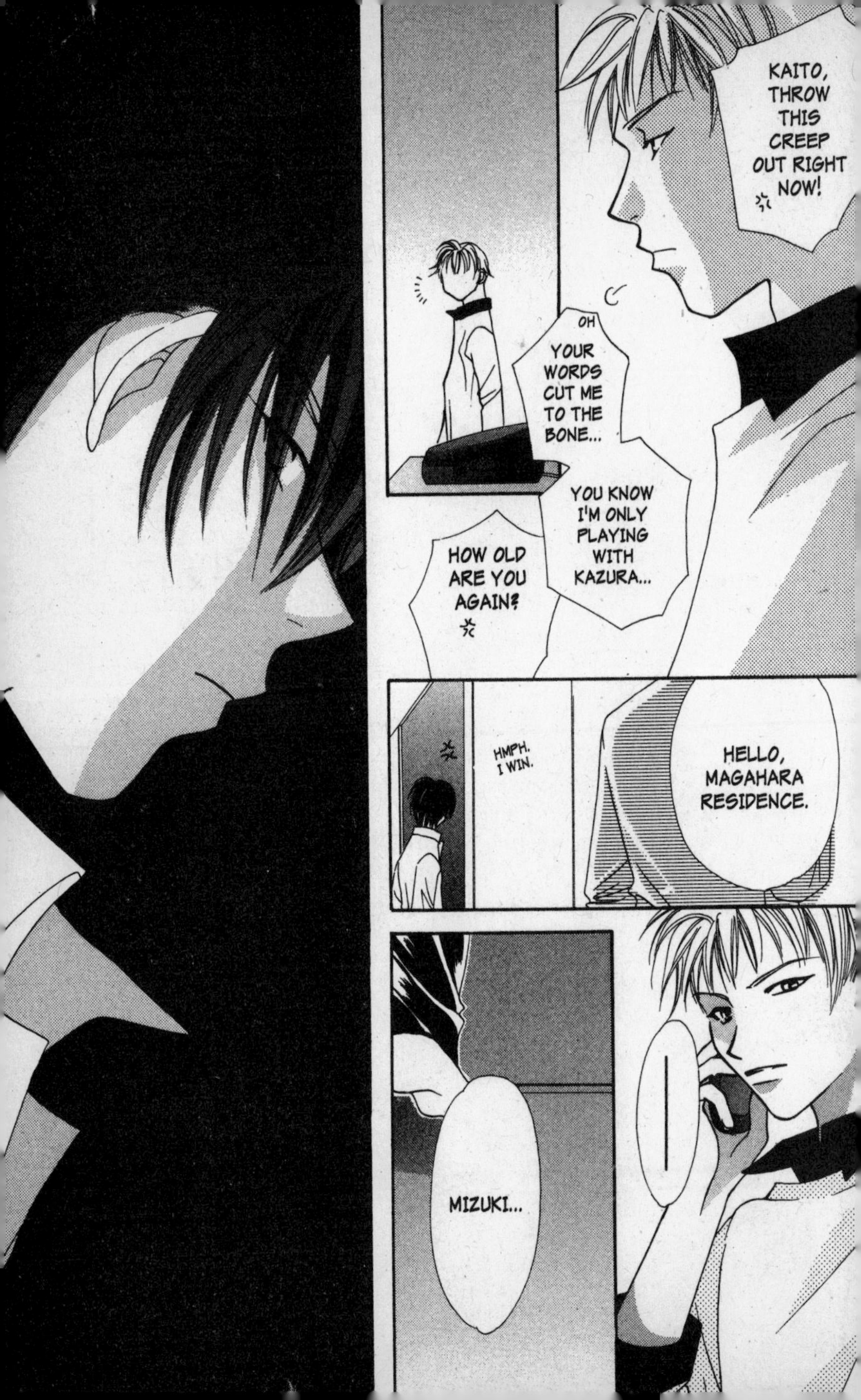
KAITO, THROW THIS CREEP OUT RIGHT NOW!
OH
YOUR WORDS CUT ME TO THE BONE...
YOU KNOW I'M ONLY PLAYING WITH KAZURA...
HOW OLD ARE YOU AGAIN?
HELLO, MAGAHARA RESIDENCE.
HMPH. I WIN.
—
MIZUKI...

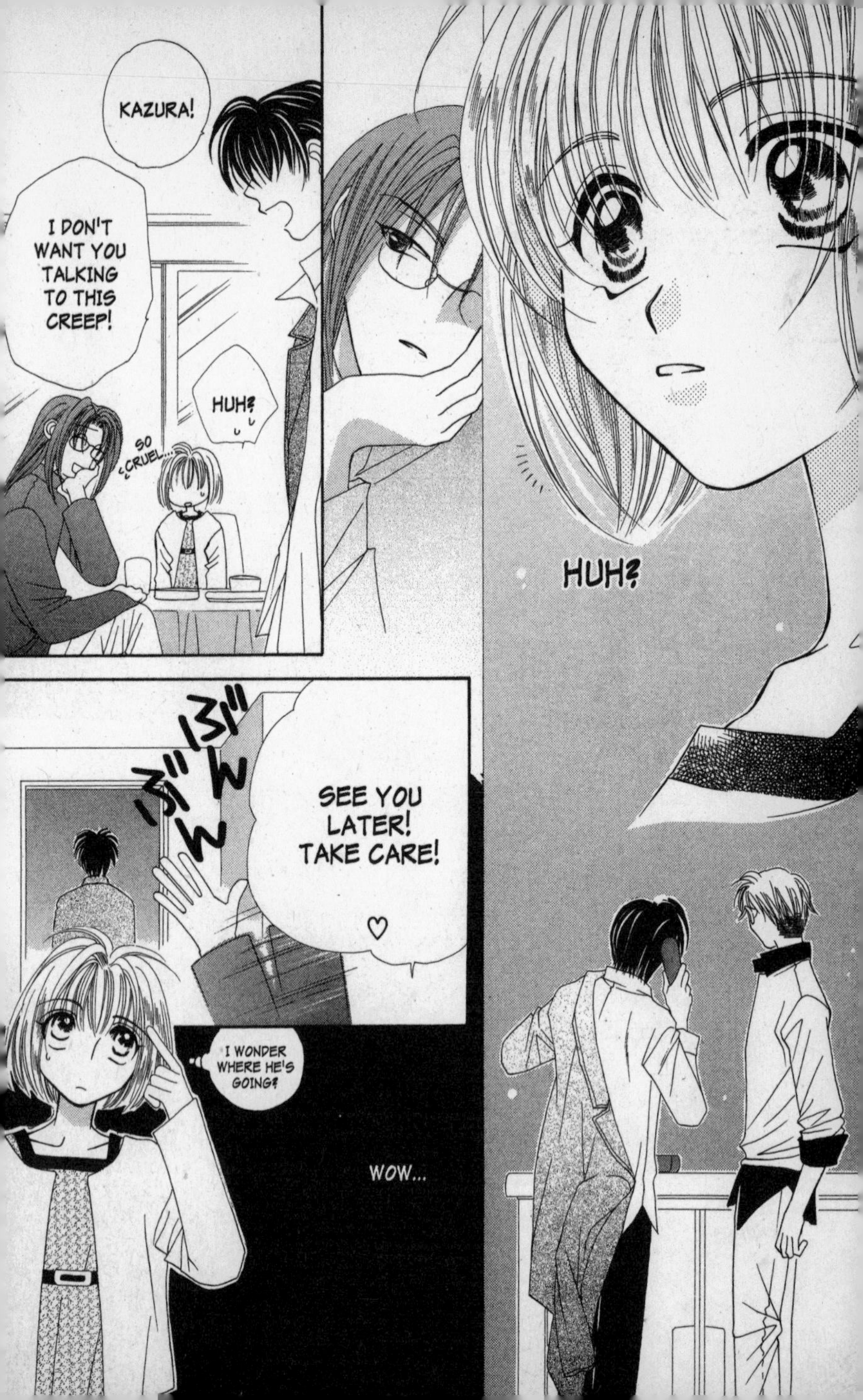
HUH?
KAZURA!
I DON'T WANT YOU TALKING TO THIS CREEP!
HUH?
SO CRUEL...
ぶんぶん
SEE YOU LATER! TAKE CARE! ♡
I WONDER WHERE HE'S GOING?
WOW...

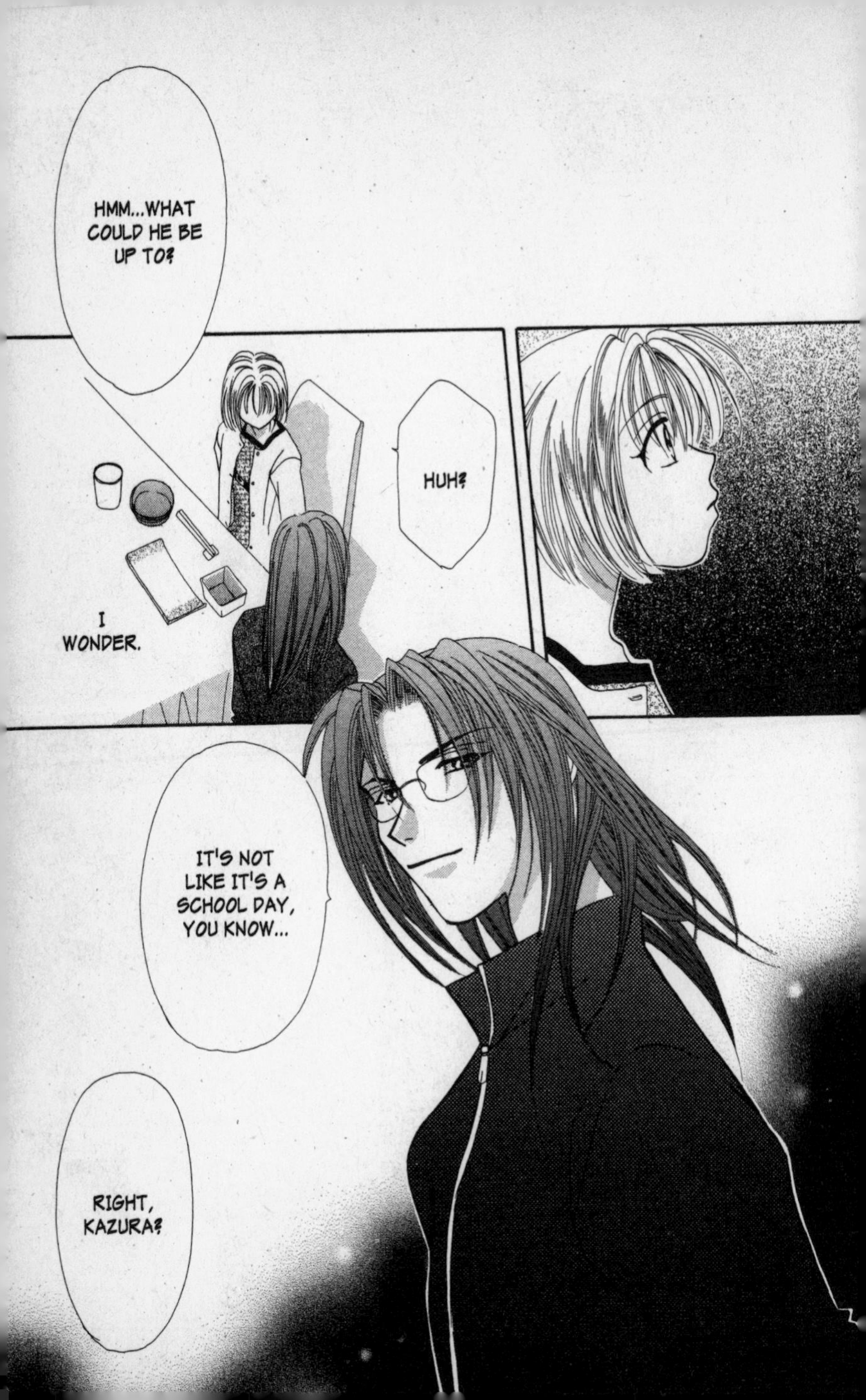
HMM...WHAT COULD HE BE UP TO?
I WONDER.
HUH?
IT'S NOT LIKE IT'S A SCHOOL DAY, YOU KNOW...
RIGHT, KAZURA?

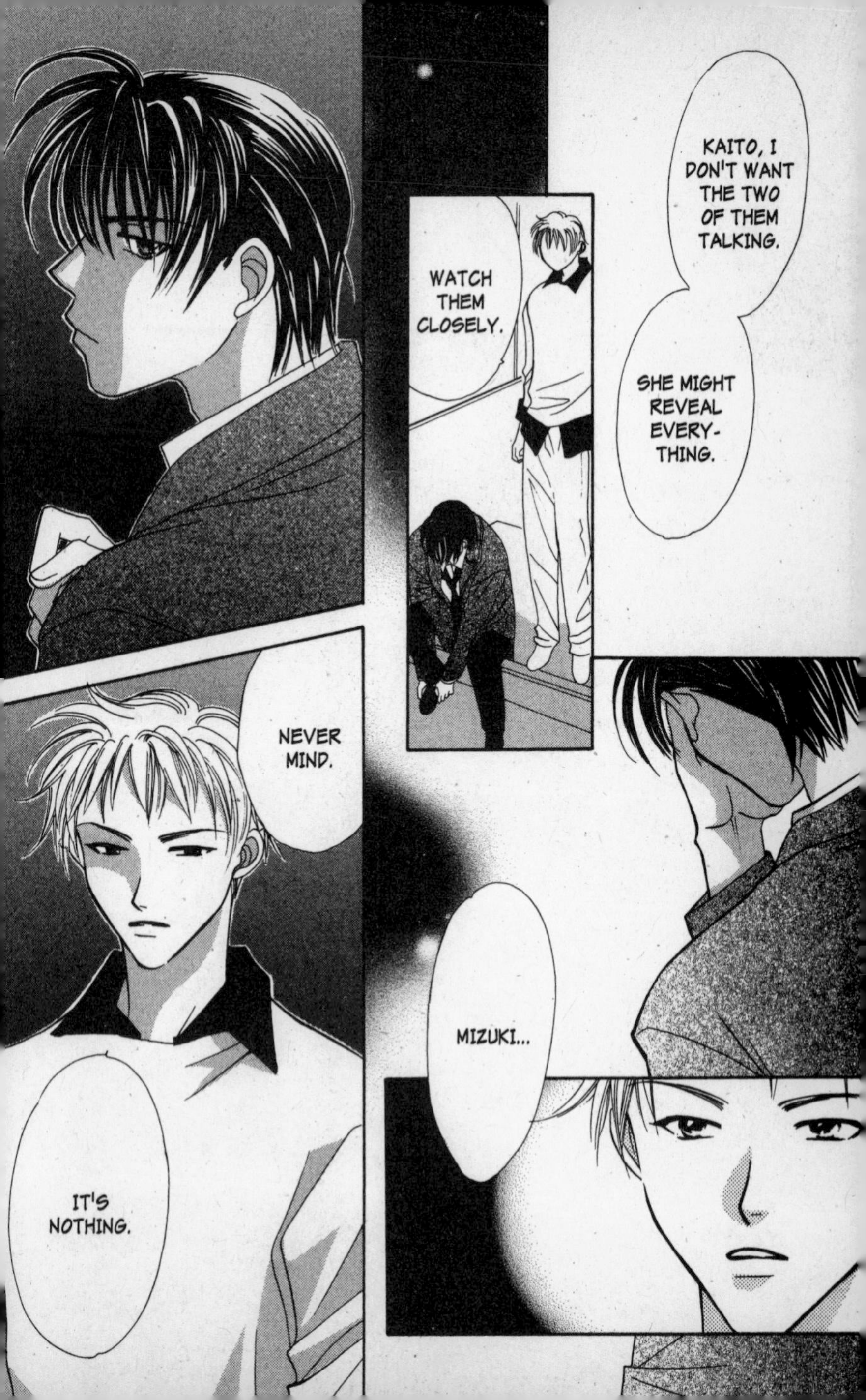
KAITO, I DON'T WANT THE TWO OF THEM TALKING.
SHE MIGHT REVEAL EVERY-THING.
WATCH THEM CLOSELY.
MIZUKI...
NEVER MIND.
IT'S NOTHING.

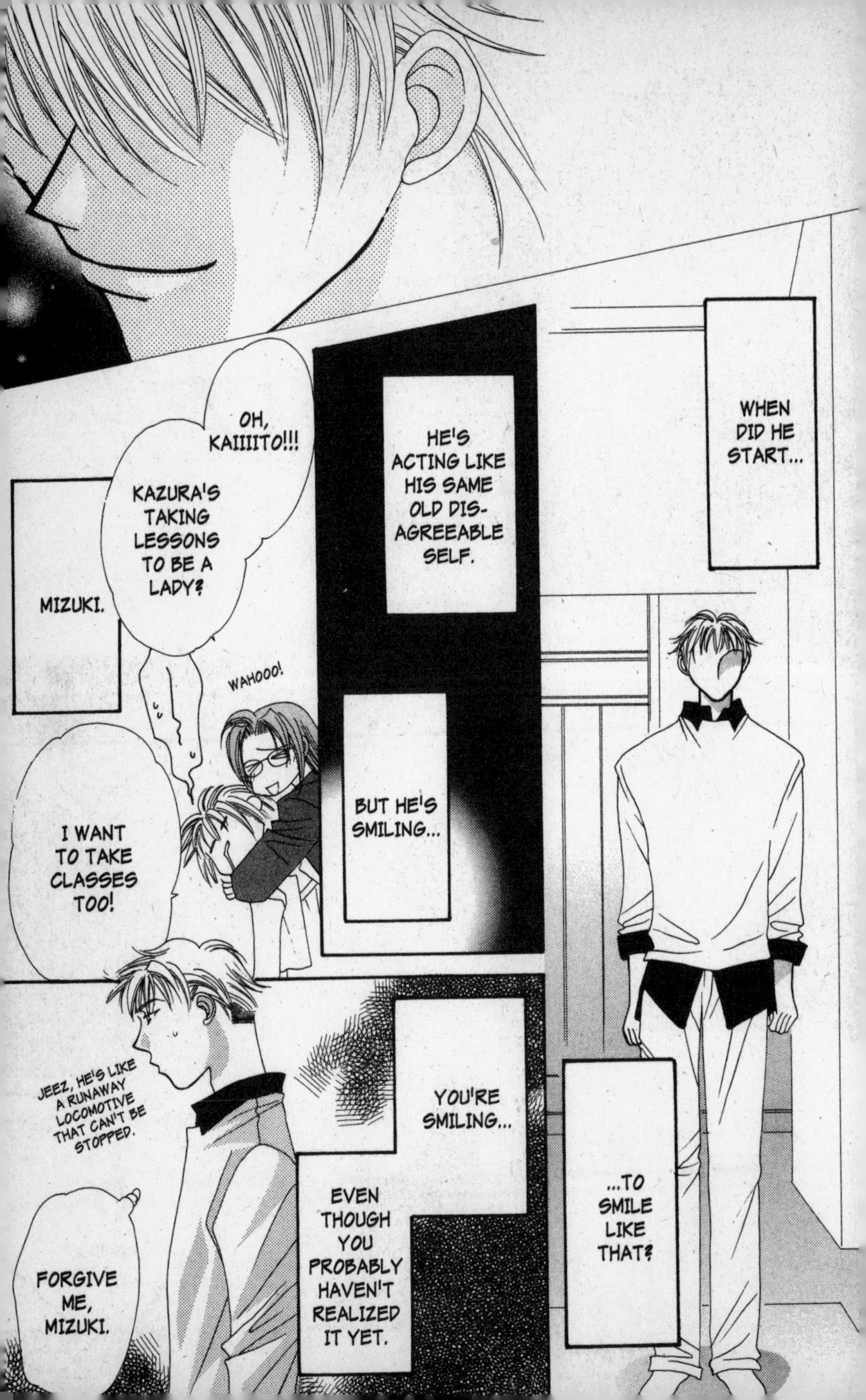
WHEN DID HE START...
...TO SMILE LIKE THAT?
HE'S ACTING LIKE HIS SAME OLD DIS-AGREEABLE SELF.
BUT HE'S SMILING...
OH, KAIIIITO!!!
KAZURA'S TAKING LESSONS TO BE A LADY?
WAHOOO!
MIZUKI.
I WANT TO TAKE CLASSES TOO!
YOU'RE SMILING...
EVEN THOUGH YOU PROBABLY HAVEN'T REALIZED IT YET.
JEEZ, HE'S LIKE A RUNAWAY LOCOMOTIVE THAT CAN'T BE STOPPED.
FORGIVE ME, MIZUKI.

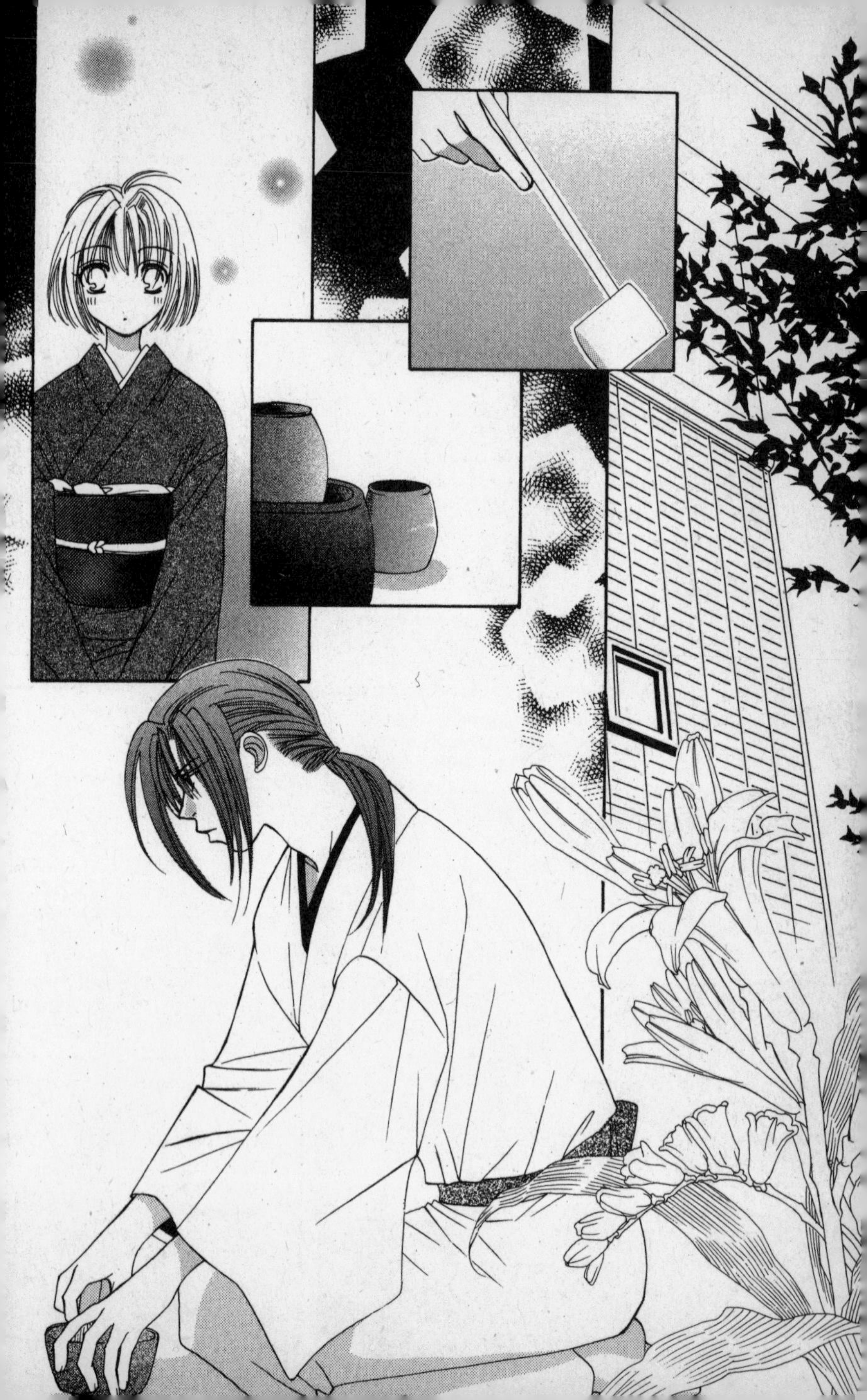

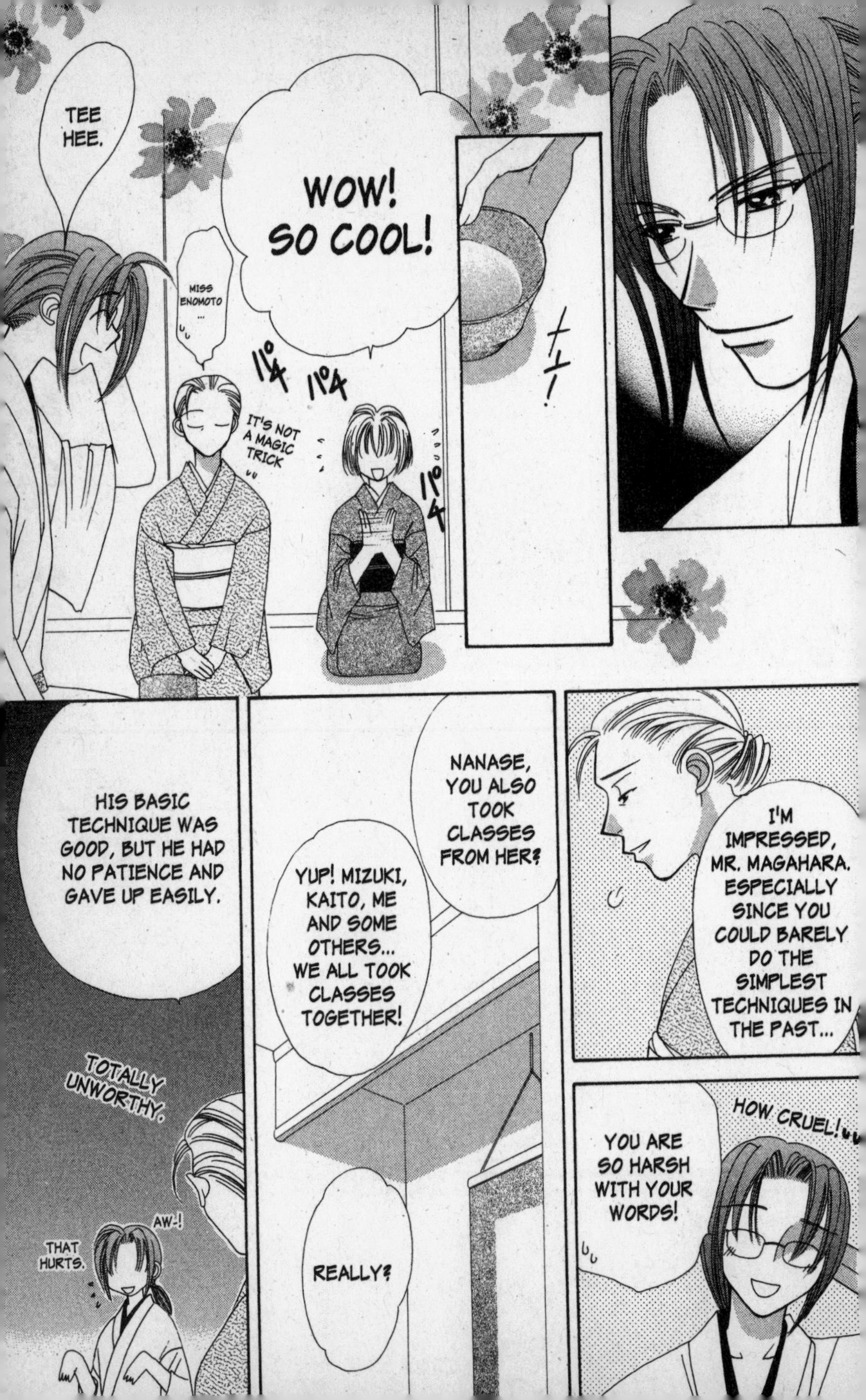
WOW! SO COOL!
TEE HEE.
MISS ENOMOTO...
パチ パチ
IT'S NOT A MAGIC TRICK
パチ
I'M IMPRESSED, MR. MAGAHARA. ESPECIALLY SINCE YOU COULD BARELY DO THE SIMPLEST TECHNIQUES IN THE PAST...
HOW CRUEL!
YOU ARE SO HARSH WITH YOUR WORDS!
NANASE, YOU ALSO TOOK CLASSES FROM HER?
YUP! MIZUKI, KAITO, ME AND SOME OTHERS... WE ALL TOOK CLASSES TOGETHER!
REALLY?
HIS BASIC TECHNIQUE WAS GOOD, BUT HE HAD NO PATIENCE AND GAVE UP EASILY.
TOTALLY UNWORTHY.
AW-!
THAT HURTS.

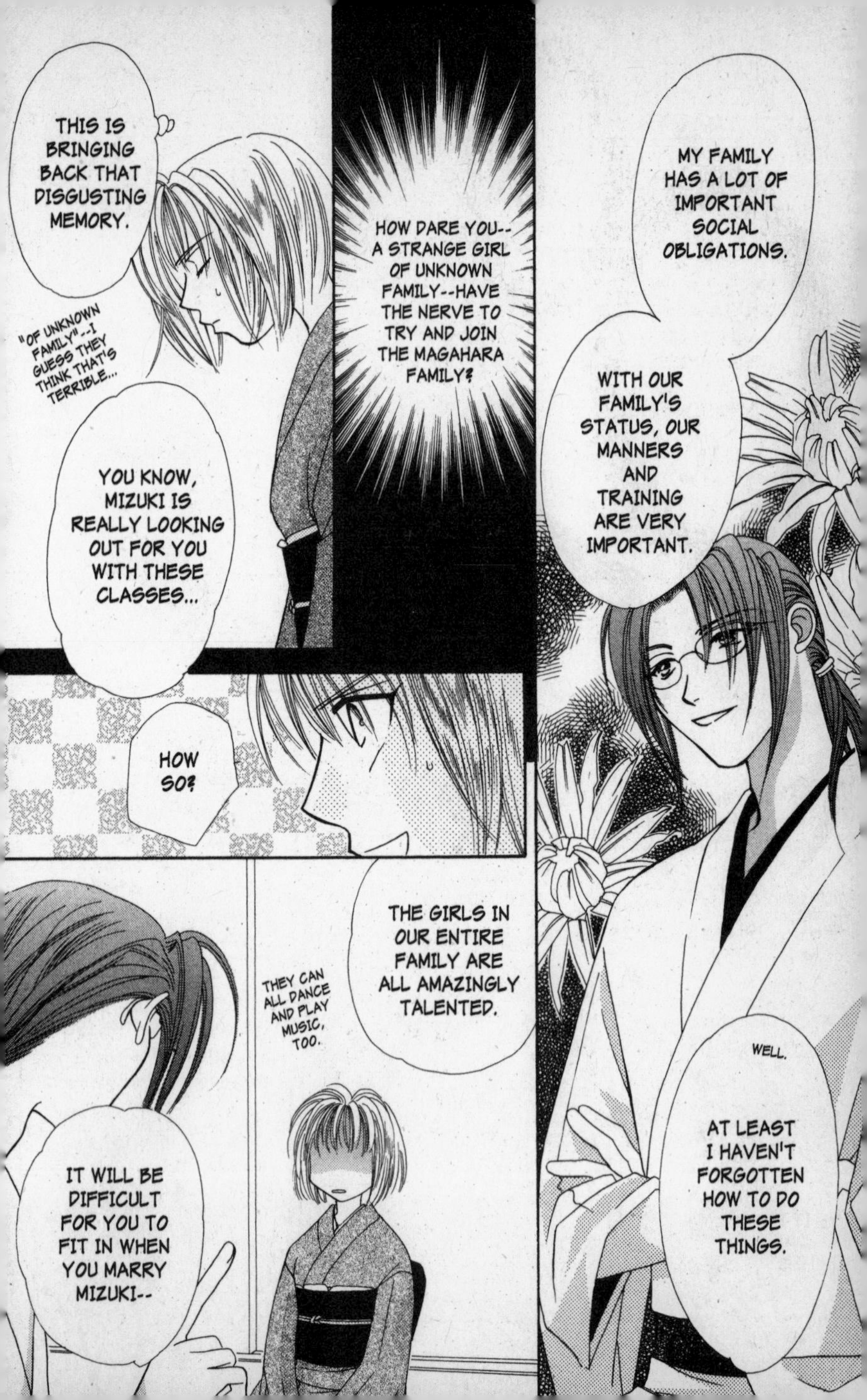
MY FAMILY HAS A LOT OF IMPORTANT SOCIAL OBLIGATIONS.
WITH OUR FAMILY'S STATUS, OUR MANNERS AND TRAINING ARE VERY IMPORTANT.
WELL.
AT LEAST I HAVEN'T FORGOTTEN HOW TO DO THESE THINGS.
HOW DARE YOU-- A STRANGE GIRL OF UNKNOWN FAMILY--HAVE THE NERVE TO TRY AND JOIN THE MAGAHARA FAMILY?
THIS IS BRINGING BACK THAT DISGUSTING MEMORY.
"OF UNKNOWN FAMILY"--I GUESS THEY THINK THAT'S TERRIBLE...
YOU KNOW, MIZUKI IS REALLY LOOKING OUT FOR YOU WITH THESE CLASSES...
HOW SO?
THE GIRLS IN OUR ENTIRE FAMILY ARE ALL AMAZINGLY TALENTED.
THEY CAN ALL DANCE AND PLAY MUSIC, TOO.
IT WILL BE DIFFICULT FOR YOU TO FIT IN WHEN YOU MARRY MIZUKI--

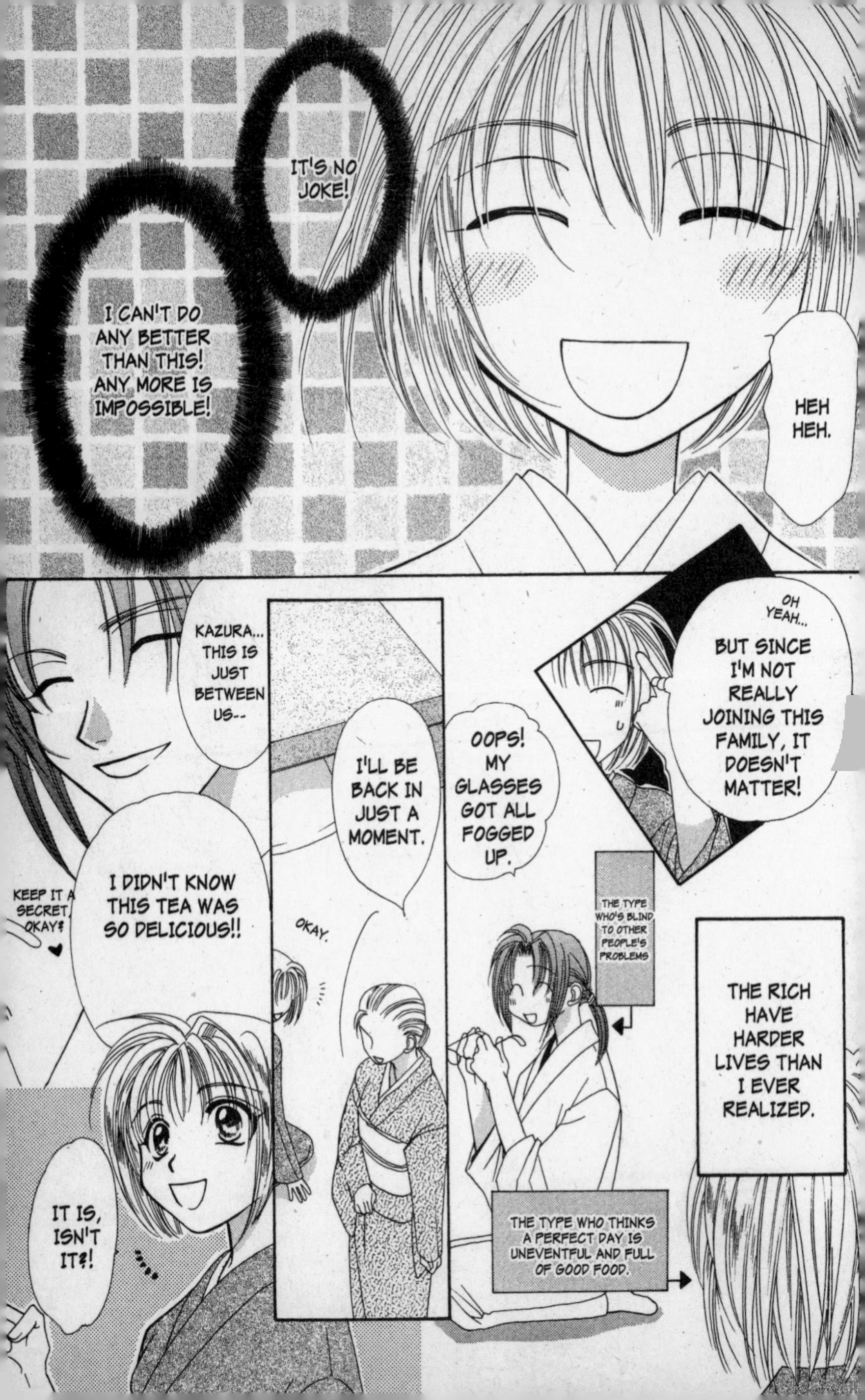
HEH HEH.
IT'S NO JOKE!
I CAN'T DO ANY BETTER THAN THIS! ANY MORE IS IMPOSSIBLE!
OH YEAH...
BUT SINCE I'M NOT REALLY JOINING THIS FAMILY, IT DOESN'T MATTER!
OOPS! MY GLASSES GOT ALL FOGGED UP.
THE TYPE WHO'S BLIND TO OTHER PEOPLE'S PROBLEMS
THE RICH HAVE HARDER LIVES THAN I EVER REALIZED.
THE TYPE WHO THINKS A PERFECT DAY IS UNEVENTFUL AND FULL OF GOOD FOOD.
I'LL BE BACK IN JUST A MOMENT.
OKAY.
KAZURA... THIS IS JUST BETWEEN US--
I DIDN'T KNOW THIS TEA WAS SO DELICIOUS!!
KEEP IT A SECRET, OKAY?
IT IS, ISN'T IT?!

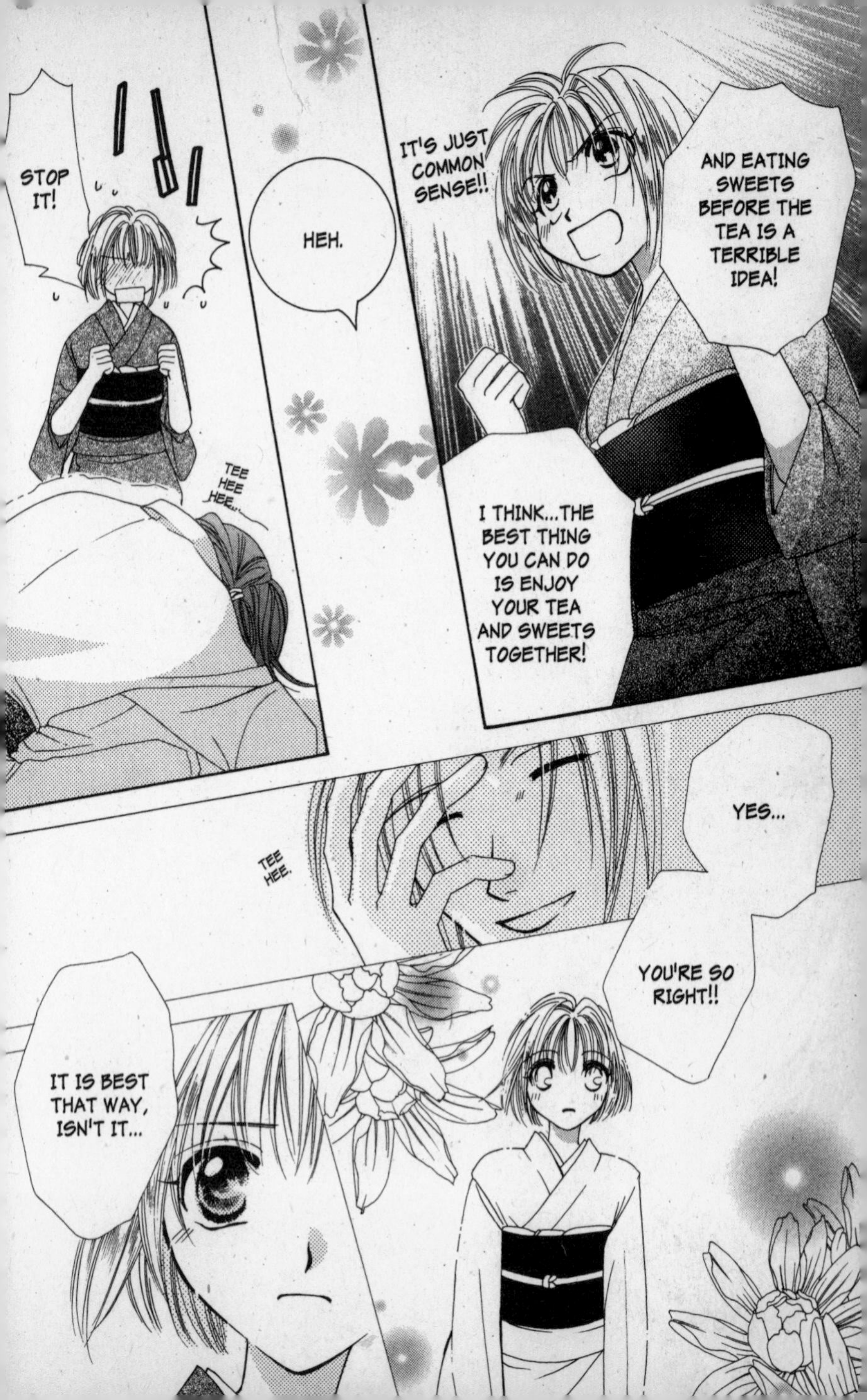
AND EATING SWEETS BEFORE THE TEA IS A TERRIBLE IDEA!
IT'S JUST COMMON SENSE!!
I THINK...THE BEST THING YOU CAN DO IS ENJOY YOUR TEA AND SWEETS TOGETHER!
HEH.
STOP IT!
TEE HEE HEE...
YES...
TEE HEE.
YOU'RE SO RIGHT!!
IT IS BEST THAT WAY, ISN'T IT...

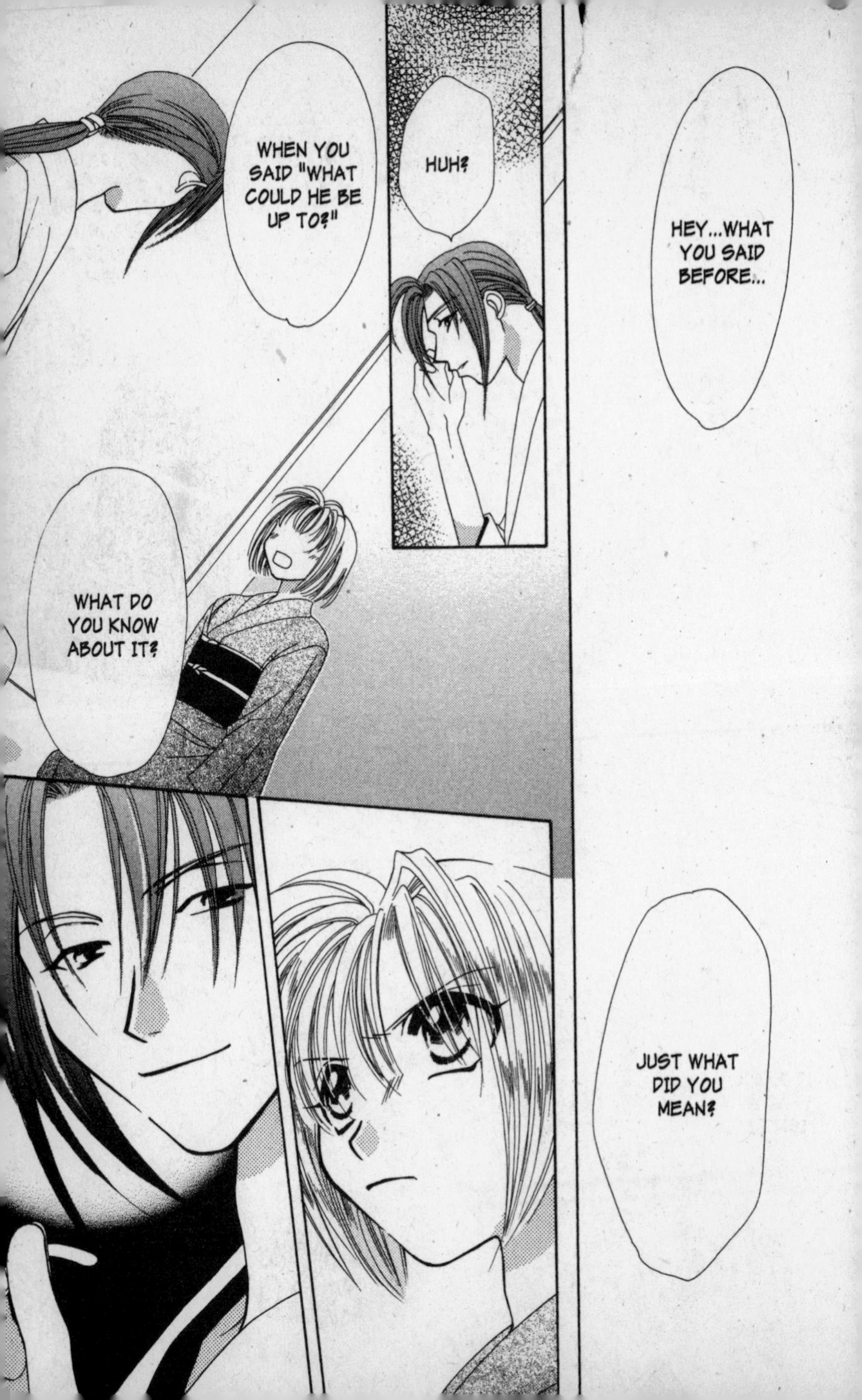
HEY...WHAT YOU SAID BEFORE...
HUH?
WHEN YOU SAID "WHAT COULD HE BE UP TO?"
WHAT DO YOU KNOW ABOUT IT?
JUST WHAT DID YOU MEAN?

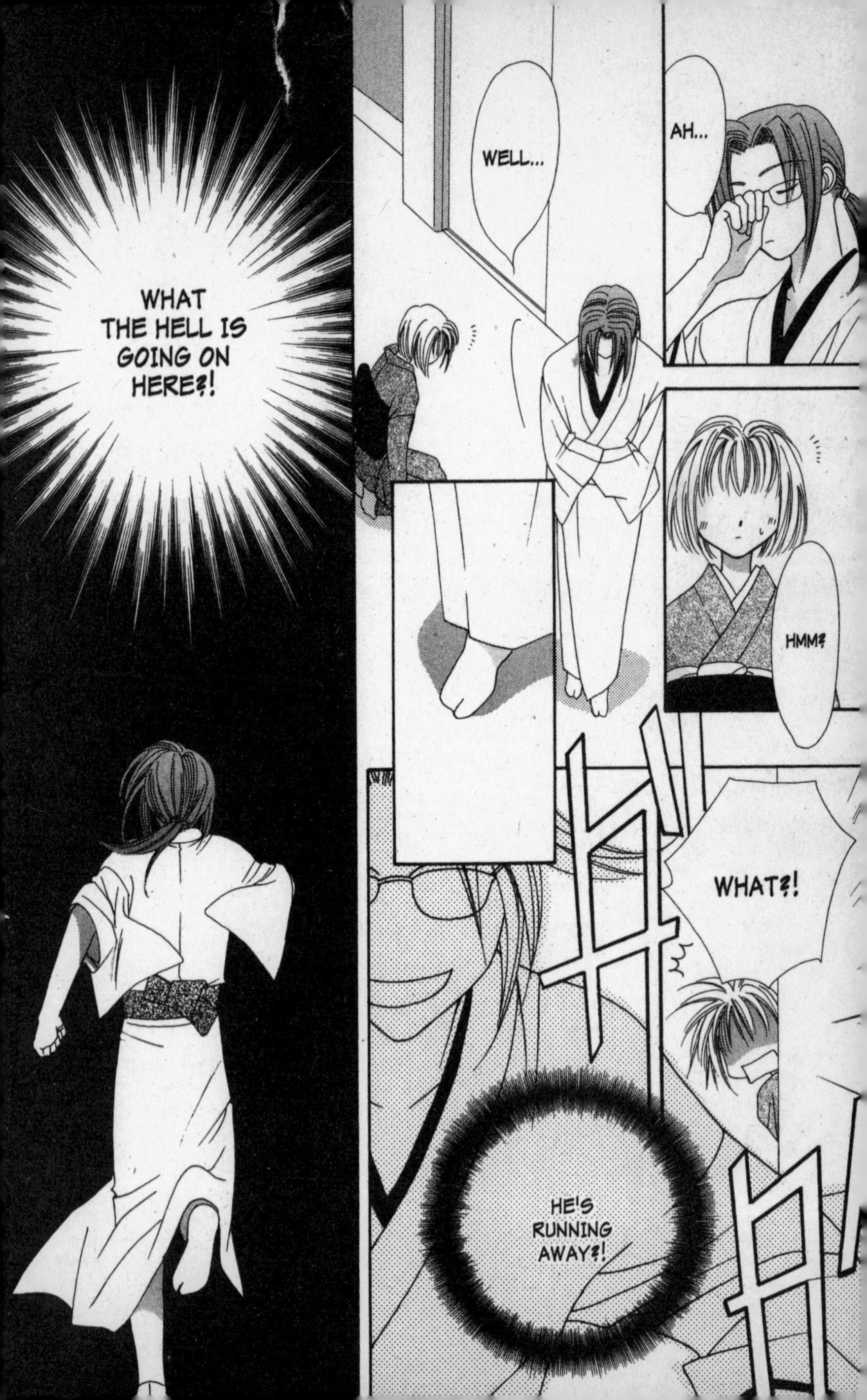
AH...
WELL...
HMM?
WHAT?!
HE'S RUNNING AWAY?!
WHAT THE HELL IS GOING ON HERE?!

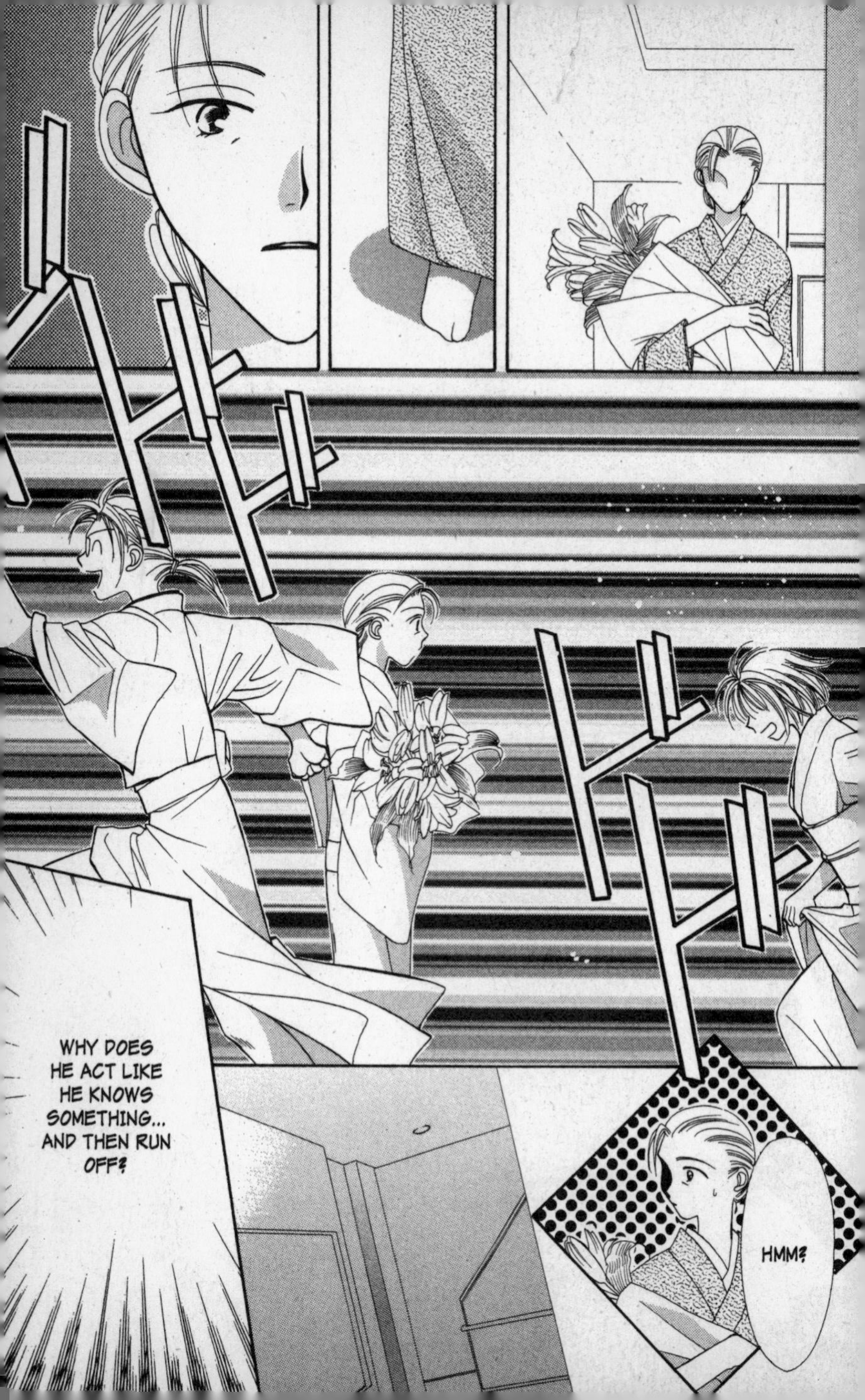
HMM?
WHY DOES HE ACT LIKE HE KNOWS SOMETHING... AND THEN RUN OFF?

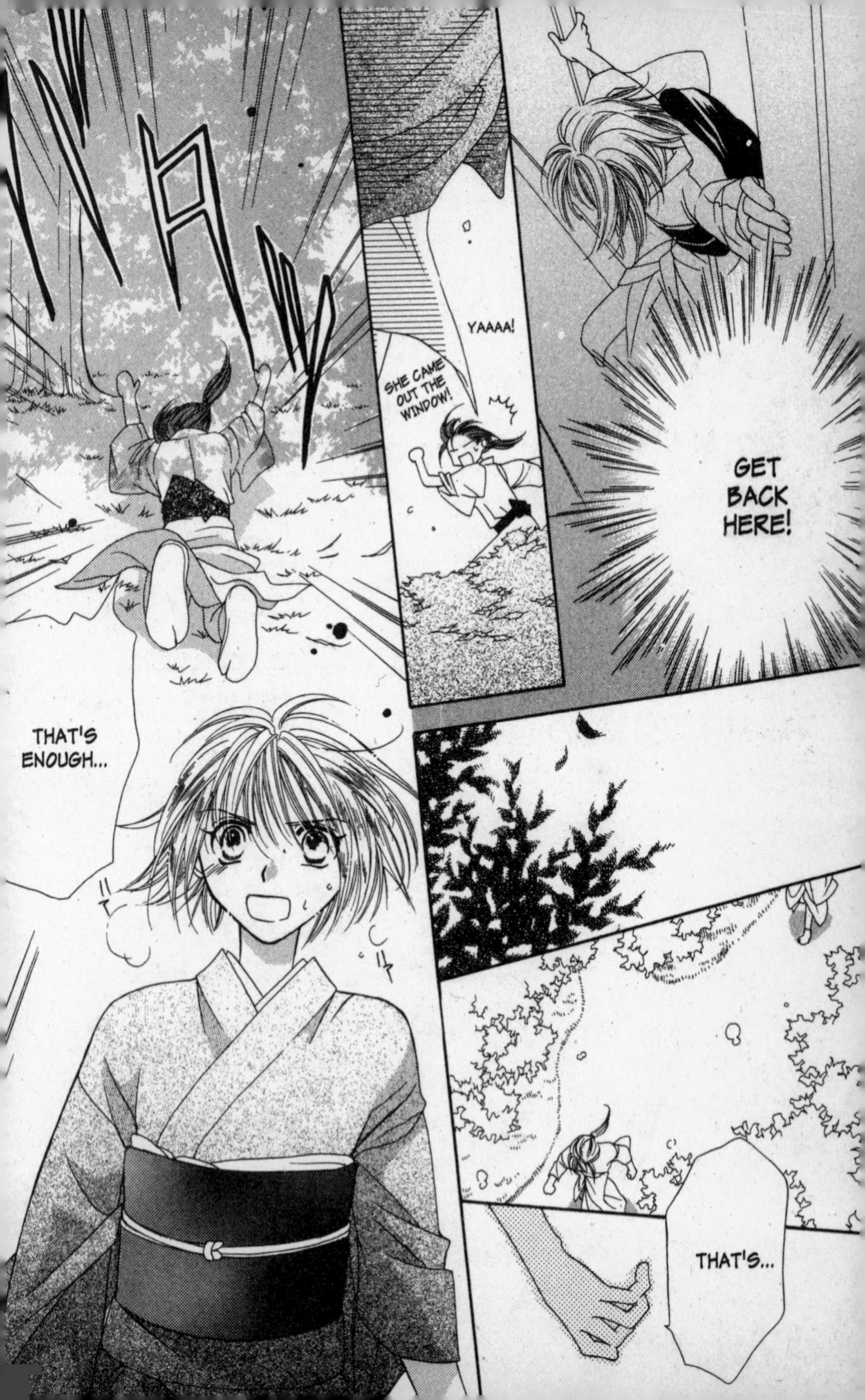
GET BACK HERE!
YAAAA!
SHE CAME OUT THE WINDOW!
THAT'S...
THAT'S ENOUGH...

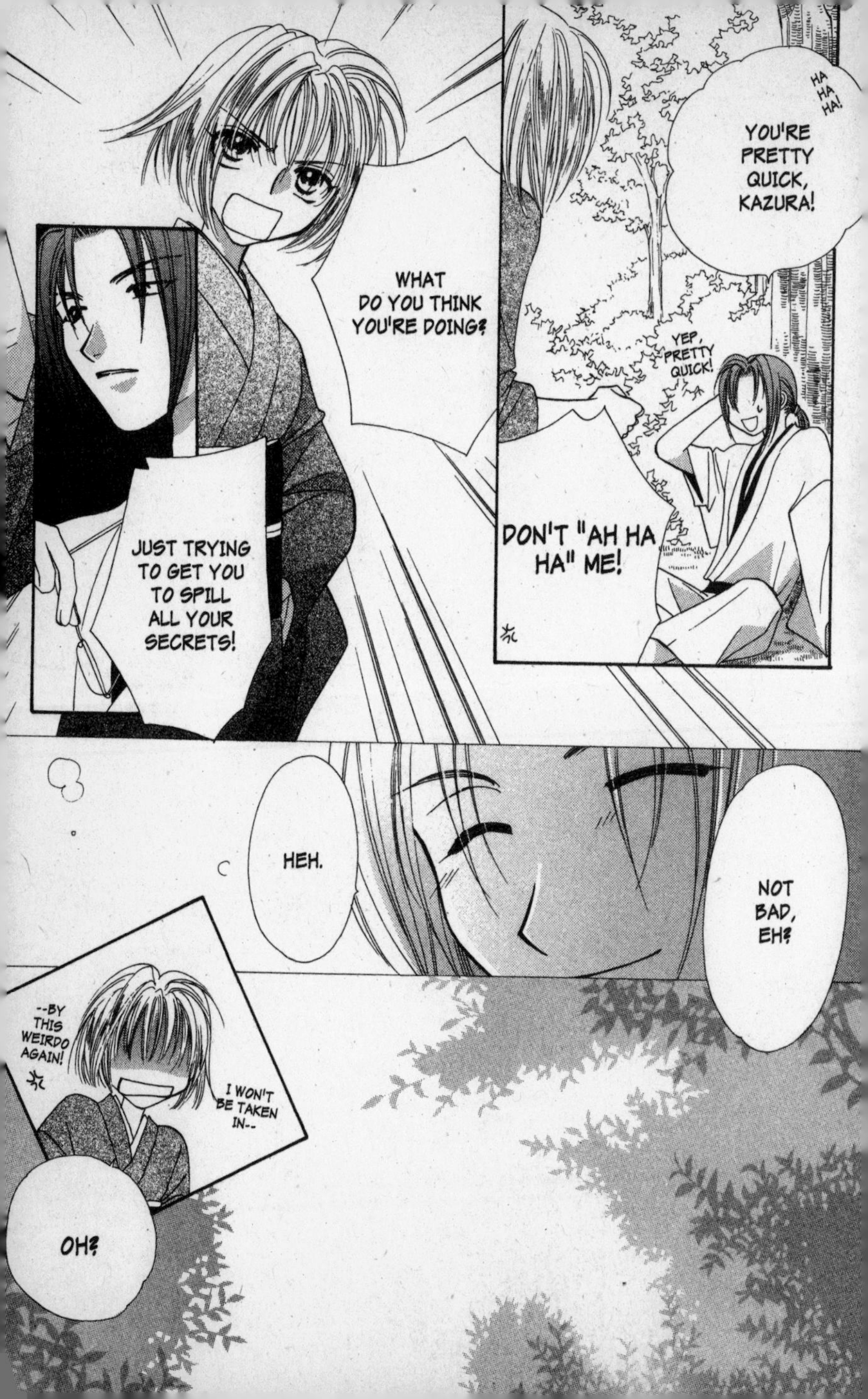
HA HA HA!
YOU'RE PRETTY QUICK, KAZURA!
YEP, PRETTY QUICK!
DON'T "AH HA HA" ME!
WHAT DO YOU THINK YOU'RE DOING?
JUST TRYING TO GET YOU TO SPILL ALL YOUR SECRETS!
HEH.
NOT BAD, EH?
I WON'T BE TAKEN IN--
--BY THIS WEIRDO AGAIN!
OH?

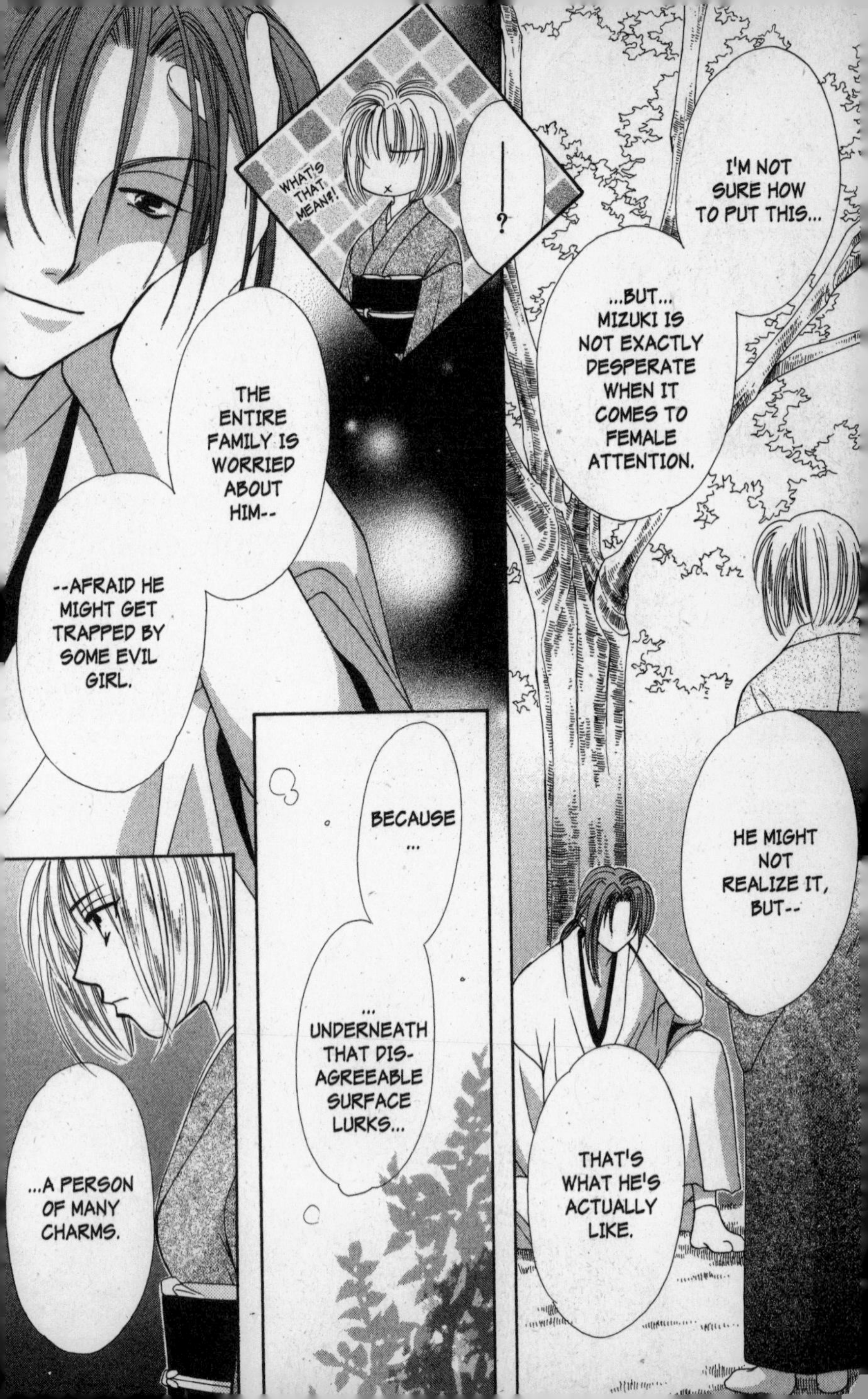
I'M NOT SURE HOW TO PUT THIS...
...BUT... MIZUKI IS NOT EXACTLY DESPERATE WHEN IT COMES TO FEMALE ATTENTION.
HE MIGHT NOT REALIZE IT, BUT--
THAT'S WHAT HE'S ACTUALLY LIKE.
---?
WHAT'S THAT MEAN?!
THE ENTIRE FAMILY IS WORRIED ABOUT HIM--
--AFRAID HE MIGHT GET TRAPPED BY SOME EVIL GIRL.
BECAUSE ...
... UNDERNEATH THAT DIS-AGREEABLE SURFACE LURKS...
...A PERSON OF MANY CHARMS.

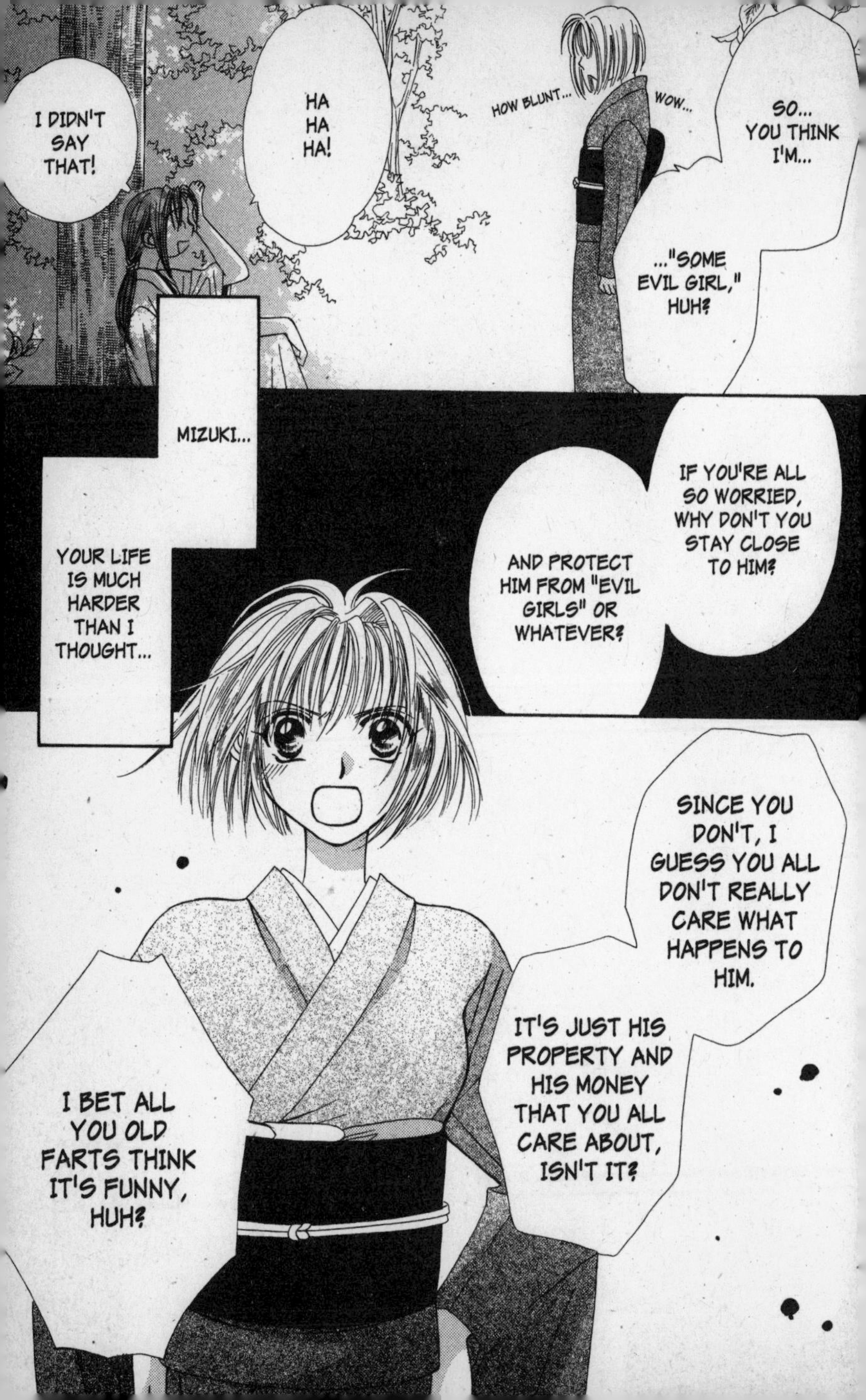
SO... YOU THINK I'M...
..."SOME EVIL GIRL," HUH?
WOW...
HOW BLUNT...
HA HA HA!
I DIDN'T SAY THAT!
IF YOU'RE ALL SO WORRIED, WHY DON'T YOU STAY CLOSE TO HIM?
AND PROTECT HIM FROM "EVIL GIRLS" OR WHATEVER?
MIZUKI...
YOUR LIFE IS MUCH HARDER THAN I THOUGHT...
SINCE YOU DON'T, I GUESS YOU ALL DON'T REALLY CARE WHAT HAPPENS TO HIM.
IT'S JUST HIS PROPERTY AND HIS MONEY THAT YOU ALL CARE ABOUT, ISN'T IT?
I BET ALL YOU OLD FARTS THINK IT'S FUNNY, HUH?

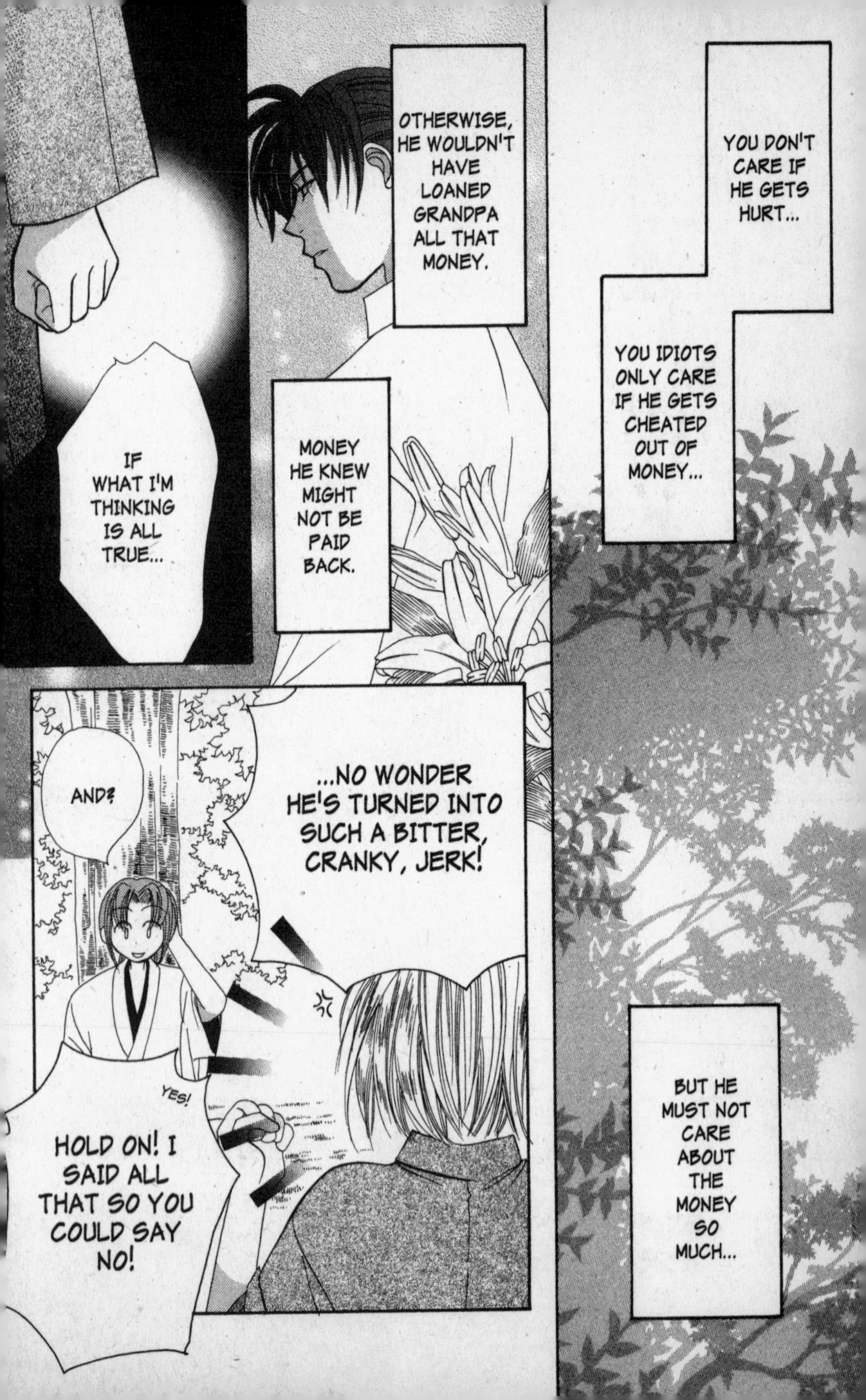
YOU DON'T CARE IF HE GETS HURT...
YOU IDIOTS ONLY CARE IF HE GETS CHEATED OUT OF MONEY...
BUT HE MUST NOT CARE ABOUT THE MONEY SO MUCH...
OTHERWISE, HE WOULDN'T HAVE LOANED GRANDPA ALL THAT MONEY.
MONEY HE KNEW MIGHT NOT BE PAID BACK.
IF WHAT I'M THINKING IS ALL TRUE...
...NO WONDER HE'S TURNED INTO SUCH A BITTER, CRANKY, JERK!
AND?
YES!
HOLD ON! I SAID ALL THAT SO YOU COULD SAY NO!

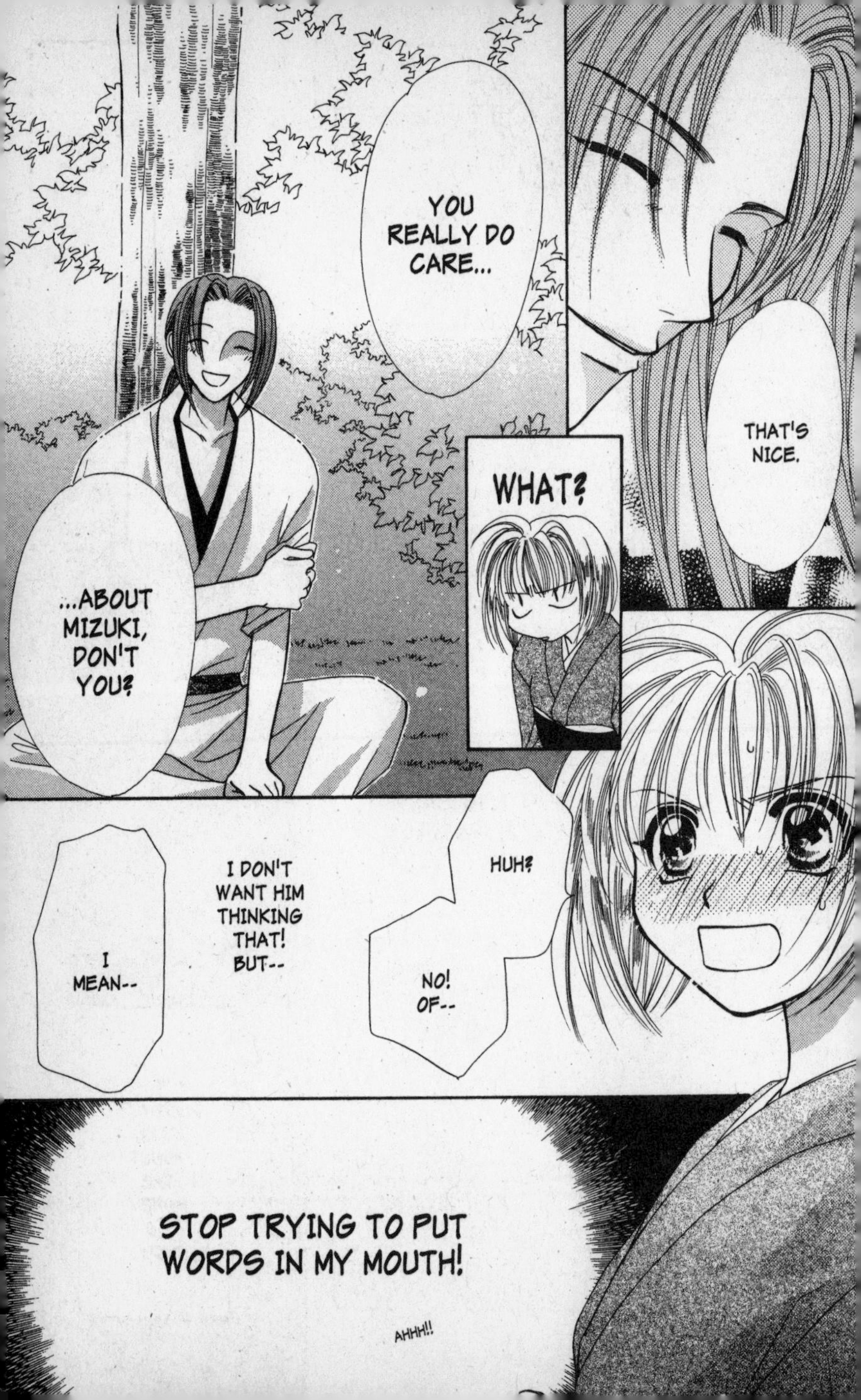
THAT'S NICE.
YOU REALLY DO CARE...
...ABOUT MIZUKI, DON'T YOU?
WHAT?
HUH?
NO! OF--
I DON'T WANT HIM THINKING THAT! BUT--
I MEAN--
STOP TRYING TO PUT WORDS IN MY MOUTH!
AHHH!!

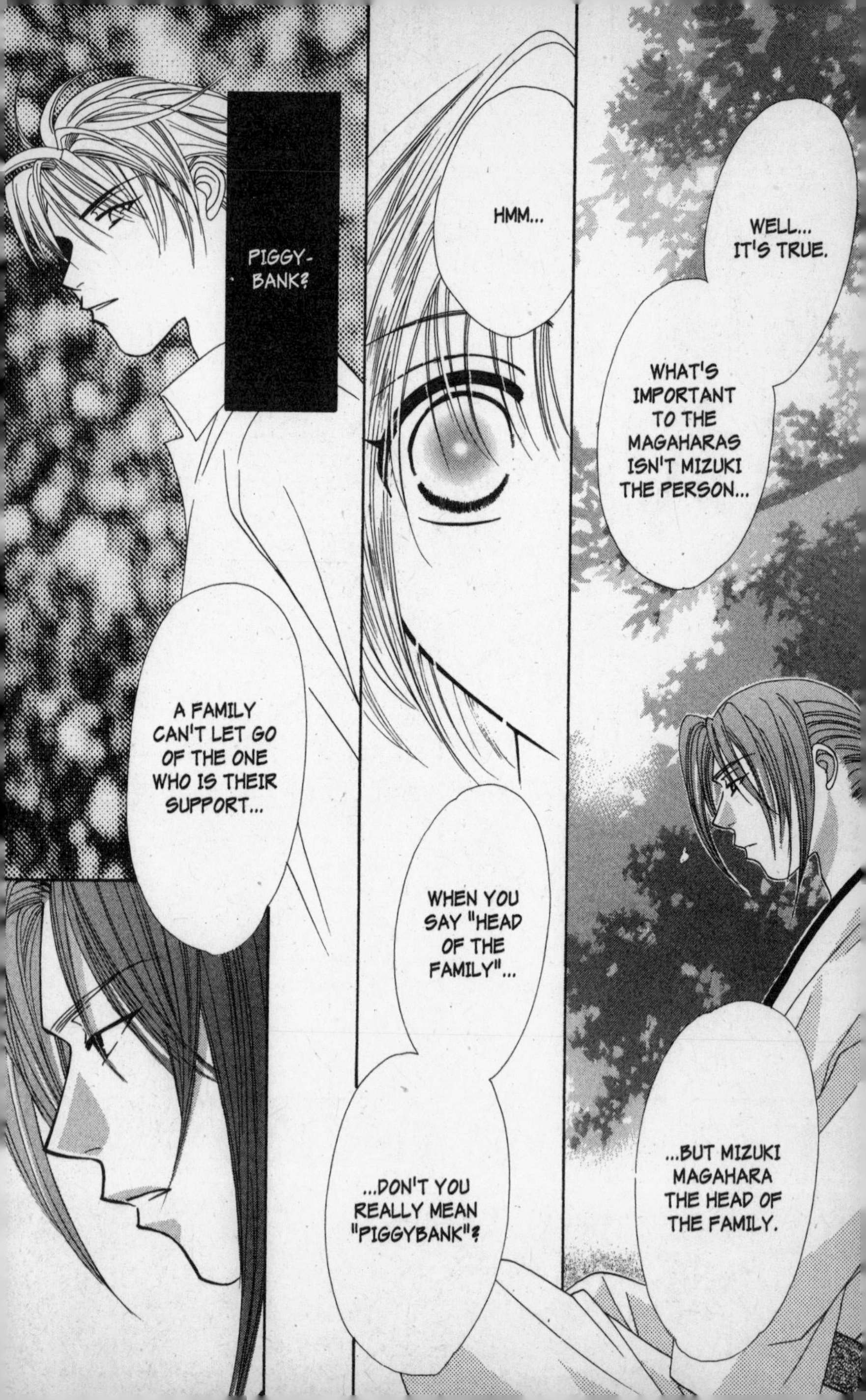
WELL... IT'S TRUE.
WHAT'S IMPORTANT TO THE MAGAHARAS ISN'T MIZUKI THE PERSON...
...BUT MIZUKI MAGAHARA THE HEAD OF THE FAMILY.
HMM...
WHEN YOU SAY "HEAD OF THE FAMILY"...
...DON'T YOU REALLY MEAN "PIGGYBANK"?
PIGGY-BANK?
A FAMILY CAN'T LET GO OF THE ONE WHO IS THEIR SUPPORT...

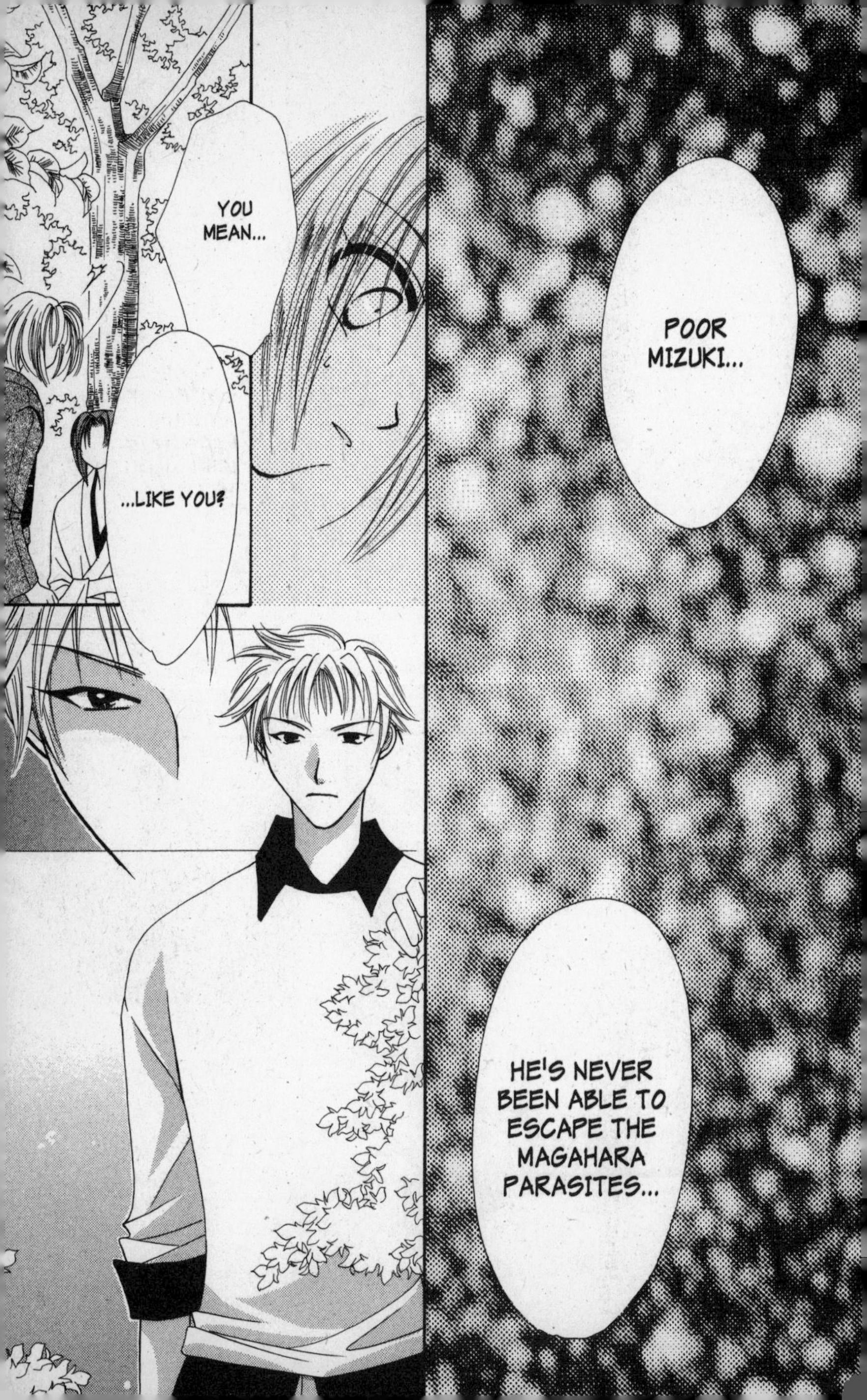
POOR MIZUKI...
HE'S NEVER BEEN ABLE TO ESCAPE THE MAGAHARA PARASITES...
YOU MEAN...
...LIKE YOU?

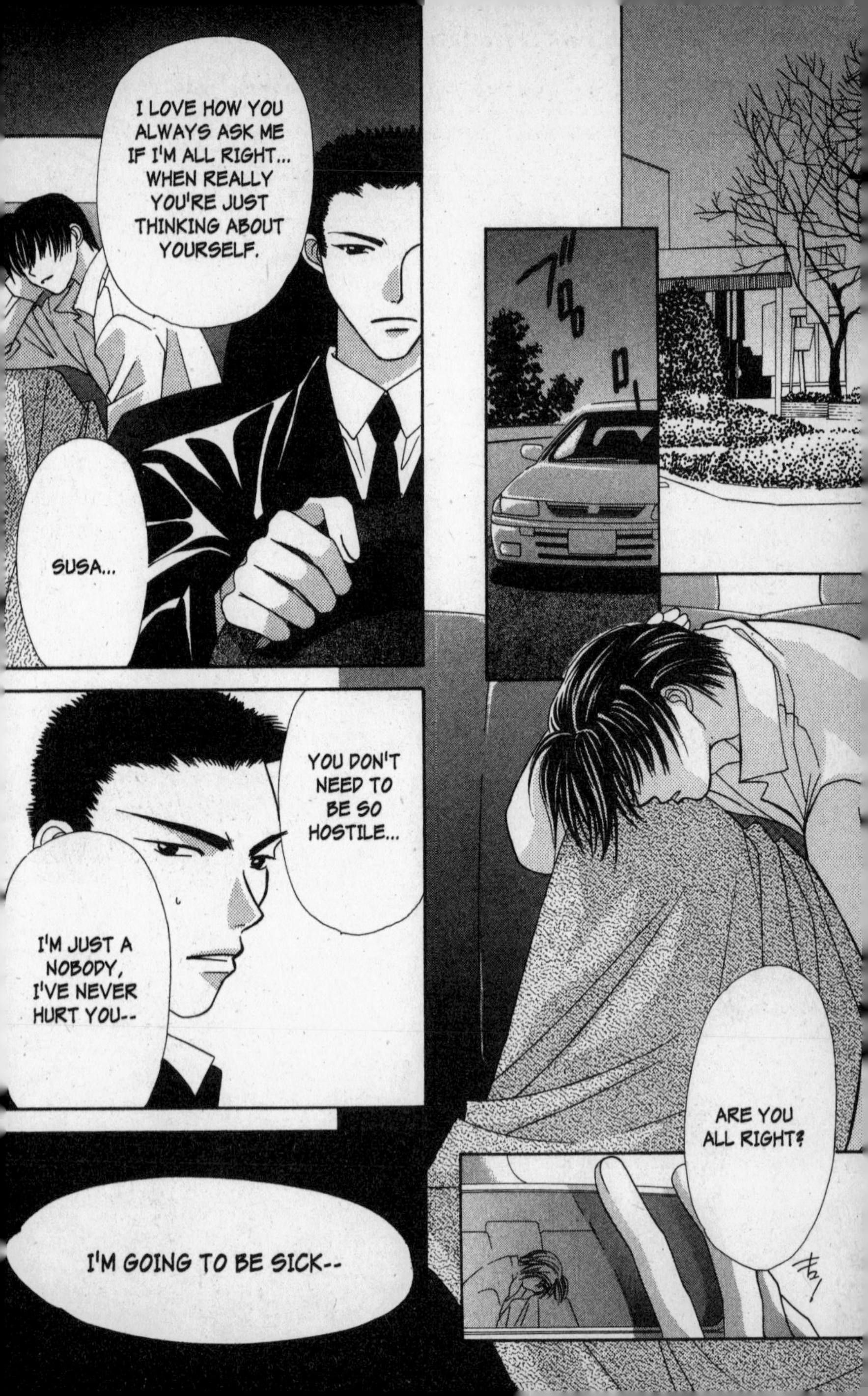
I LOVE HOW YOU ALWAYS ASK ME IF I'M ALL RIGHT... WHEN REALLY YOU'RE JUST THINKING ABOUT YOURSELF.
SUSA...
ARE YOU ALL RIGHT?
YOU DON'T NEED TO BE SO HOSTILE...
I'M JUST A NOBODY, I'VE NEVER HURT YOU--
I'M GOING TO BE SICK--

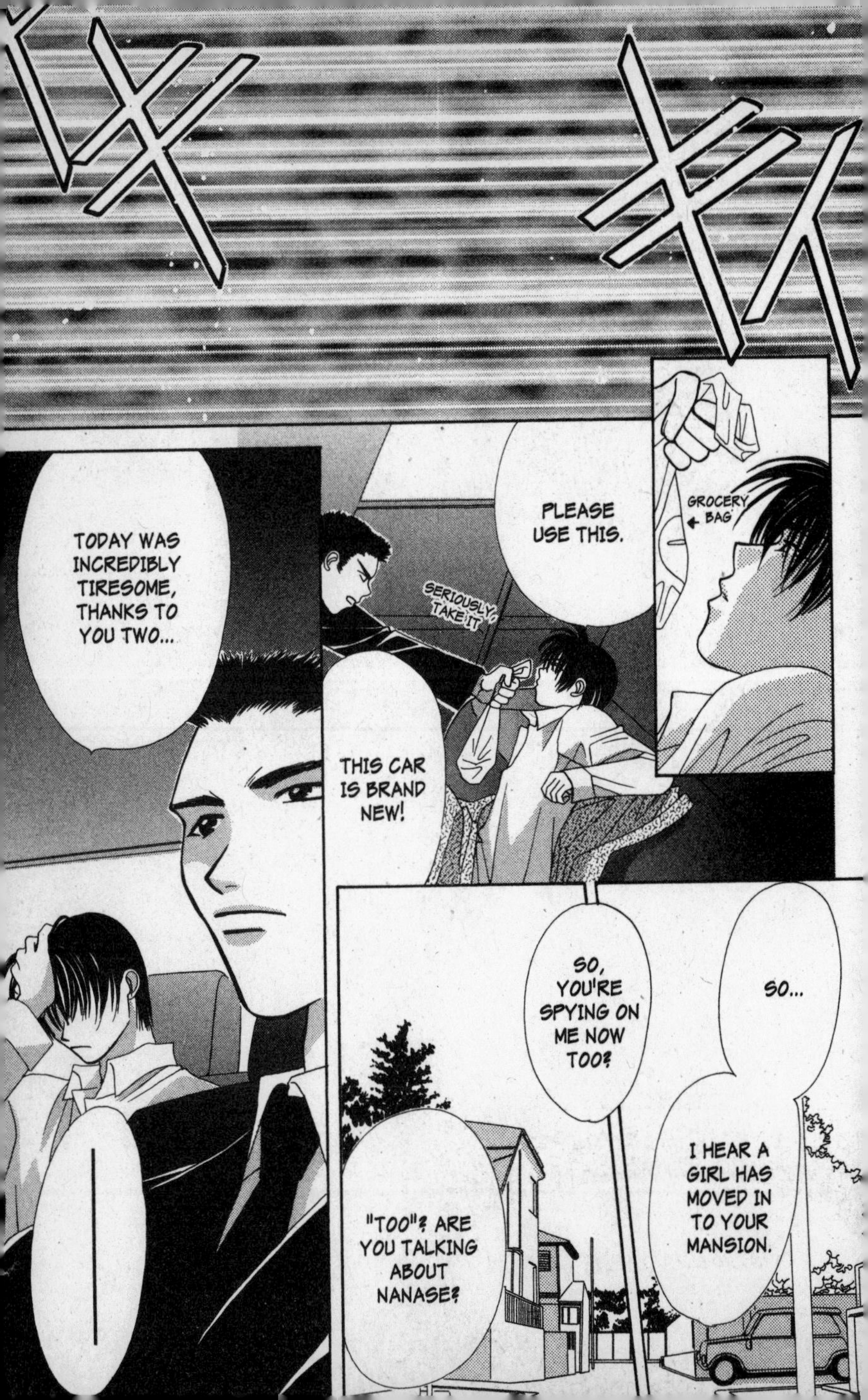
GROCERY ← BAG
PLEASE USE THIS.
SERIOUSLY, TAKE IT
THIS CAR IS BRAND NEW!
SO...
I HEAR A GIRL HAS MOVED IN TO YOUR MANSION.
SO, YOU'RE SPYING ON ME NOW TOO?
"TOO"? ARE YOU TALKING ABOUT NANASE?
TODAY WAS INCREDIBLY TIRESOME, THANKS TO YOU TWO...

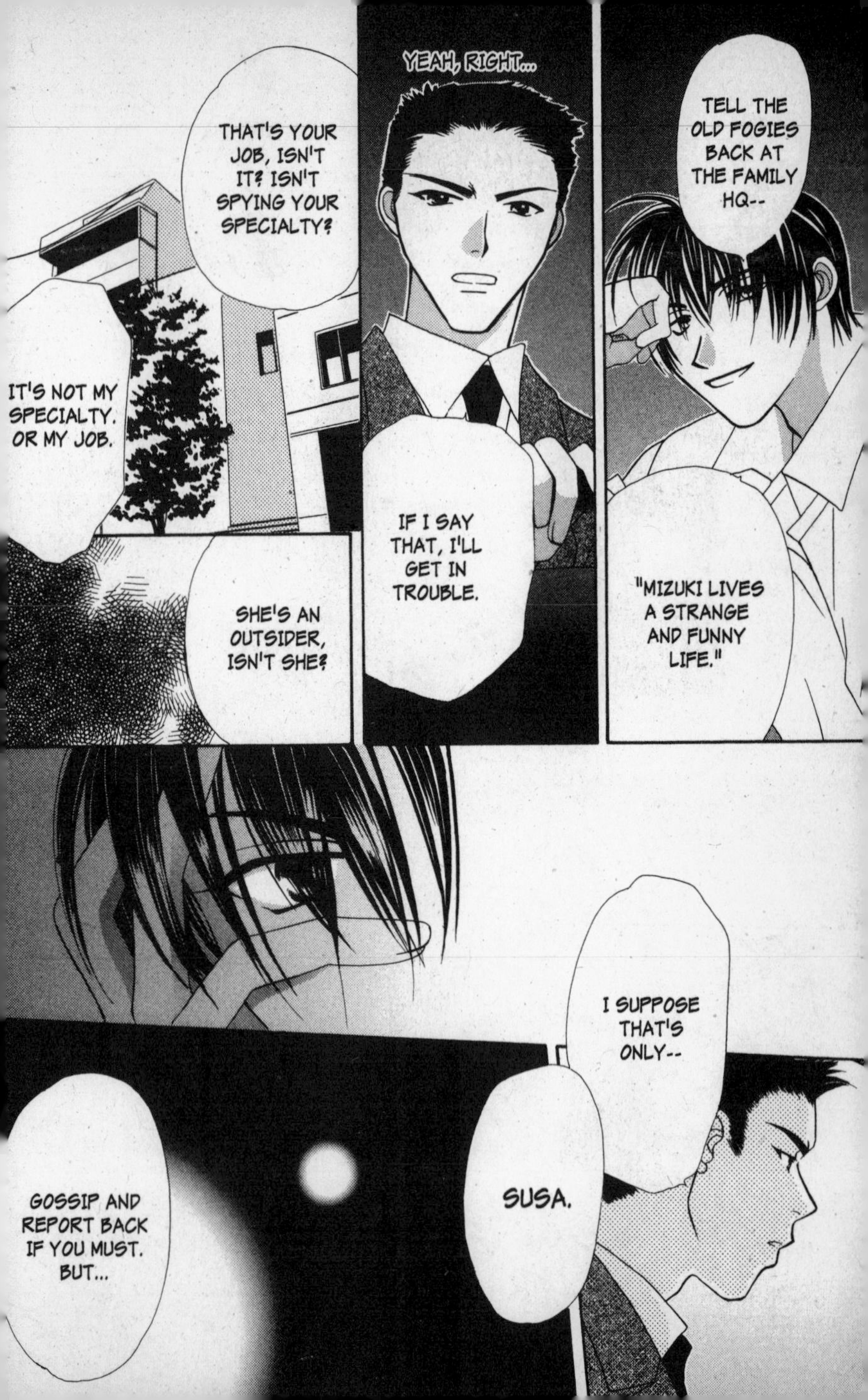
TELL THE OLD FOGIES BACK AT THE FAMILY HQ--
"MIZUKI LIVES A STRANGE AND FUNNY LIFE."
YEAH, RIGHT...
IF I SAY THAT, I'LL GET IN TROUBLE.
THAT'S YOUR JOB, ISN'T IT? ISN'T SPYING YOUR SPECIALTY?
IT'S NOT MY SPECIALTY. OR MY JOB.
SHE'S AN OUTSIDER, ISN'T SHE?
I SUPPOSE THAT'S ONLY--
SUSA.
GOSSIP AND REPORT BACK IF YOU MUST. BUT...

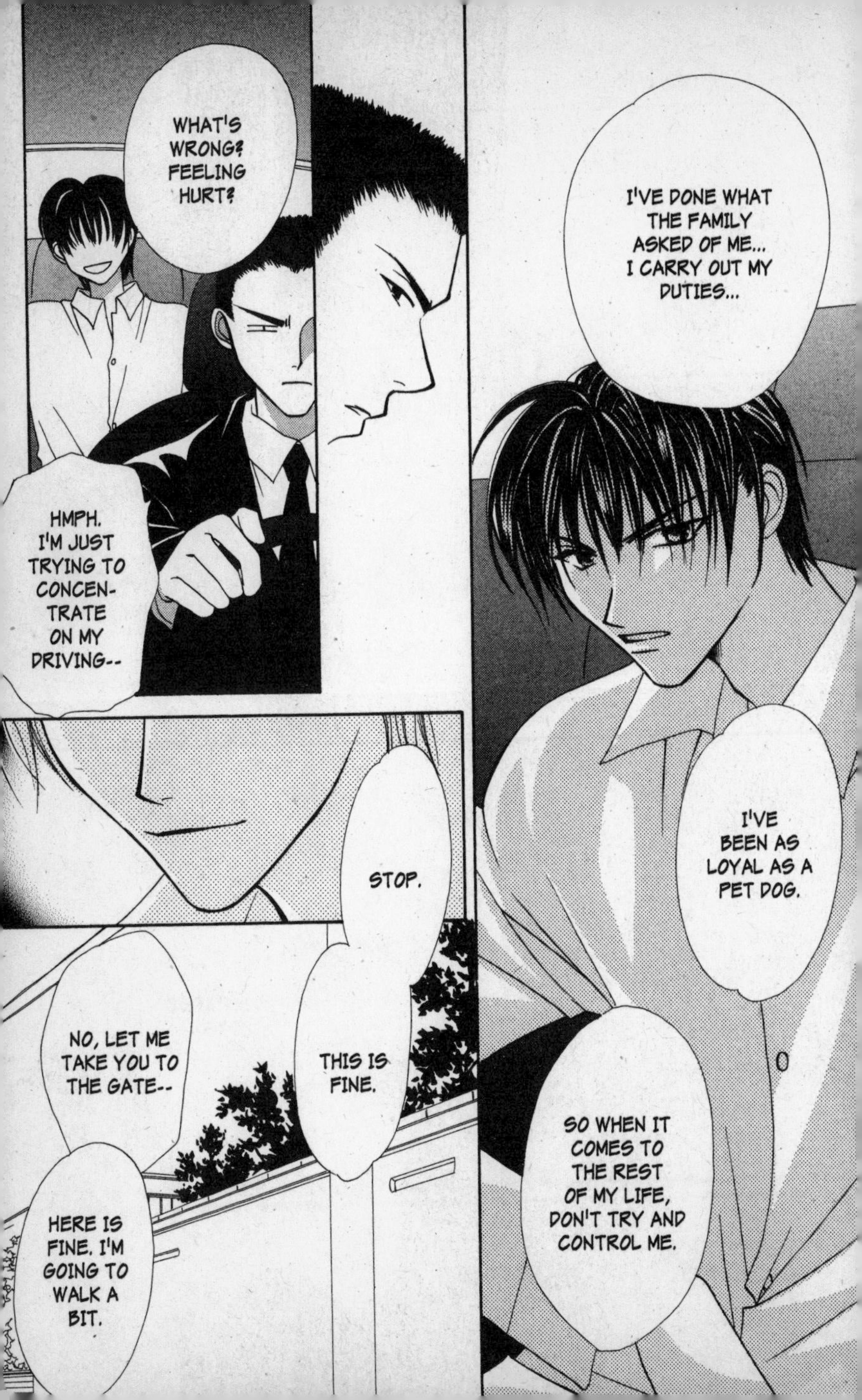
I'VE DONE WHAT THE FAMILY ASKED OF ME... I CARRY OUT MY DUTIES...
I'VE BEEN AS LOYAL AS A PET DOG.
SO WHEN IT COMES TO THE REST OF MY LIFE, DON'T TRY AND CONTROL ME.
WHAT'S WRONG? FEELING HURT?
HMPH. I'M JUST TRYING TO CONCEN-TRATE ON MY DRIVING--
STOP.
THIS IS FINE.
NO, LET ME TAKE YOU TO THE GATE--
HERE IS FINE. I'M GOING TO WALK A BIT.

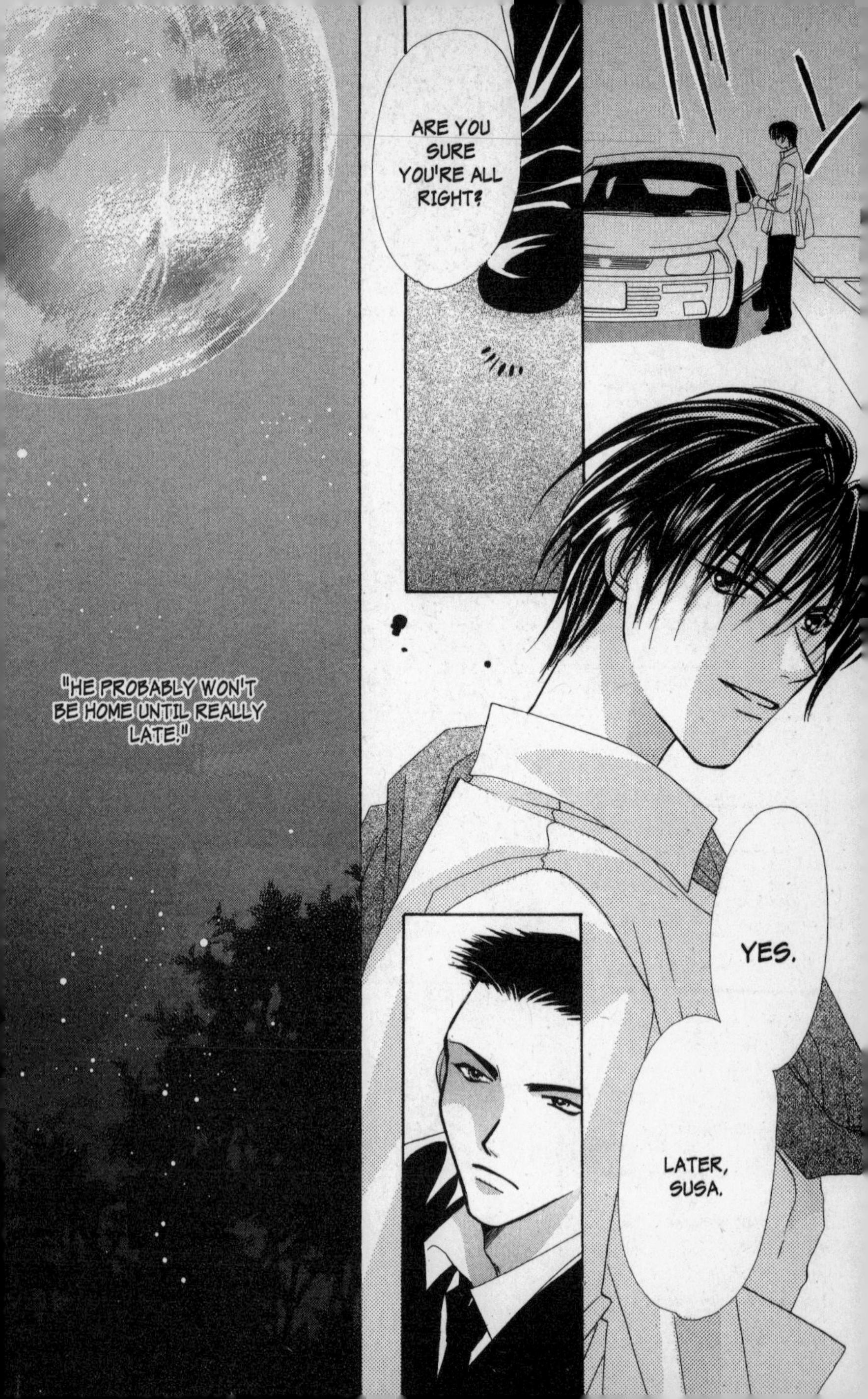
ARE YOU SURE YOU'RE ALL RIGHT?
YES.
LATER, SUSA.
"HE PROBABLY WON'T BE HOME UNTIL REALLY LATE."

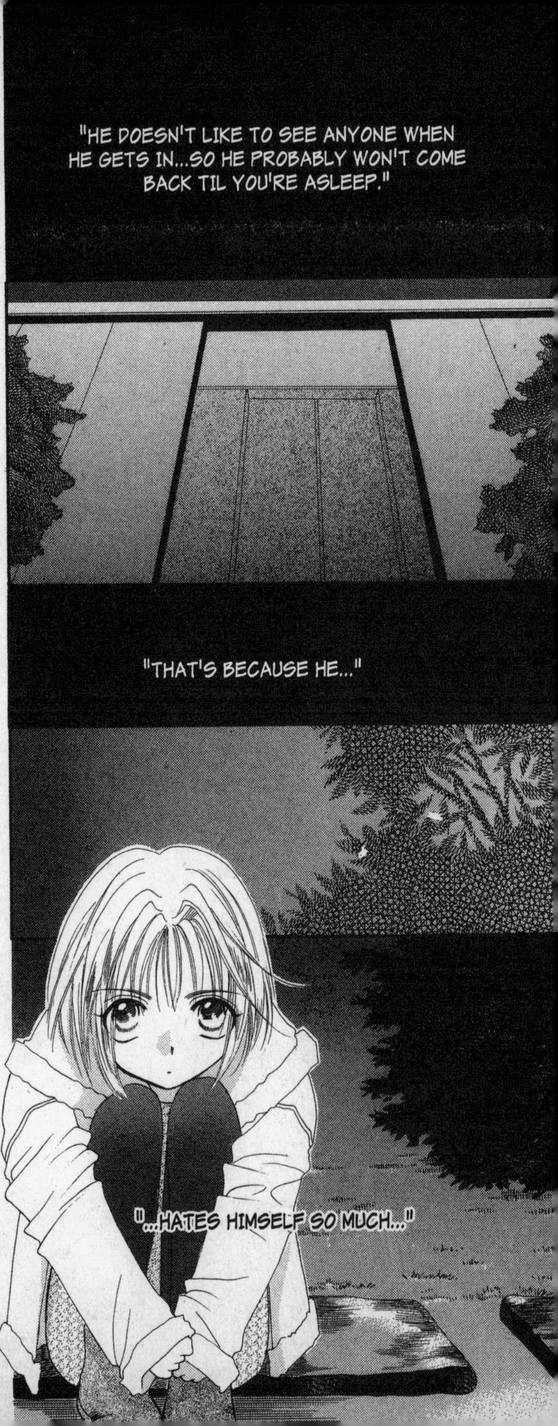
"HE DOESN'T LIKE TO SEE ANYONE WHEN HE GETS IN...SO HE PROBABLY WON'T COME BACK TIL YOU'RE ASLEEP."
"THAT'S BECAUSE HE..."
"...HATES HIMSELF SO MUCH..."

IDIOTIC RAMBLINGS II

THE LYRICAL INCIDENT OF THE LOVELORN

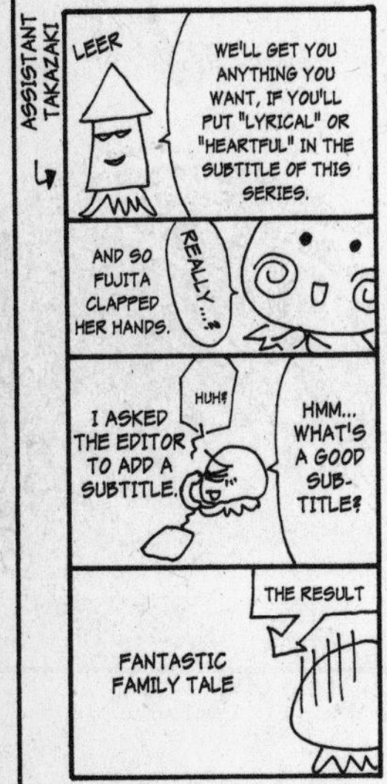
ASSISTANT TAKAZAKI
LEER
WE'LL GET YOU ANYTHING YOU WANT, IF YOU'LL PUT "LYRICAL" OR "HEARTFUL" IN THE SUBTITLE OF THIS SERIES.
REALLY...?
AND SO FUJITA CLAPPED HER HANDS.
HMM... WHAT'S A GOOD SUB-TITLE?
HUH?
I ASKED THE EDITOR TO ADD A SUBTITLE.
THE RESULT
FANTASTIC FAMILY TALE

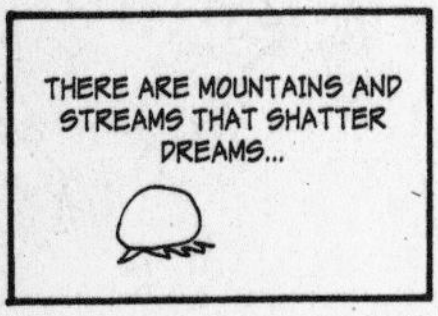
THERE ARE MOUNTAINS AND STREAMS THAT SHATTER DREAMS...

EXCITING SCHOOL DAYS
↓
HYPER MIRACULOUS STORY
↓
IT'S MY EXCITING LIFE
↓
FANTASTIC FAMILY TALE

NEXT TIME FOR SURE!

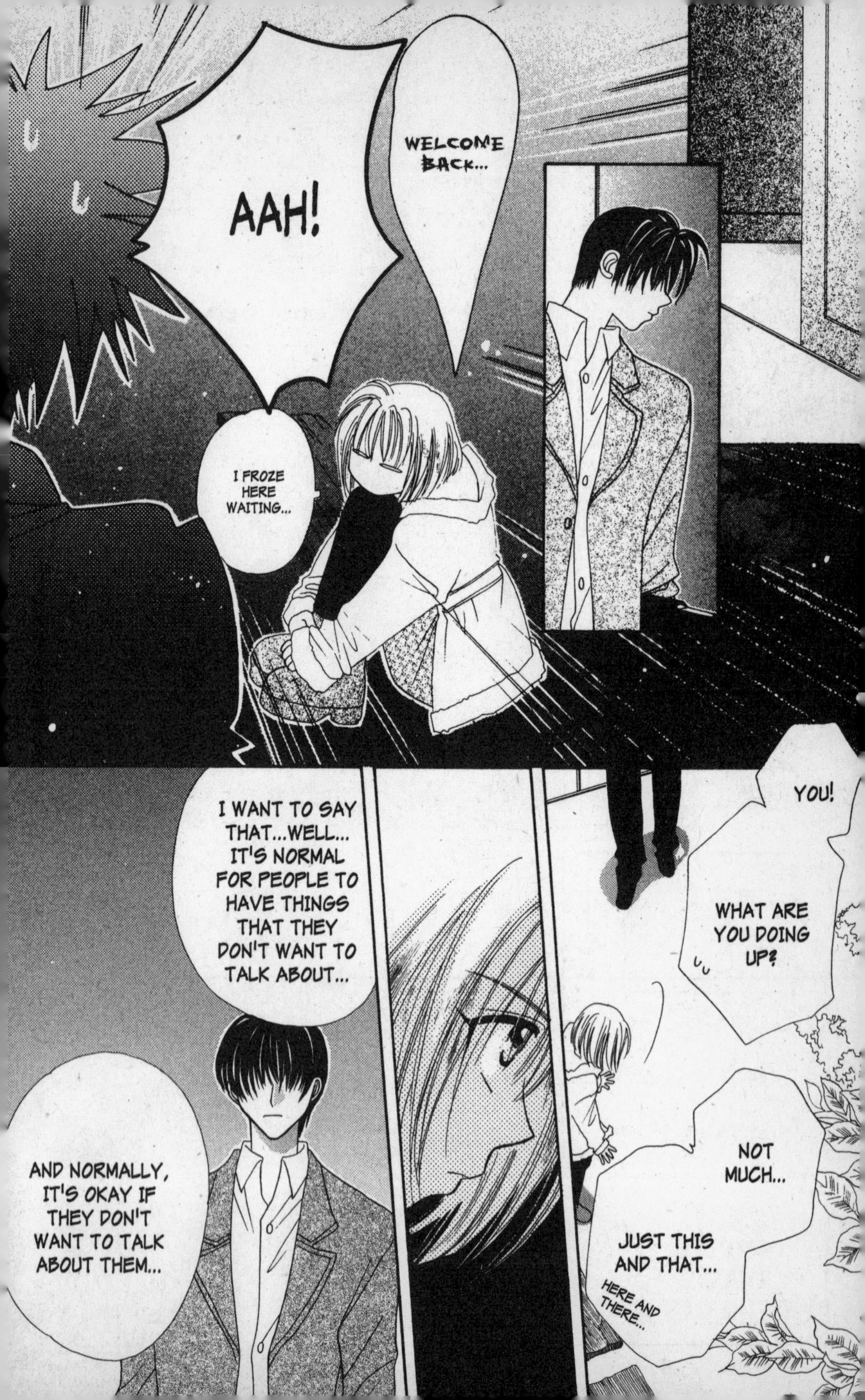
WELCOME BACK...
AAH!
I FROZE HERE WAITING...
YOU!
WHAT ARE YOU DOING UP?
NOT MUCH...
JUST THIS AND THAT...
HERE AND THERE...
I WANT TO SAY THAT...WELL... IT'S NORMAL FOR PEOPLE TO HAVE THINGS THAT THEY DON'T WANT TO TALK ABOUT...
AND NORMALLY, IT'S OKAY IF THEY DON'T WANT TO TALK ABOUT THEM...

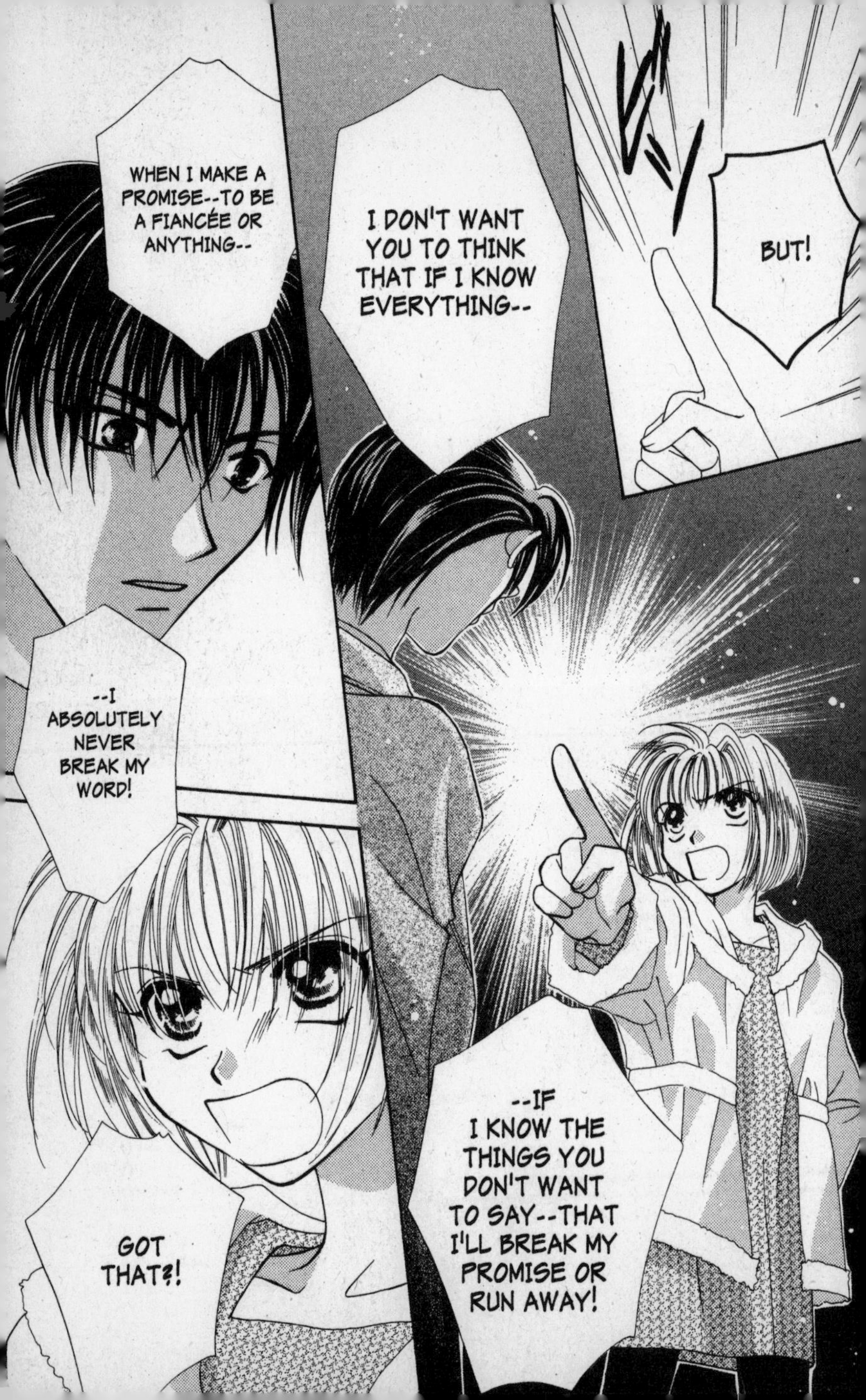
BUT!
I DON'T WANT YOU TO THINK THAT IF I KNOW EVERYTHING--
--IF I KNOW THE THINGS YOU DON'T WANT TO SAY--THAT I'LL BREAK MY PROMISE OR RUN AWAY!
WHEN I MAKE A PROMISE--TO BE A FIANCÉE OR ANYTHING--
--I ABSOLUTELY NEVER BREAK MY WORD!
GOT THAT?!

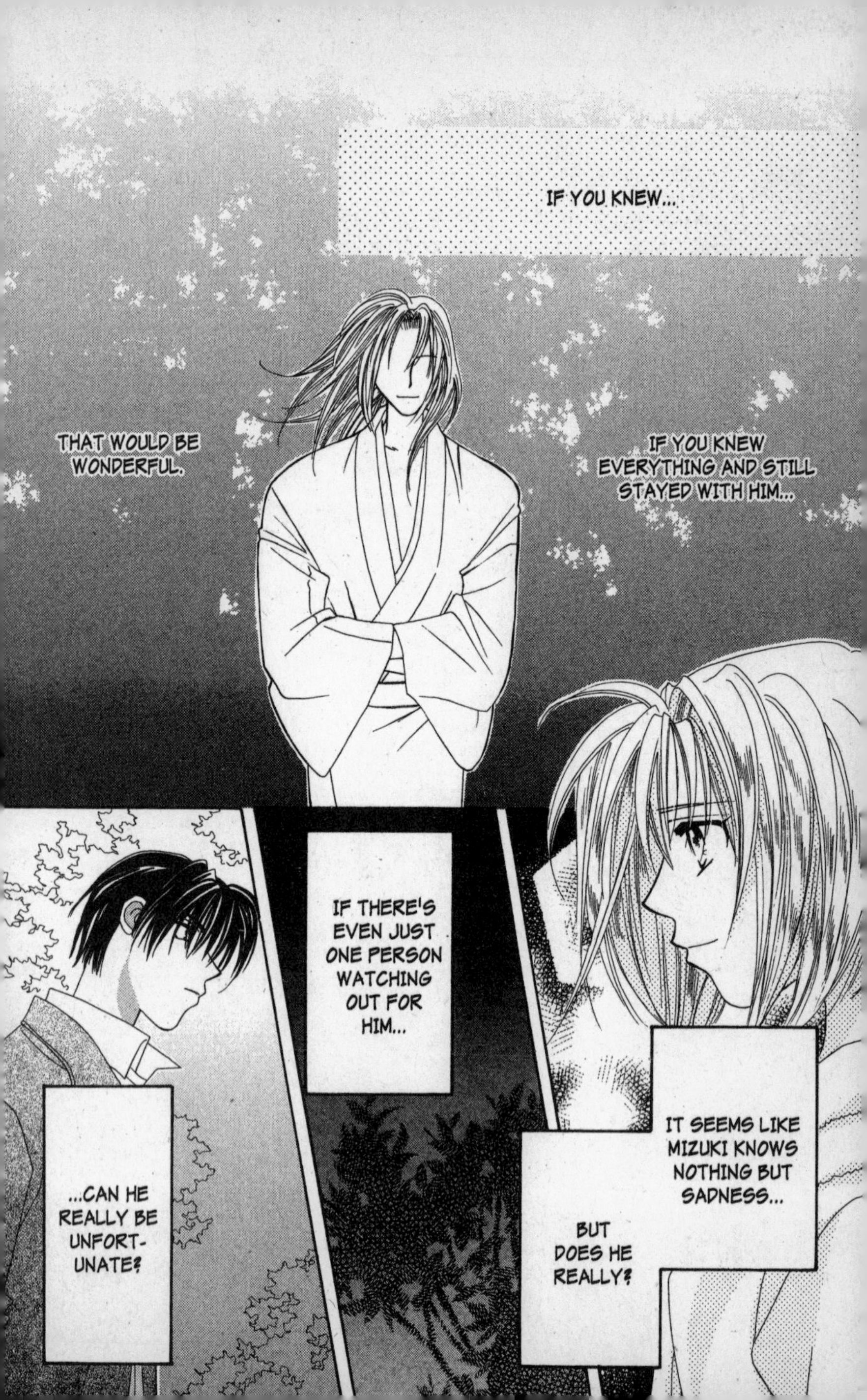
IF YOU KNEW...
IF YOU KNEW EVERYTHING AND STILL STAYED WITH HIM...
THAT WOULD BE WONDERFUL.
IT SEEMS LIKE MIZUKI KNOWS NOTHING BUT SADNESS...
BUT DOES HE REALLY?
IF THERE'S EVEN JUST ONE PERSON WATCHING OUT FOR HIM...
...CAN HE REALLY BE UNFORT-UNATE?

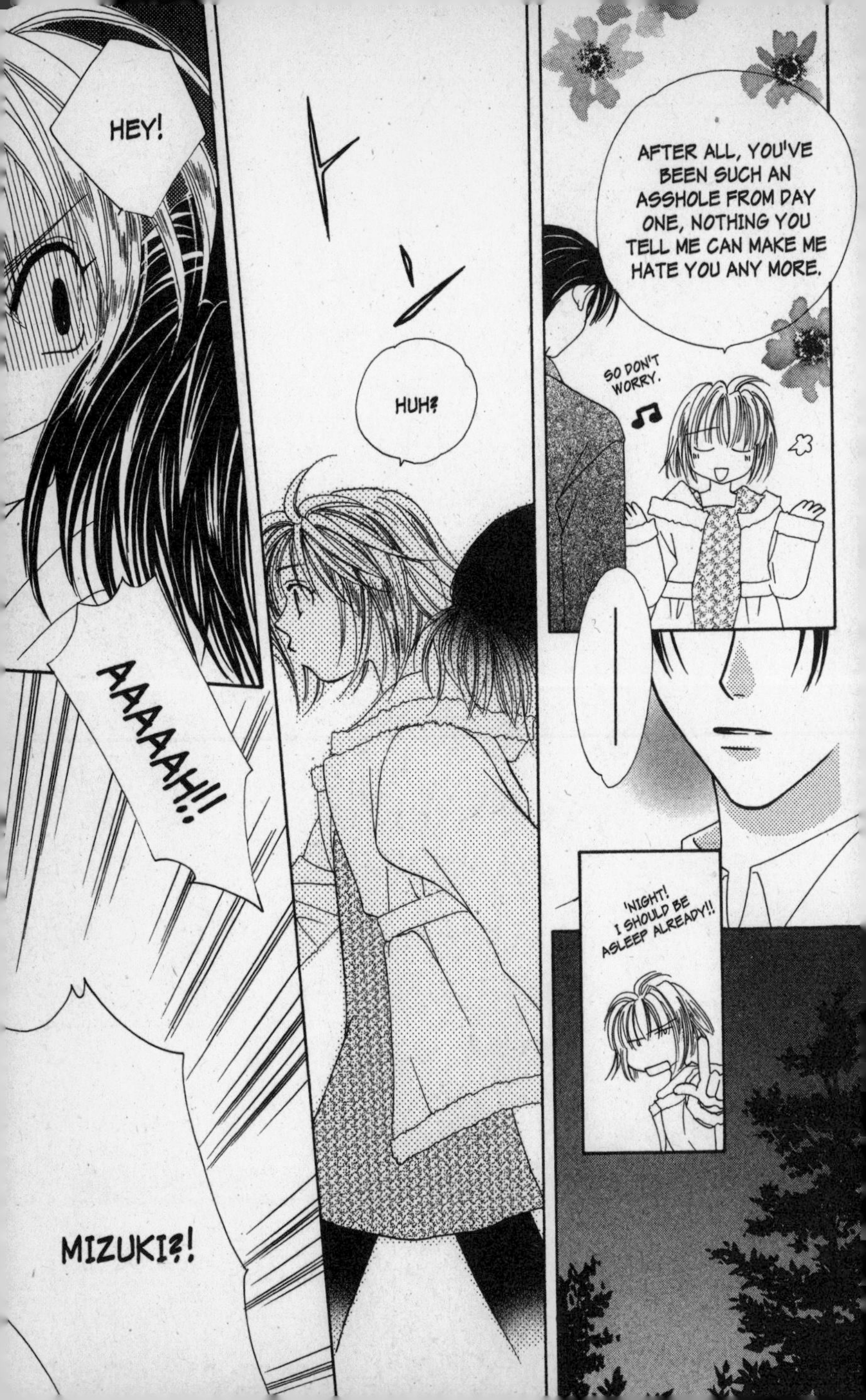
AFTER ALL, YOU'VE BEEN SUCH AN ASSHOLE FROM DAY ONE, NOTHING YOU TELL ME CAN MAKE ME HATE YOU ANY MORE.
SO DON'T WORRY.
'NIGHT! I SHOULD BE ASLEEP ALREADY!!
HUH?
HEY!
AAAAAH!!
MIZUKI?!

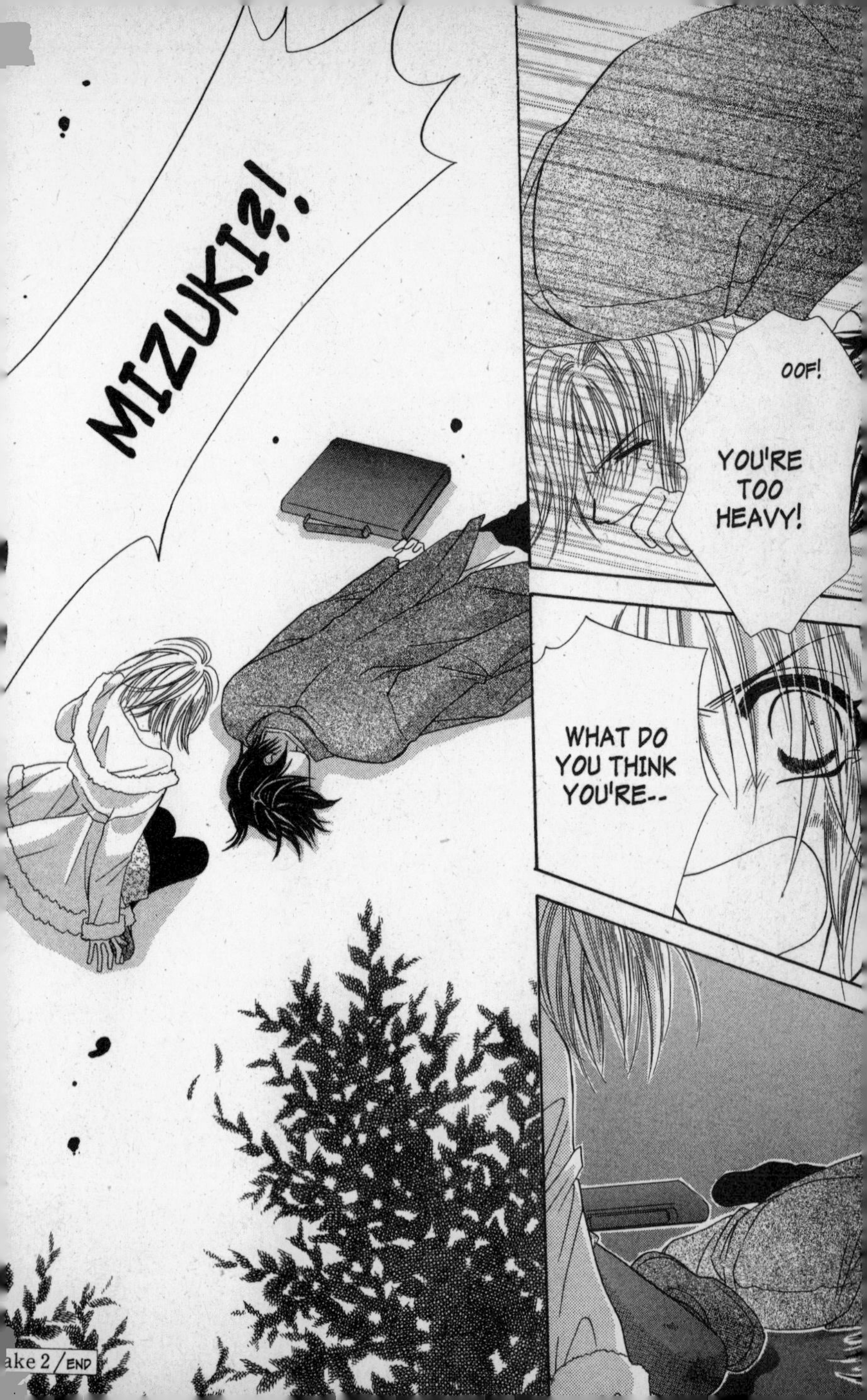
OOF!
YOU'RE TOO HEAVY!
WHAT DO YOU THINK YOU'RE--
MIZUKI?!
ake 2 / END

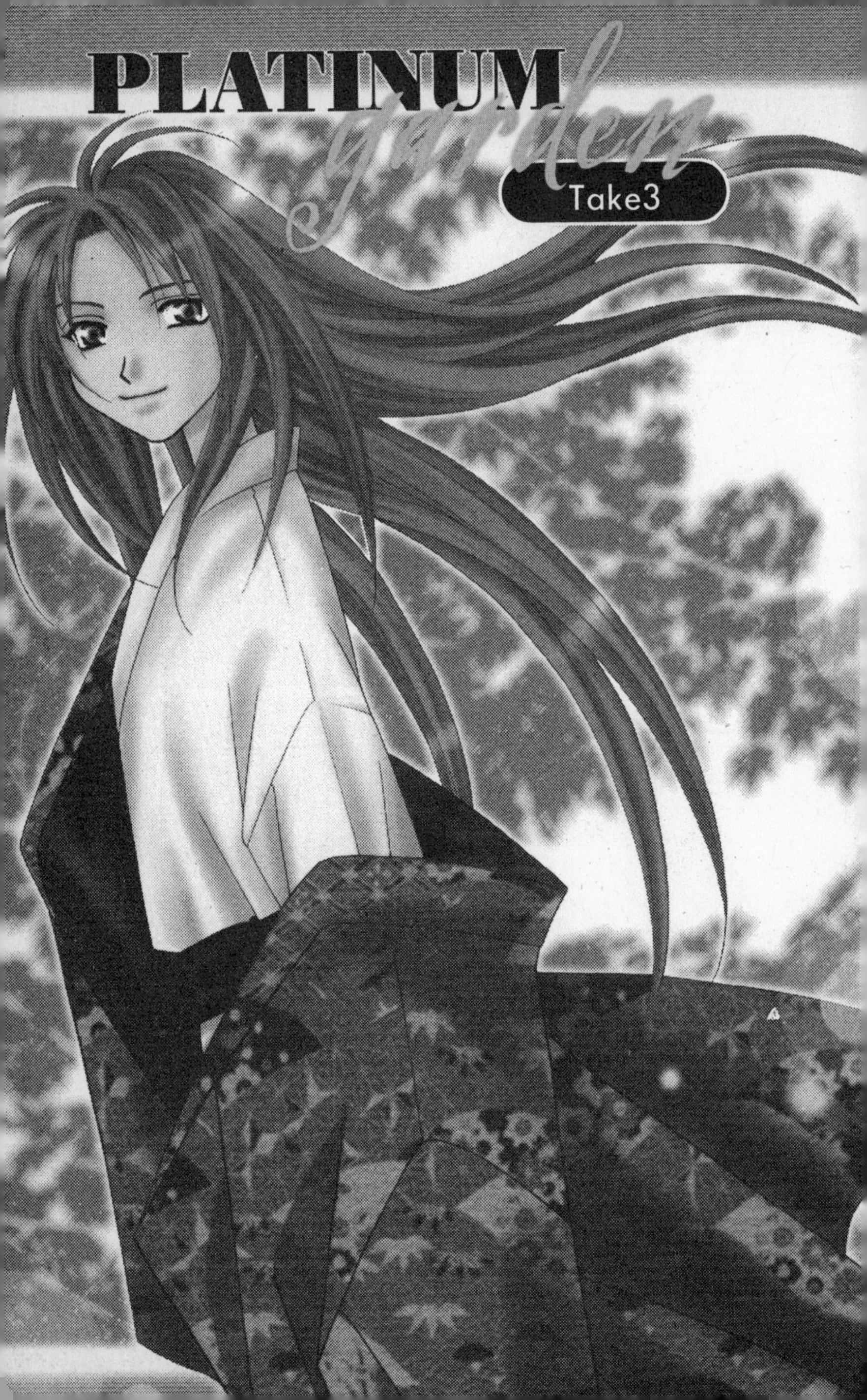
PLATINUM
garden
Take3

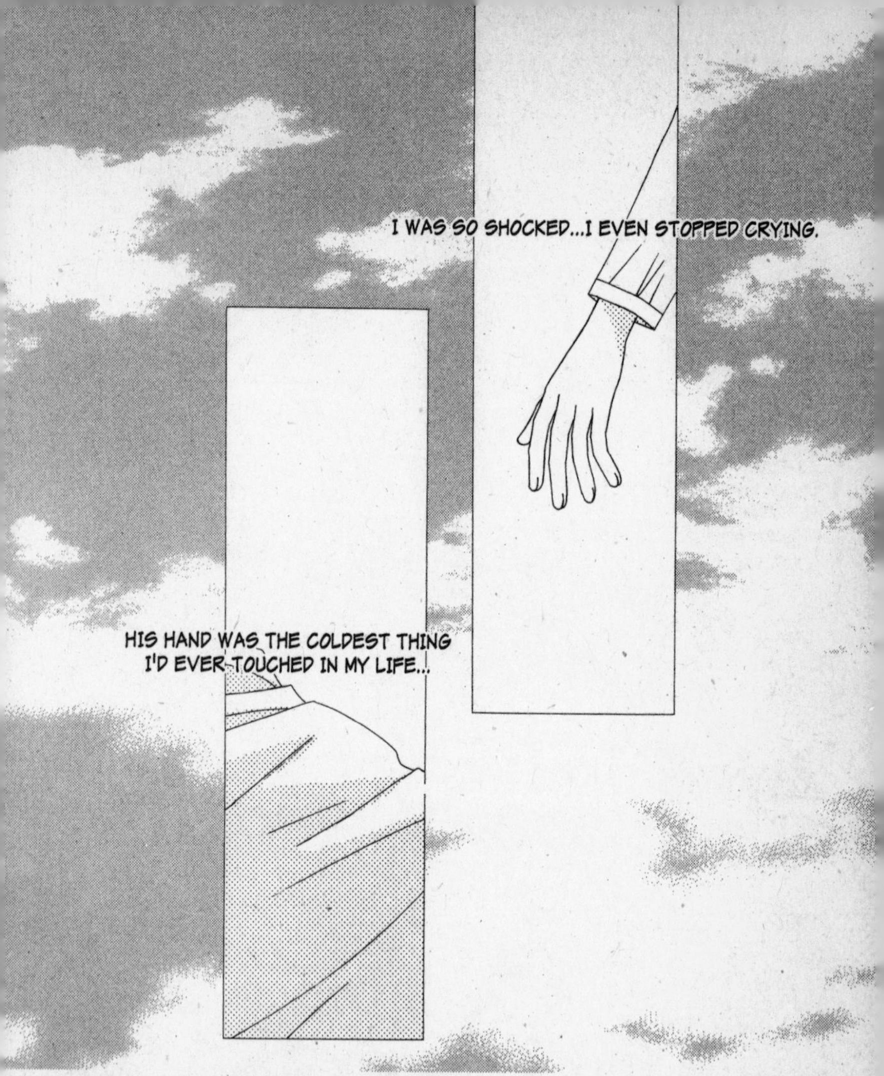
I WAS SO SHOCKED...I EVEN STOPPED CRYING.
HIS HAND WAS THE COLDEST THING I'D EVER TOUCHED IN MY LIFE...

I'VE BEEN WATCHING "A SON OF THE GOOD EARTH" (A.K.A. DAICHI NO KO) OVER AND OVER AGAIN. I ALREADY SAW IT ON TV EVERY TIME IT AIRED, BUT NOW I'M WATCHING IT ON MY OWN VIDEO COPY!! I HAVE ALWAYS BEEN A BIG FAN OF THE STAR, TATSUYA NAKADAI...BUT I REALLY LOVE ZHU XU-SAN, WHO PLAYS HIS CHINESE FATHER...* ♥

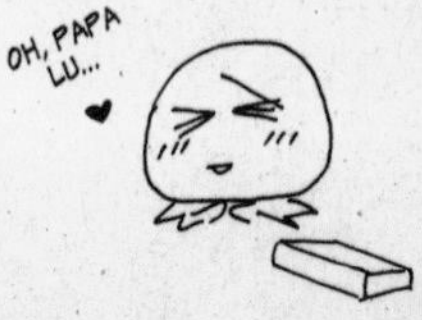
OH, PAPA LU...

FUJITA'S WINTER, 2001

*DAICHI NO KO: A POPULAR SERIES FROM 1995 ABOUT A JAPANESE BOY WHO IS RAISED IN CHINA AFTER WORLD WAR II.

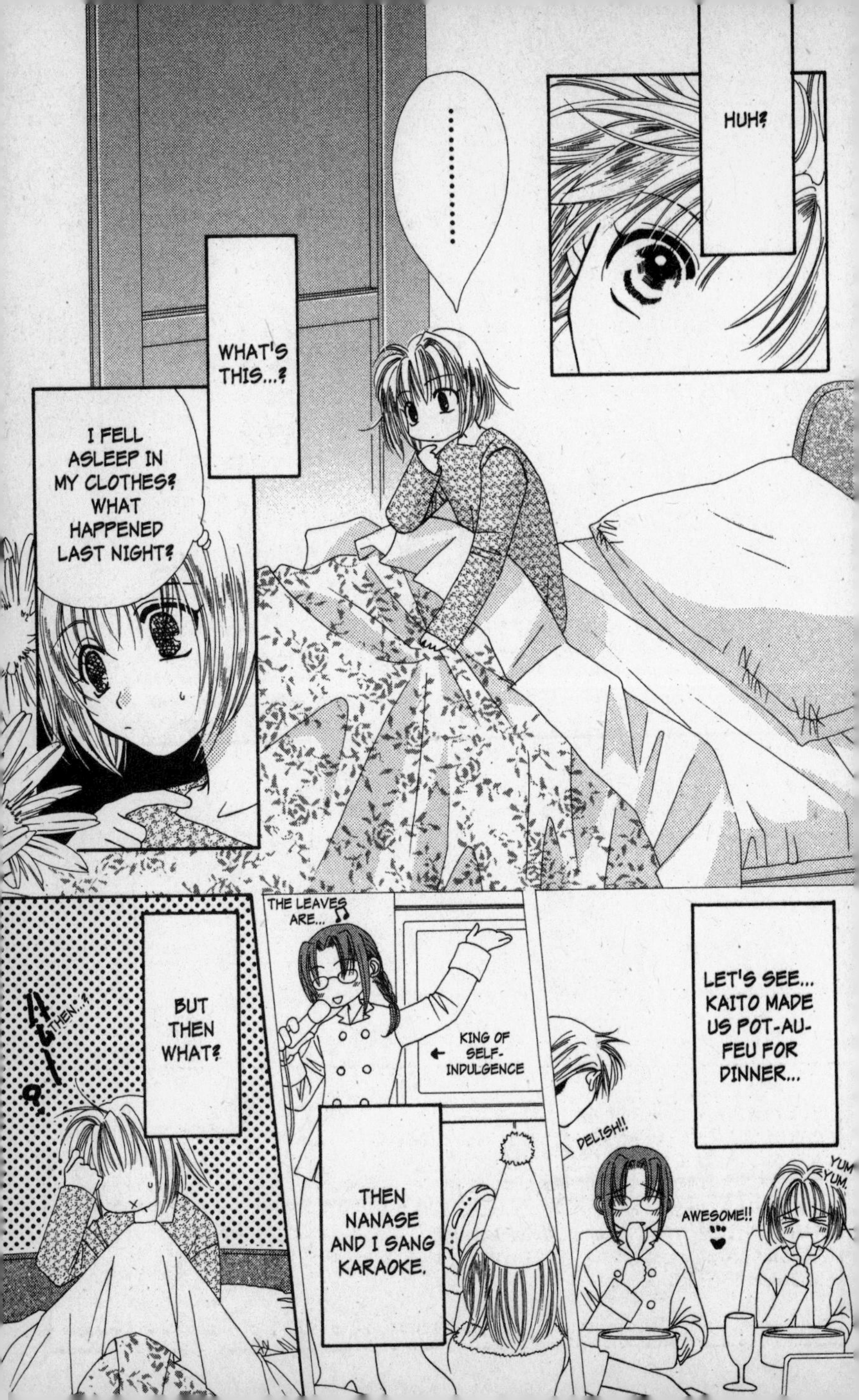
HUH?
......
WHAT'S THIS...?
I FELL ASLEEP IN MY CLOTHES? WHAT HAPPENED LAST NIGHT?
LET'S SEE... KAITO MADE US POT-AU-FEU FOR DINNER...
YUM YUM.
DELISH!!
AWESOME!!
THE LEAVES ARE...
KING OF SELF-INDULGENCE
THEN NANASE AND I SANG KARAOKE.
BUT THEN WHAT?
THEN...?

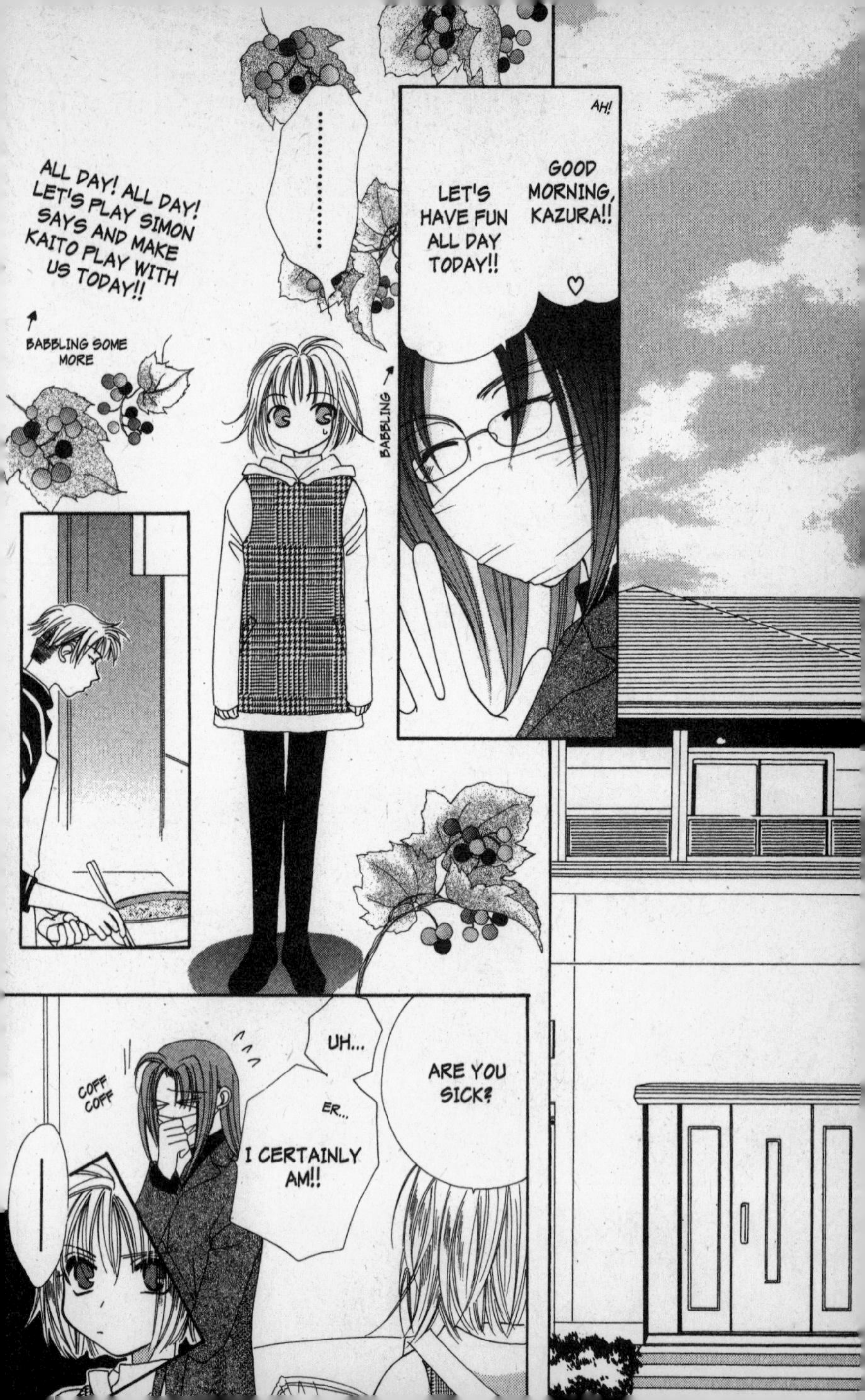
AH!
GOOD MORNING, KAZURA!!
LET'S HAVE FUN ALL DAY TODAY!! ♡
BABBLING
......
ALL DAY! ALL DAY! LET'S PLAY SIMON SAYS AND MAKE KAITO PLAY WITH US TODAY!!
BABBLING SOME MORE
ARE YOU SICK?
UH...
ER...
I CERTAINLY AM!!
COFF COFF

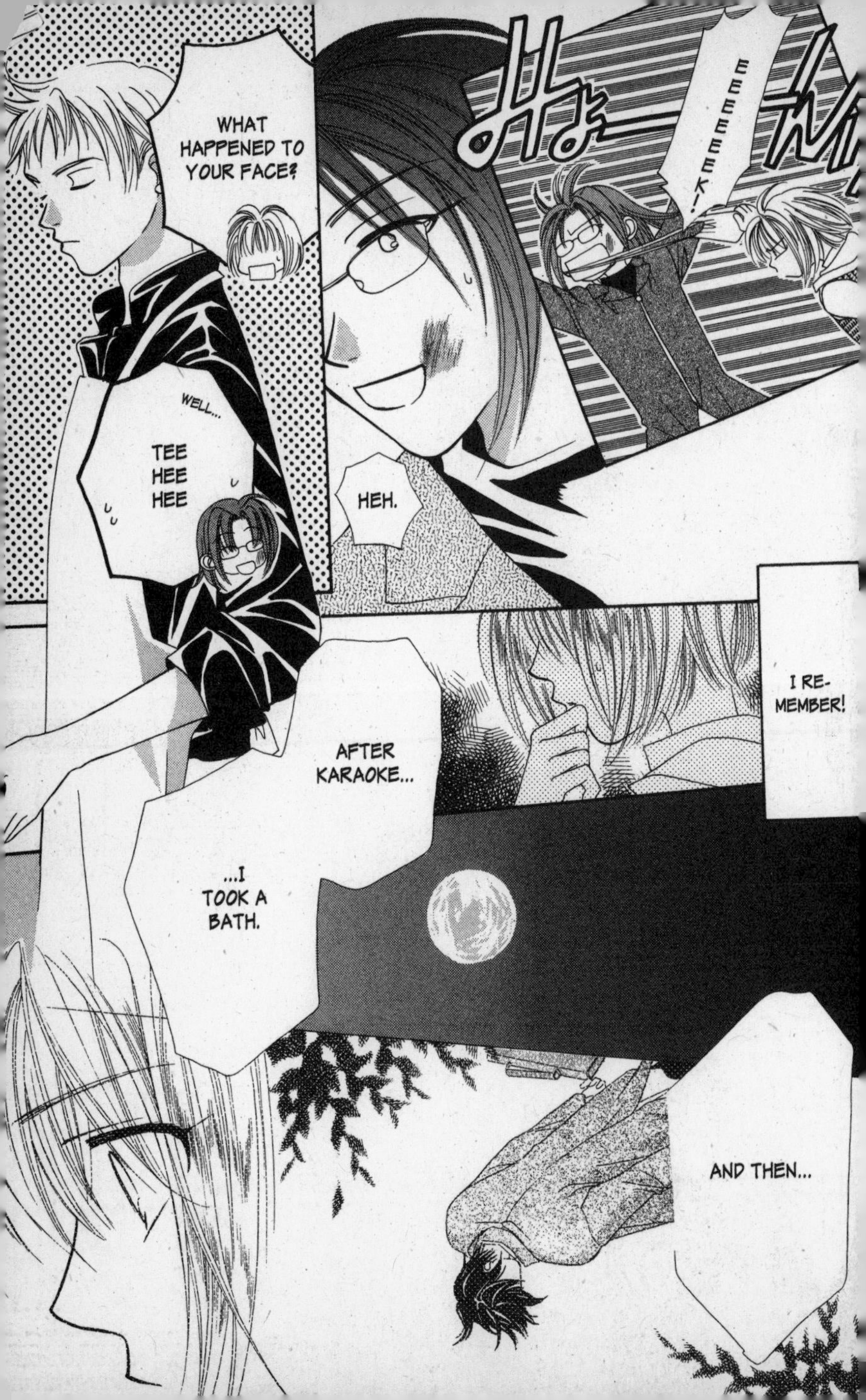
EEEEEEEK!
HEH.
WHAT HAPPENED TO YOUR FACE?
WELL...
TEE HEE HEE
I RE-MEMBER!
AFTER KARAOKE...
...I TOOK A BATH.
AND THEN...

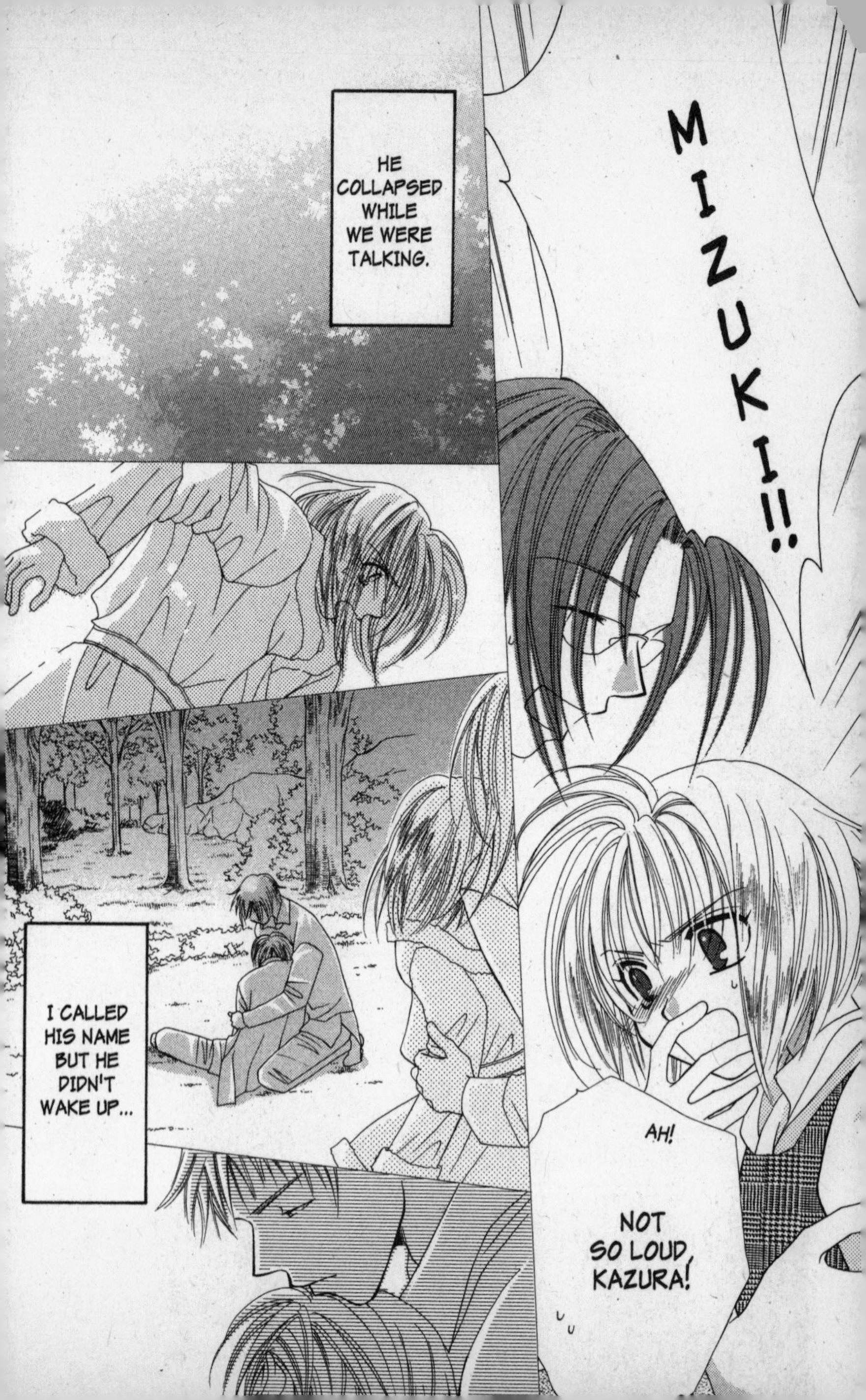
MIZUKI!!
AH!
NOT SO LOUD, KAZURA!
HE COLLAPSED WHILE WE WERE TALKING.
I CALLED HIS NAME BUT HE DIDN'T WAKE UP...

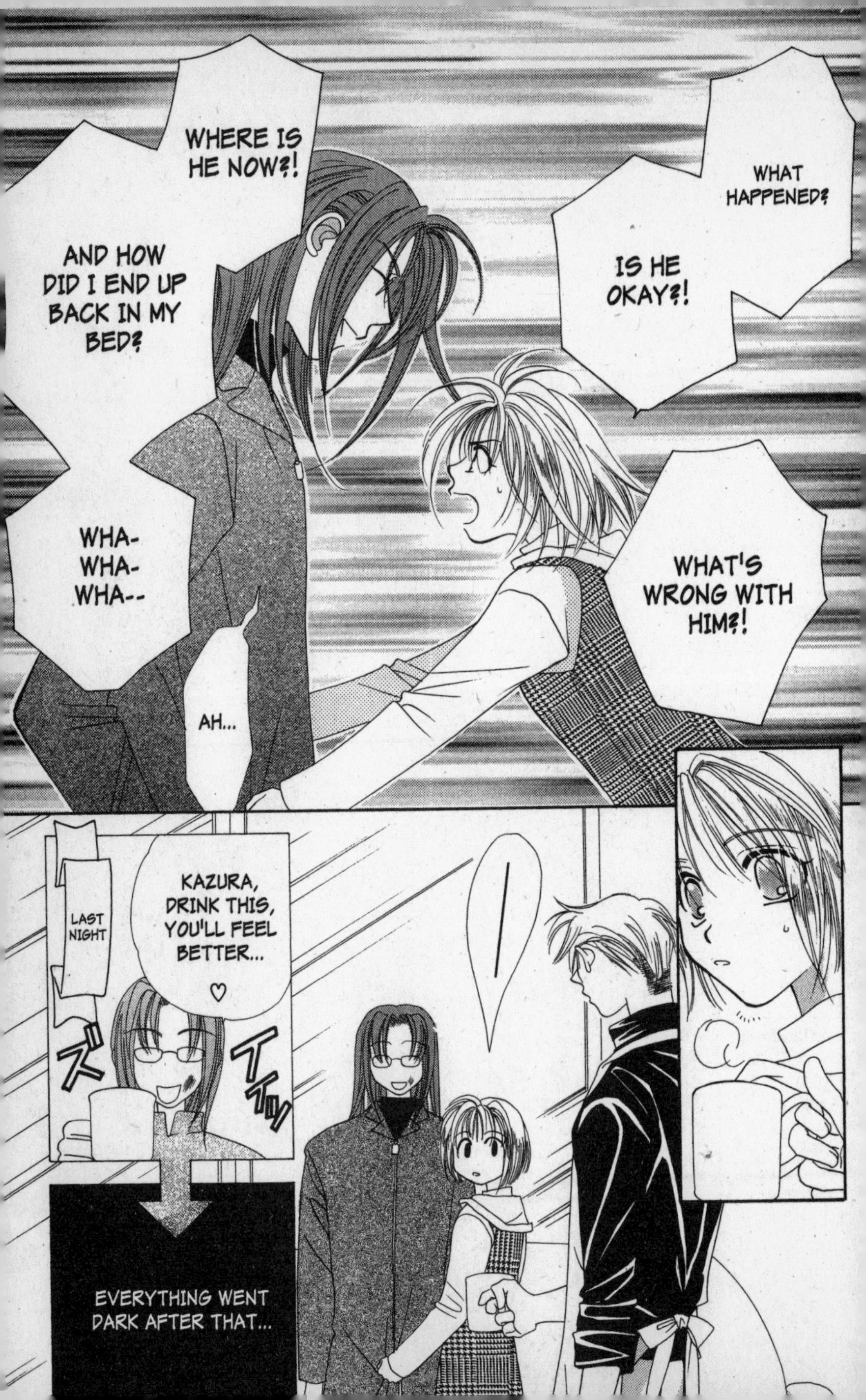
WHAT HAPPENED?
IS HE OKAY?!
WHERE IS HE NOW?!
AND HOW DID I END UP BACK IN MY BED?
WHAT'S WRONG WITH HIM?!
WHA-WHA-WHA--
AH...
!
LAST NIGHT
KAZURA, DRINK THIS, YOU'LL FEEL BETTER... ♡
EVERYTHING WENT DARK AFTER THAT...

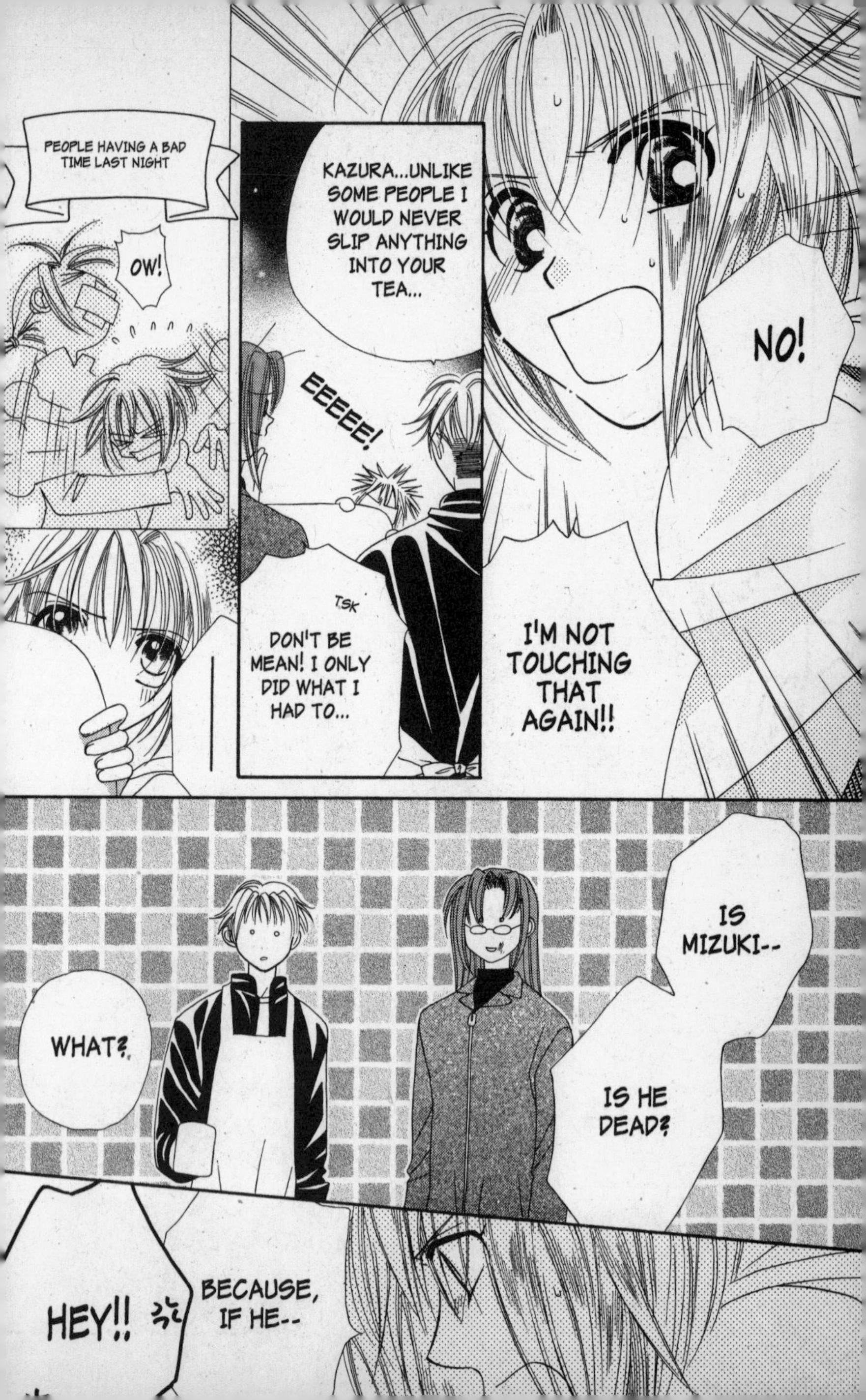
NO!
I'M NOT TOUCHING THAT AGAIN!!
KAZURA...UNLIKE SOME PEOPLE I WOULD NEVER SLIP ANYTHING INTO YOUR TEA...
EEEEE!
TSK
DON'T BE MEAN! I ONLY DID WHAT I HAD TO...
PEOPLE HAVING A BAD TIME LAST NIGHT
OW!
IS MIZUKI--
IS HE DEAD?
WHAT?
BECAUSE, IF HE--
HEY!!

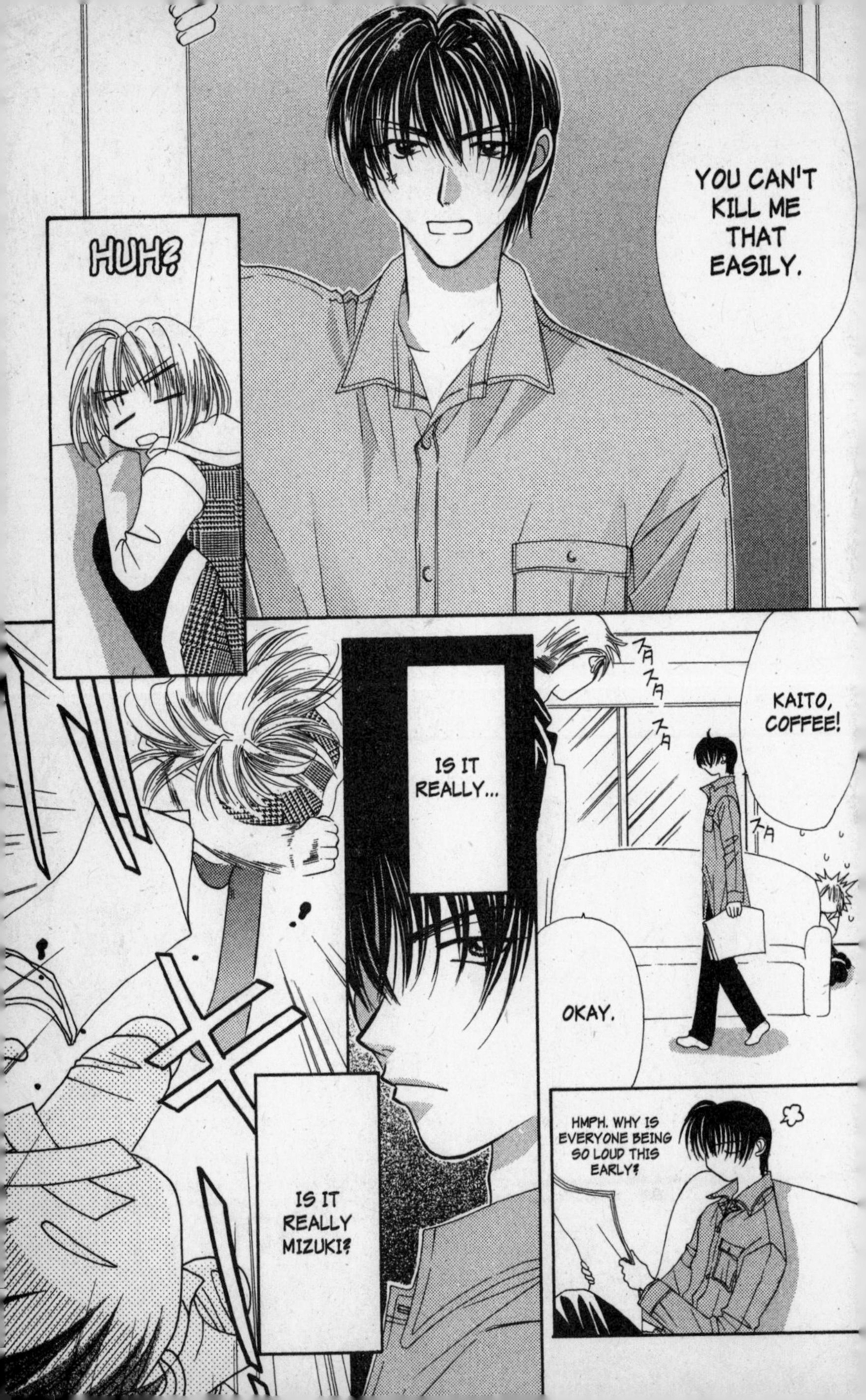
YOU CAN'T KILL ME THAT EASILY.
HUH?
KAITO, COFFEE!
スタ
スタ
スタ
スタ
OKAY.
HMPH. WHY IS EVERYONE BEING SO LOUD THIS EARLY?
IS IT REALLY...
IS IT REALLY MIZUKI?

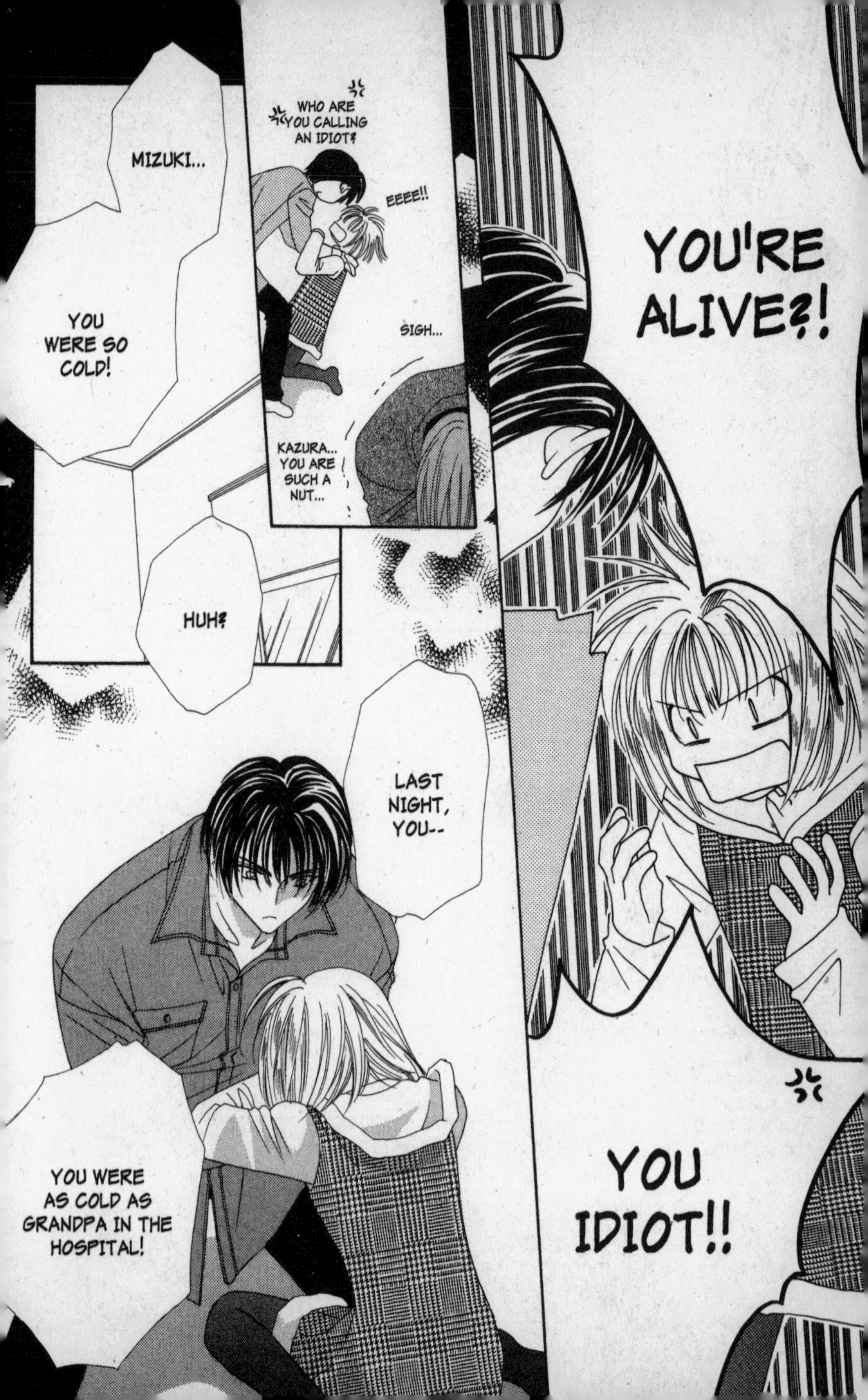
YOU'RE ALIVE?!
YOU IDIOT!!
WHO ARE YOU CALLING AN IDIOT?
EEEE!!
SIGH...
KAZURA... YOU ARE SUCH A NUT...
MIZUKI...
YOU WERE SO COLD!
HUH?
LAST NIGHT, YOU--
YOU WERE AS COLD AS GRANDPA IN THE HOSPITAL!

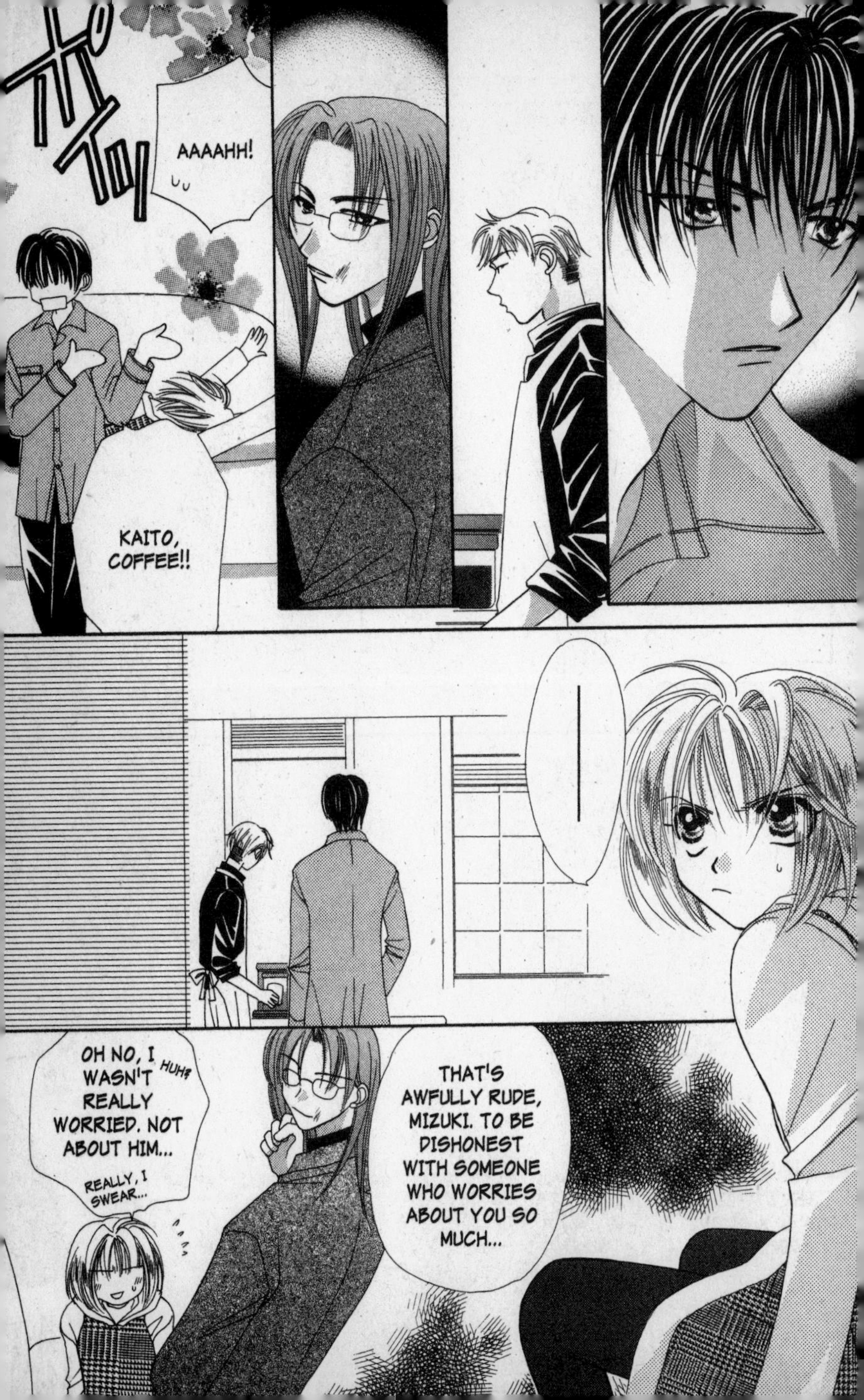

ポイッ
AAAAHH!
KAITO, COFFEE!!
THAT'S AWFULLY RUDE, MIZUKI. TO BE DISHONEST WITH SOMEONE WHO WORRIES ABOUT YOU SO MUCH...
OH NO, I WASN'T REALLY WORRIED. NOT ABOUT HIM...
HUH?
REALLY, I SWEAR...

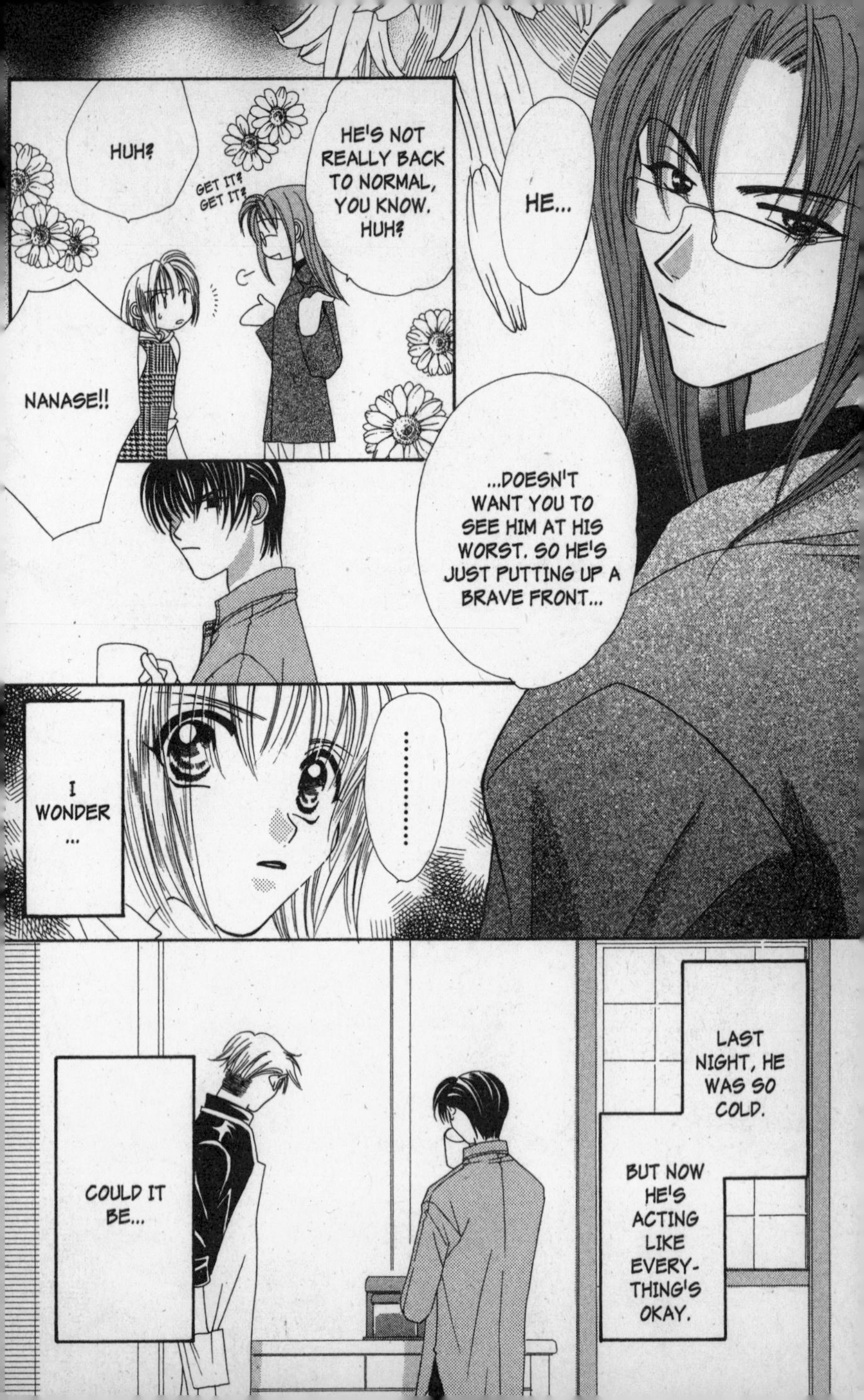
HE...
...DOESN'T WANT YOU TO SEE HIM AT HIS WORST. SO HE'S JUST PUTTING UP A BRAVE FRONT...
HE'S NOT REALLY BACK TO NORMAL, YOU KNOW. HUH?
GET IT? GET IT?
HUH?
NANASE!!
......
I WONDER ...
LAST NIGHT, HE WAS SO COLD.
BUT NOW HE'S ACTING LIKE EVERY-THING'S OKAY.
COULD IT BE...

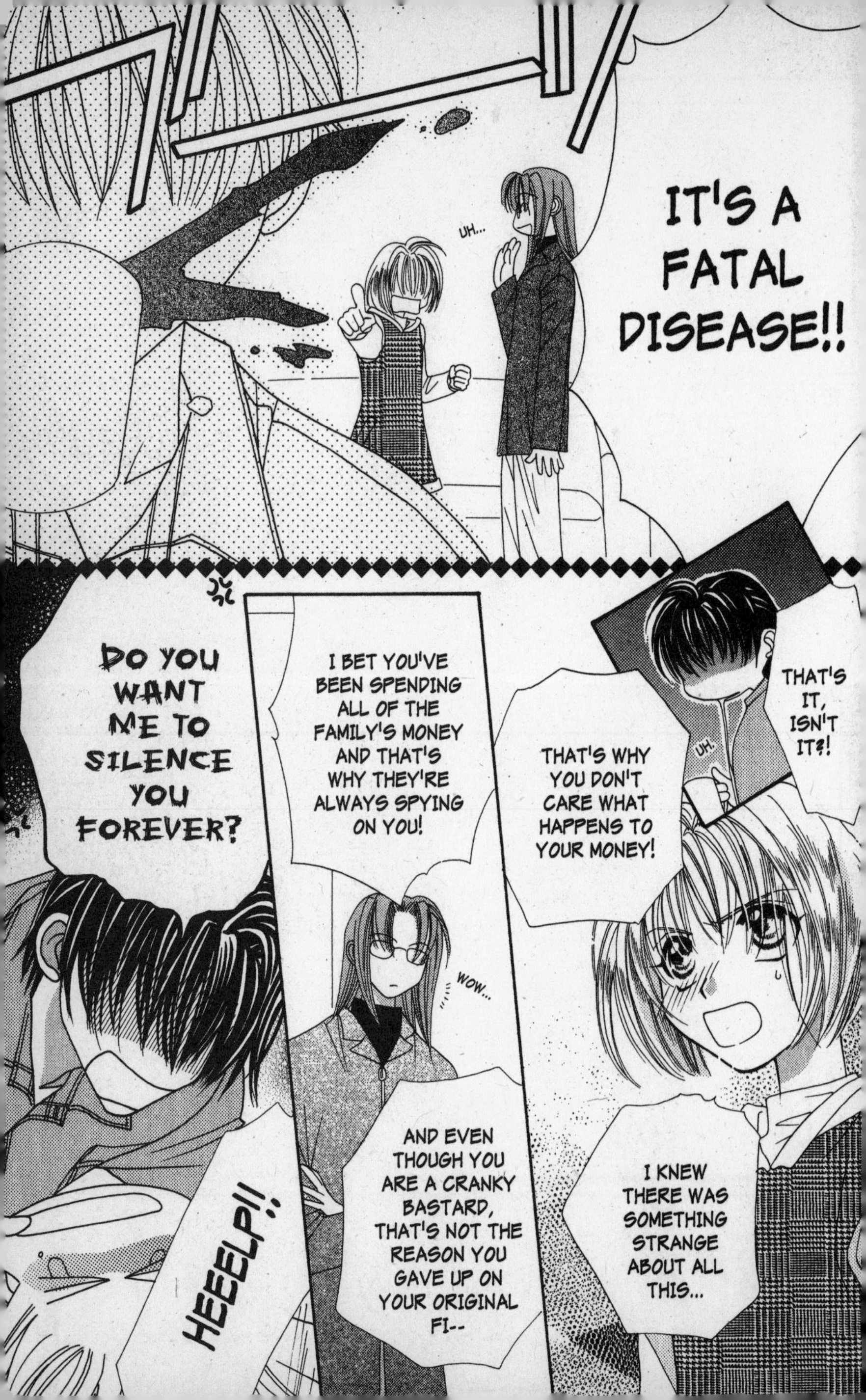
IT'S A FATAL DISEASE!!
UH...
THAT'S IT, ISN'T IT?!
UH.
THAT'S WHY YOU DON'T CARE WHAT HAPPENS TO YOUR MONEY!
I KNEW THERE WAS SOMETHING STRANGE ABOUT ALL THIS...
I BET YOU'VE BEEN SPENDING ALL OF THE FAMILY'S MONEY AND THAT'S WHY THEY'RE ALWAYS SPYING ON YOU!
WOW...
AND EVEN THOUGH YOU ARE A CRANKY BASTARD, THAT'S NOT THE REASON YOU GAVE UP ON YOUR ORIGINAL FI--
DO YOU WANT ME TO SILENCE YOU FOREVER?
HEEELP!!

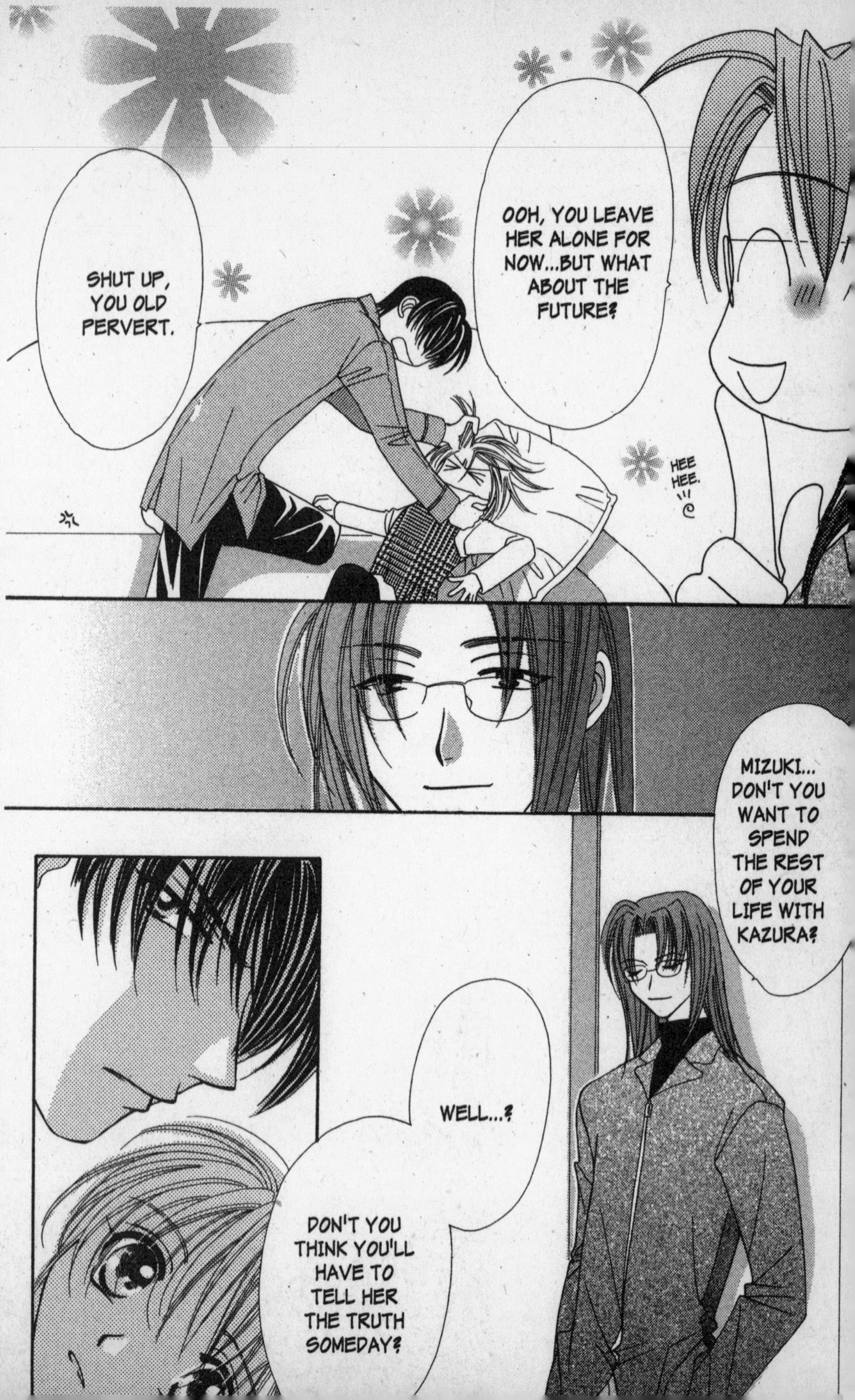
OOH, YOU LEAVE HER ALONE FOR NOW...BUT WHAT ABOUT THE FUTURE?
HEE HEE.
SHUT UP, YOU OLD PERVERT.
MIZUKI... DON'T YOU WANT TO SPEND THE REST OF YOUR LIFE WITH KAZURA?
WELL...?
DON'T YOU THINK YOU'LL HAVE TO TELL HER THE TRUTH SOMEDAY?

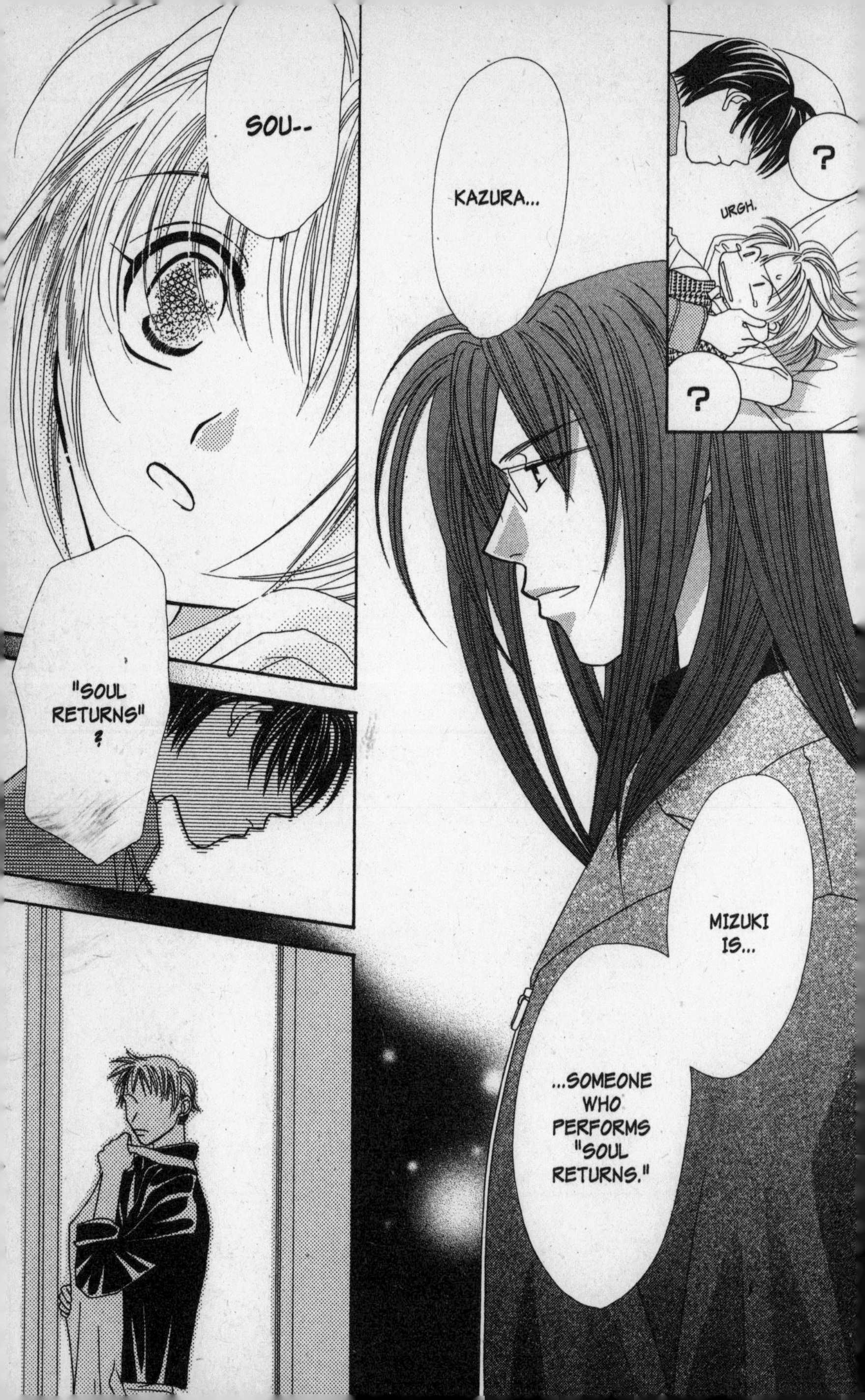
?
URGH.
?
KAZURA...
MIZUKI IS...
...SOMEONE WHO PERFORMS "SOUL RETURNS."
SOU--
"SOUL RETURNS"?

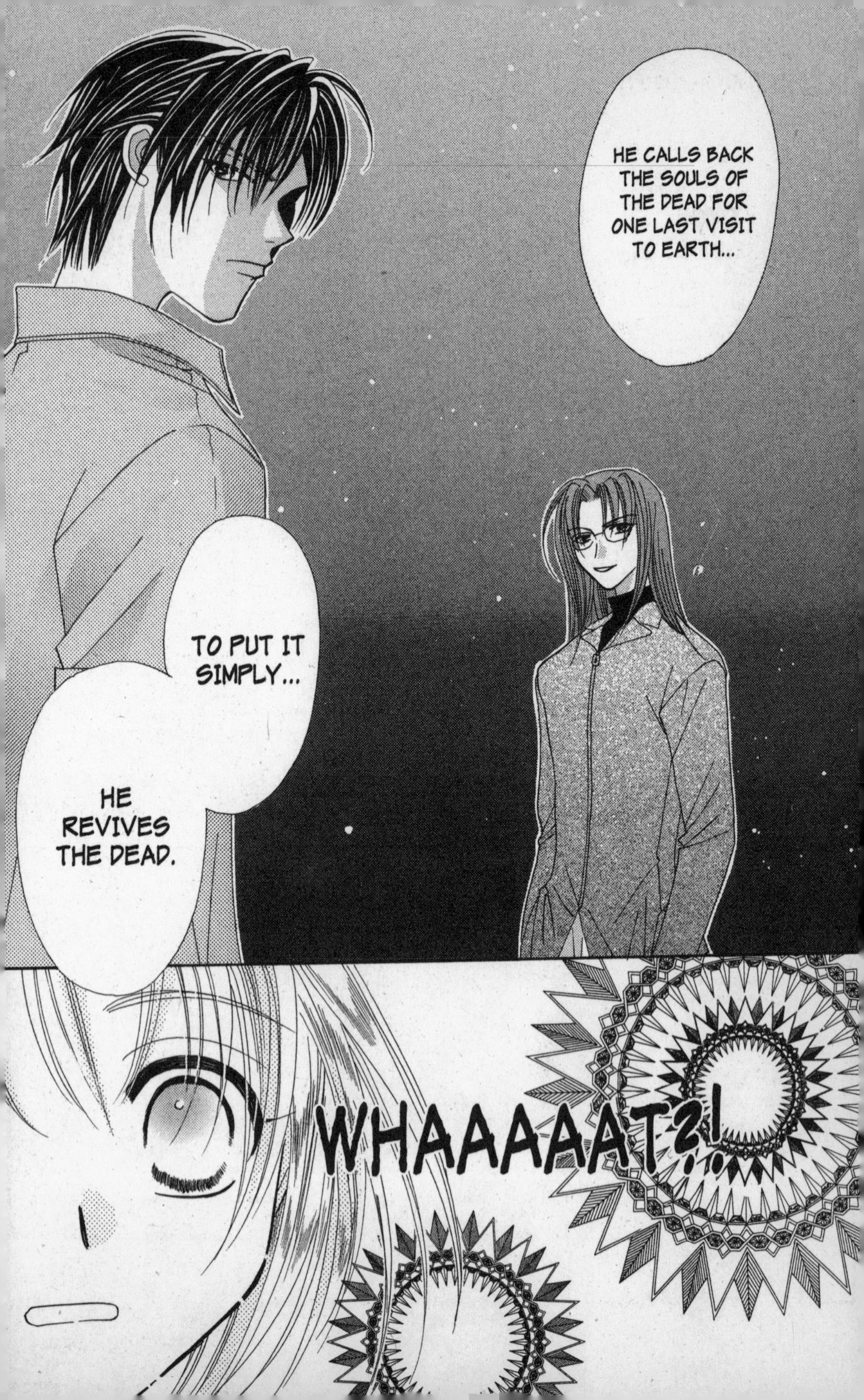
HE CALLS BACK THE SOULS OF THE DEAD FOR ONE LAST VISIT TO EARTH...
TO PUT IT SIMPLY...
HE REVIVES THE DEAD.
WHAAAAAT?!

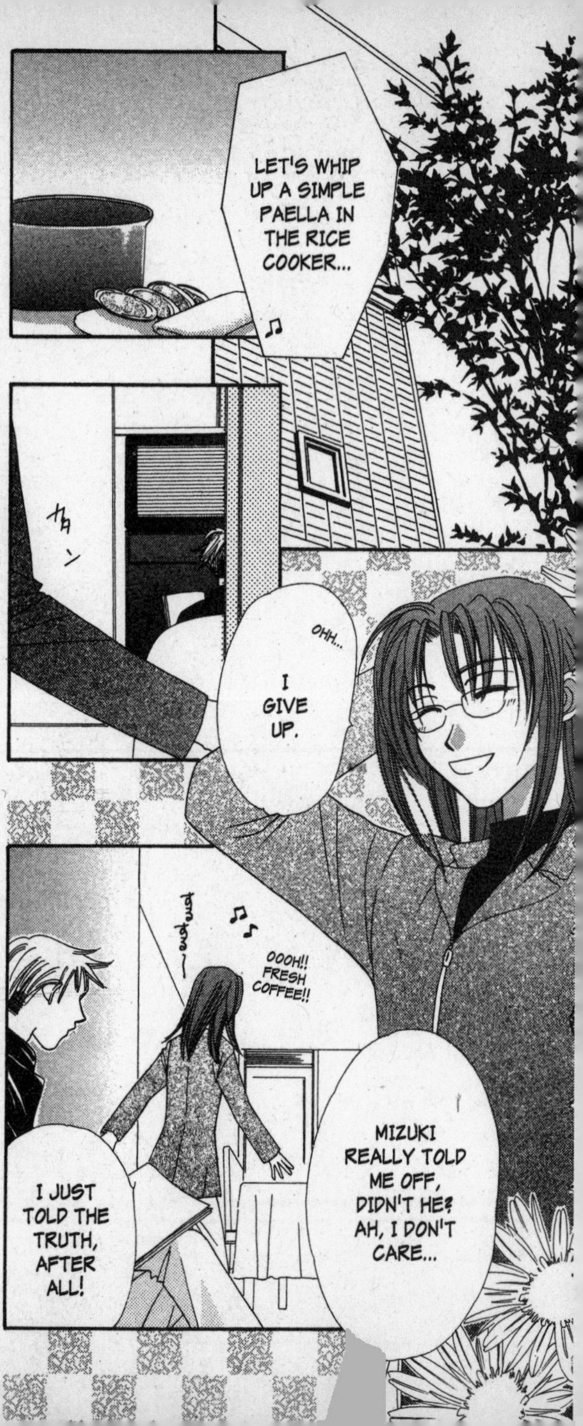
LET'S WHIP UP A SIMPLE PAELLA IN THE RICE COOKER... ♫
OHH... I GIVE UP.
MIZUKI REALLY TOLD ME OFF, DIDN'T HE? AH, I DON'T CARE...
カタン
OOOH!! FRESH COFFEE!!
I JUST TOLD THE TRUTH, AFTER ALL!

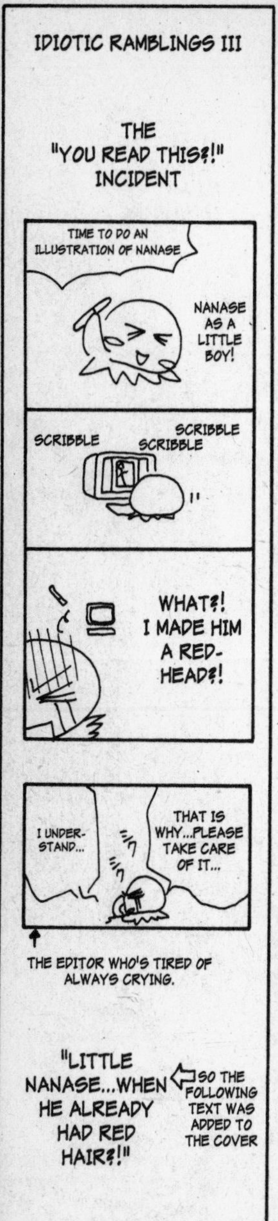
IDIOTIC RAMBLINGS III
THE "YOU READ THIS?!" INCIDENT
TIME TO DO AN ILLUSTRATION OF NANASE
NANASE AS A LITTLE BOY!
SCRIBBLE
SCRIBBLE SCRIBBLE
WHAT?! I MADE HIM A RED-HEAD?!
THAT IS WHY...PLEASE TAKE CARE OF IT...
I UNDER-STAND...
THE EDITOR WHO'S TIRED OF ALWAYS CRYING.
"LITTLE NANASE...WHEN HE ALREADY HAD RED HAIR?!"
SO THE FOLLOWING TEXT WAS ADDED TO THE COVER
I'M SUCH A DOOFUS...

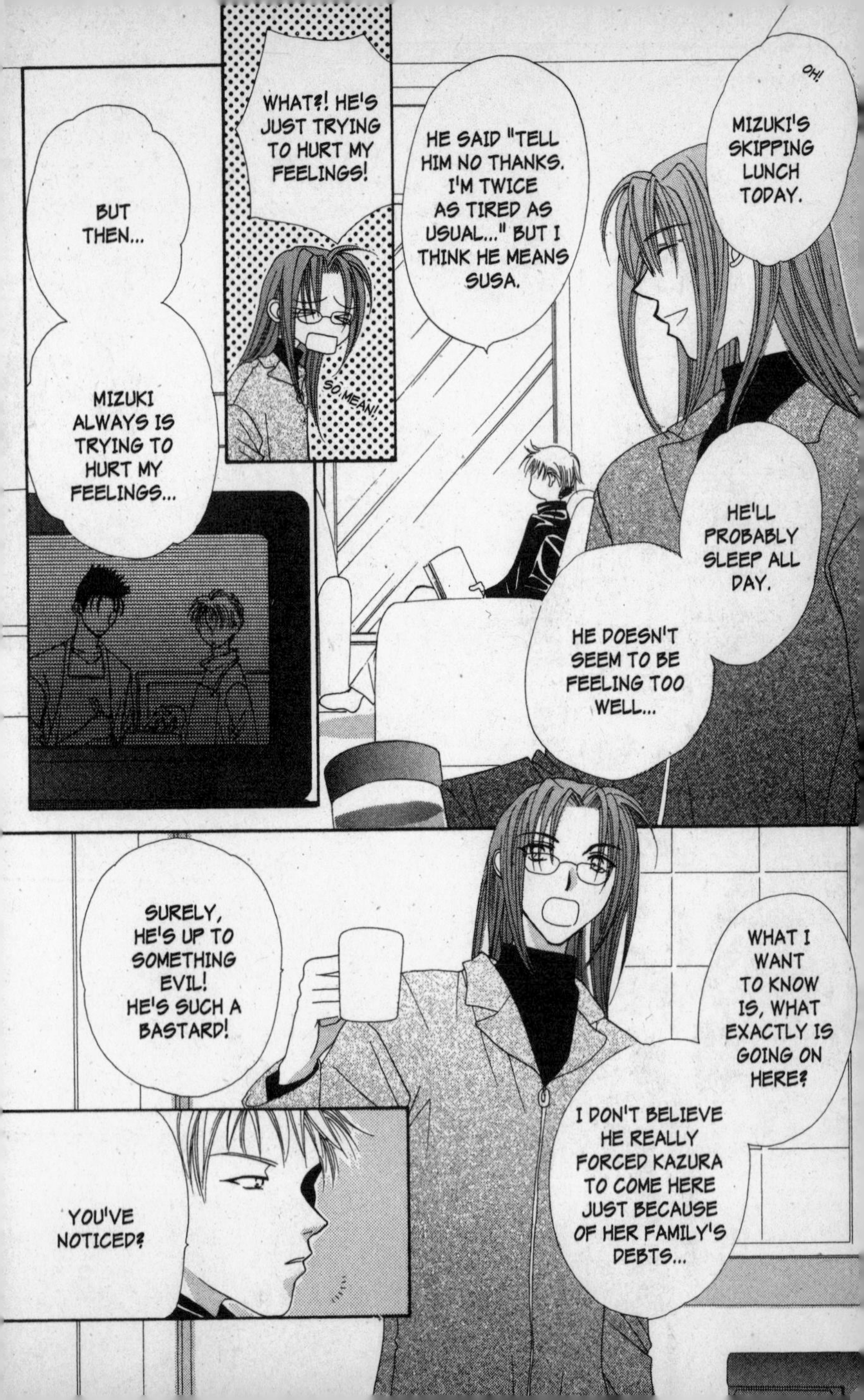
OH!
MIZUKI'S SKIPPING LUNCH TODAY.
HE'LL PROBABLY SLEEP ALL DAY.
HE DOESN'T SEEM TO BE FEELING TOO WELL...
HE SAID "TELL HIM NO THANKS. I'M TWICE AS TIRED AS USUAL..." BUT I THINK HE MEANS SUSA.
WHAT?! HE'S JUST TRYING TO HURT MY FEELINGS!
SO MEAN!!
BUT THEN...
MIZUKI ALWAYS IS TRYING TO HURT MY FEELINGS...
SURELY, HE'S UP TO SOMETHING EVIL! HE'S SUCH A BASTARD!
WHAT I WANT TO KNOW IS, WHAT EXACTLY IS GOING ON HERE?
I DON'T BELIEVE HE REALLY FORCED KAZURA TO COME HERE JUST BECAUSE OF HER FAMILY'S DEBTS...
YOU'VE NOTICED?

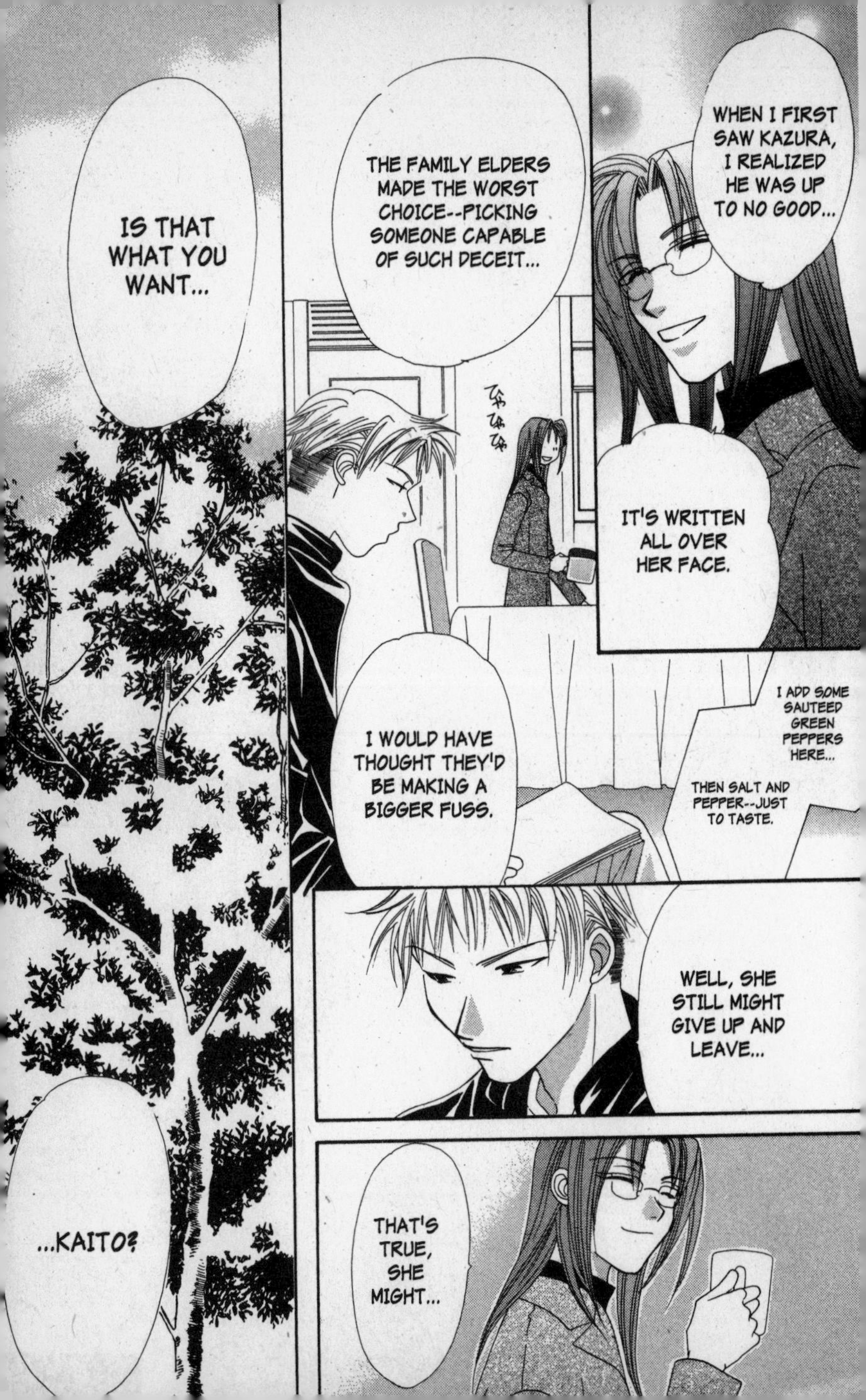
WHEN I FIRST SAW KAZURA, I REALIZED HE WAS UP TO NO GOOD...
IT'S WRITTEN ALL OVER HER FACE.
THE FAMILY ELDERS MADE THE WORST CHOICE--PICKING SOMEONE CAPABLE OF SUCH DECEIT...
I ADD SOME SAUTEED GREEN PEPPERS HERE...
THEN SALT AND PEPPER--JUST TO TASTE.
I WOULD HAVE THOUGHT THEY'D BE MAKING A BIGGER FUSS.
WELL, SHE STILL MIGHT GIVE UP AND LEAVE...
THAT'S TRUE, SHE MIGHT...
IS THAT WHAT YOU WANT...
...KAITO?

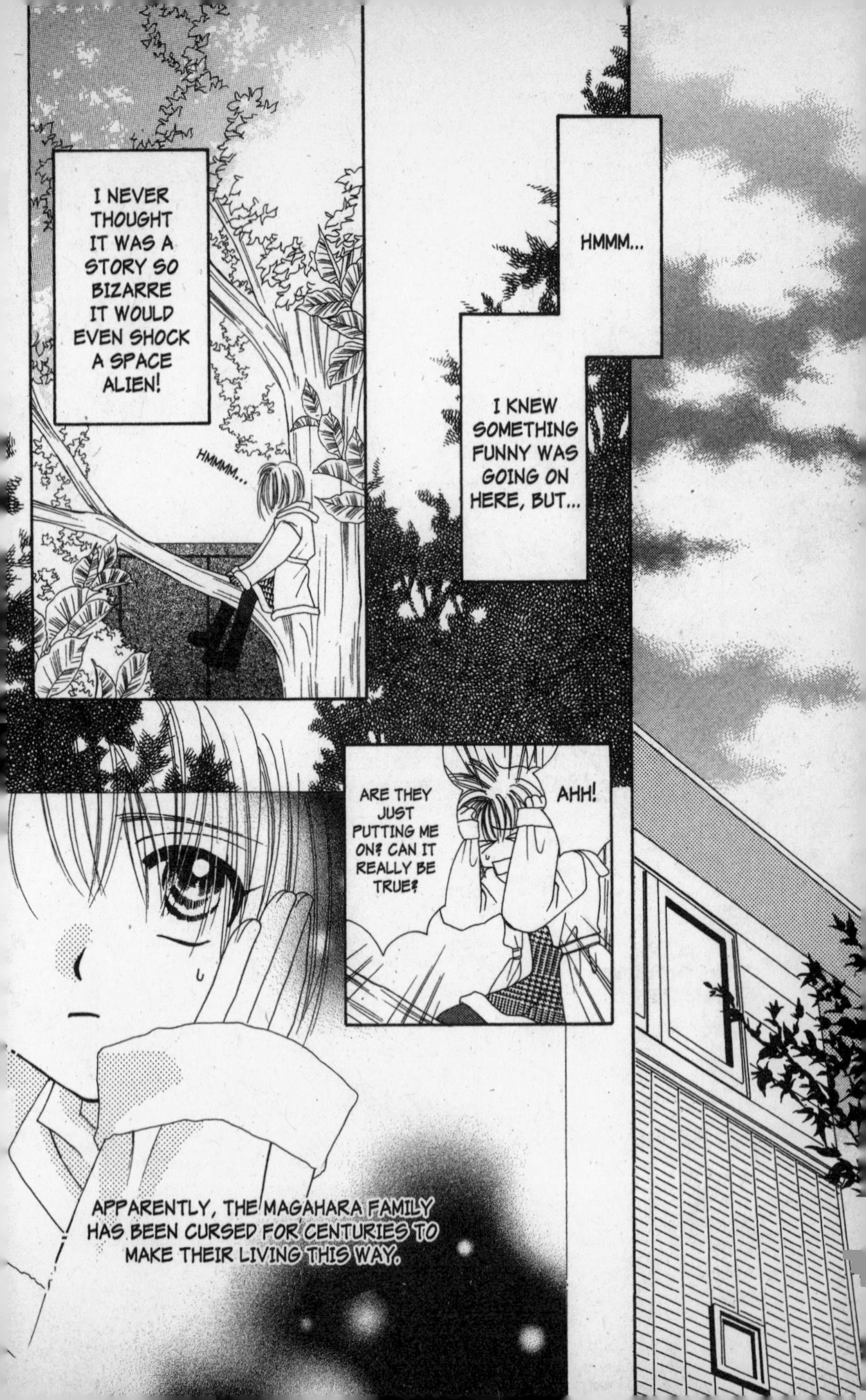
HMMM...
I KNEW SOMETHING FUNNY WAS GOING ON HERE, BUT...
I NEVER THOUGHT IT WAS A STORY SO BIZARRE IT WOULD EVEN SHOCK A SPACE ALIEN!
HMMMM...
AHH!
ARE THEY JUST PUTTING ME ON? CAN IT REALLY BE TRUE?
APPARENTLY, THE MAGAHARA FAMILY HAS BEEN CURSED FOR CENTURIES TO MAKE THEIR LIVING THIS WAY.

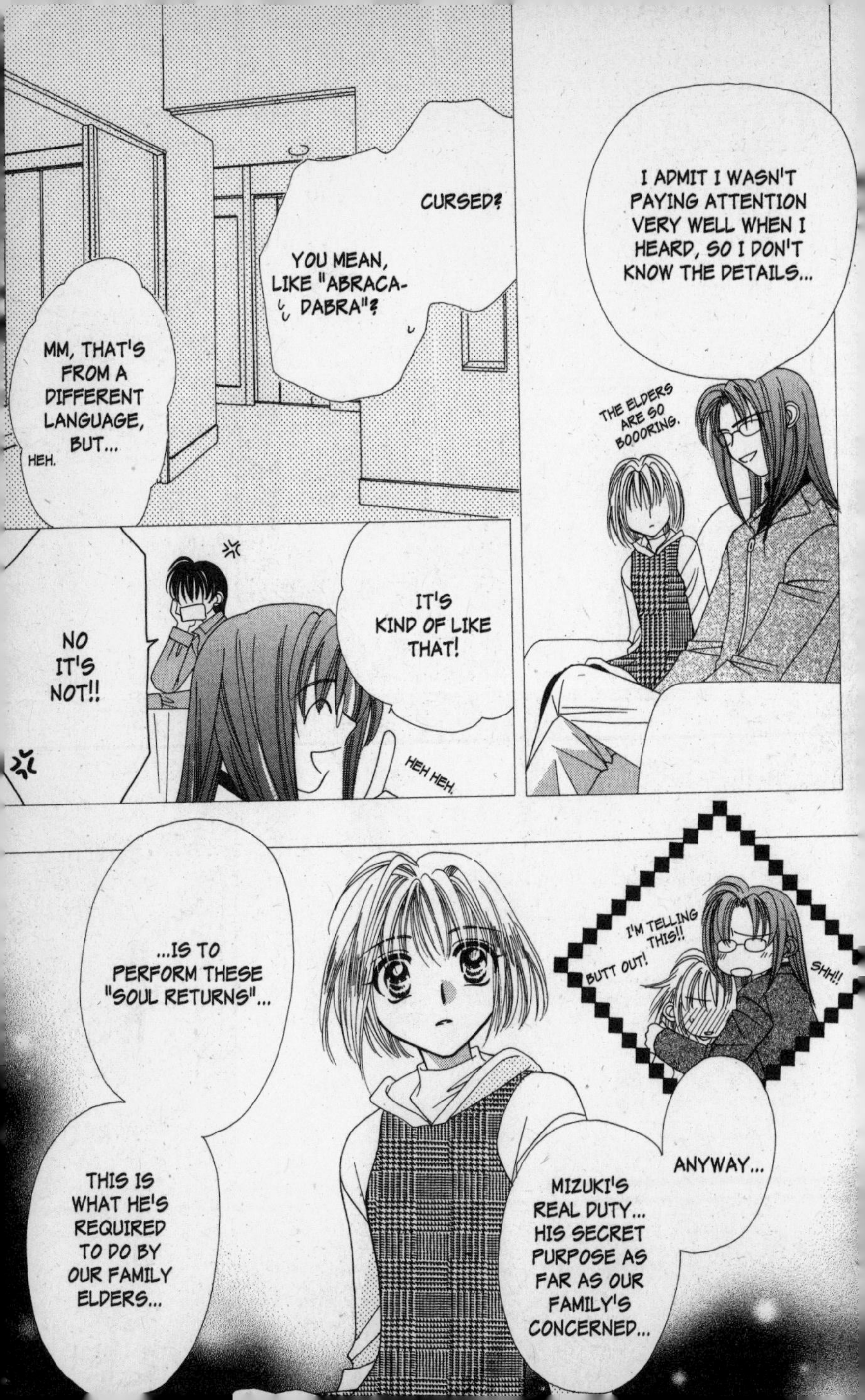
I ADMIT I WASN'T PAYING ATTENTION VERY WELL WHEN I HEARD, SO I DON'T KNOW THE DETAILS...
THE ELDERS ARE SO BOOORING.
CURSED?
YOU MEAN, LIKE "ABRACA-DABRA"?
MM, THAT'S FROM A DIFFERENT LANGUAGE, BUT...
HEH.
IT'S KIND OF LIKE THAT!
HEH HEH.
NO IT'S NOT!!
I'M TELLING THIS!!
BUTT OUT!
SHH!!
ANYWAY...
MIZUKI'S REAL DUTY... HIS SECRET PURPOSE AS FAR AS OUR FAMILY'S CONCERNED...
...IS TO PERFORM THESE "SOUL RETURNS"...
THIS IS WHAT HE'S REQUIRED TO DO BY OUR FAMILY ELDERS...

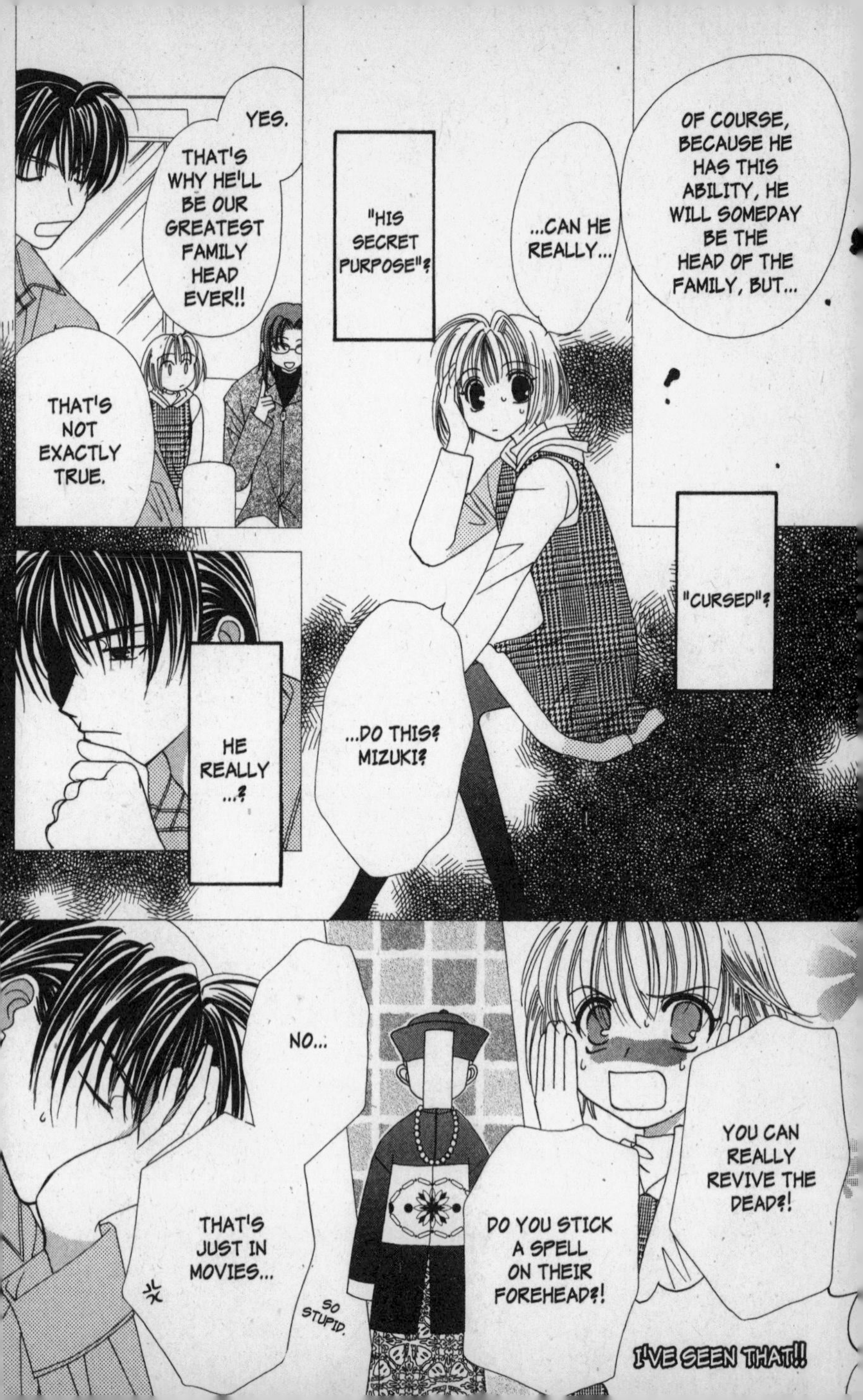
OF COURSE, BECAUSE HE HAS THIS ABILITY, HE WILL SOMEDAY BE THE HEAD OF THE FAMILY, BUT...
...CAN HE REALLY...
"CURSED"?
"HIS SECRET PURPOSE"?
...DO THIS? MIZUKI?
YES.
THAT'S WHY HE'LL BE OUR GREATEST FAMILY HEAD EVER!!
THAT'S NOT EXACTLY TRUE.
HE REALLY ...?
YOU CAN REALLY REVIVE THE DEAD?!
I'VE SEEN THAT!!
DO YOU STICK A SPELL ON THEIR FOREHEAD?!
SO STUPID.
NO...
THAT'S JUST IN MOVIES...

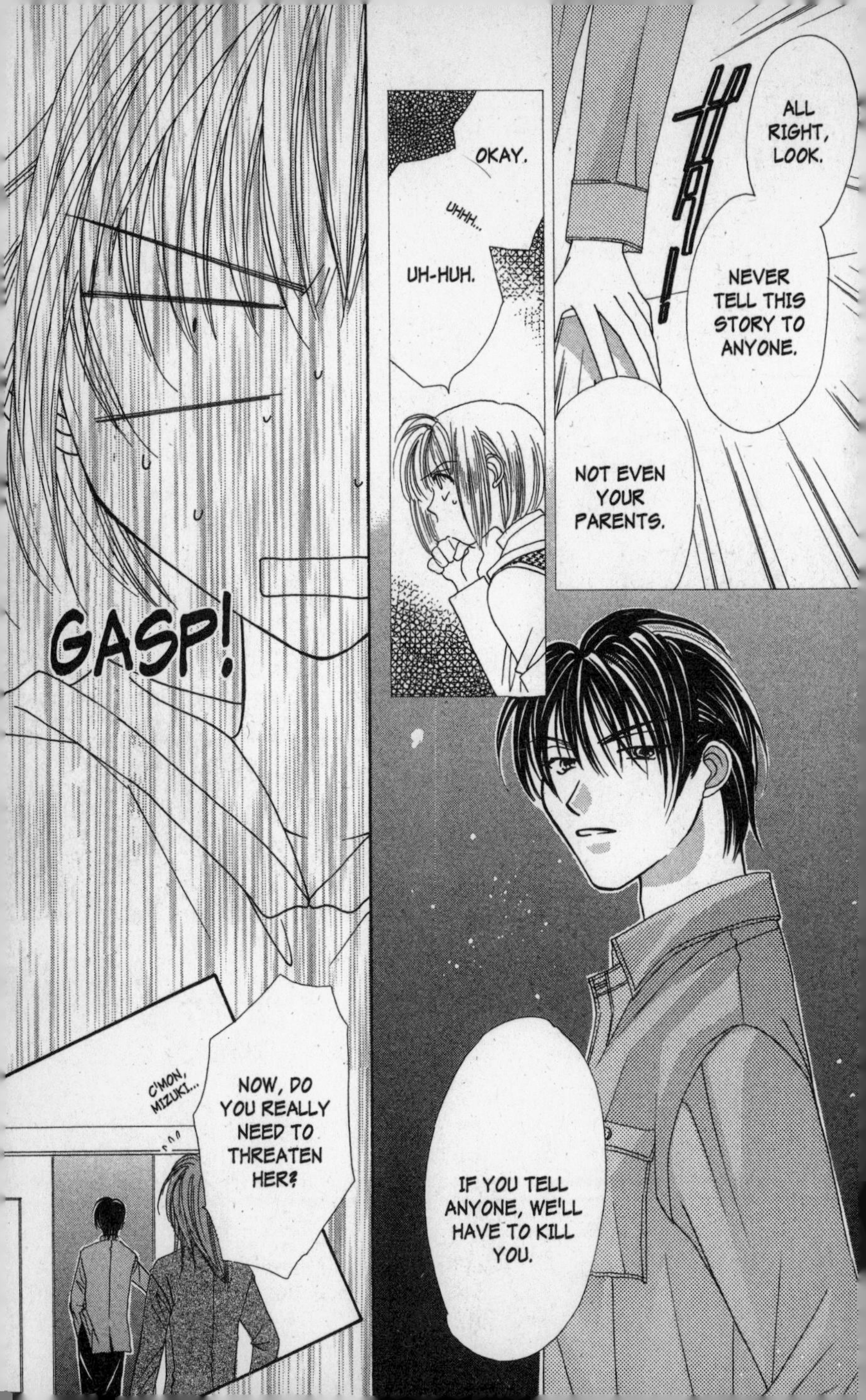
ALL RIGHT, LOOK.
NEVER TELL THIS STORY TO ANYONE.
NOT EVEN YOUR PARENTS.
OKAY.
UHHH...
UH-HUH.
IF YOU TELL ANYONE, WE'LL HAVE TO KILL YOU.
GASP!
C'MON, MIZUKI...
NOW, DO YOU REALLY NEED TO THREATEN HER?

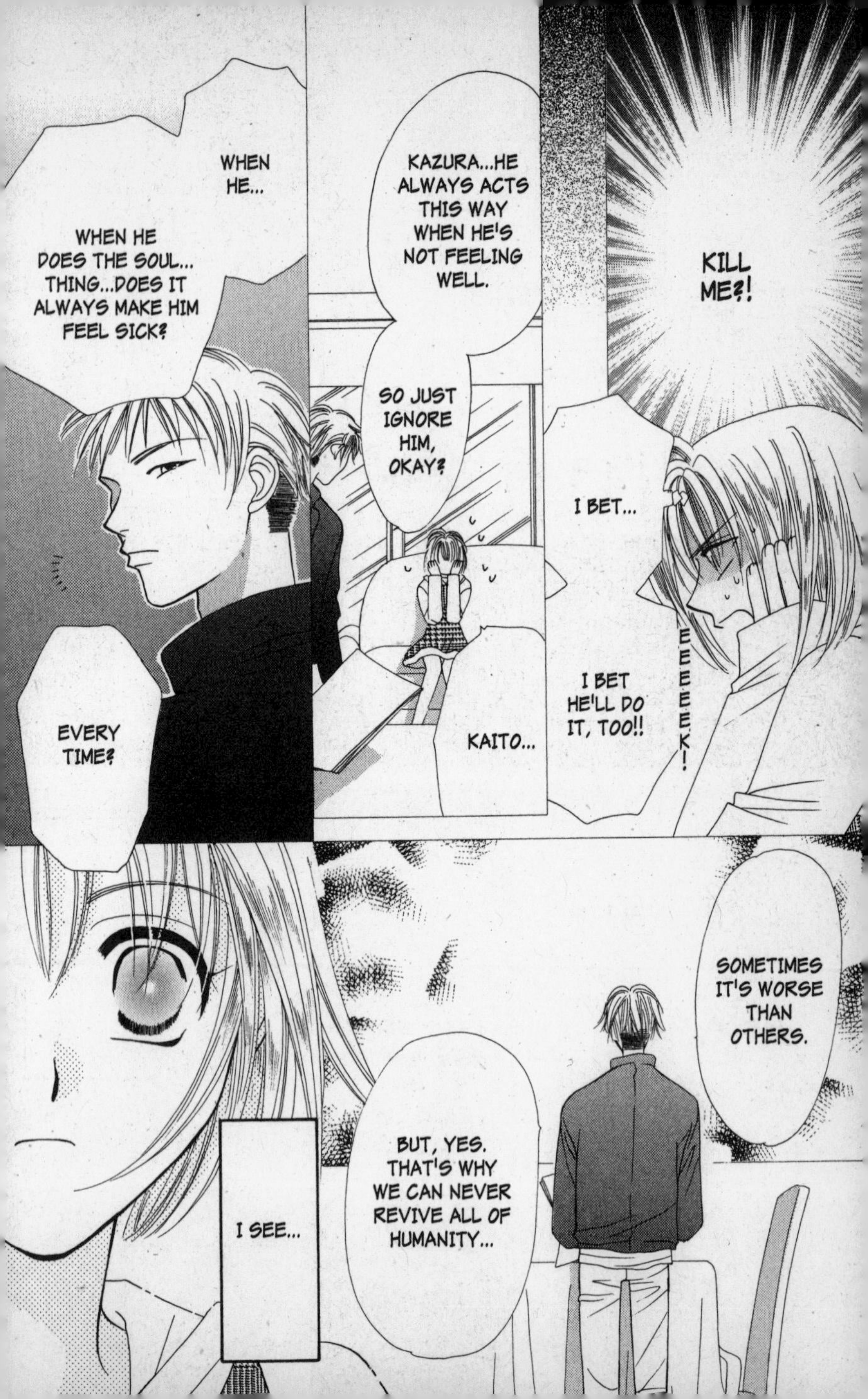
KILL ME?!
I BET...
I BET HE'LL DO IT, TOO!!
EEEEEK!
KAZURA...HE ALWAYS ACTS THIS WAY WHEN HE'S NOT FEELING WELL.
SO JUST IGNORE HIM, OKAY?
KAITO...
WHEN HE...
WHEN HE DOES THE SOUL... THING...DOES IT ALWAYS MAKE HIM FEEL SICK?
EVERY TIME?
SOMETIMES IT'S WORSE THAN OTHERS.
BUT, YES. THAT'S WHY WE CAN NEVER REVIVE ALL OF HUMANITY...
I SEE...

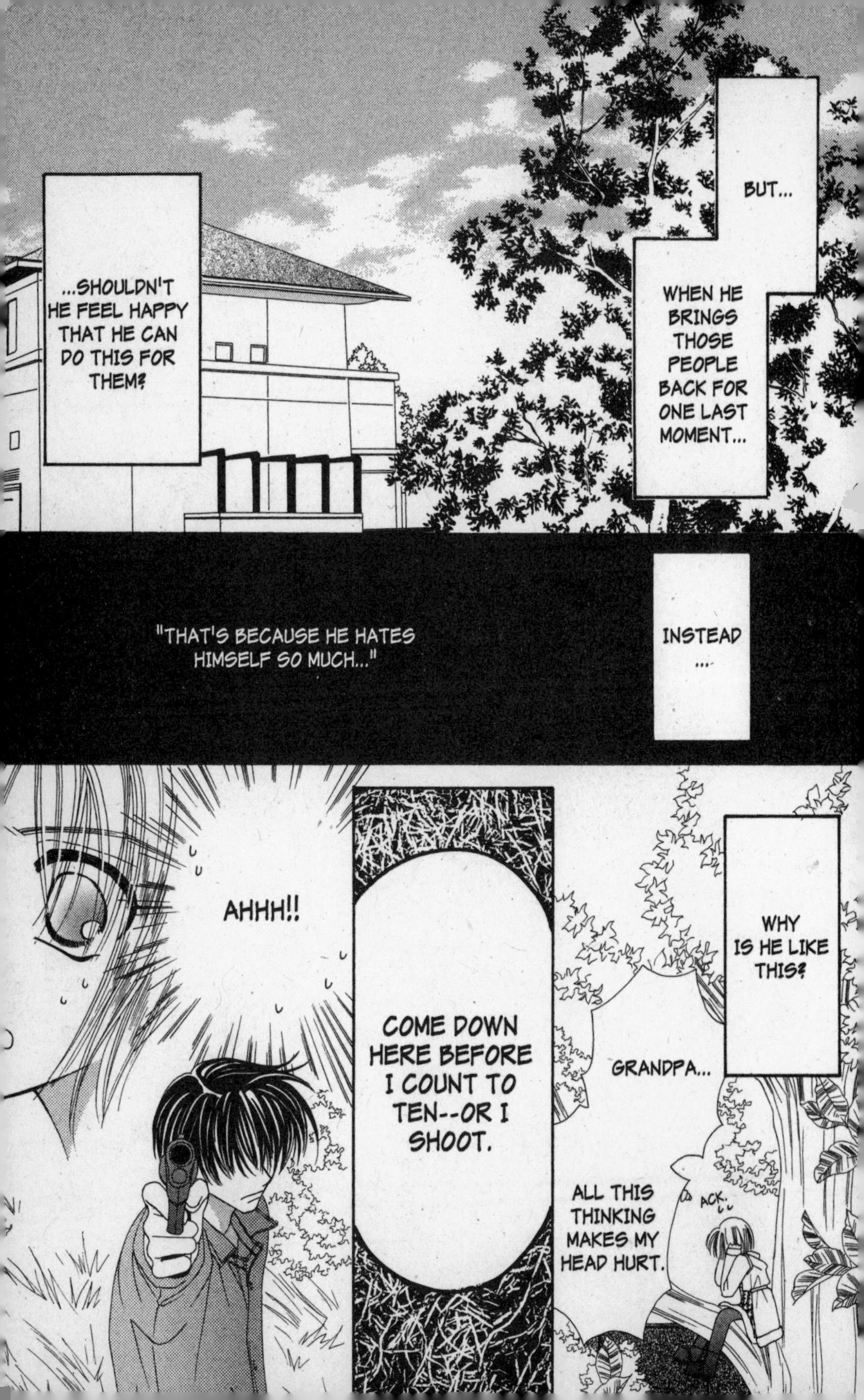
BUT...
WHEN HE BRINGS THOSE PEOPLE BACK FOR ONE LAST MOMENT...
...SHOULDN'T HE FEEL HAPPY THAT HE CAN DO THIS FOR THEM?
INSTEAD...
"THAT'S BECAUSE HE HATES HIMSELF SO MUCH..."
WHY IS HE LIKE THIS?
GRANDPA...
ALL THIS THINKING MAKES MY HEAD HURT.
ACK.
COME DOWN HERE BEFORE I COUNT TO TEN--OR I SHOOT.
AHHH!!

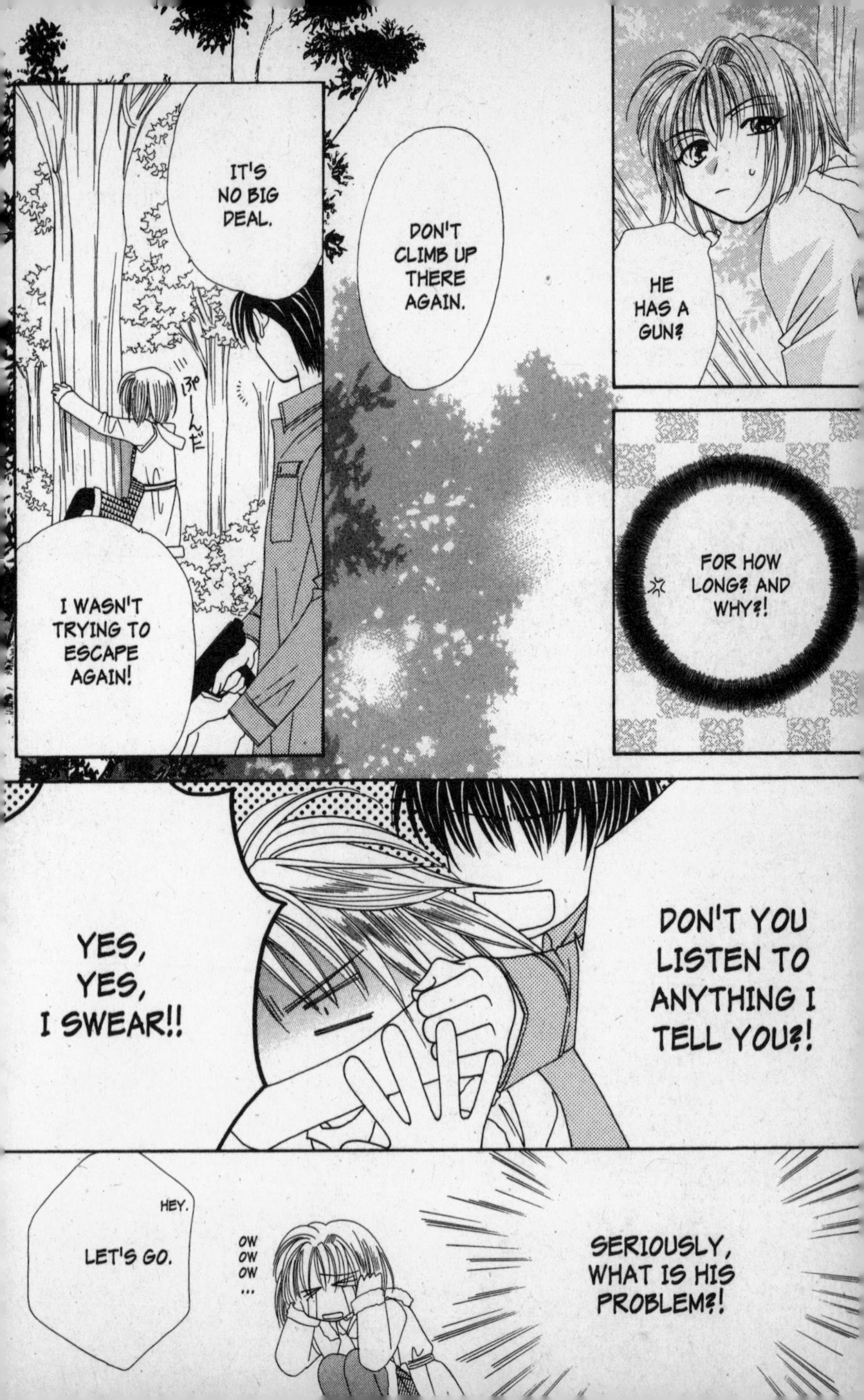
HE HAS A GUN?
FOR HOW LONG? AND WHY?!
DON'T CLIMB UP THERE AGAIN.
IT'S NO BIG DEAL.
ぷーんだ
I WASN'T TRYING TO ESCAPE AGAIN!
DON'T YOU LISTEN TO ANYTHING I TELL YOU?!
YES, YES, I SWEAR!!
SERIOUSLY, WHAT IS HIS PROBLEM?!
OW OW OW ...
HEY.
LET'S GO.

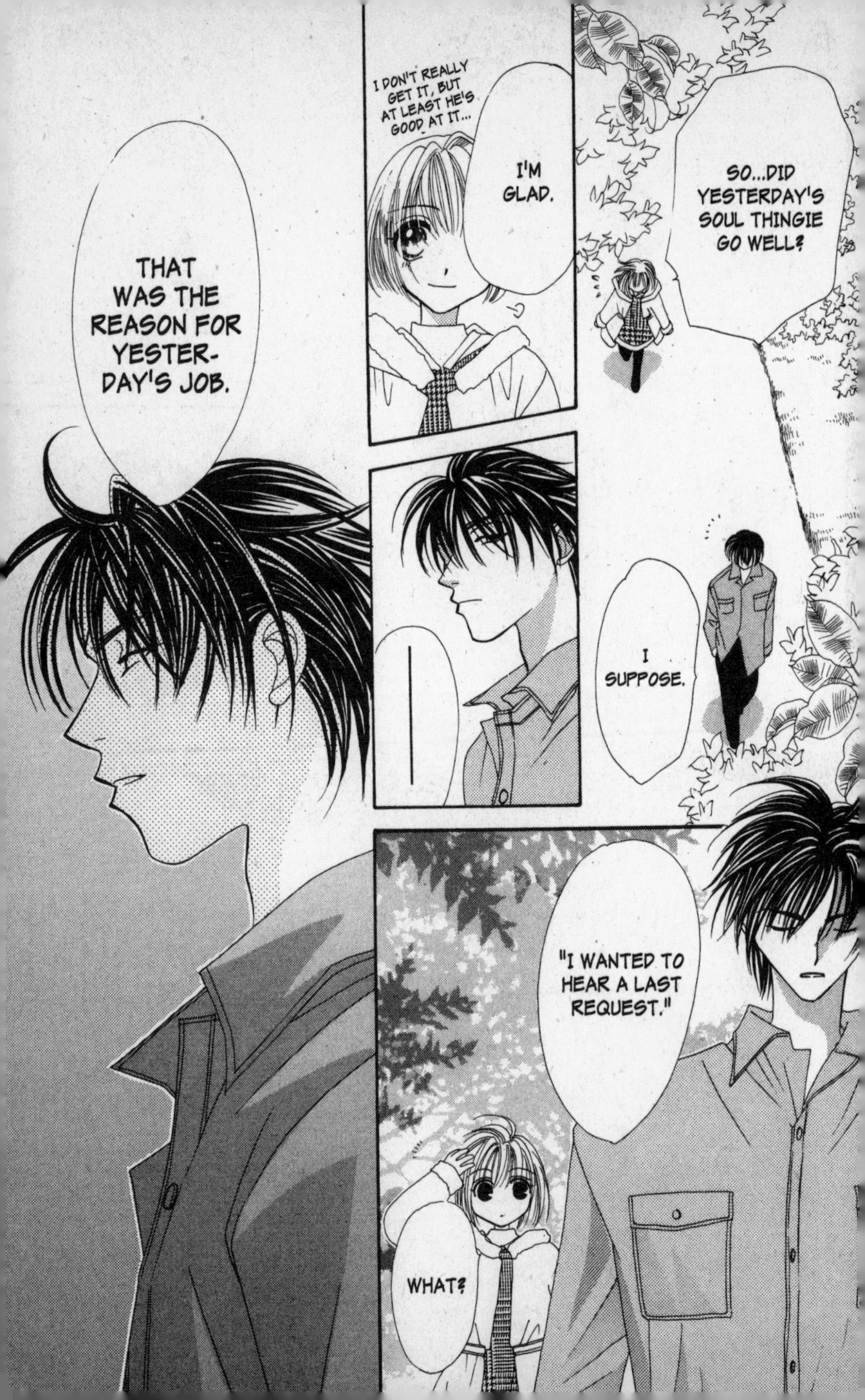
SO...DID YESTERDAY'S SOUL THINGIE GO WELL?
I SUPPOSE.
I'M GLAD.
I DON'T REALLY GET IT, BUT AT LEAST HE'S GOOD AT IT...
"I WANTED TO HEAR A LAST REQUEST."
WHAT?
THAT WAS THE REASON FOR YESTER-DAY'S JOB.

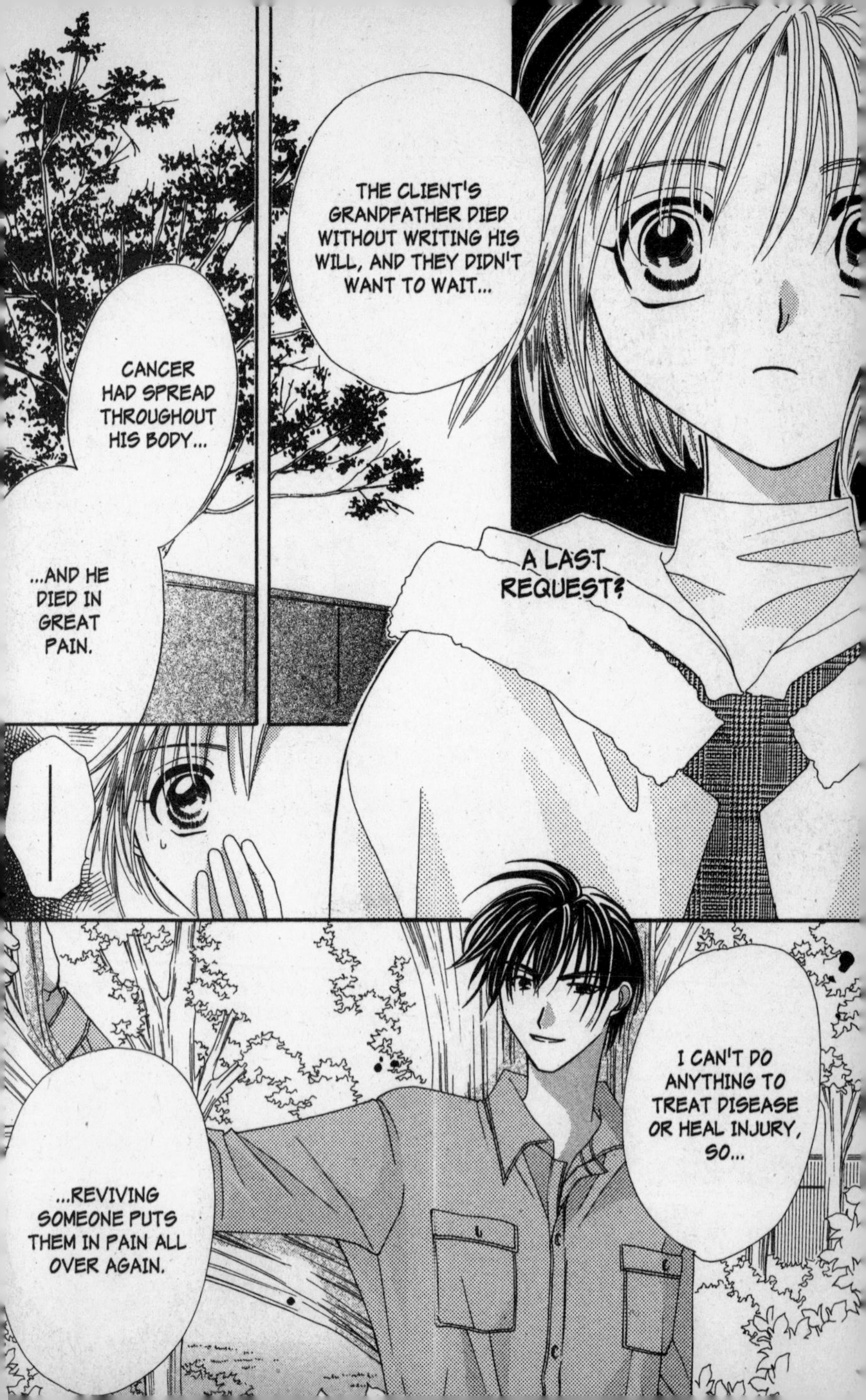

A LAST REQUEST?
THE CLIENT'S GRANDFATHER DIED WITHOUT WRITING HIS WILL, AND THEY DIDN'T WANT TO WAIT...
CANCER HAD SPREAD THROUGHOUT HIS BODY...
...AND HE DIED IN GREAT PAIN.
I CAN'T DO ANYTHING TO TREAT DISEASE OR HEAL INJURY, SO...
...REVIVING SOMEONE PUTS THEM IN PAIN ALL OVER AGAIN.

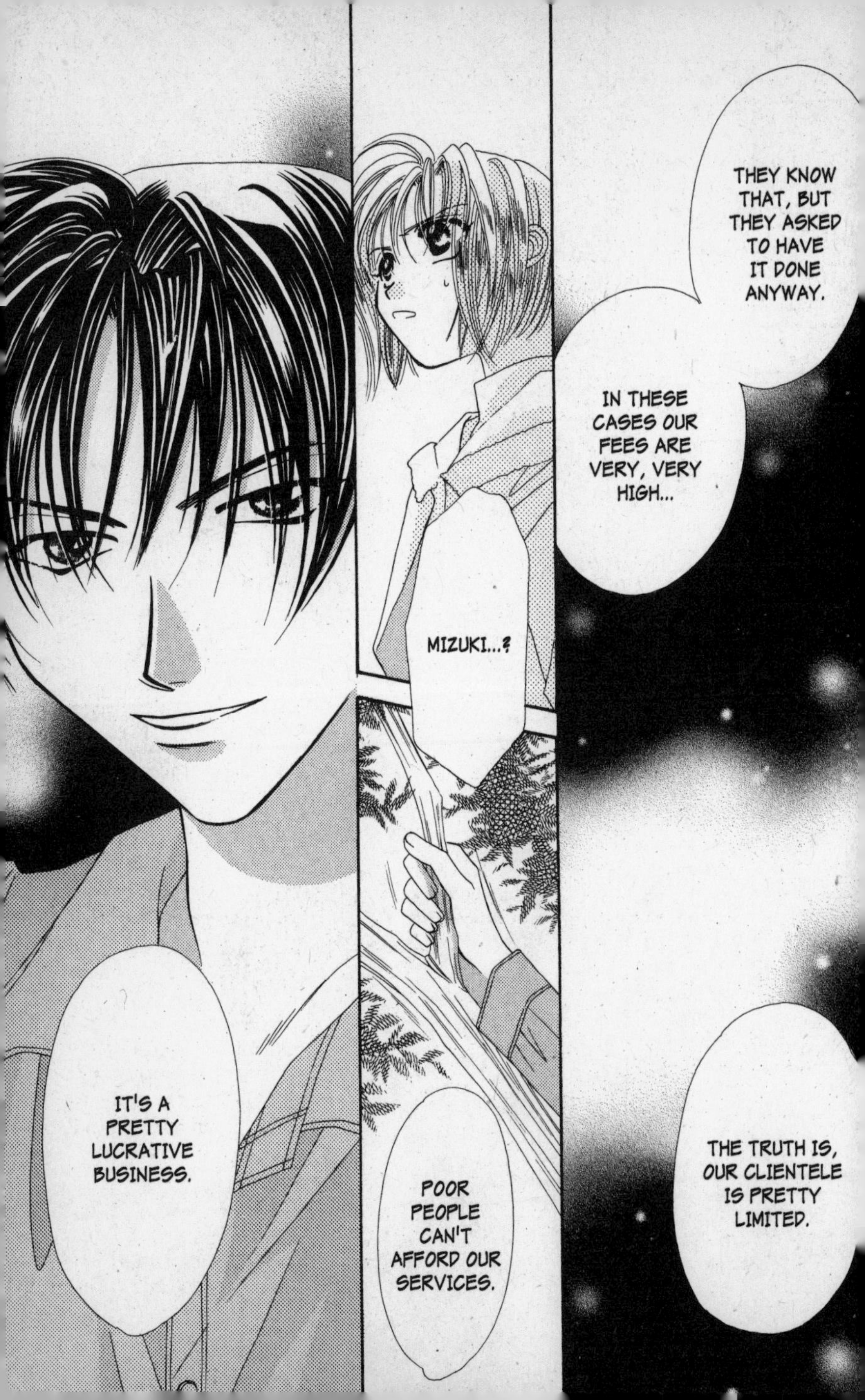
THEY KNOW THAT, BUT THEY ASKED TO HAVE IT DONE ANYWAY.
IN THESE CASES OUR FEES ARE VERY, VERY HIGH...
THE TRUTH IS, OUR CLIENTELE IS PRETTY LIMITED.
MIZUKI...?
POOR PEOPLE CAN'T AFFORD OUR SERVICES.
IT'S A PRETTY LUCRATIVE BUSINESS.

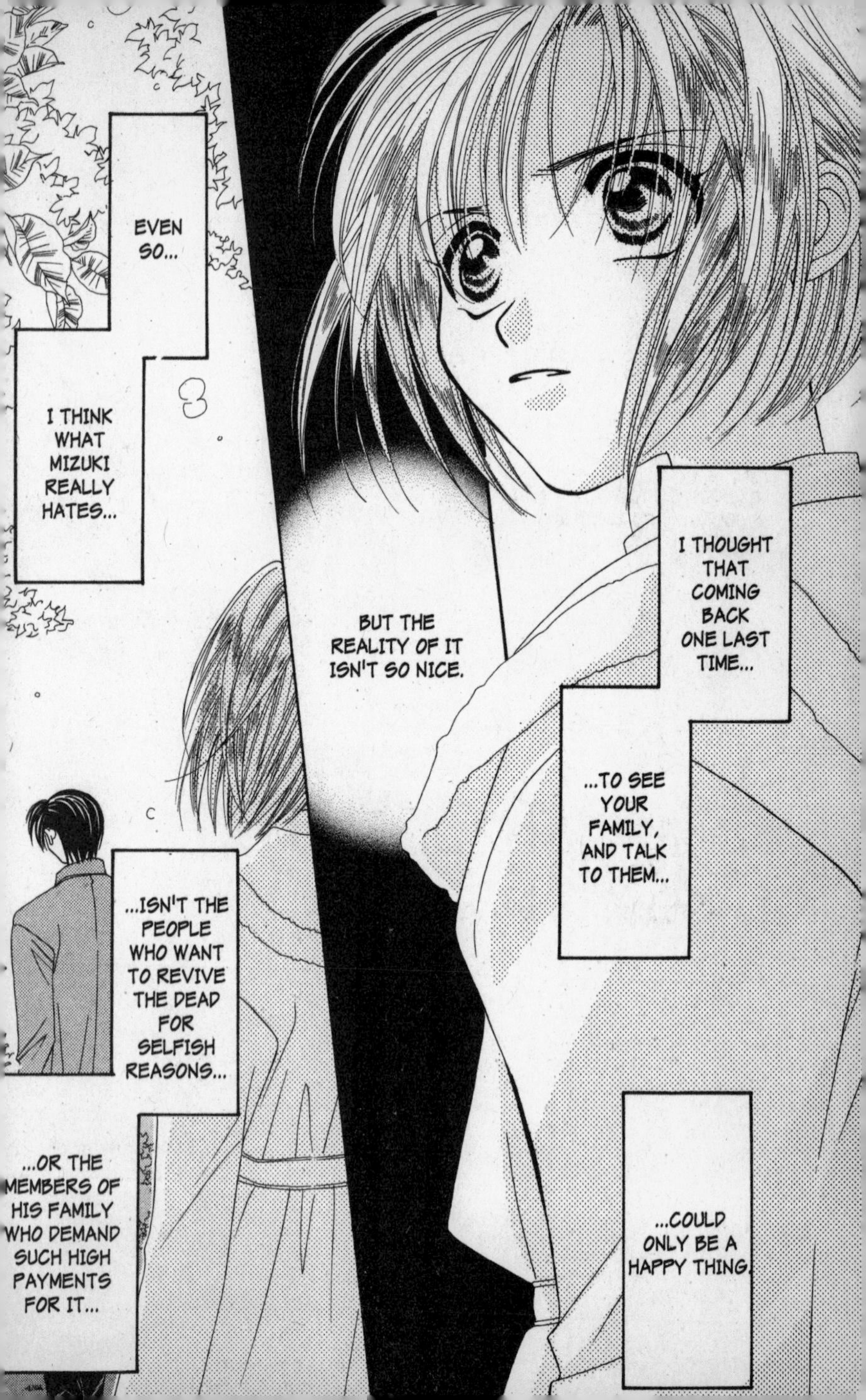
I THOUGHT THAT COMING BACK ONE LAST TIME...
...TO SEE YOUR FAMILY, AND TALK TO THEM...
...COULD ONLY BE A HAPPY THING.
BUT THE REALITY OF IT ISN'T SO NICE.
EVEN SO...
I THINK WHAT MIZUKI REALLY HATES...
...ISN'T THE PEOPLE WHO WANT TO REVIVE THE DEAD FOR SELFISH REASONS...
...OR THE MEMBERS OF HIS FAMILY WHO DEMAND SUCH HIGH PAYMENTS FOR IT...

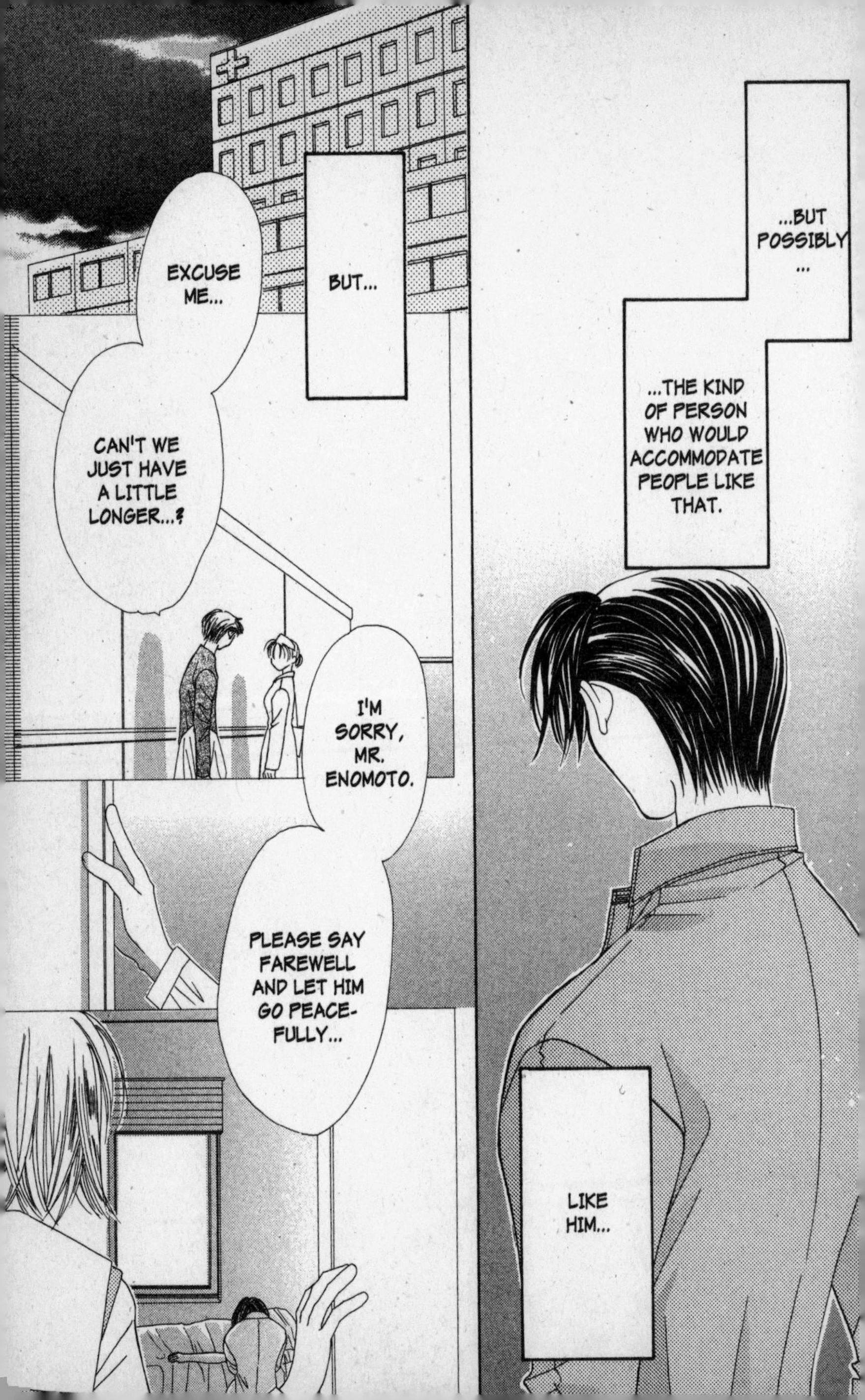
...BUT POSSIBLY ...
...THE KIND OF PERSON WHO WOULD ACCOMMODATE PEOPLE LIKE THAT.
LIKE HIM...
BUT...
EXCUSE ME...
CAN'T WE JUST HAVE A LITTLE LONGER...?
I'M SORRY, MR. ENOMOTO.
PLEASE SAY FAREWELL AND LET HIM GO PEACEFULLY...

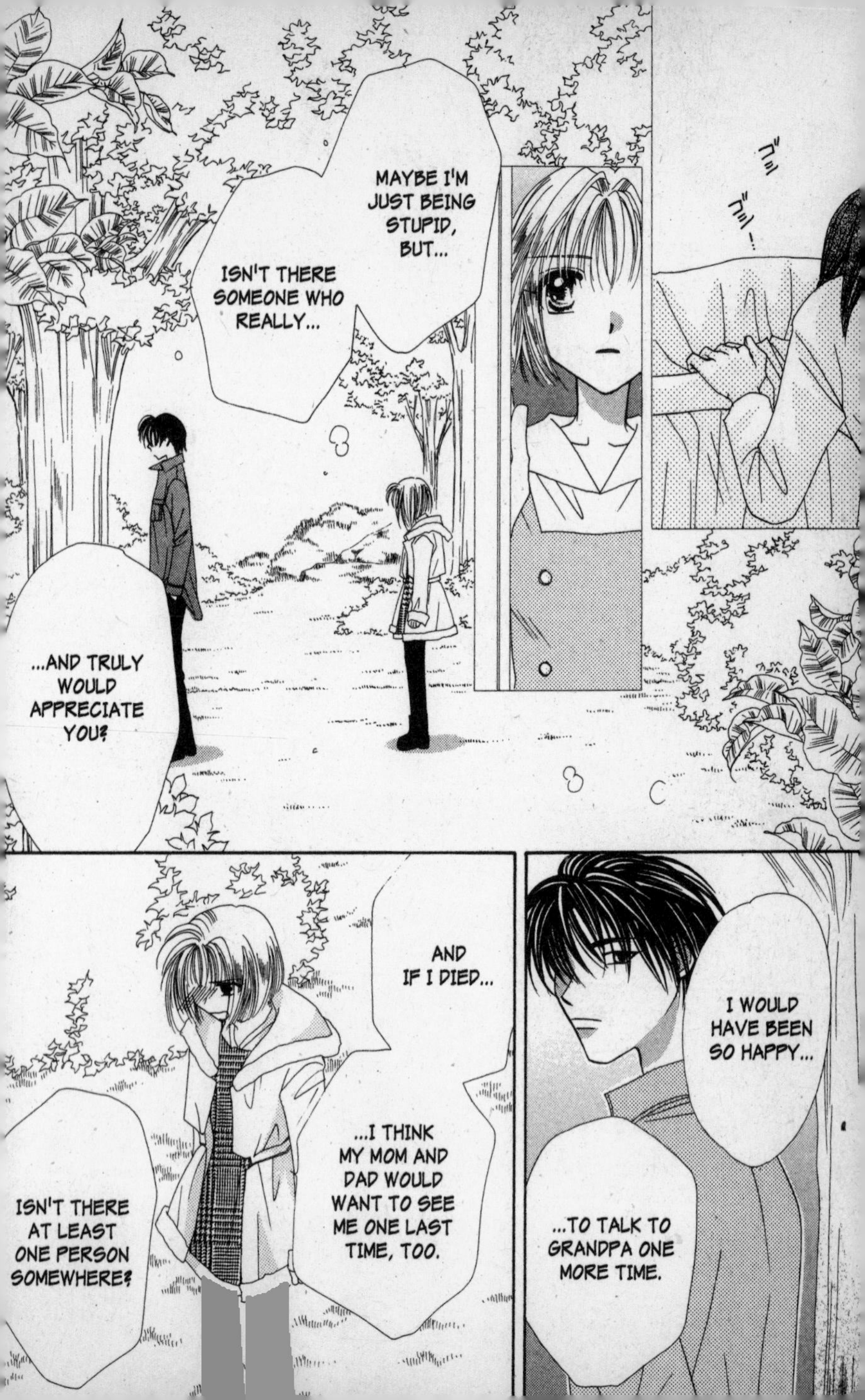
MAYBE I'M JUST BEING STUPID, BUT...
ISN'T THERE SOMEONE WHO REALLY...
...AND TRULY WOULD APPRECIATE YOU?
I WOULD HAVE BEEN SO HAPPY...
...TO TALK TO GRANDPA ONE MORE TIME.
AND IF I DIED...
...I THINK MY MOM AND DAD WOULD WANT TO SEE ME ONE LAST TIME, TOO.
ISN'T THERE AT LEAST ONE PERSON SOMEWHERE?

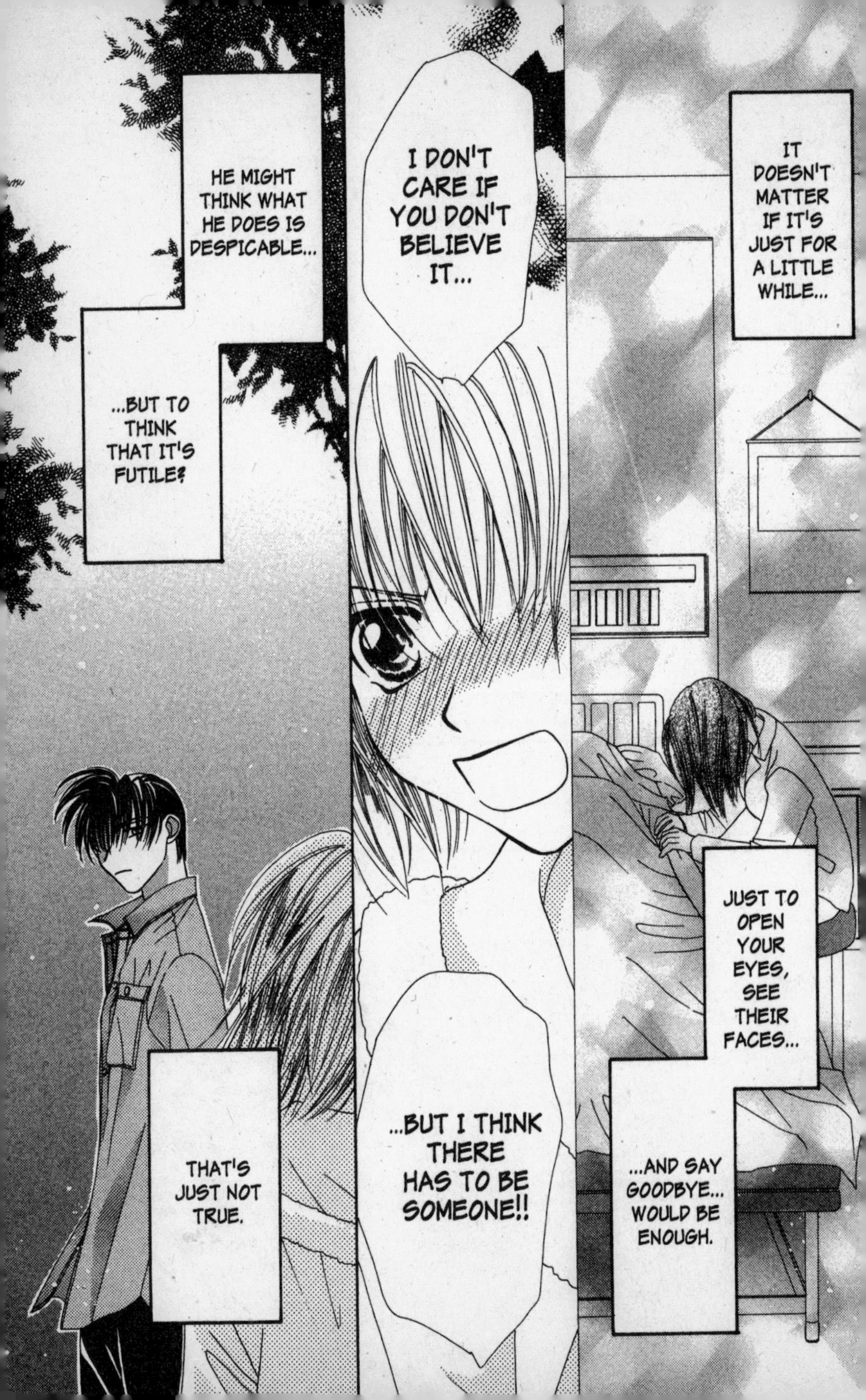
IT DOESN'T MATTER IF IT'S JUST FOR A LITTLE WHILE...
JUST TO OPEN YOUR EYES, SEE THEIR FACES...
...AND SAY GOODBYE... WOULD BE ENOUGH.
I DON'T CARE IF YOU DON'T BELIEVE IT...
...BUT I THINK THERE HAS TO BE SOMEONE!!
HE MIGHT THINK WHAT HE DOES IS DESPICABLE...
...BUT TO THINK THAT IT'S FUTILE?
THAT'S JUST NOT TRUE.

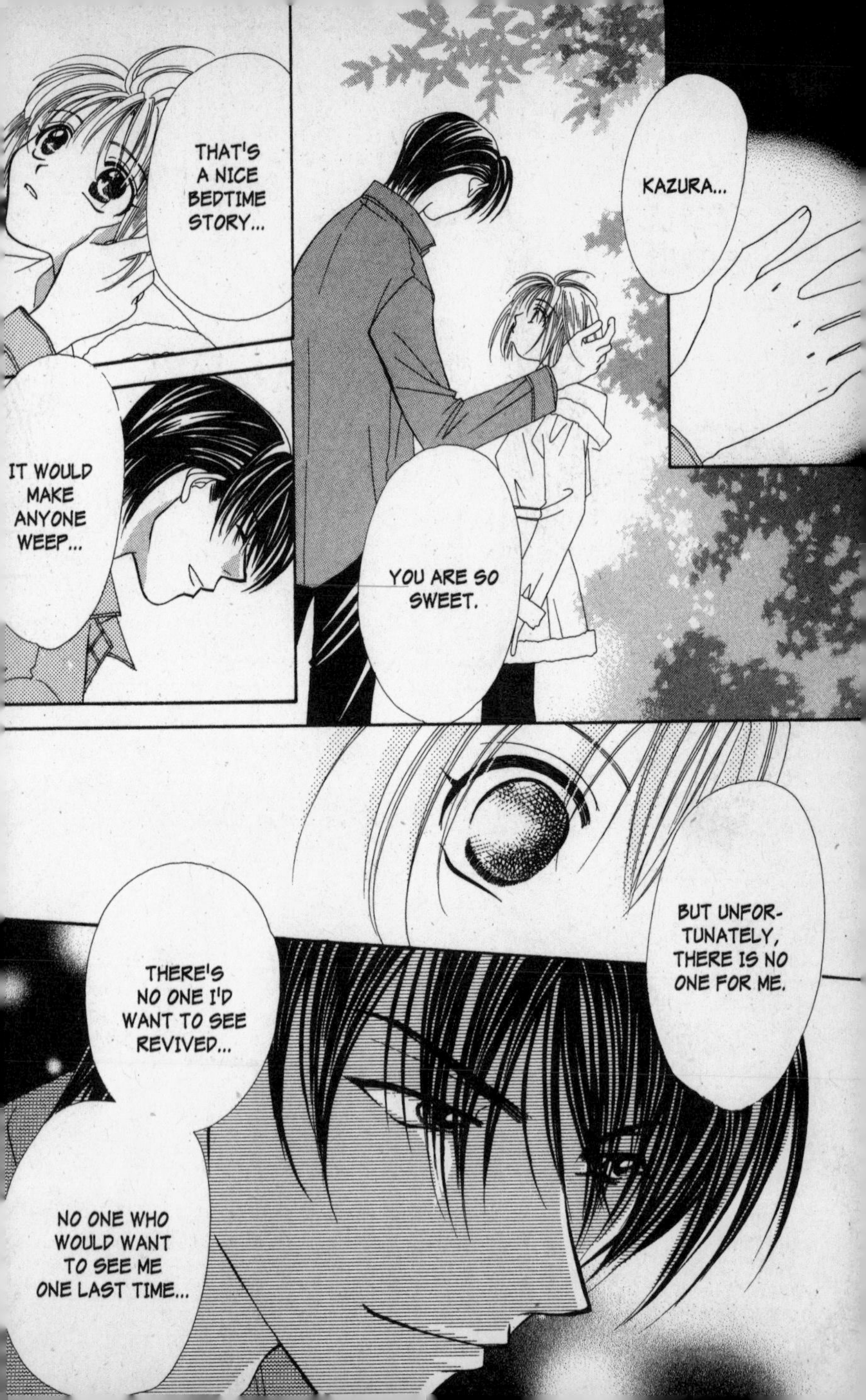
KAZURA...
YOU ARE SO SWEET.
THAT'S A NICE BEDTIME STORY...
IT WOULD MAKE ANYONE WEEP...
BUT UNFOR-TUNATELY, THERE IS NO ONE FOR ME.
THERE'S NO ONE I'D WANT TO SEE REVIVED...
NO ONE WHO WOULD WANT TO SEE ME ONE LAST TIME...

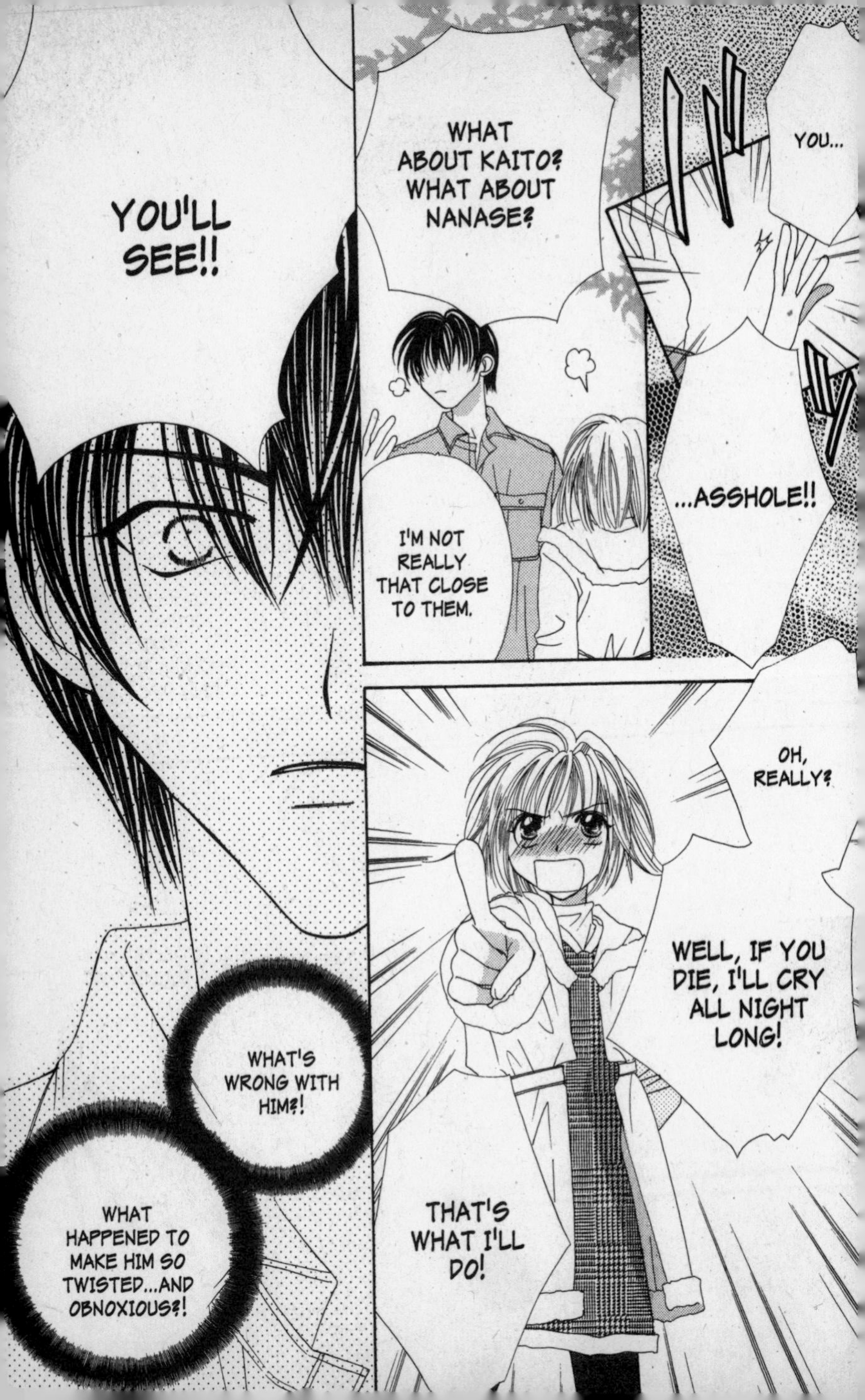
YOU...
...ASSHOLE!!
WHAT ABOUT KAITO? WHAT ABOUT NANASE?
I'M NOT REALLY THAT CLOSE TO THEM.
OH, REALLY?
WELL, IF YOU DIE, I'LL CRY ALL NIGHT LONG!
THAT'S WHAT I'LL DO!
YOU'LL SEE!!
WHAT'S WRONG WITH HIM?!
WHAT HAPPENED TO MAKE HIM SO TWISTED...AND OBNOXIOUS?!

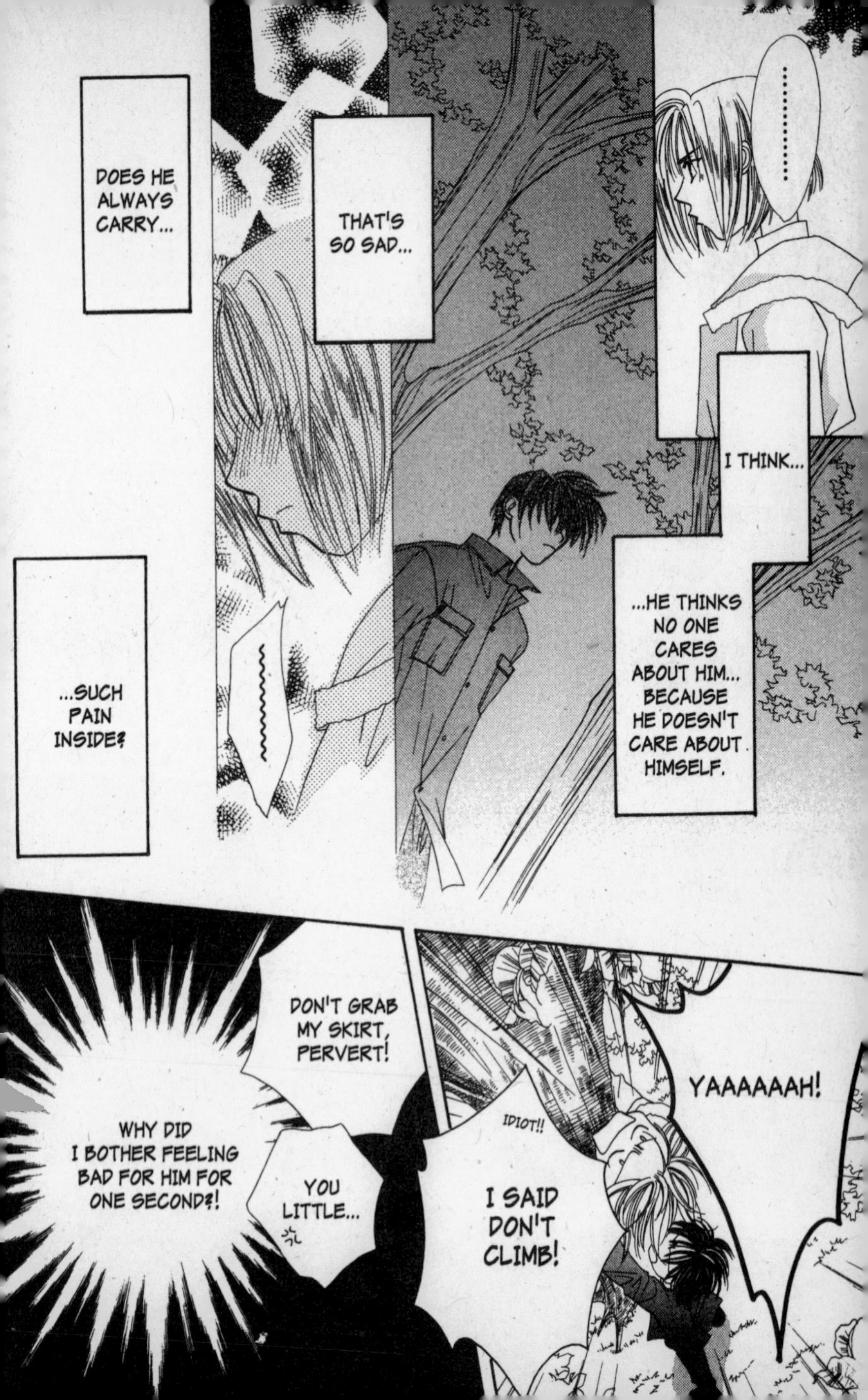
......
I THINK...
...HE THINKS NO ONE CARES ABOUT HIM... BECAUSE HE DOESN'T CARE ABOUT HIMSELF.
THAT'S SO SAD...
DOES HE ALWAYS CARRY...
...SUCH PAIN INSIDE?
YAAAAAAH!
IDIOT!!
I SAID DON'T CLIMB!
DON'T GRAB MY SKIRT, PERVERT!
YOU LITTLE...
WHY DID I BOTHER FEELING BAD FOR HIM FOR ONE SECOND?!

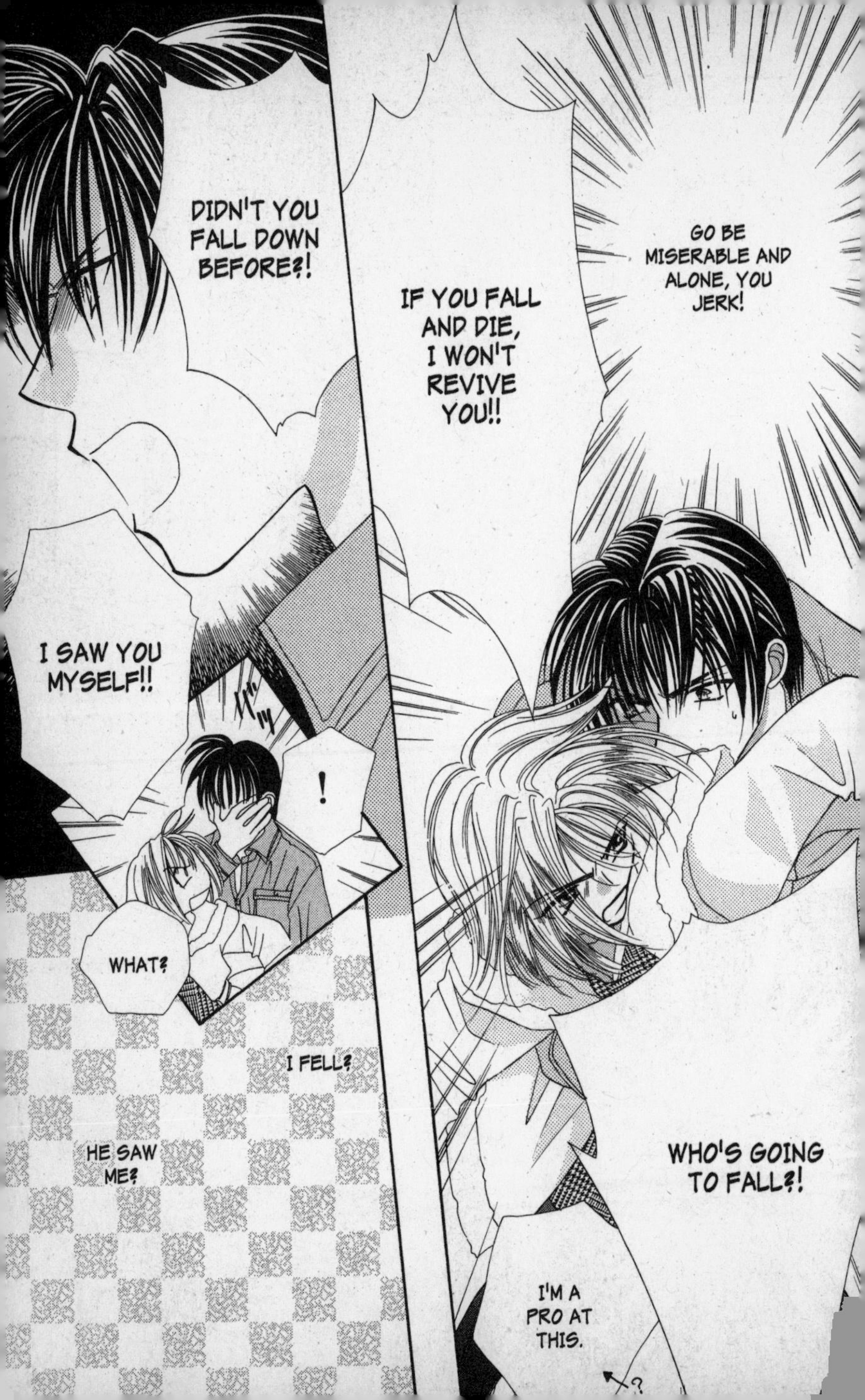
GO BE MISERABLE AND ALONE, YOU JERK!
IF YOU FALL AND DIE, I WON'T REVIVE YOU!!
WHO'S GOING TO FALL?!
I'M A PRO AT THIS.
?
DIDN'T YOU FALL DOWN BEFORE?!
I SAW YOU MYSELF!!
!
WHAT?
I FELL?
HE SAW ME?

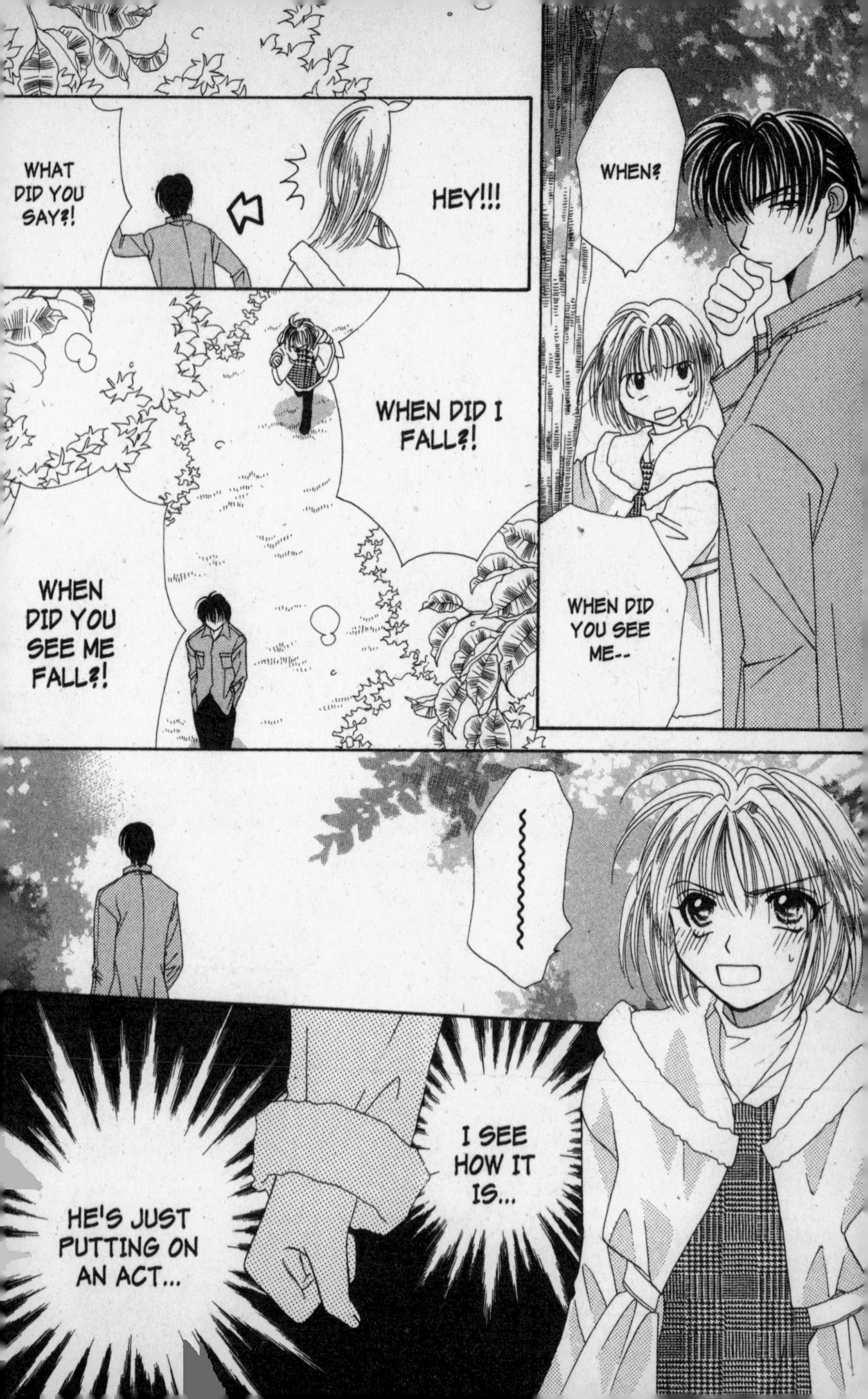
WHEN?
WHEN DID YOU SEE ME--
HEY!!!
WHAT DID YOU SAY?!
WHEN DID I FALL?!
WHEN DID YOU SEE ME FALL?!
I SEE HOW IT IS...
HE'S JUST PUTTING ON AN ACT...

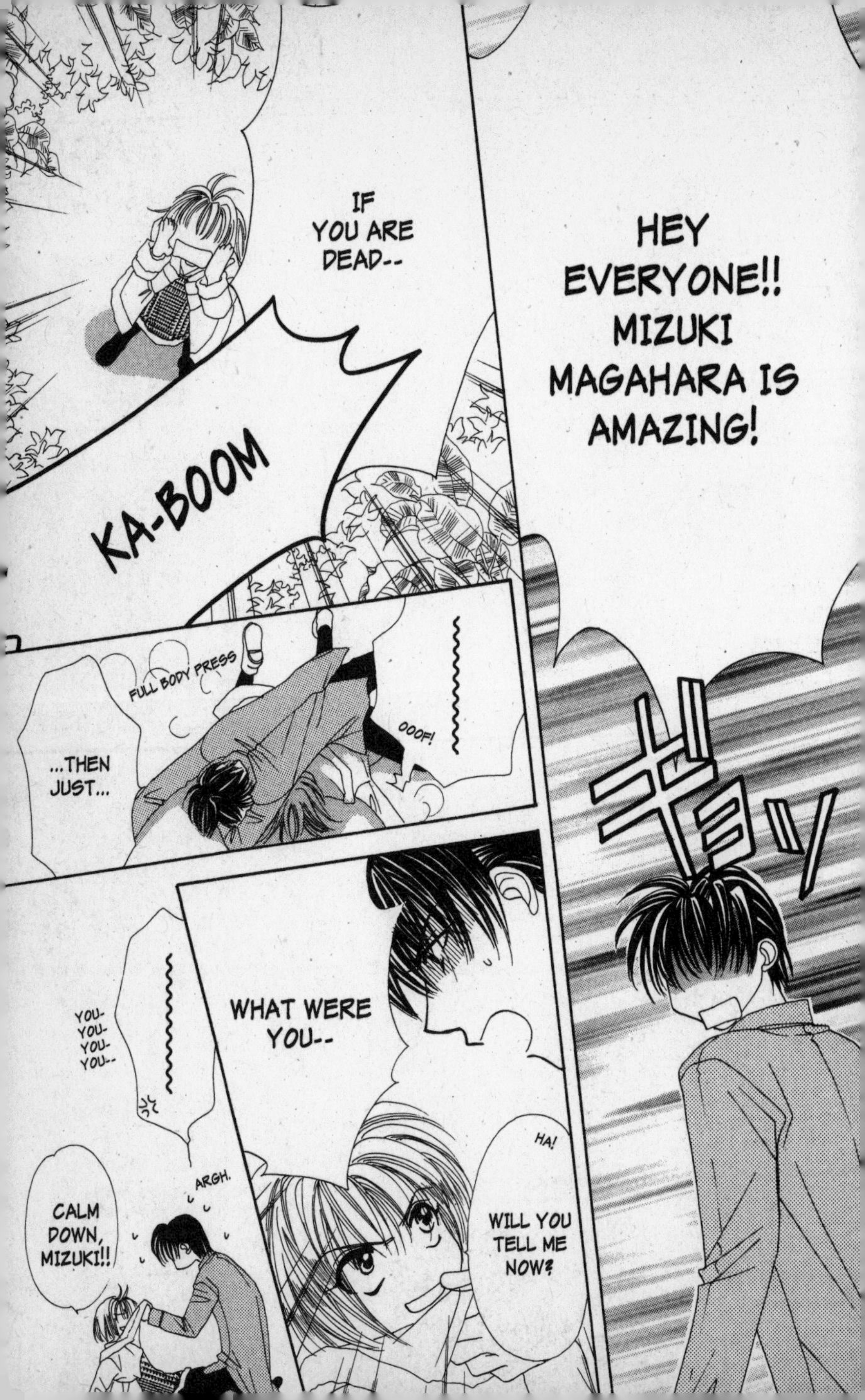
HEY EVERYONE!! MIZUKI MAGAHARA IS AMAZING!
ギョッ
IF YOU ARE DEAD--
KA-BOOM
OOOF!
FULL BODY PRESS
...THEN JUST...
WHAT WERE YOU--
YOU-YOU-YOU-YOU--
HA!
WILL YOU TELL ME NOW?
ARGH.
CALM DOWN, MIZUKI!!

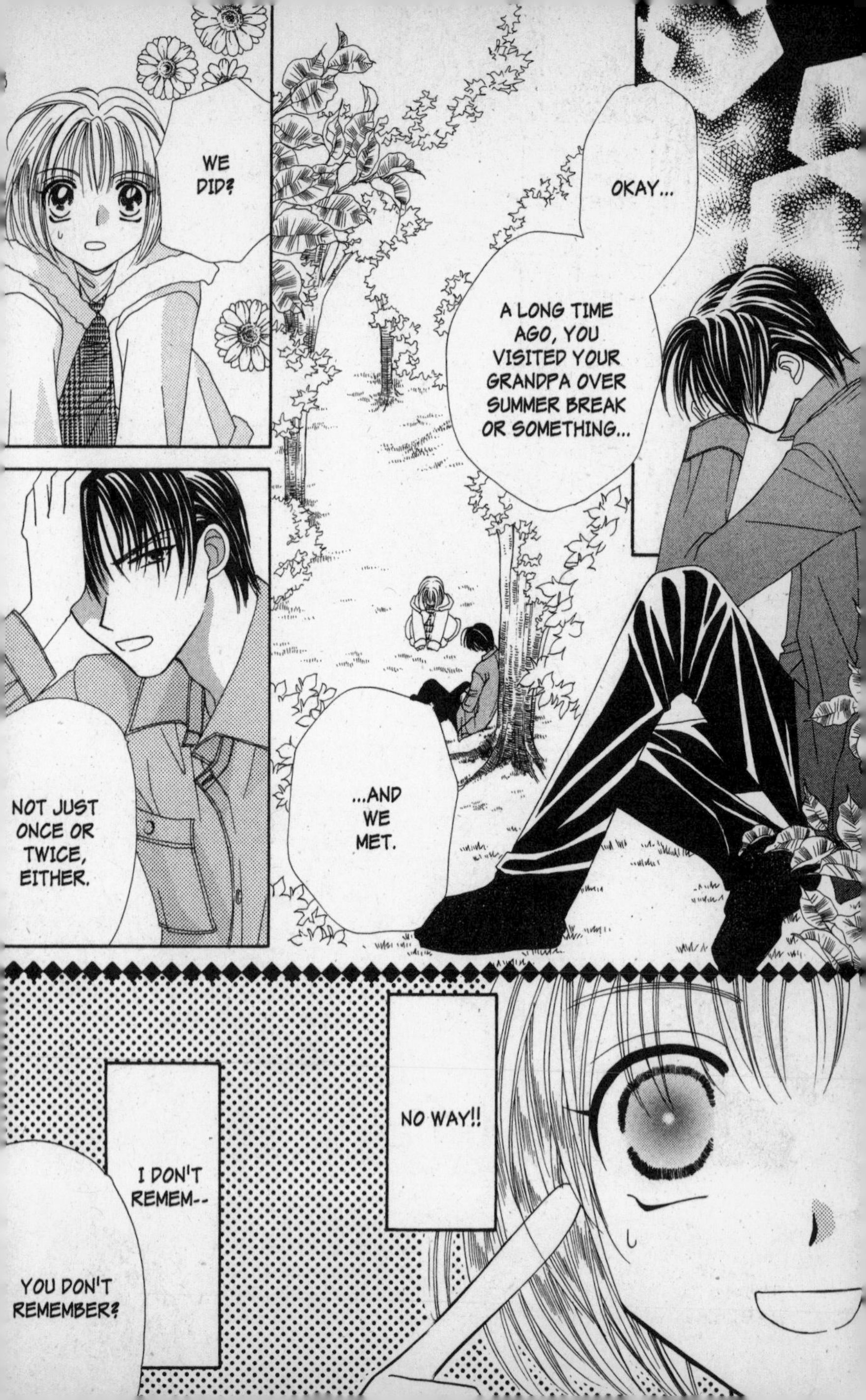
OKAY...
A LONG TIME AGO, YOU VISITED YOUR GRANDPA OVER SUMMER BREAK OR SOMETHING...
...AND WE MET.
WE DID?
NOT JUST ONCE OR TWICE, EITHER.
NO WAY!!
I DON'T REMEM--
YOU DON'T REMEMBER?

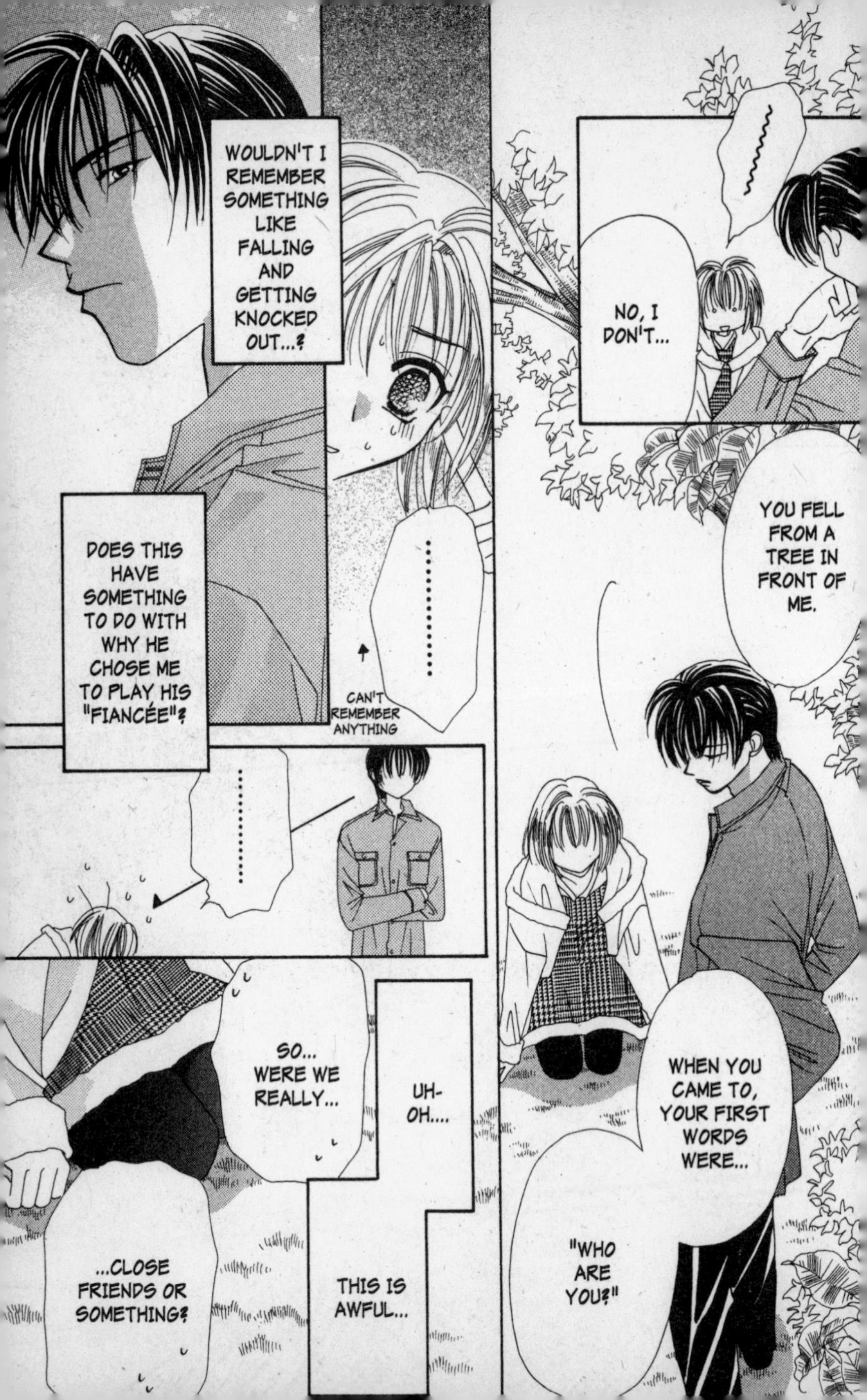
NO, I DON'T...
YOU FELL FROM A TREE IN FRONT OF ME.
WHEN YOU CAME TO, YOUR FIRST WORDS WERE...
"WHO ARE YOU?"
WOULDN'T I REMEMBER SOMETHING LIKE FALLING AND GETTING KNOCKED OUT...?
....
CAN'T REMEMBER ANYTHING
DOES THIS HAVE SOMETHING TO DO WITH WHY HE CHOSE ME TO PLAY HIS "FIANCÉE"?
....
UH-OH....
THIS IS AWFUL...
SO... WERE WE REALLY...
...CLOSE FRIENDS OR SOMETHING?

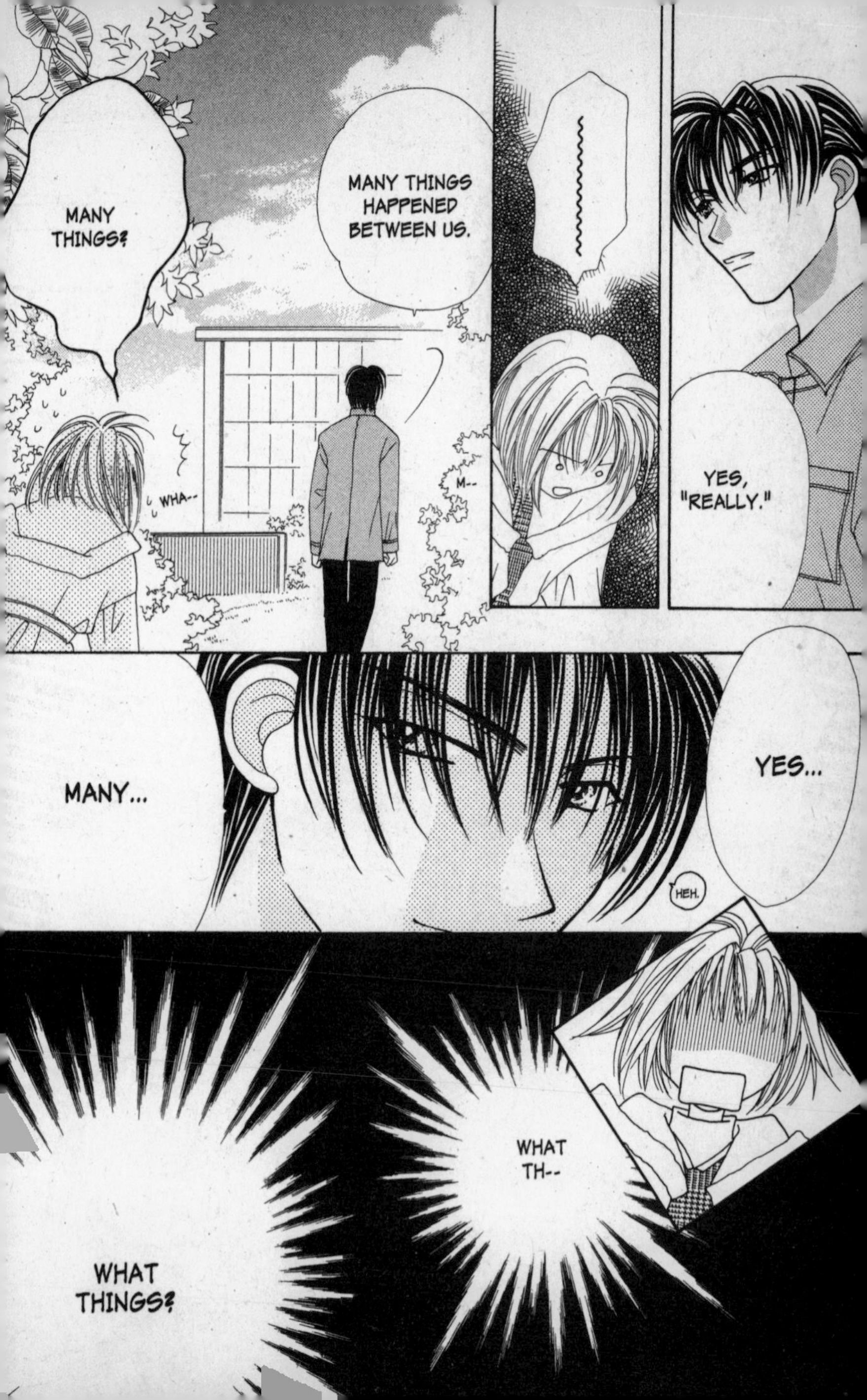
YES, "REALLY."
MANY THINGS HAPPENED BETWEEN US.
MANY THINGS?
M--
WHA--
YES...
HEH.
MANY...
WHAT TH--
WHAT THINGS?

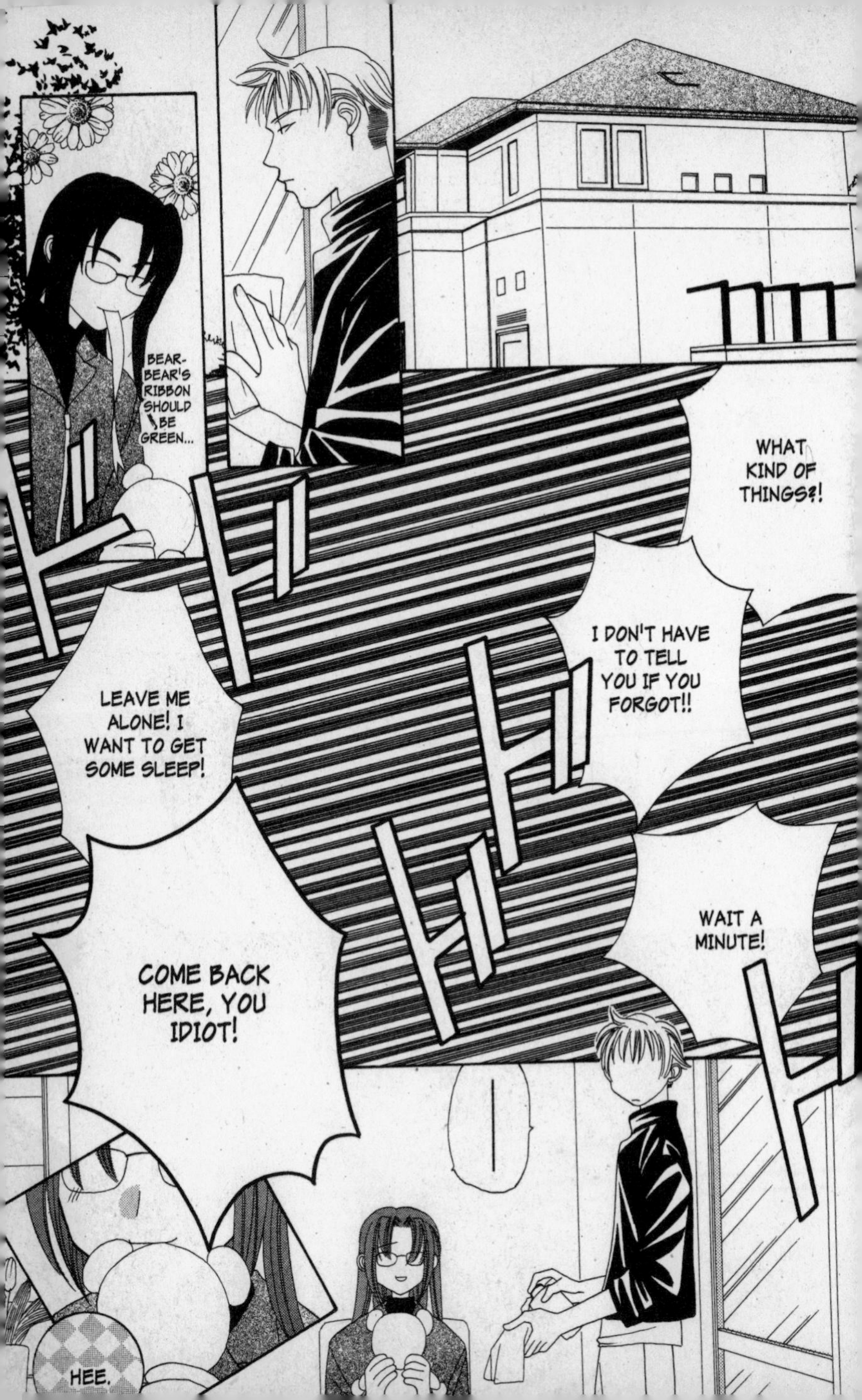
BEAR-BEAR'S RIBBON SHOULD BE GREEN...
WHAT KIND OF THINGS?!
I DON'T HAVE TO TELL YOU IF YOU FORGOT!!
LEAVE ME ALONE! I WANT TO GET SOME SLEEP!
WAIT A MINUTE!
COME BACK HERE, YOU IDIOT!
HEE.

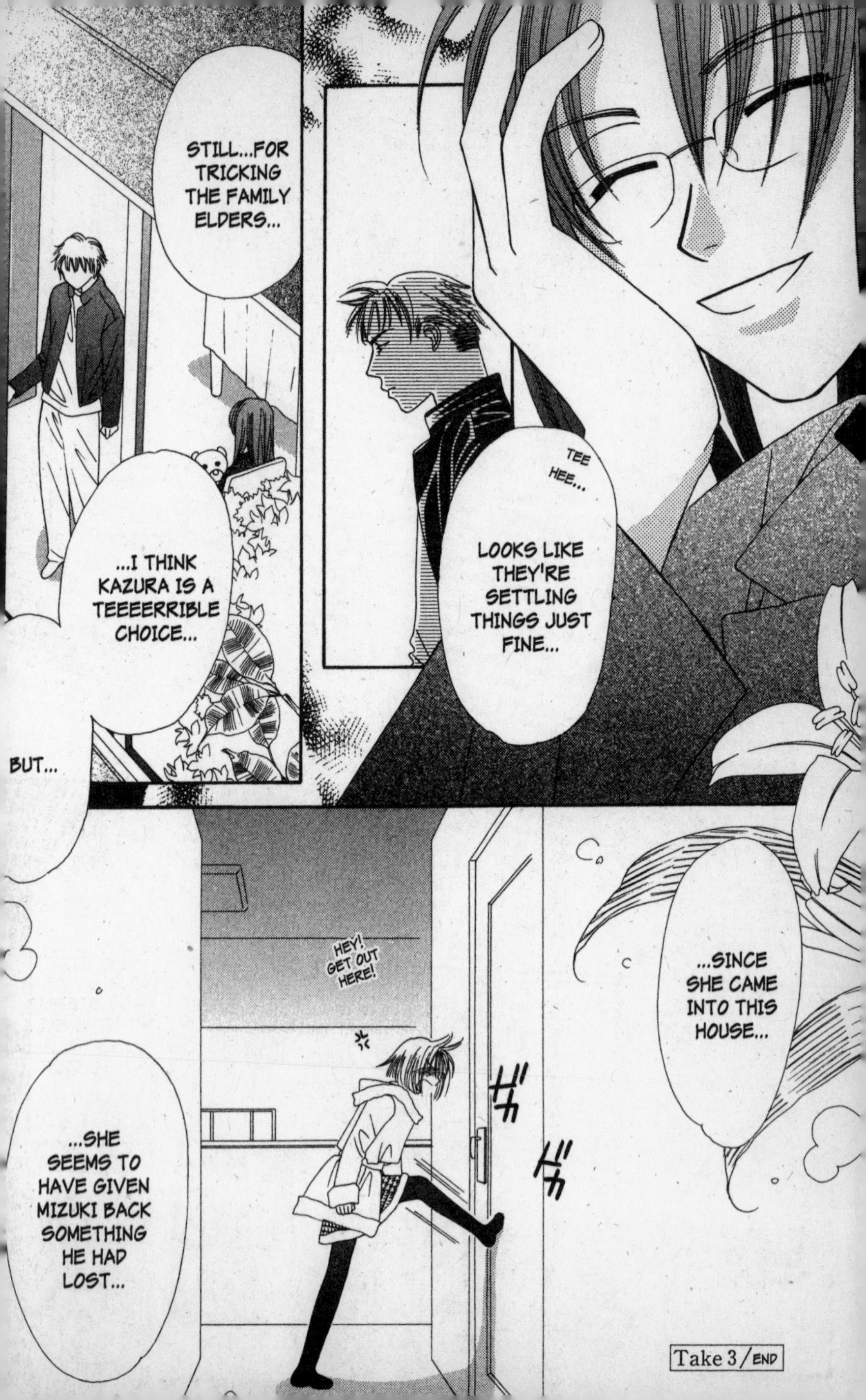
TEE HEE...
LOOKS LIKE THEY'RE SETTLING THINGS JUST FINE...
STILL...FOR TRICKING THE FAMILY ELDERS...
...I THINK KAZURA IS A TEEEERRIBLE CHOICE...
BUT...
...SINCE SHE CAME INTO THIS HOUSE...
HEY! GET OUT HERE!
...SHE SEEMS TO HAVE GIVEN MIZUKI BACK SOMETHING HE HAD LOST...
Take 3/END

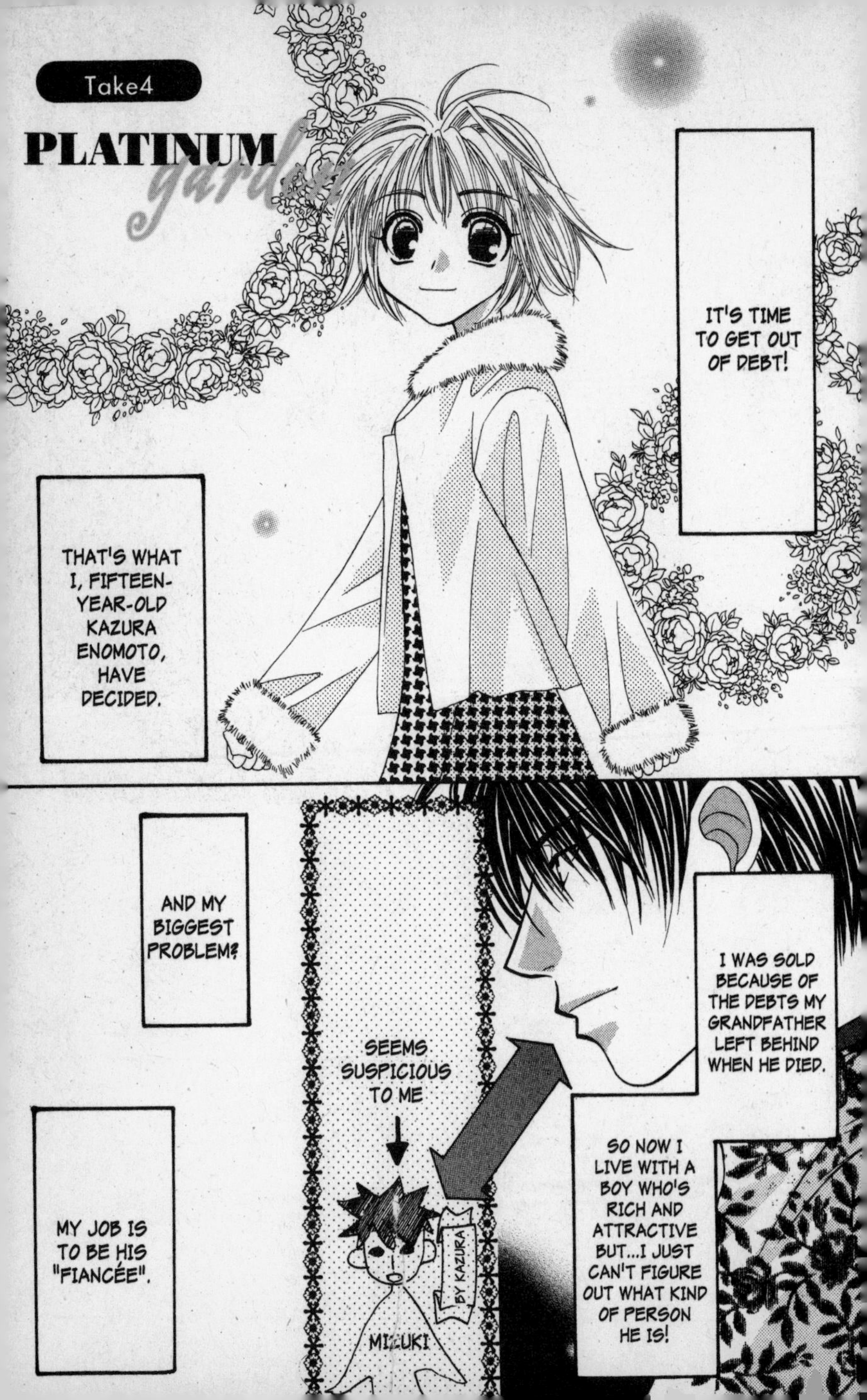
Take4
PLATINUM garden
IT'S TIME TO GET OUT OF DEBT!
THAT'S WHAT I, FIFTEEN-YEAR-OLD KAZURA ENOMOTO, HAVE DECIDED.
I WAS SOLD BECAUSE OF THE DEBTS MY GRANDFATHER LEFT BEHIND WHEN HE DIED.
SO NOW I LIVE WITH A BOY WHO'S RICH AND ATTRACTIVE BUT...I JUST CAN'T FIGURE OUT WHAT KIND OF PERSON HE IS!
MY JOB IS TO BE HIS "FIANCÉE".
AND MY BIGGEST PROBLEM?
SEEMS SUSPICIOUS TO ME
BY KAZURA

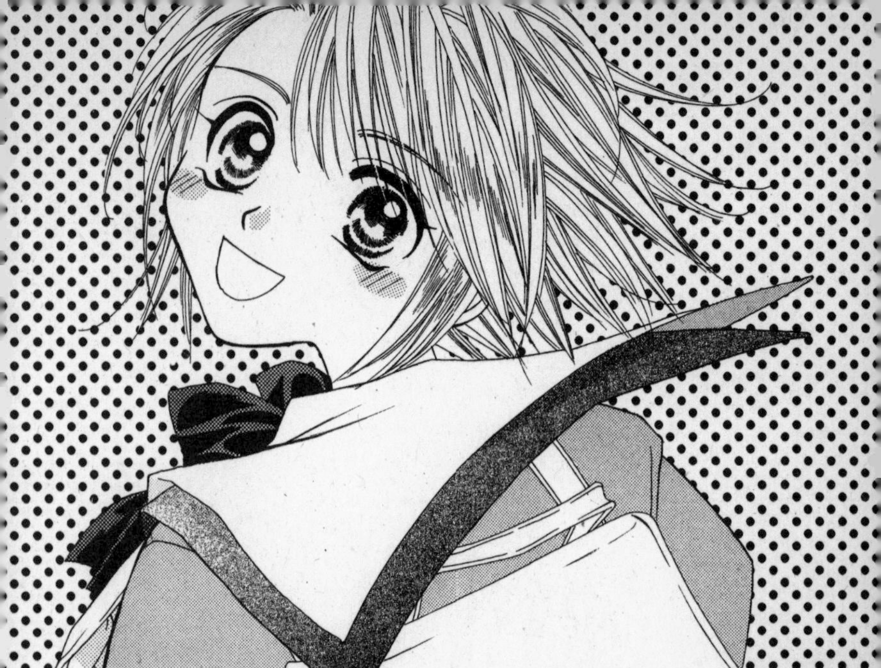
PLATINUM garden
Take4

FUJITA'S WINTER, 2001

SAY GOODBYE TO BOO-CHAN, WHO PASSED AWAY A WHILE AGO.

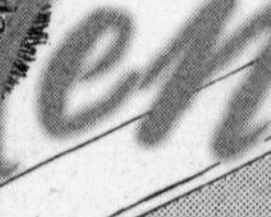

WHILE I WAS DRAWING THIS CHAPTER'S CONFLICT SCENE, YUKI 13 DIED. SHE WAS A CUTE, OLD HAMSTER.

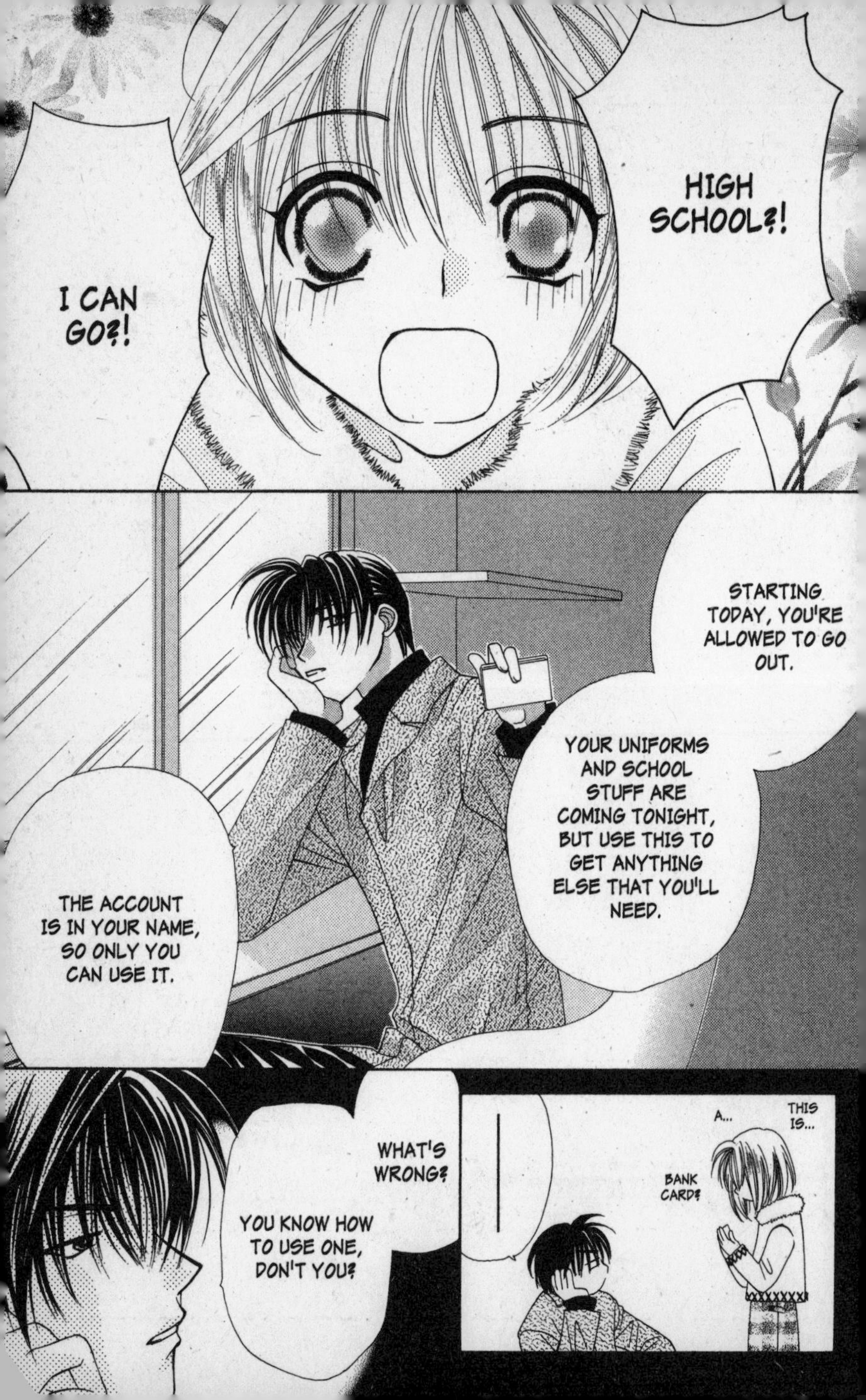

HIGH SCHOOL?!
I CAN GO?!
STARTING TODAY, YOU'RE ALLOWED TO GO OUT.
YOUR UNIFORMS AND SCHOOL STUFF ARE COMING TONIGHT, BUT USE THIS TO GET ANYTHING ELSE THAT YOU'LL NEED.
THE ACCOUNT IS IN YOUR NAME, SO ONLY YOU CAN USE IT.
THIS IS...
A...
BANK CARD?
WHAT'S WRONG?
YOU KNOW HOW TO USE ONE, DON'T YOU?

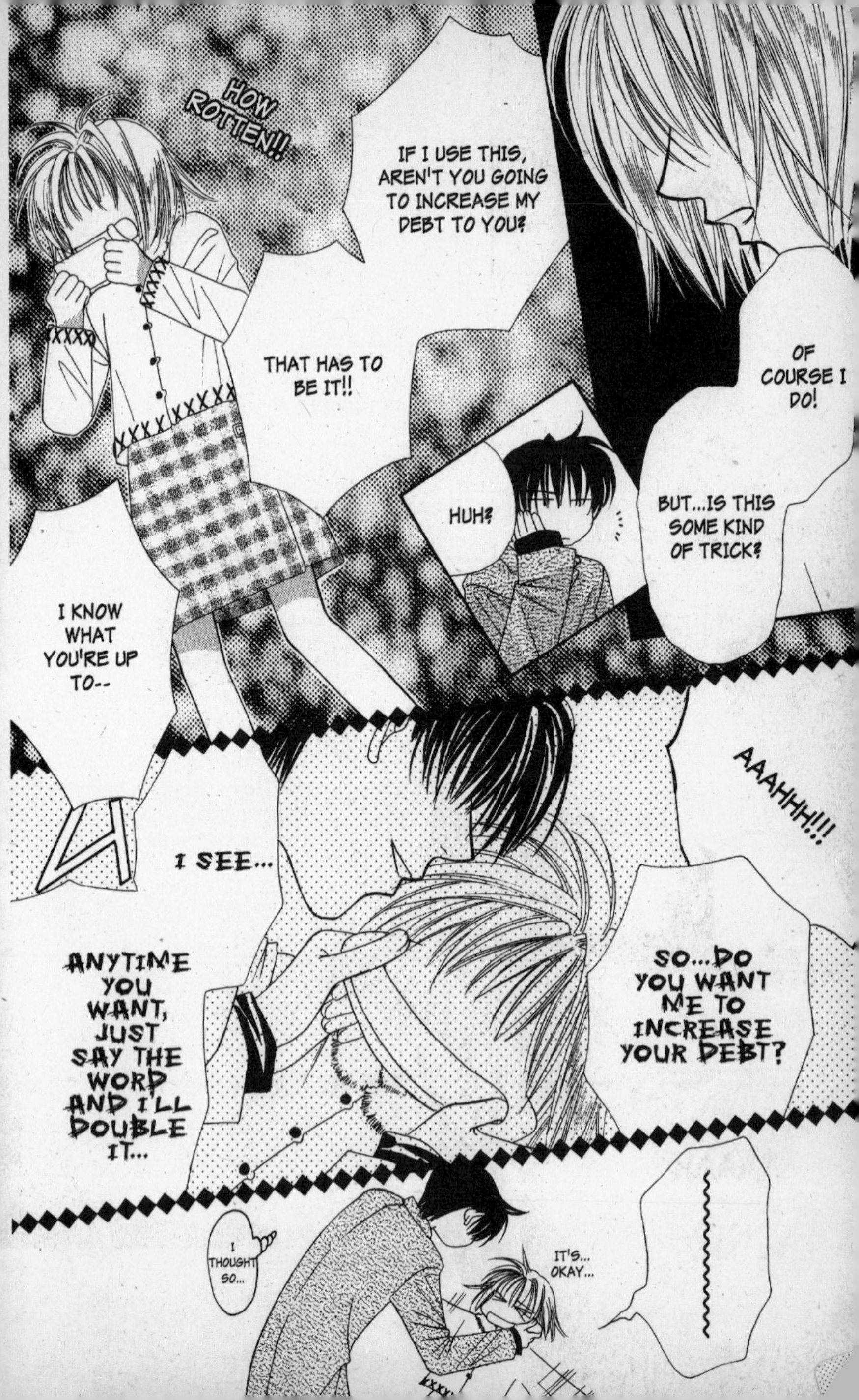
OF COURSE I DO!
BUT...IS THIS SOME KIND OF TRICK?
HUH?
IF I USE THIS, AREN'T YOU GOING TO INCREASE MY DEBT TO YOU?
HOW ROTTEN!!
THAT HAS TO BE IT!!
I KNOW WHAT YOU'RE UP TO--
AAAHHH!!!
SO...DO YOU WANT ME TO INCREASE YOUR DEBT?
I SEE...
ANYTIME YOU WANT, JUST SAY THE WORD AND I'LL DOUBLE IT...
IT'S... OKAY...
I THOUGHT SO...

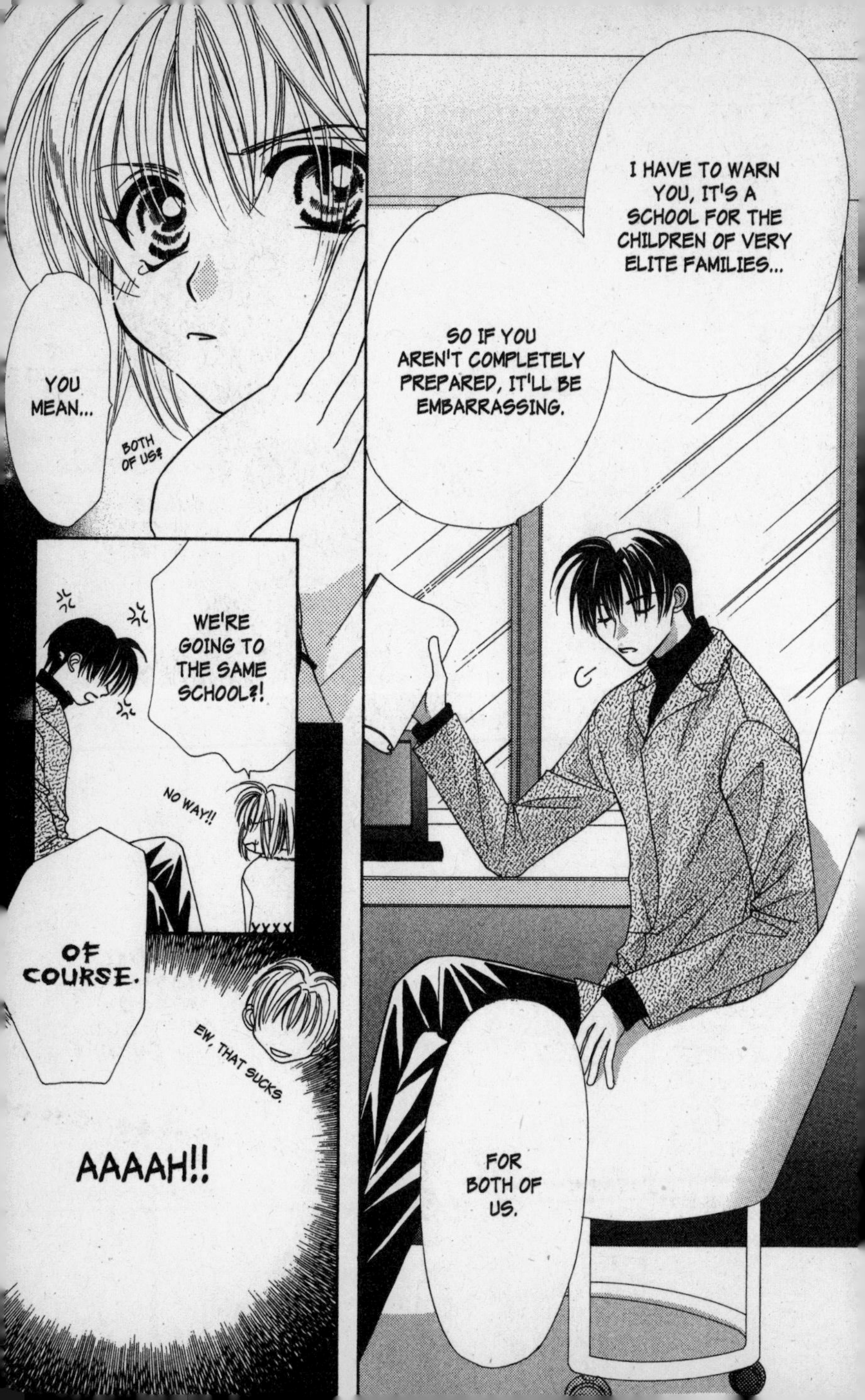
I HAVE TO WARN YOU, IT'S A SCHOOL FOR THE CHILDREN OF VERY ELITE FAMILIES...
SO IF YOU AREN'T COMPLETELY PREPARED, IT'LL BE EMBARRASSING.
FOR BOTH OF US.
YOU MEAN...
BOTH OF US?
WE'RE GOING TO THE SAME SCHOOL?!
NO WAY!!
OF COURSE.
EW, THAT SUCKS.
AAAAH!!

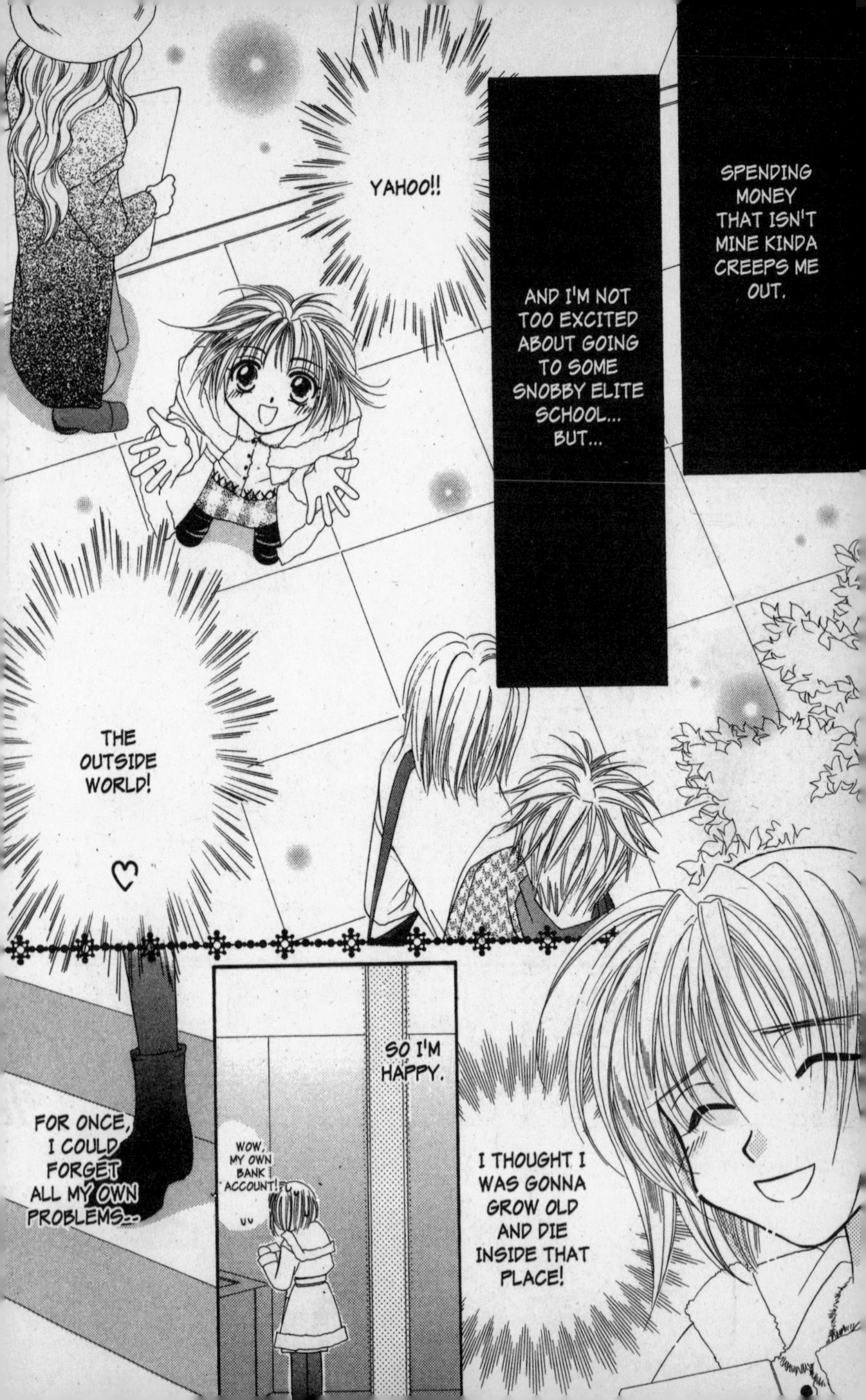
SPENDING MONEY THAT ISN'T MINE KINDA CREEPS ME OUT.
AND I'M NOT TOO EXCITED ABOUT GOING TO SOME SNOBBY ELITE SCHOOL... BUT...
YAHOO!!
THE OUTSIDE WORLD! ♡
I THOUGHT I WAS GONNA GROW OLD AND DIE INSIDE THAT PLACE!
SO I'M HAPPY.
WOW, MY OWN BANK ACCOUNT!
FOR ONCE, I COULD FORGET ALL MY OWN PROBLEMS...

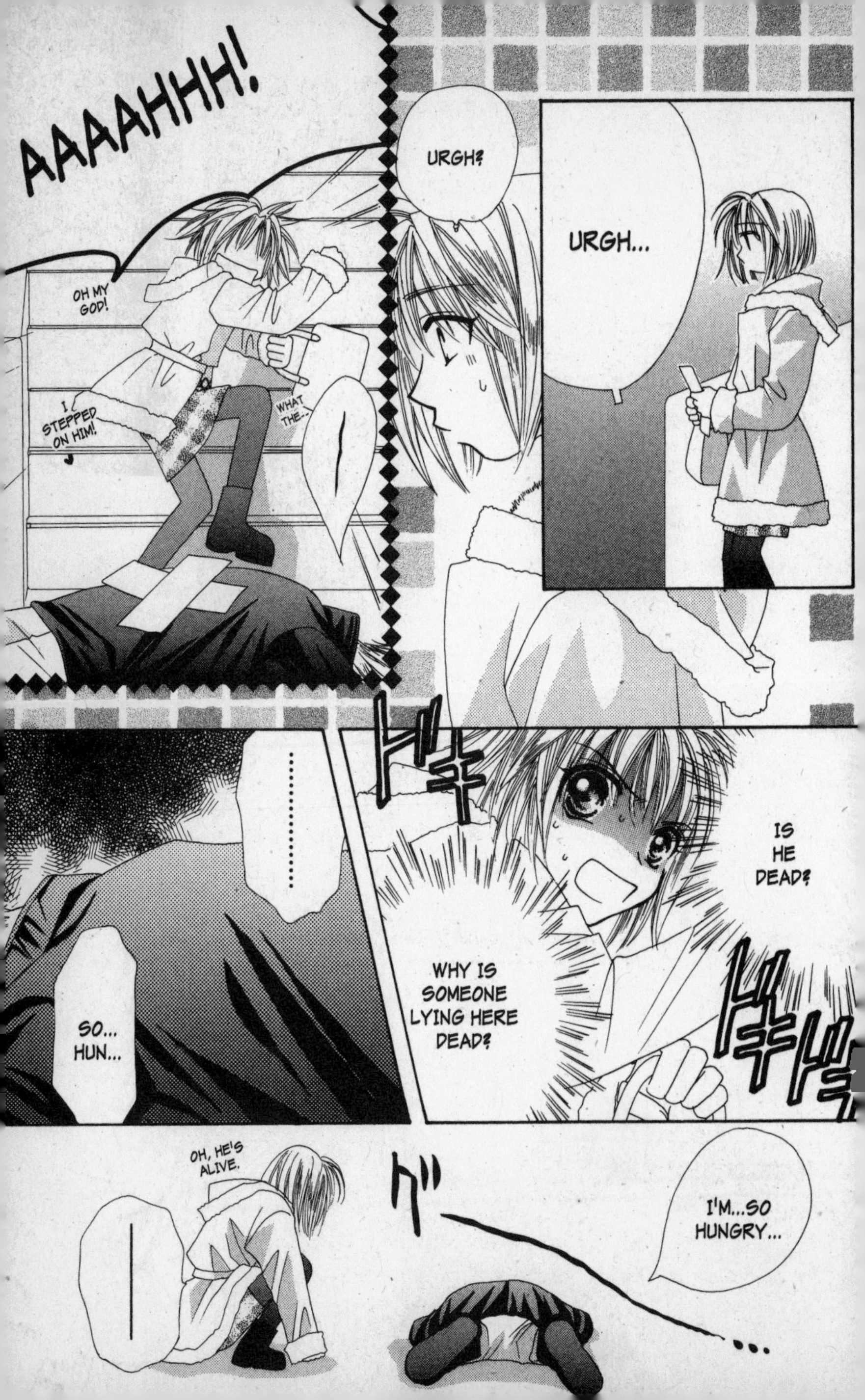
URGH...
URGH?
AAAAHHH!
OH MY GOD!
WHAT THE...
I STEPPED ON HIM!
IS HE DEAD?
WHY IS SOMEONE LYING HERE DEAD?
......
SO... HUN...
I'M...SO HUNGRY...
OH, HE'S ALIVE.
—

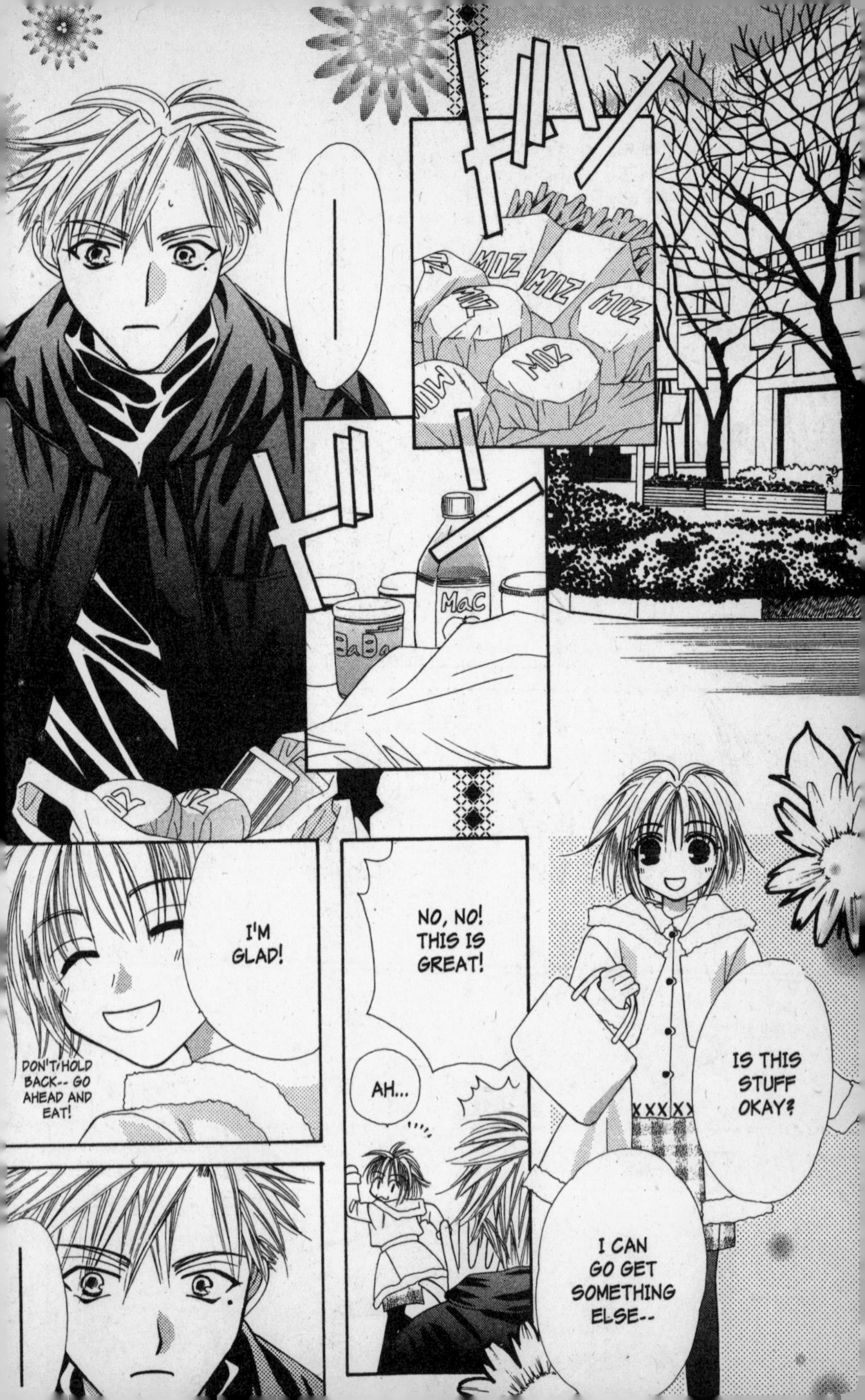
IS THIS STUFF OKAY?
I CAN GO GET SOMETHING ELSE--
NO, NO! THIS IS GREAT!
AH...
I'M GLAD!
DON'T HOLD BACK-- GO AHEAD AND EAT!

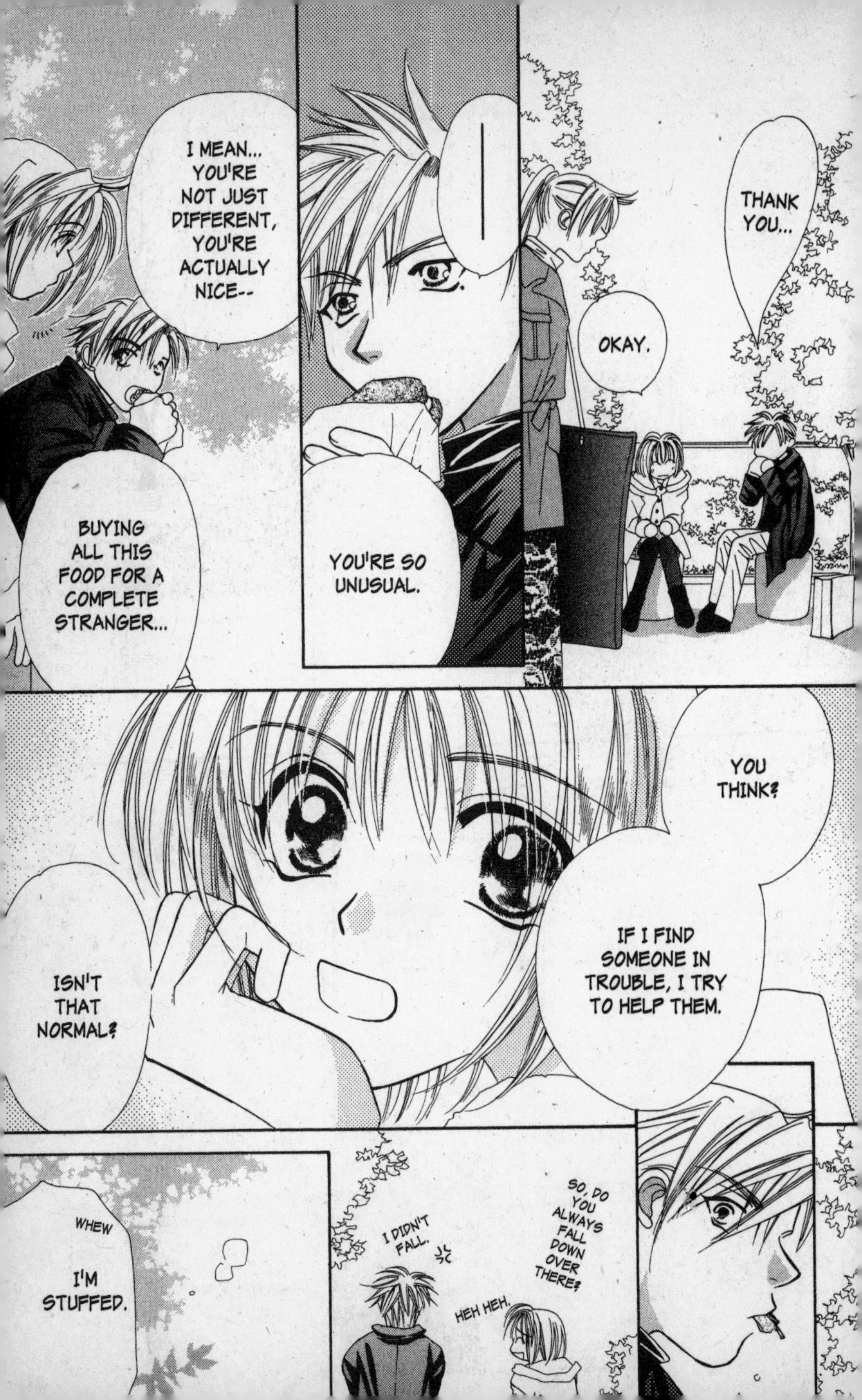
THANK YOU...
OKAY.
—
YOU'RE SO UNUSUAL.
I MEAN... YOU'RE NOT JUST DIFFERENT, YOU'RE ACTUALLY NICE--
BUYING ALL THIS FOOD FOR A COMPLETE STRANGER...
YOU THINK?
IF I FIND SOMEONE IN TROUBLE, I TRY TO HELP THEM.
ISN'T THAT NORMAL?
SO, DO YOU ALWAYS FALL DOWN OVER THERE?
I DIDN'T FALL.
HEH HEH.
WHEW
I'M STUFFED.

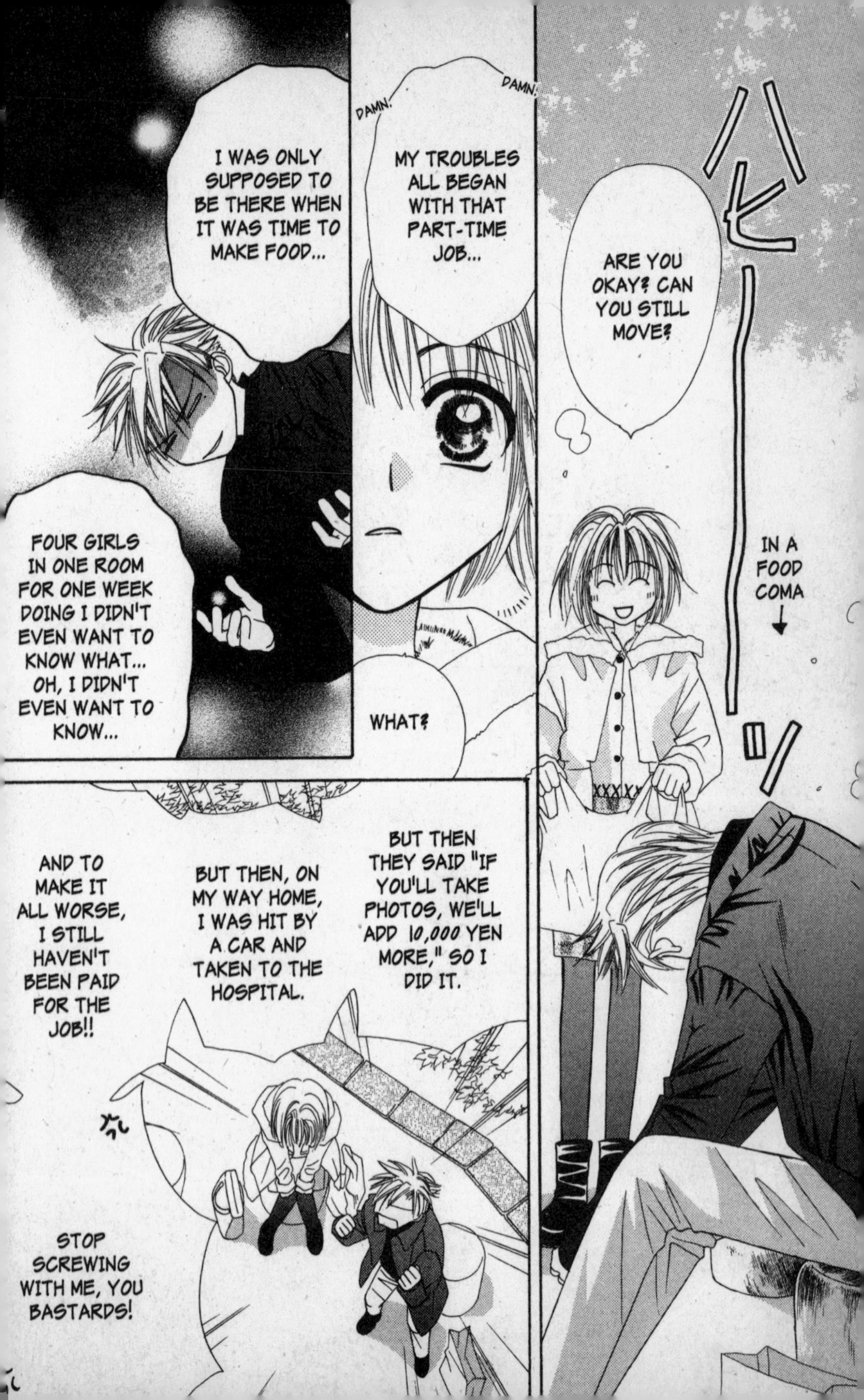
ハヒー
ARE YOU OKAY? CAN YOU STILL MOVE?
IN A FOOD COMA
DAMN. DAMN.
MY TROUBLES ALL BEGAN WITH THAT PART-TIME JOB...
WHAT?
I WAS ONLY SUPPOSED TO BE THERE WHEN IT WAS TIME TO MAKE FOOD...
FOUR GIRLS IN ONE ROOM FOR ONE WEEK DOING I DIDN'T EVEN WANT TO KNOW WHAT... OH, I DIDN'T EVEN WANT TO KNOW...
BUT THEN THEY SAID "IF YOU'LL TAKE PHOTOS, WE'LL ADD 10,000 YEN MORE," SO I DID IT.
BUT THEN, ON MY WAY HOME, I WAS HIT BY A CAR AND TAKEN TO THE HOSPITAL.
AND TO MAKE IT ALL WORSE, I STILL HAVEN'T BEEN PAID FOR THE JOB!!
STOP SCREWING WITH ME, YOU BASTARDS!

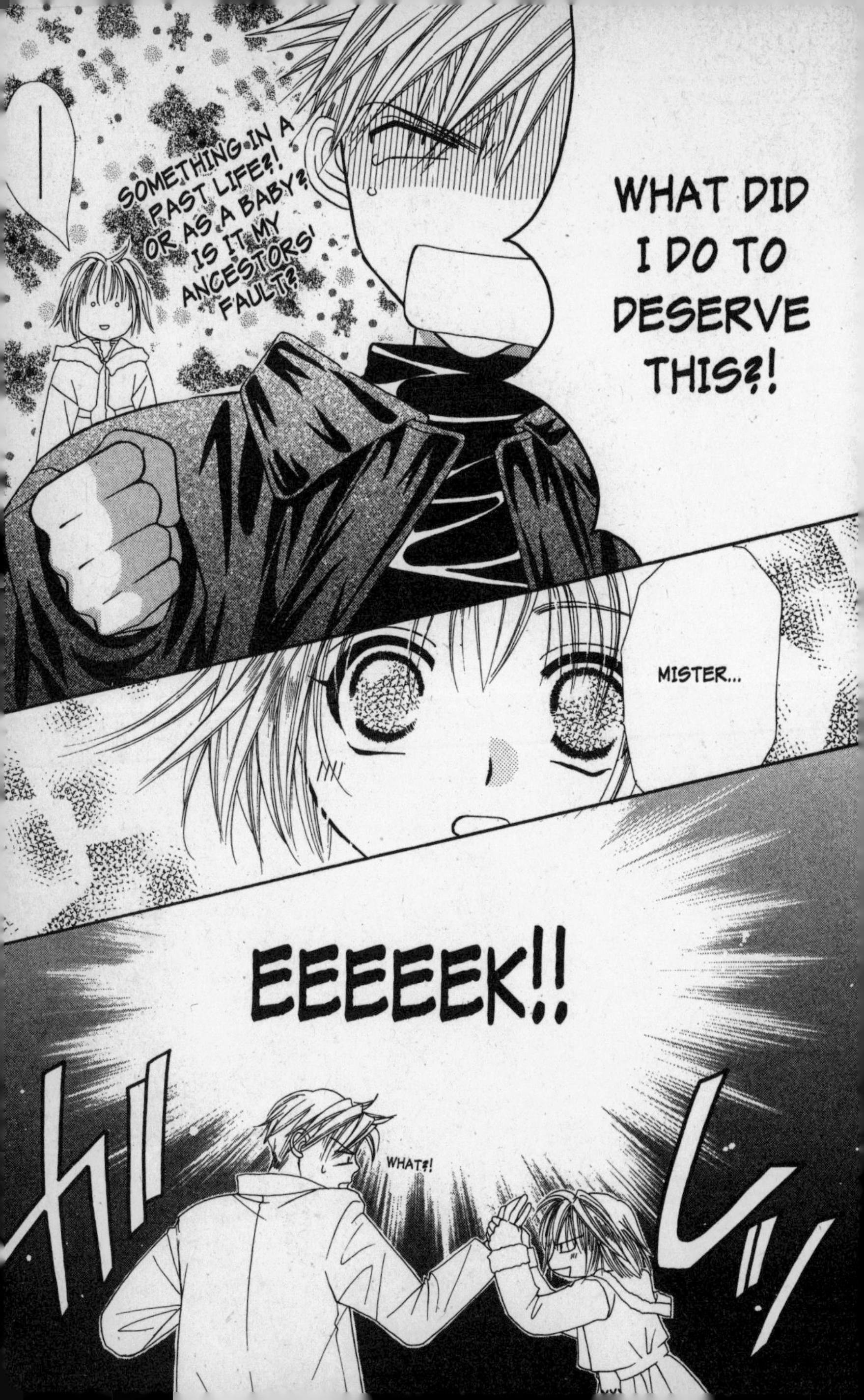
WHAT DID I DO TO DESERVE THIS?!
SOMETHING IN A PAST LIFE?! OR AS A BABY? IS IT MY ANCESTORS' FAULT?
!
MISTER...
EEEEEK!!
WHAT?!

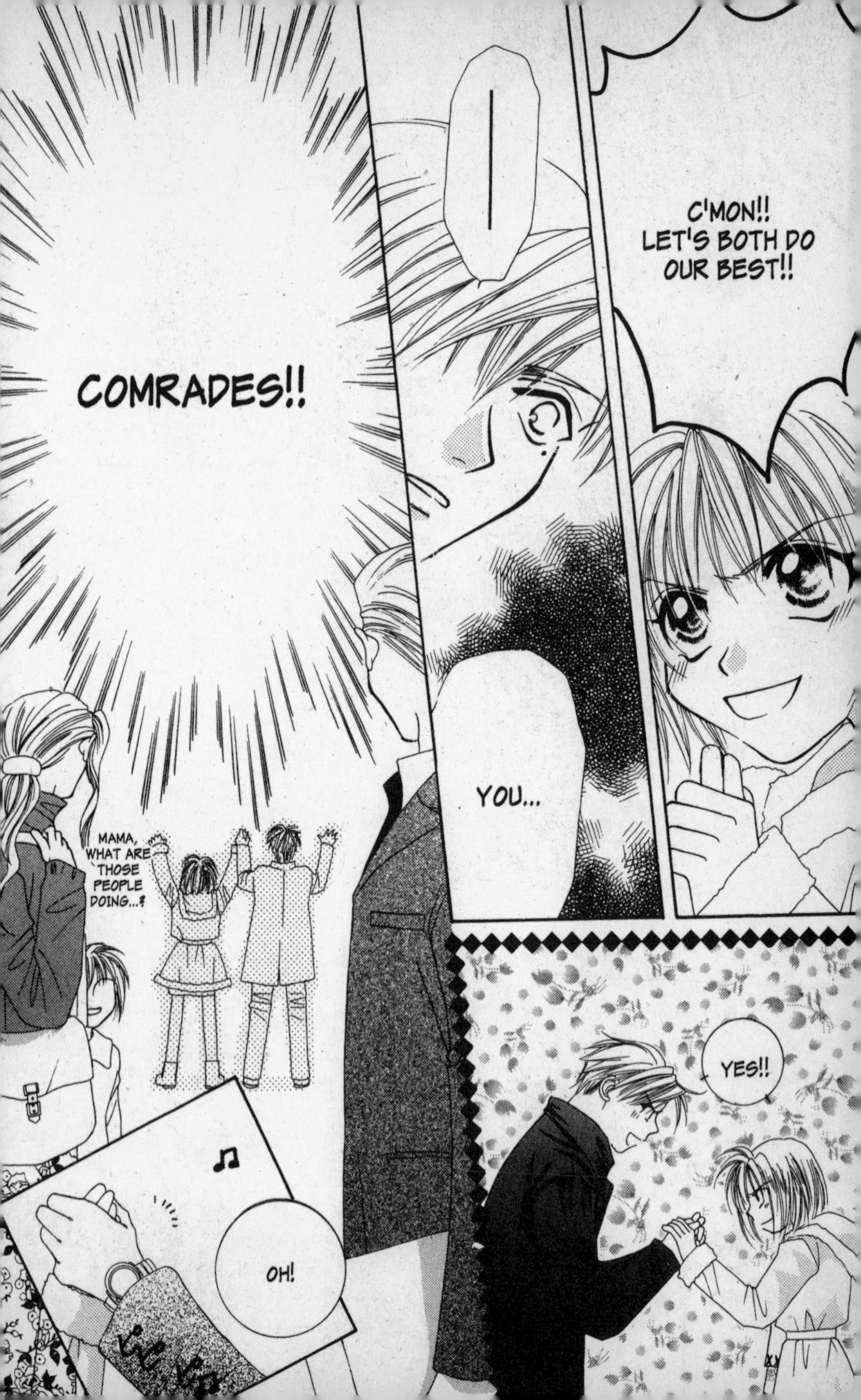
C'MON!! LET'S BOTH DO OUR BEST!!
!
YOU...
COMRADES!!
MAMA, WHAT ARE THOSE PEOPLE DOING...?
YES!!
OH!

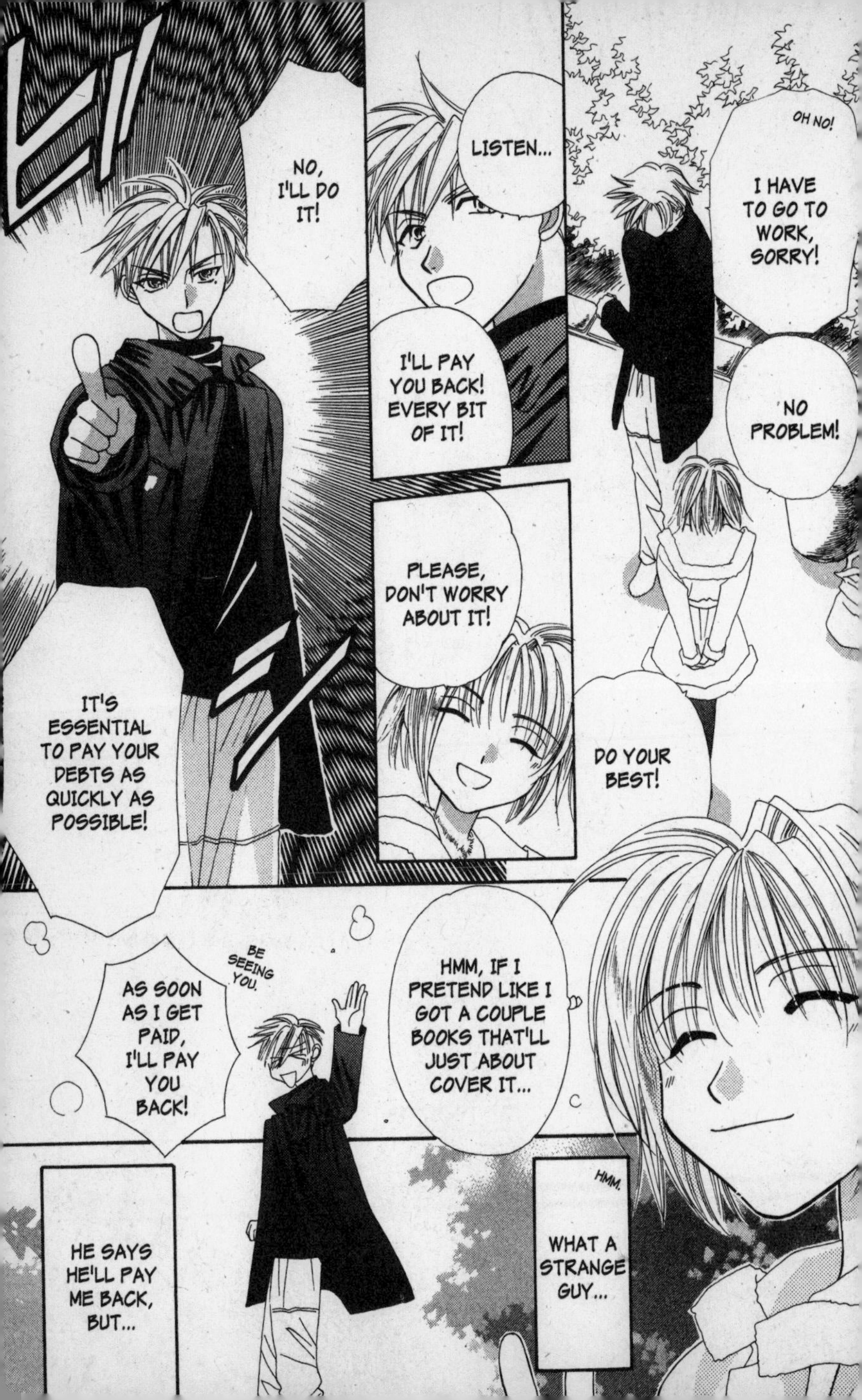
OH NO!
I HAVE TO GO TO WORK, SORRY!
NO PROBLEM!
DO YOUR BEST!
LISTEN...
I'LL PAY YOU BACK! EVERY BIT OF IT!
PLEASE, DON'T WORRY ABOUT IT!
NO, I'LL DO IT!
IT'S ESSENTIAL TO PAY YOUR DEBTS AS QUICKLY AS POSSIBLE!
HMM, IF I PRETEND LIKE I GOT A COUPLE BOOKS THAT'LL JUST ABOUT COVER IT...
HMM.
WHAT A STRANGE GUY...
BE SEEING YOU.
AS SOON AS I GET PAID, I'LL PAY YOU BACK!
HE SAYS HE'LL PAY ME BACK, BUT...

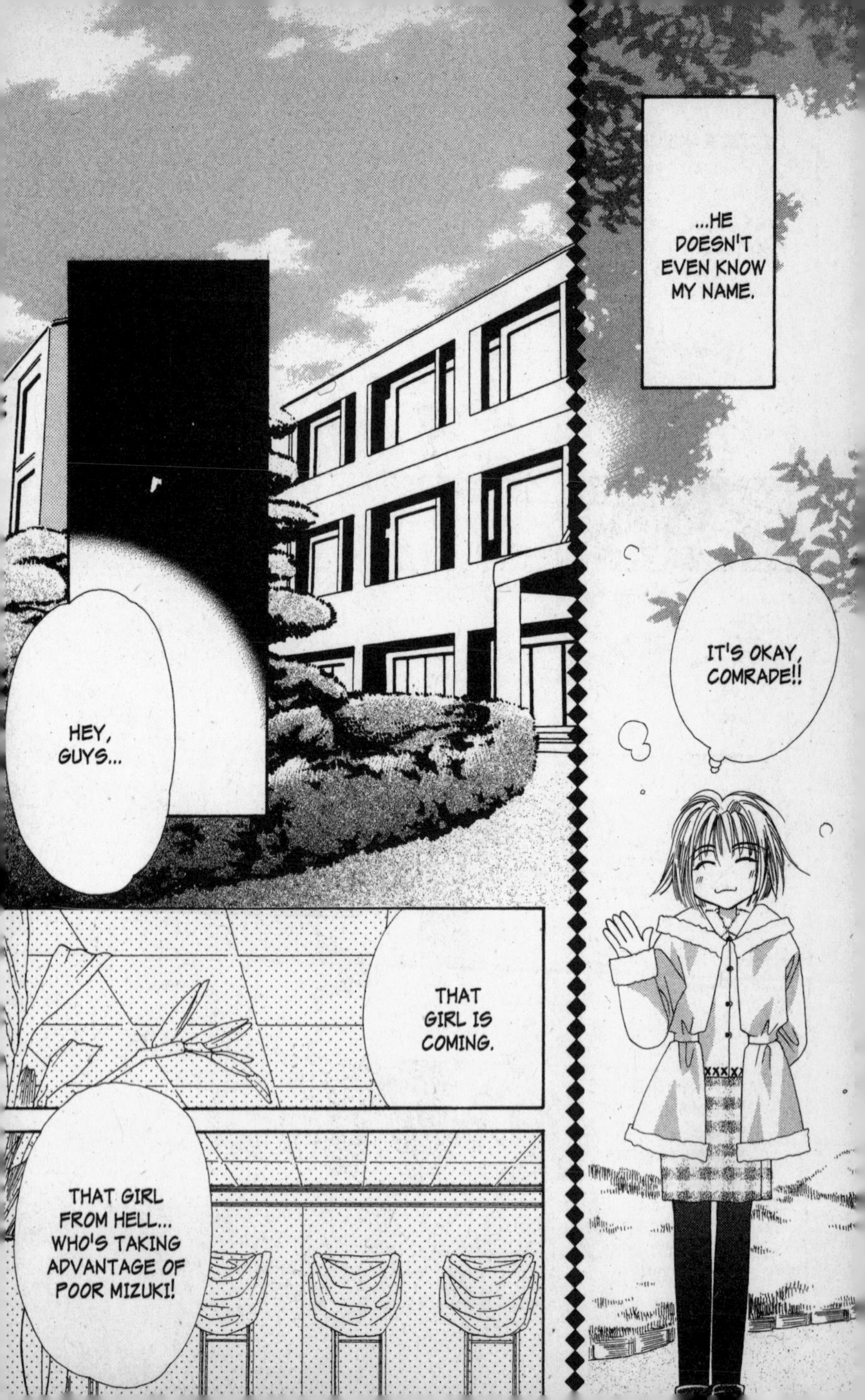
...HE DOESN'T EVEN KNOW MY NAME.
IT'S OKAY, COMRADE!!
HEY, GUYS...
THAT GIRL IS COMING.
THAT GIRL FROM HELL... WHO'S TAKING ADVANTAGE OF POOR MIZUKI!

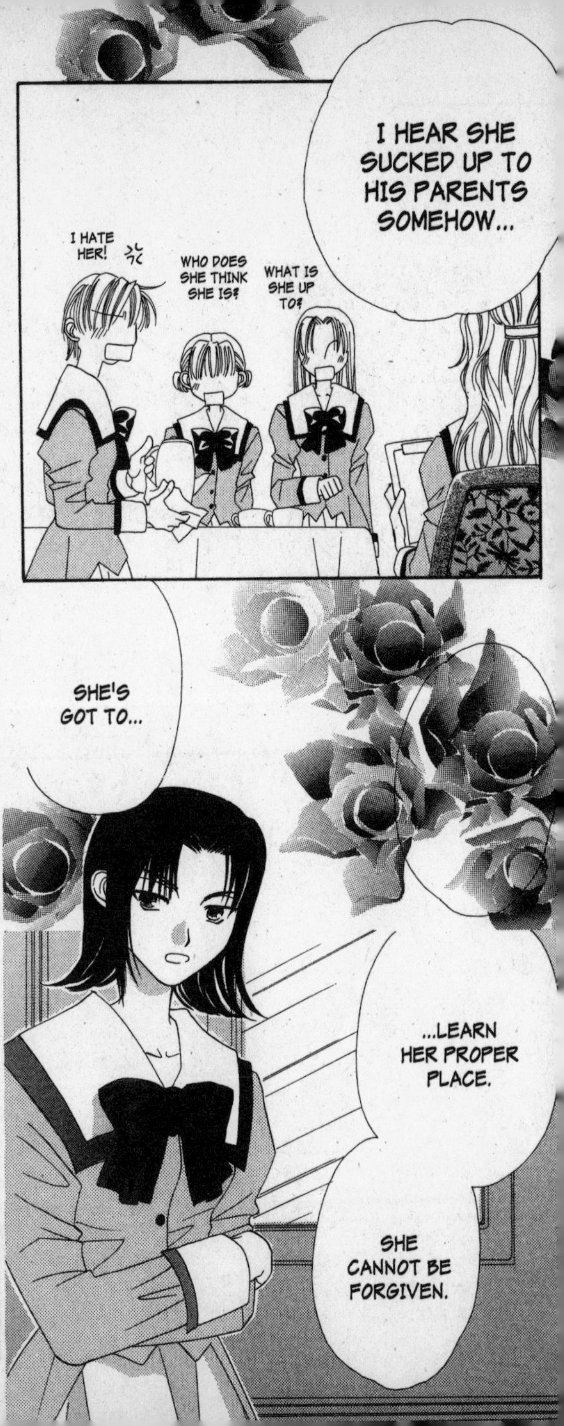
I HEAR SHE SUCKED UP TO HIS PARENTS SOMEHOW...
WHAT IS SHE UP TO?
WHO DOES SHE THINK SHE IS?
I HATE HER!
SHE'S GOT TO...
...LEARN HER PROPER PLACE.
SHE CANNOT BE FORGIVEN.

IDIOTIC RAMBLINGS IV

THE GREAT UNIFORM UNPOPULARITY INCIDENT (HAHA)

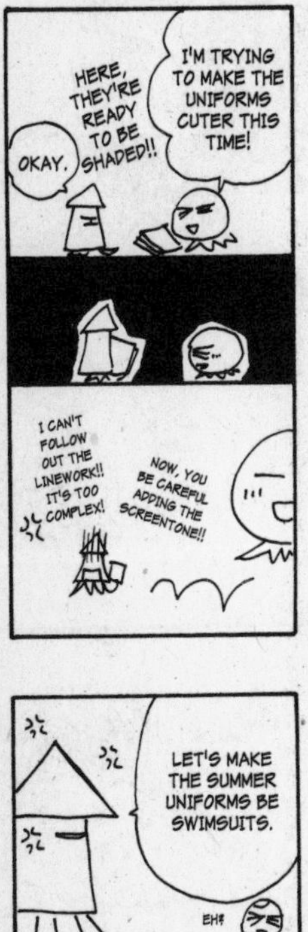
I'M TRYING TO MAKE THE UNIFORMS CUTER THIS TIME!
HERE, THEY'RE READY TO BE SHADED!!
OKAY.
NOW, YOU BE CAREFUL ADDING THE SCREENTONE!!
I CAN'T FOLLOW OUT THE LINEWORK!! IT'S TOO COMPLEX!
LET'S MAKE THE SUMMER UNIFORMS BE SWIMSUITS.
EH?

FOR MY ASSISTANTS WHO LAY DOWN THE SCREENTONES, THE UNIFORMS THIS TIME WERE VERY UNPOPULAR!! HEE HEE!! I'M SORRY, MY LITTLE ANGELS! KEEP UP THE GOOD WORK.

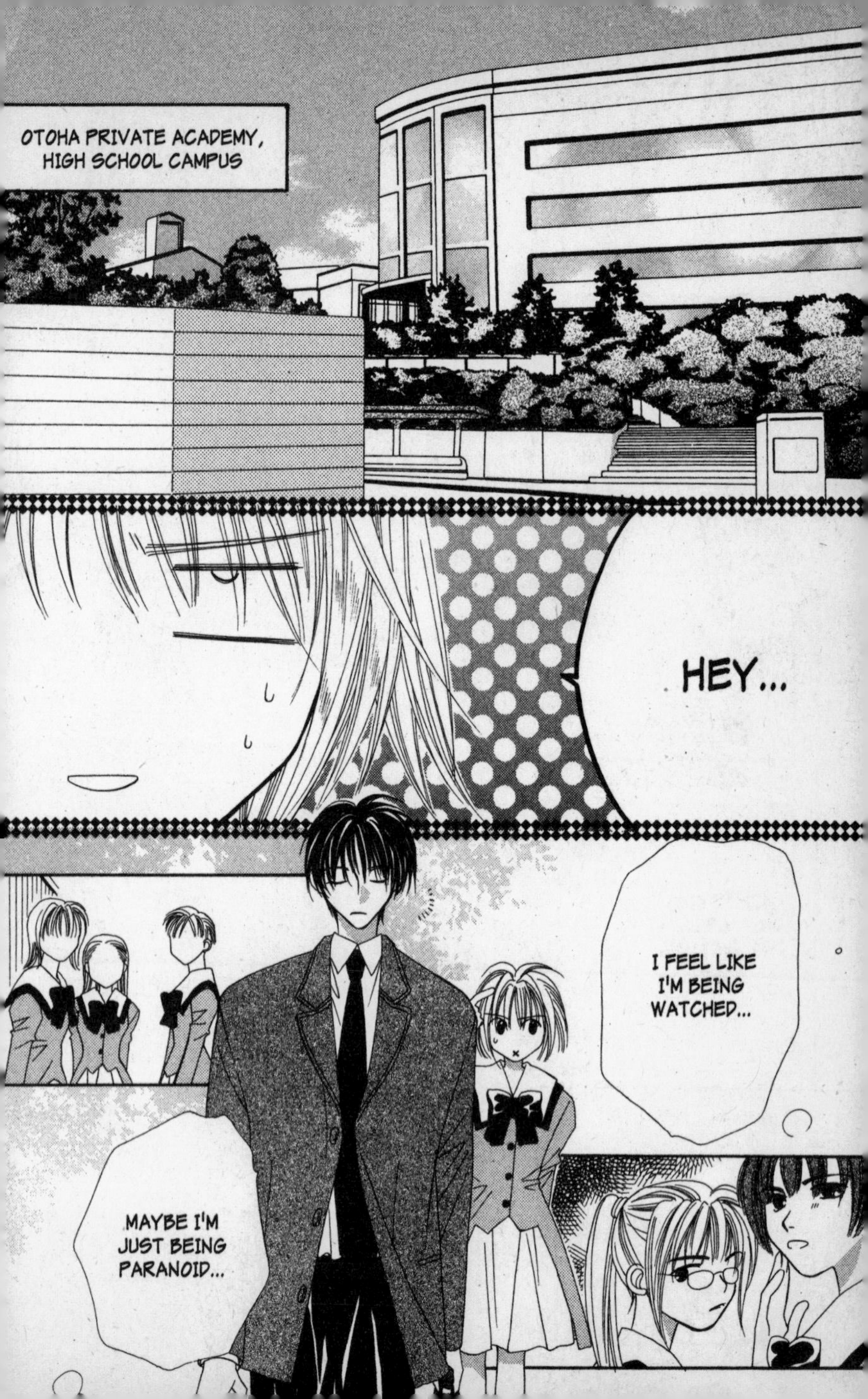

OTOHA PRIVATE ACADEMY, HIGH SCHOOL CAMPUS
HEY...
I FEEL LIKE I'M BEING WATCHED...
MAYBE I'M JUST BEING PARANOID...

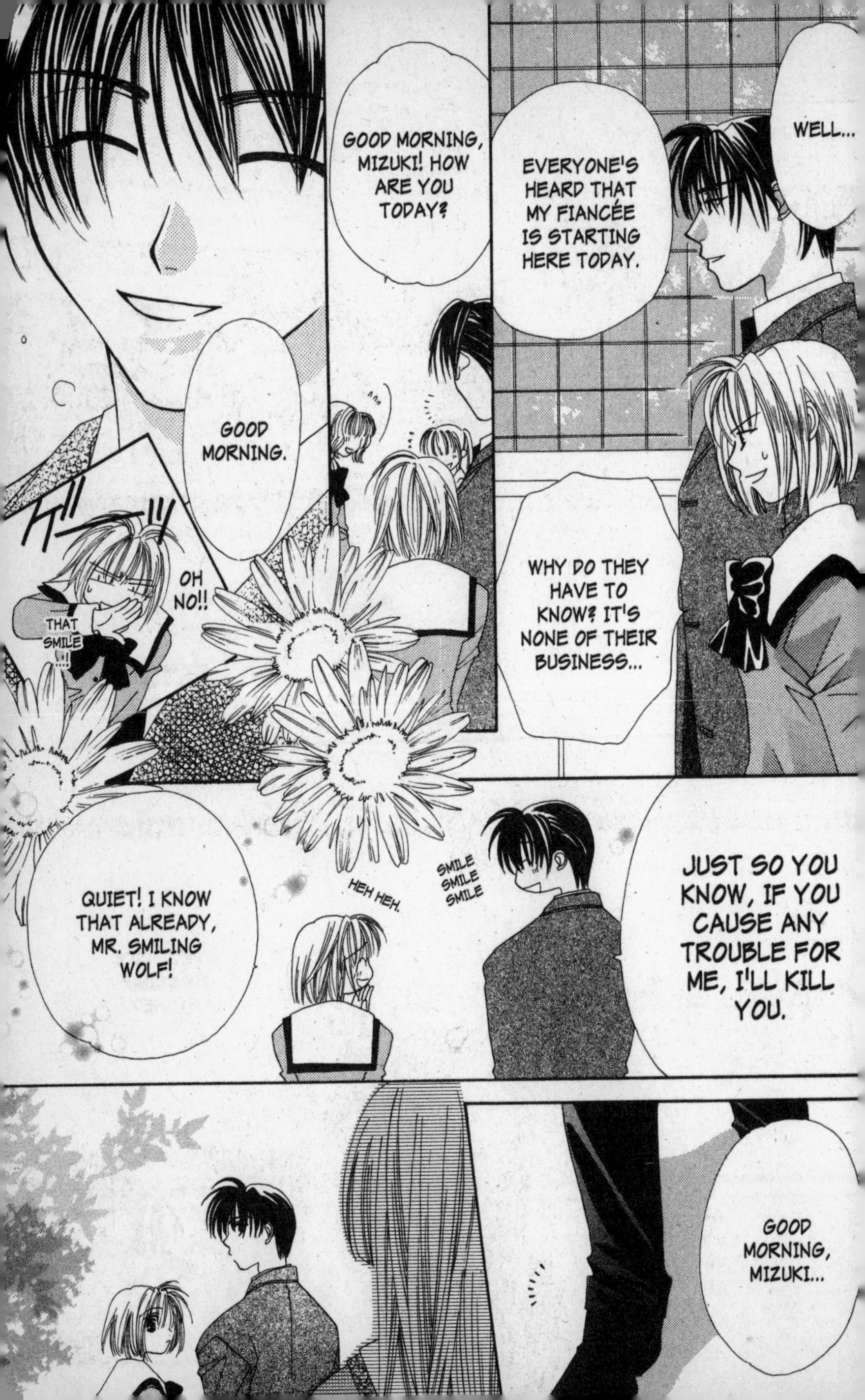
WELL...
EVERYONE'S HEARD THAT MY FIANCÉE IS STARTING HERE TODAY.
WHY DO THEY HAVE TO KNOW? IT'S NONE OF THEIR BUSINESS...
GOOD MORNING, MIZUKI! HOW ARE YOU TODAY?
GOOD MORNING.
OH NO!!
THAT SMILE...!
JUST SO YOU KNOW, IF YOU CAUSE ANY TROUBLE FOR ME, I'LL KILL YOU.
SMILE SMILE SMILE
HEH HEH.
QUIET! I KNOW THAT ALREADY, MR. SMILING WOLF!
GOOD MORNING, MIZUKI...

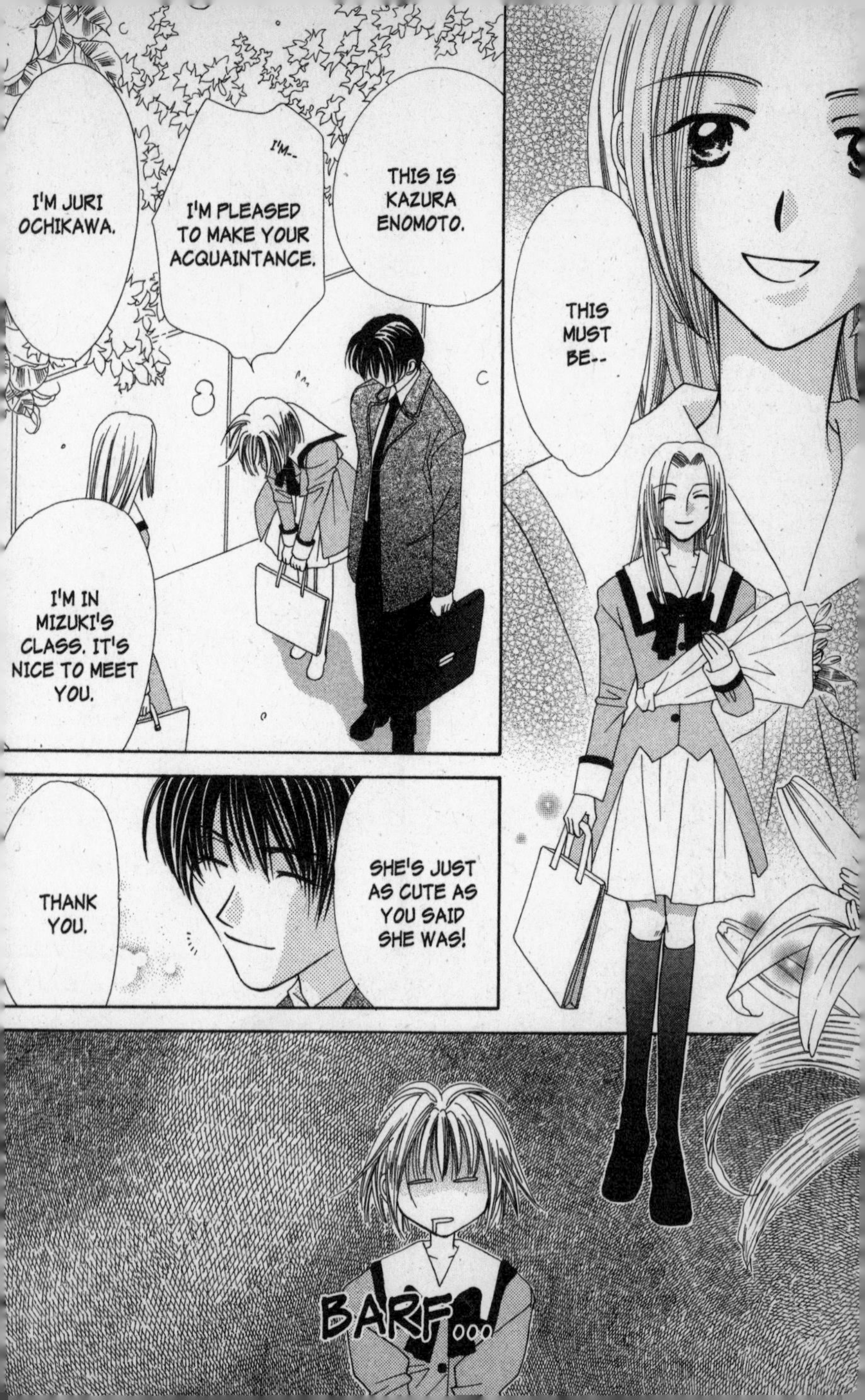
THIS MUST BE--
THIS IS KAZURA ENOMOTO.
I'M--
I'M PLEASED TO MAKE YOUR ACQUAINTANCE.
I'M JURI OCHIKAWA.
I'M IN MIZUKI'S CLASS. IT'S NICE TO MEET YOU.
SHE'S JUST AS CUTE AS YOU SAID SHE WAS!
THANK YOU.
BARF...

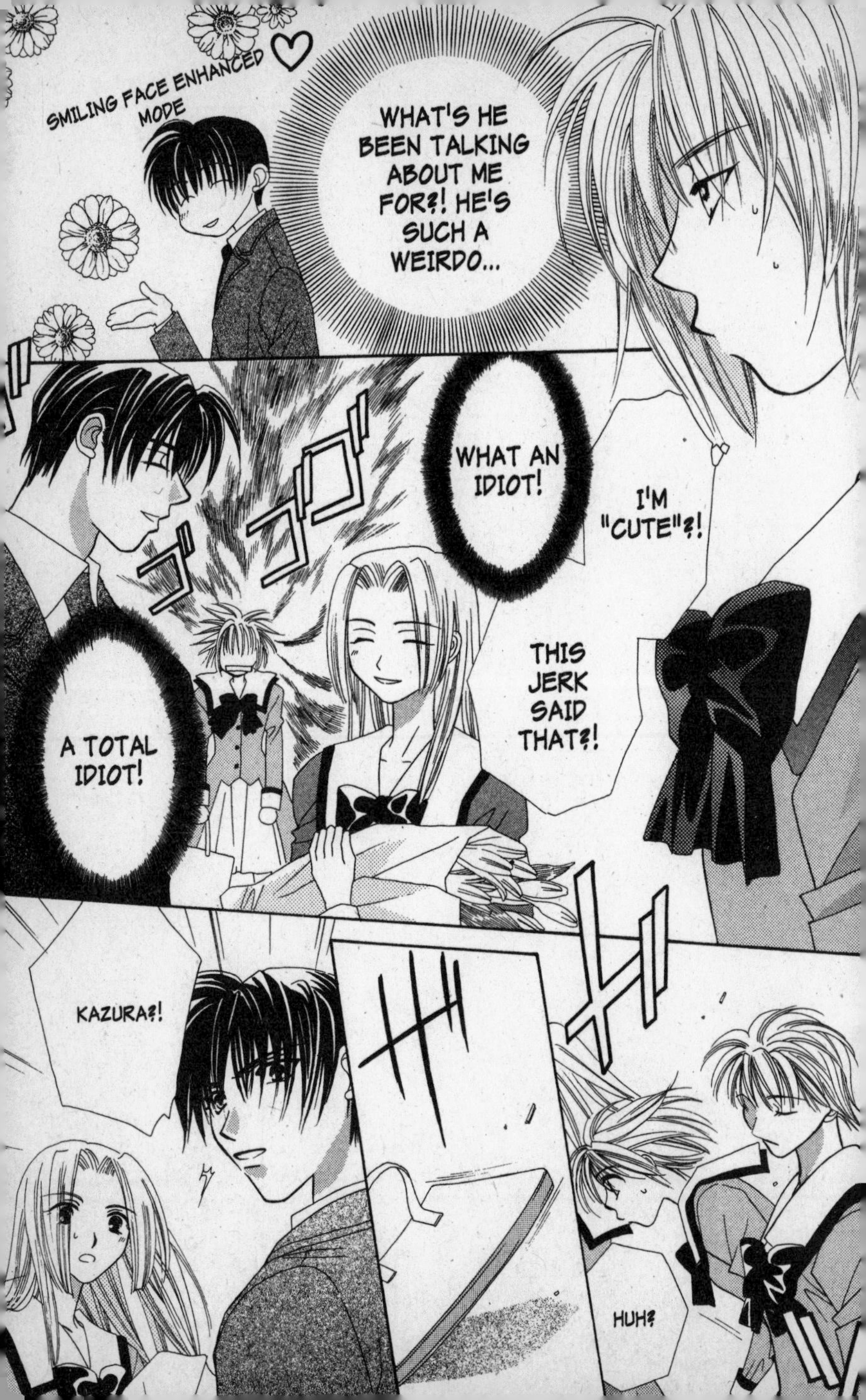
WHAT'S HE BEEN TALKING ABOUT ME FOR?! HE'S SUCH A WEIRDO...
SMILING FACE ENHANCED MODE
I'M "CUTE"?!
THIS JERK SAID THAT?!
WHAT AN IDIOT!
A TOTAL IDIOT!
HUH?
KAZURA?!

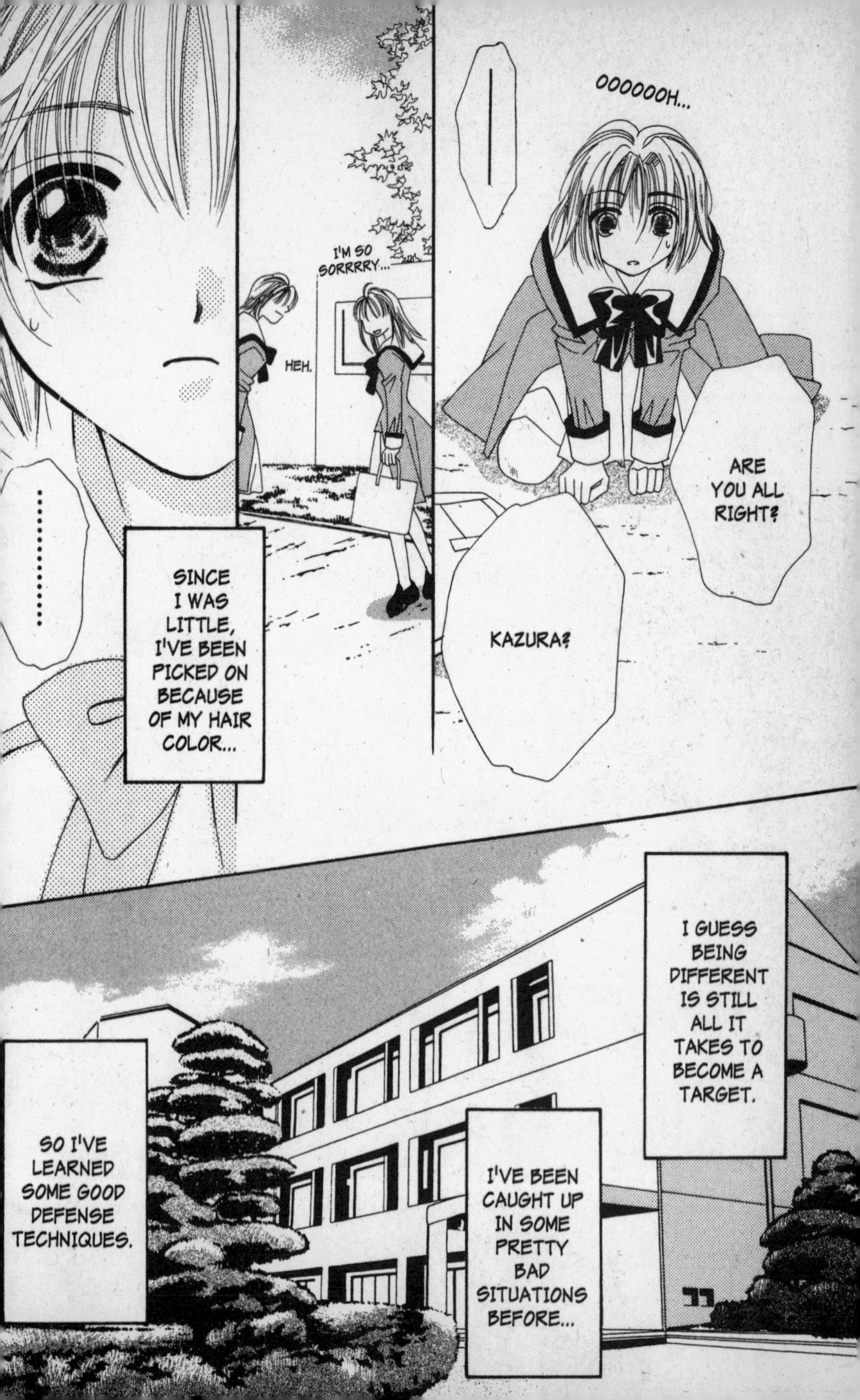
OOOOOOH...
ARE YOU ALL RIGHT?
KAZURA?
I'M SO SORRRRY...
HEH.
SINCE I WAS LITTLE, I'VE BEEN PICKED ON BECAUSE OF MY HAIR COLOR...
......
I GUESS BEING DIFFERENT IS STILL ALL IT TAKES TO BECOME A TARGET.
I'VE BEEN CAUGHT UP IN SOME PRETTY BAD SITUATIONS BEFORE...
SO I'VE LEARNED SOME GOOD DEFENSE TECHNIQUES.

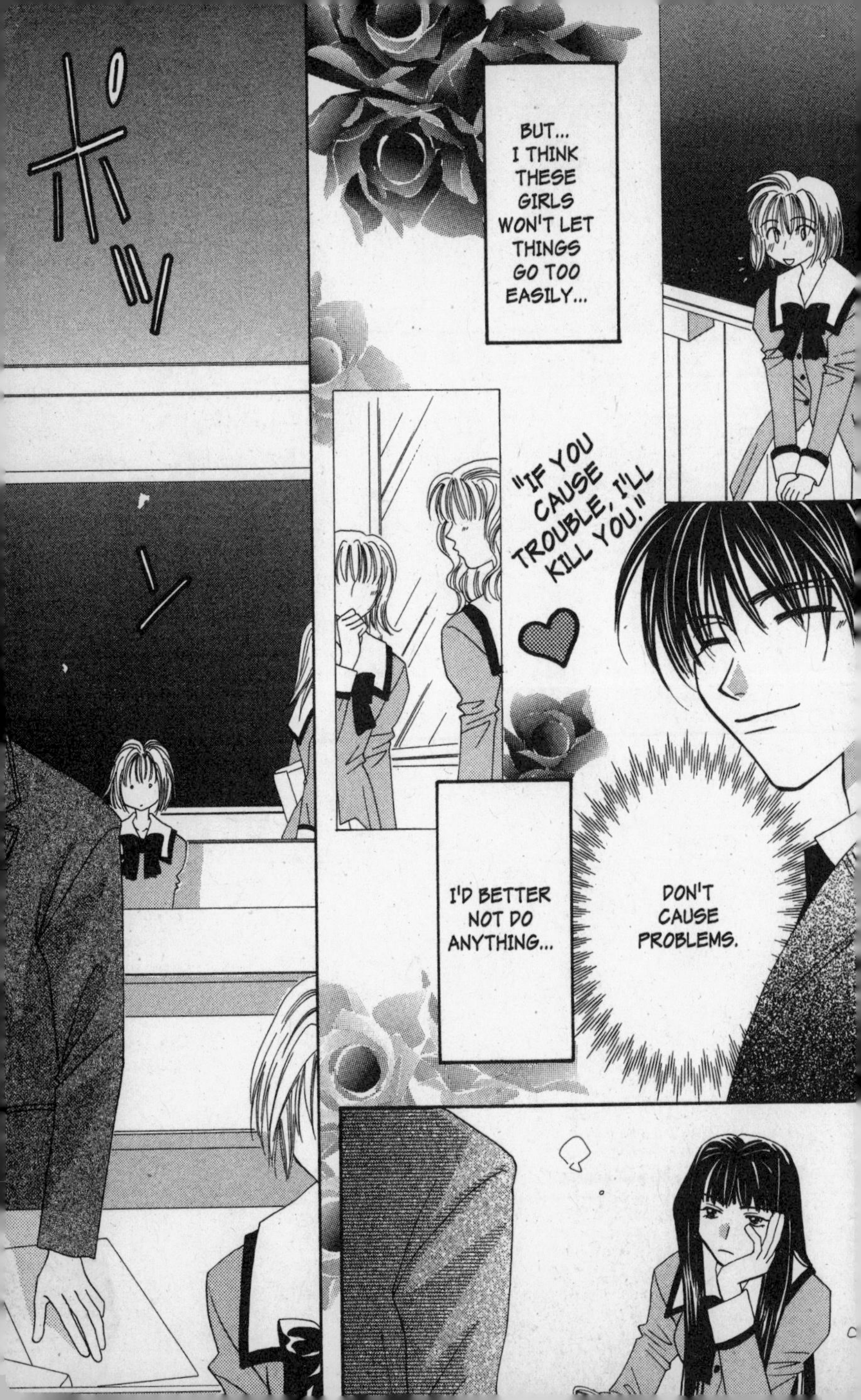
BUT... I THINK THESE GIRLS WON'T LET THINGS GO TOO EASILY...
"IF YOU CAUSE TROUBLE, I'LL KILL YOU!"
DON'T CAUSE PROBLEMS.
I'D BETTER NOT DO ANYTHING...
ポッ

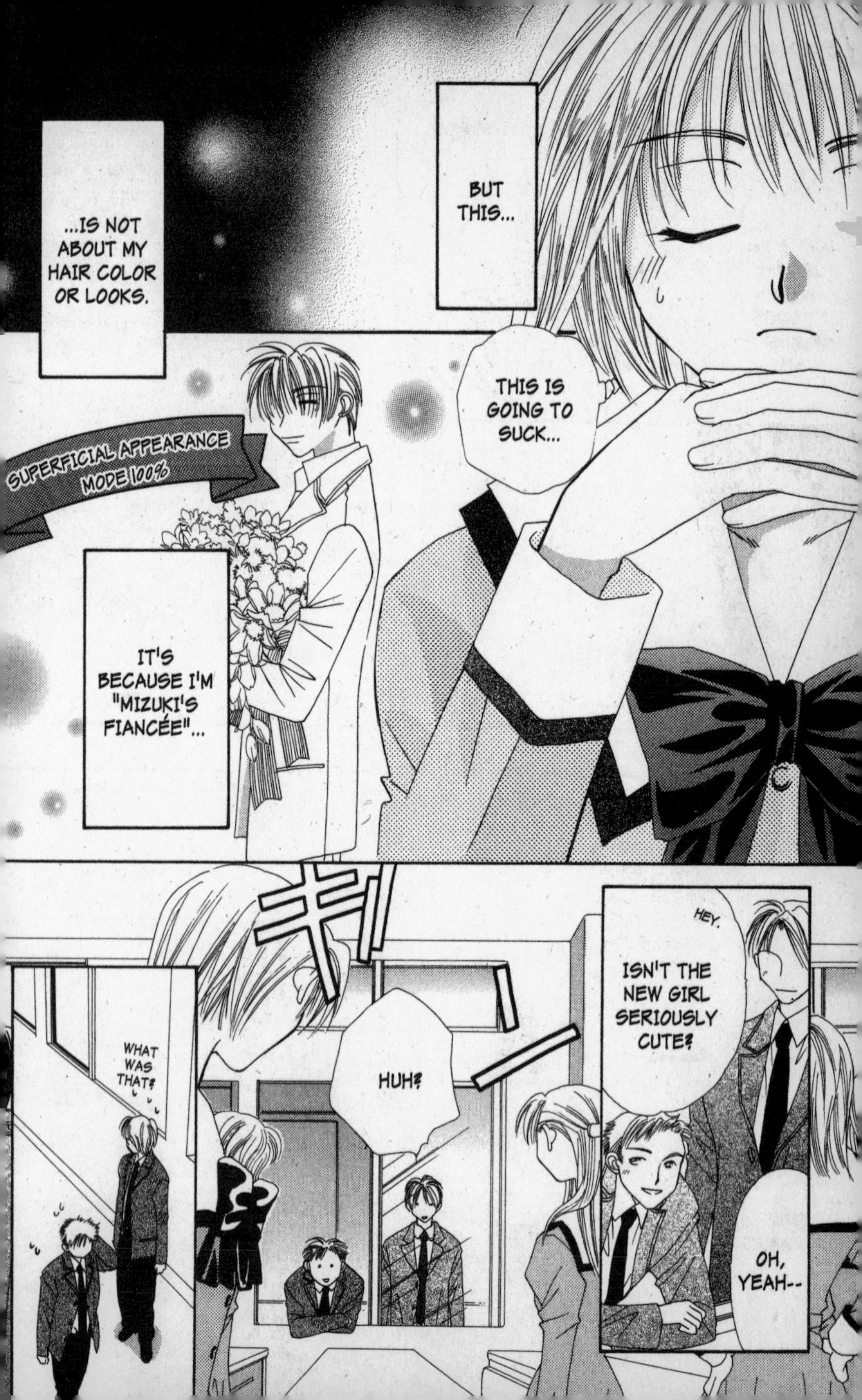
BUT THIS...
...IS NOT ABOUT MY HAIR COLOR OR LOOKS.
THIS IS GOING TO SUCK...
SUPERFICIAL APPEARANCE MODE 100%
IT'S BECAUSE I'M "MIZUKI'S FIANCÉE"...
HEY.
ISN'T THE NEW GIRL SERIOUSLY CUTE?
OH, YEAH--
キ
HUH?
WHAT WAS THAT?

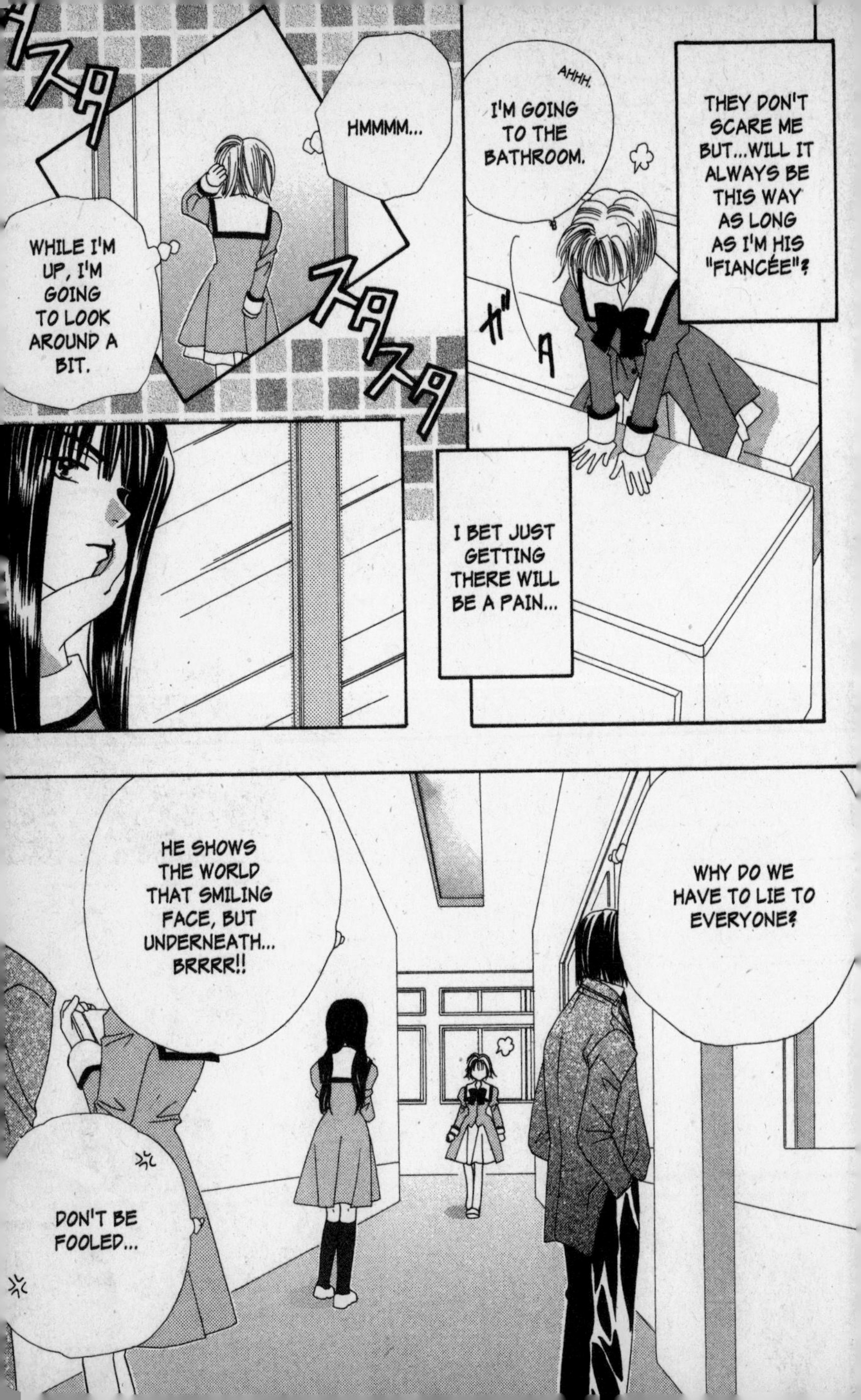
THEY DON'T SCARE ME BUT...WILL IT ALWAYS BE THIS WAY AS LONG AS I'M HIS "FIANCÉE"?
AHHH.
I'M GOING TO THE BATHROOM.
ガタ
I BET JUST GETTING THERE WILL BE A PAIN...
スタスタ
HMMMM...
WHILE I'M UP, I'M GOING TO LOOK AROUND A BIT.
スタスタ
WHY DO WE HAVE TO LIE TO EVERYONE?
HE SHOWS THE WORLD THAT SMILING FACE, BUT UNDERNEATH... BRRRR!!
DON'T BE FOOLED...

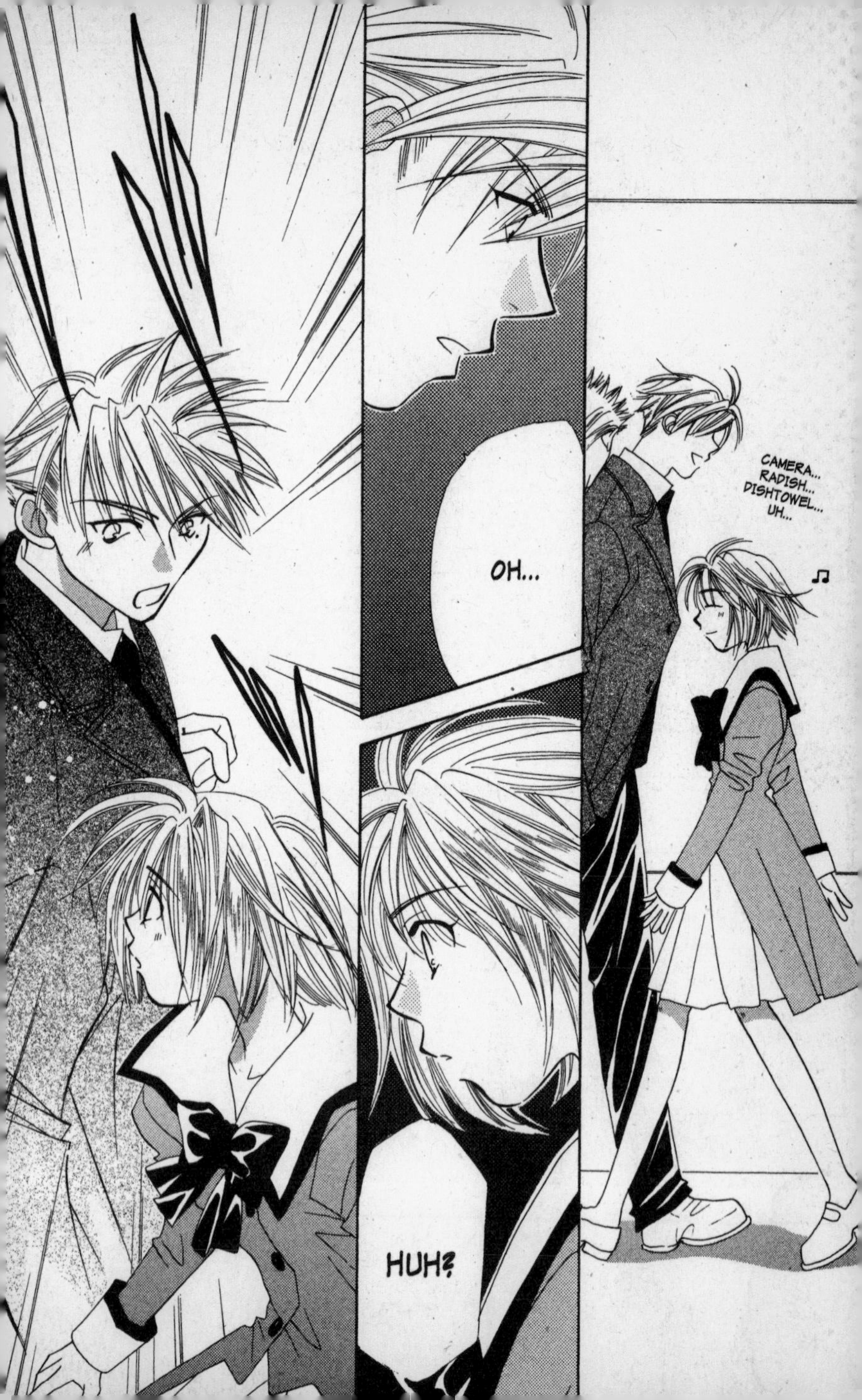
CAMERA... RADISH... DISHTOWEL... UH...
♫
OH...
HUH?

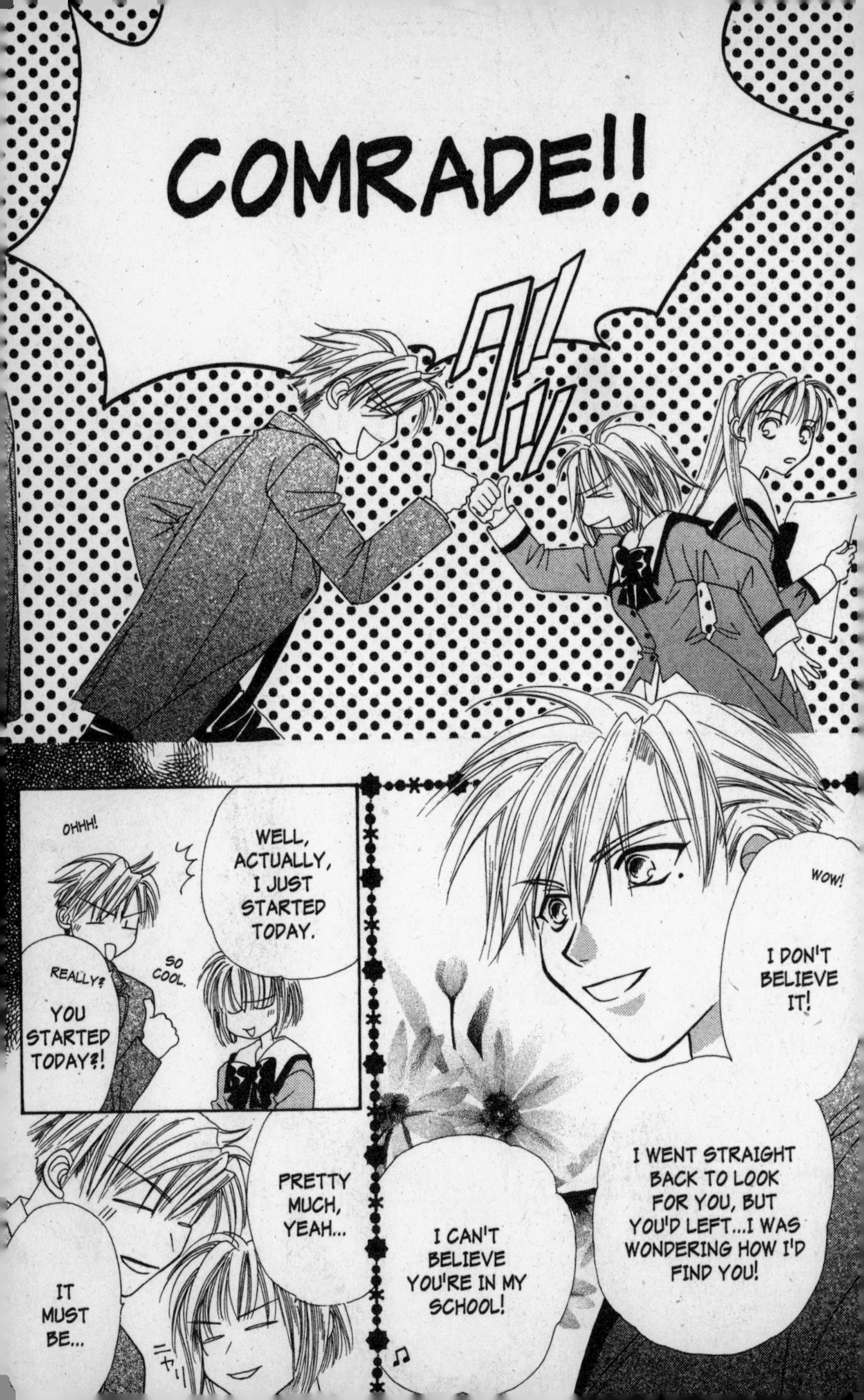
COMRADE!!
WOW!
I DON'T BELIEVE IT!
I WENT STRAIGHT BACK TO LOOK FOR YOU, BUT YOU'D LEFT...I WAS WONDERING HOW I'D FIND YOU!
I CAN'T BELIEVE YOU'RE IN MY SCHOOL!
WELL, ACTUALLY, I JUST STARTED TODAY.
OHHH!
SO COOL.
REALLY? YOU STARTED TODAY?!
PRETTY MUCH, YEAH...
IT MUST BE...

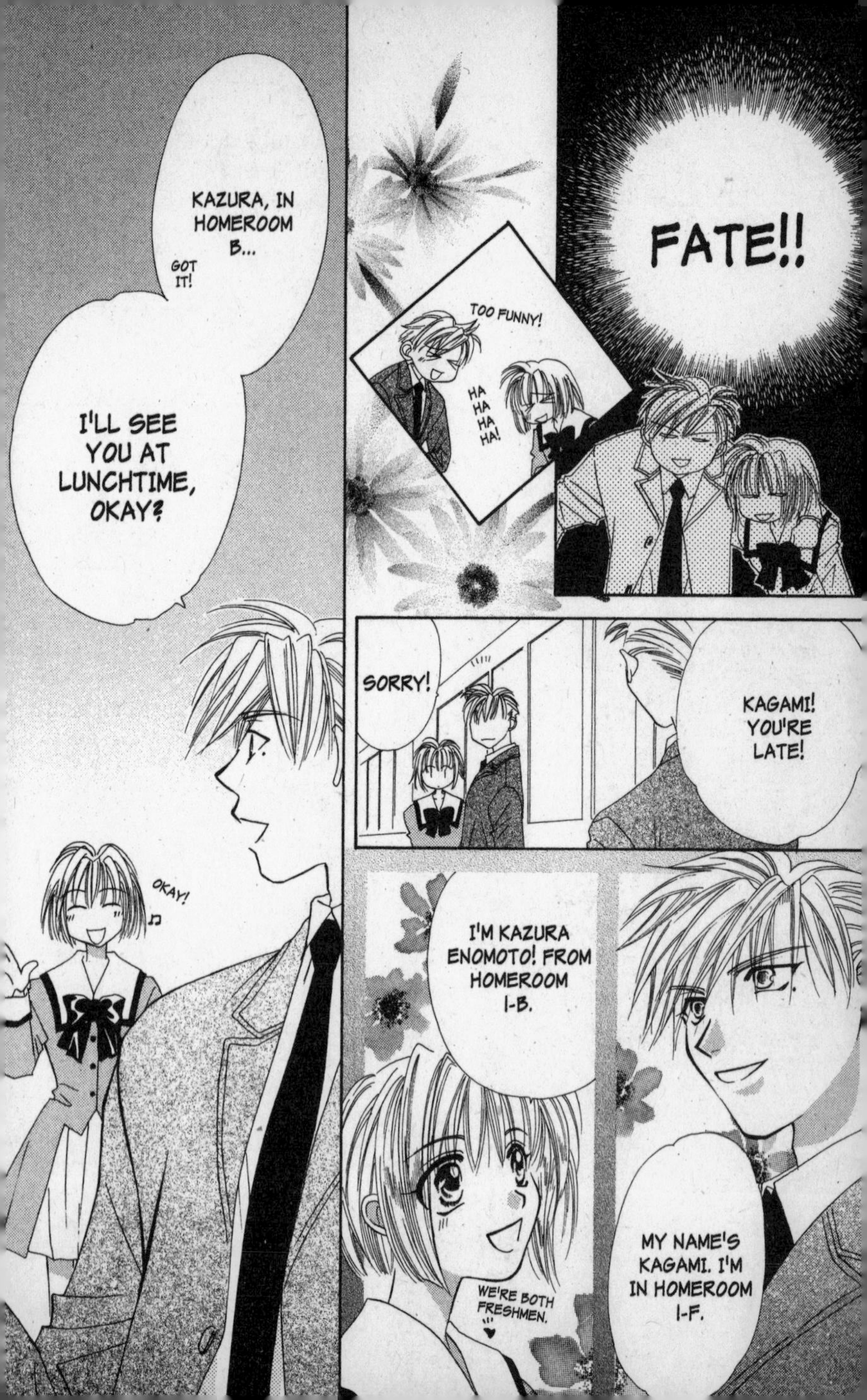
FATE!!
TOO FUNNY!
HA HA HA HA!
KAGAMI! YOU'RE LATE!
SORRY!
MY NAME'S KAGAMI. I'M IN HOMEROOM I-F.
I'M KAZURA ENOMOTO! FROM HOMEROOM I-B.
WE'RE BOTH FRESHMEN.
KAZURA, IN HOMEROOM B...
GOT IT!
I'LL SEE YOU AT LUNCHTIME, OKAY?
OKAY!

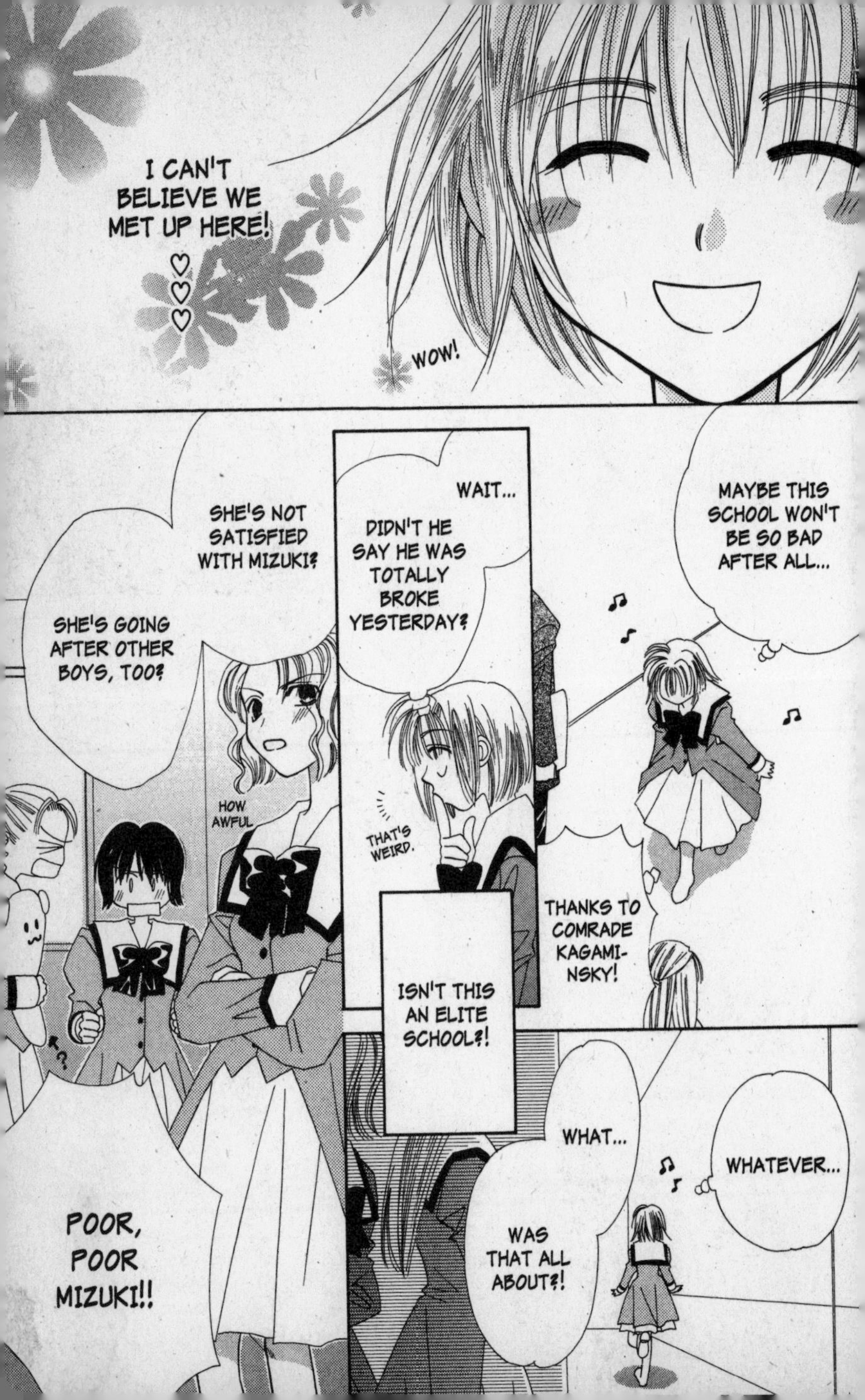
I CAN'T BELIEVE WE MET UP HERE! ♡♡♡
WOW!
MAYBE THIS SCHOOL WON'T BE SO BAD AFTER ALL...
THANKS TO COMRADE KAGAMI-NSKY!
WAIT...
DIDN'T HE SAY HE WAS TOTALLY BROKE YESTERDAY?
THAT'S WEIRD.
ISN'T THIS AN ELITE SCHOOL?!
WHATEVER...
WHAT...
WAS THAT ALL ABOUT?!
SHE'S NOT SATISFIED WITH MIZUKI?
SHE'S GOING AFTER OTHER BOYS, TOO?
HOW AWFUL
POOR, POOR MIZUKI!!

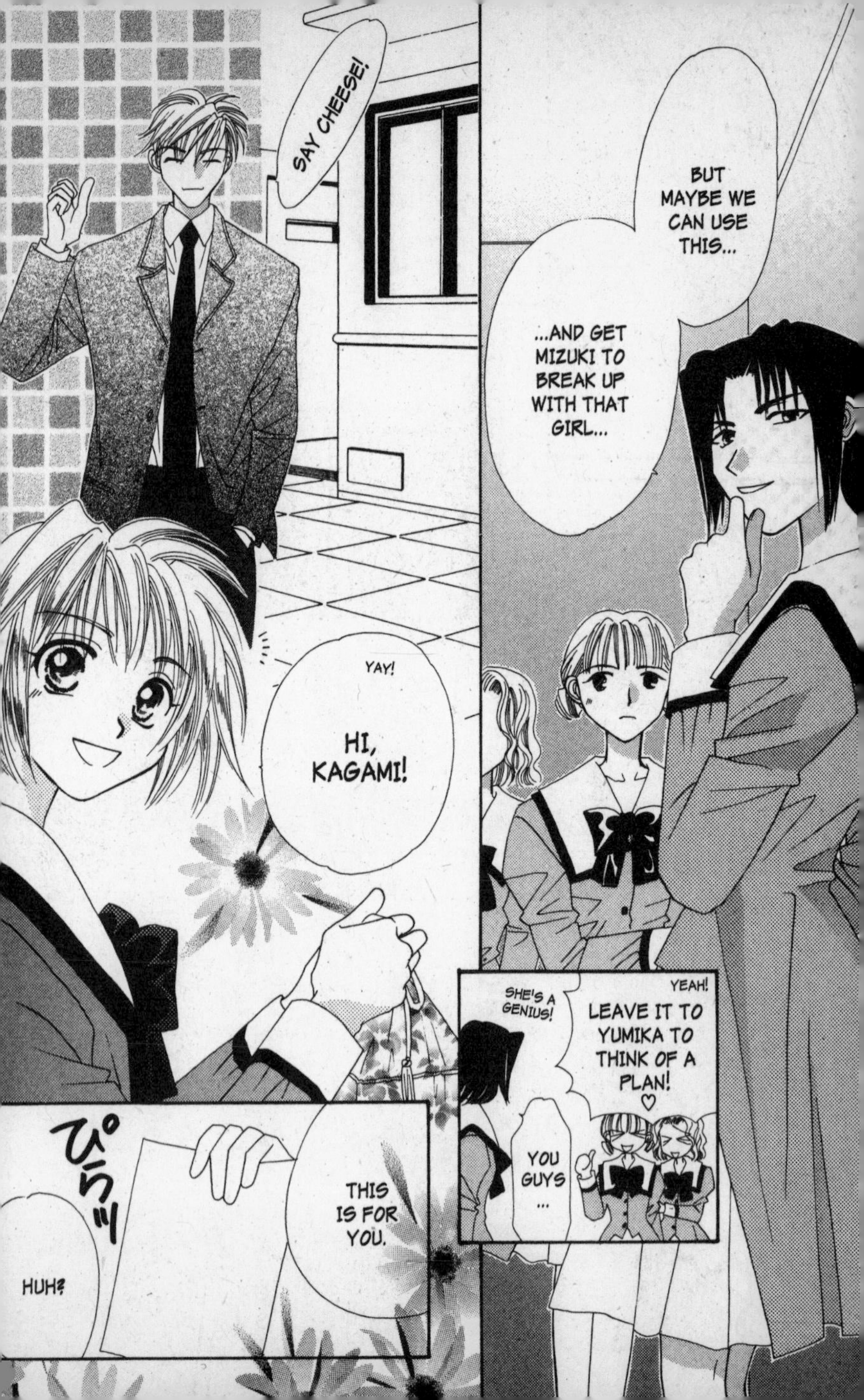
BUT MAYBE WE CAN USE THIS...
...AND GET MIZUKI TO BREAK UP WITH THAT GIRL...
YEAH!
LEAVE IT TO YUMIKA TO THINK OF A PLAN! ♡
SHE'S A GENIUS!
YOU GUYS ...
SAY CHEESE!
YAY!
HI, KAGAMI!
ぴらッ
THIS IS FOR YOU.
HUH?

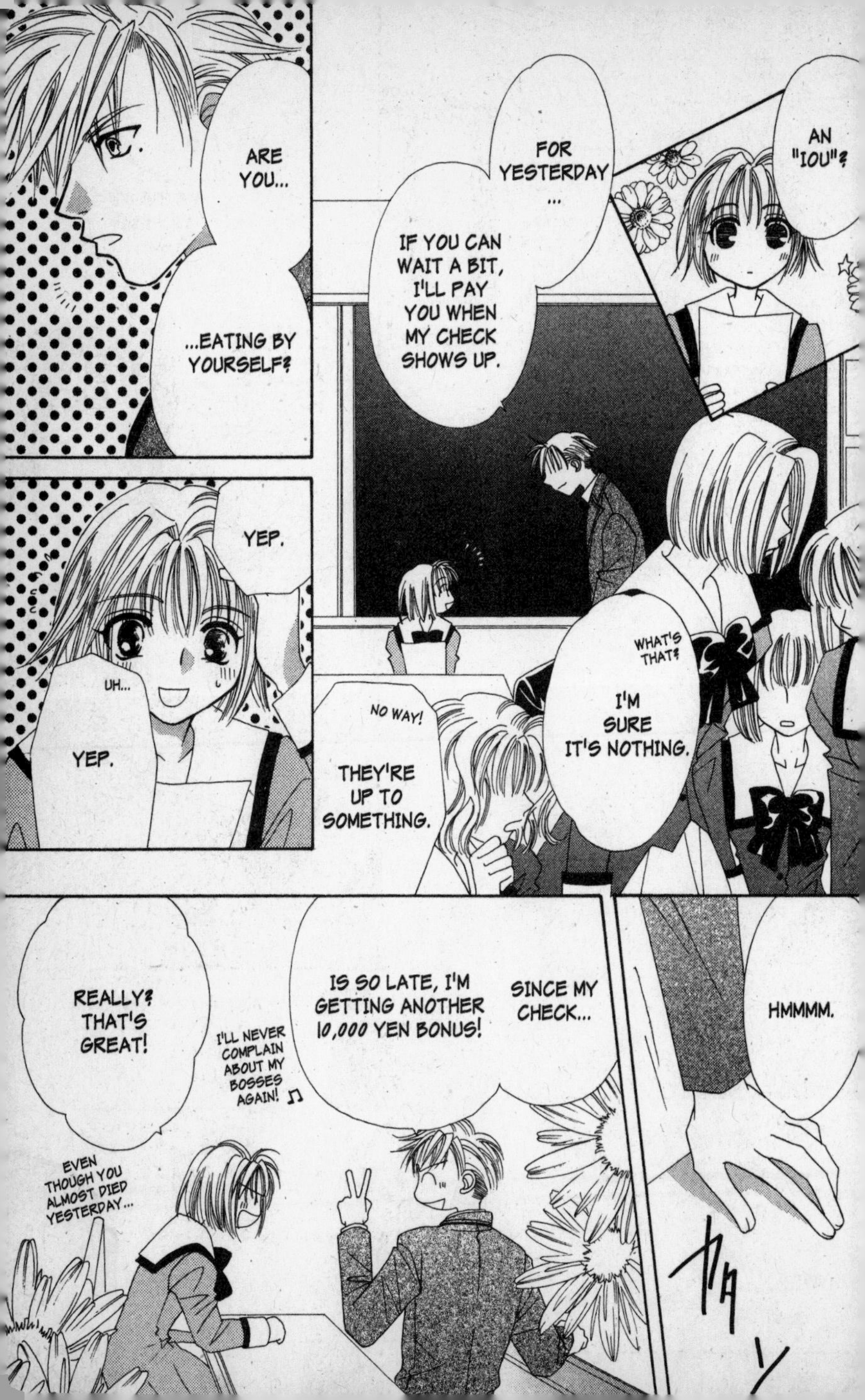
AN "IOU"?
FOR YESTERDAY ...
IF YOU CAN WAIT A BIT, I'LL PAY YOU WHEN MY CHECK SHOWS UP.
WHAT'S THAT?
I'M SURE IT'S NOTHING.
NO WAY!
THEY'RE UP TO SOMETHING.
ARE YOU...
...EATING BY YOURSELF?
YEP.
UH...
YEP.
HMMMM.
SINCE MY CHECK...
IS SO LATE, I'M GETTING ANOTHER 10,000 YEN BONUS!
I'LL NEVER COMPLAIN ABOUT MY BOSSES AGAIN! ♫
REALLY? THAT'S GREAT!
EVEN THOUGH YOU ALMOST DIED YESTERDAY...

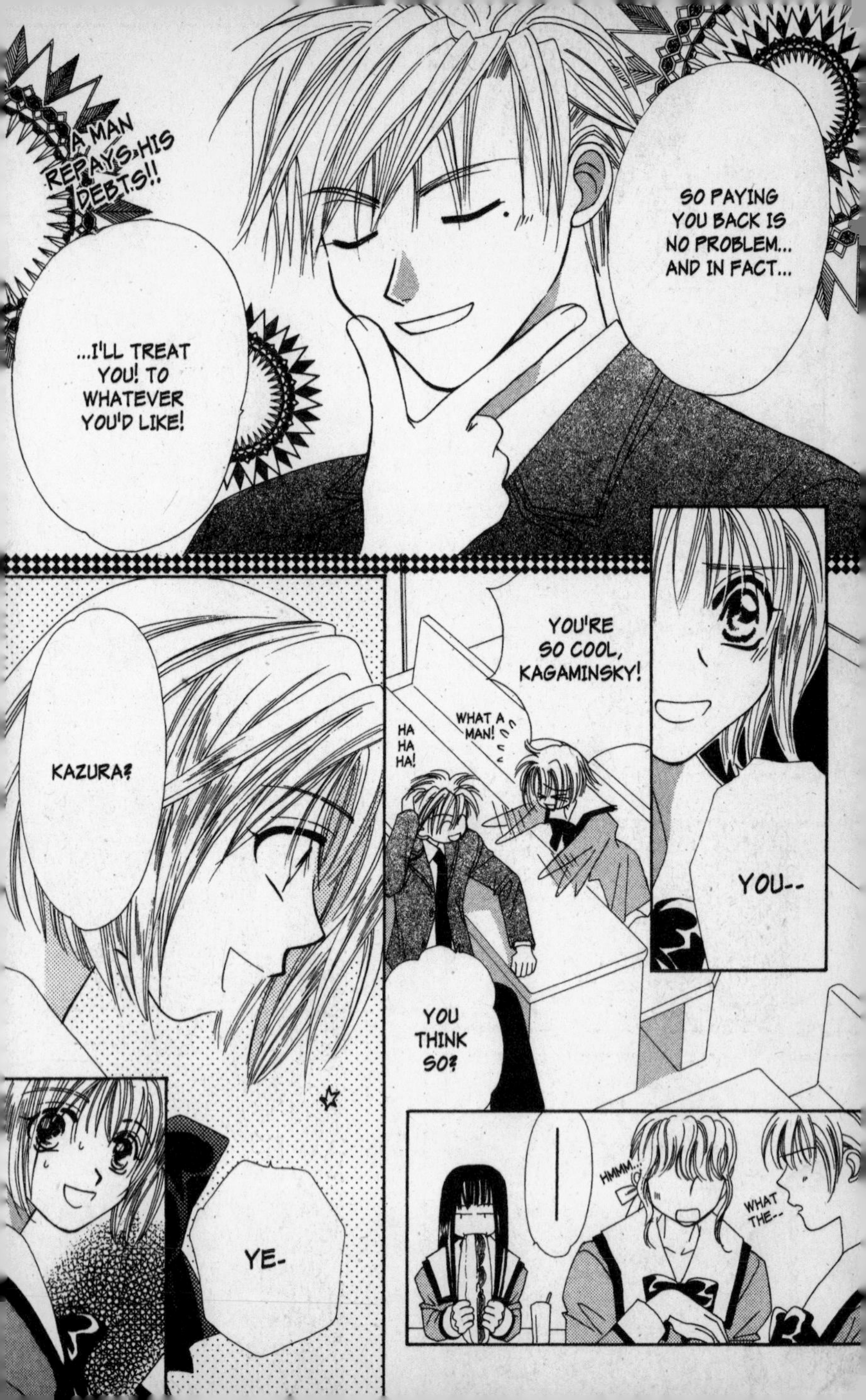

SO PAYING YOU BACK IS NO PROBLEM... AND IN FACT...
A MAN REPAYS HIS DEBTS!!
...I'LL TREAT YOU! TO WHATEVER YOU'D LIKE!
YOU--
YOU'RE SO COOL, KAGAMINSKY!
WHAT A MAN!
HA HA HA!
YOU THINK SO?
KAZURA?
YE-
|
HMMM...
WHAT THE--

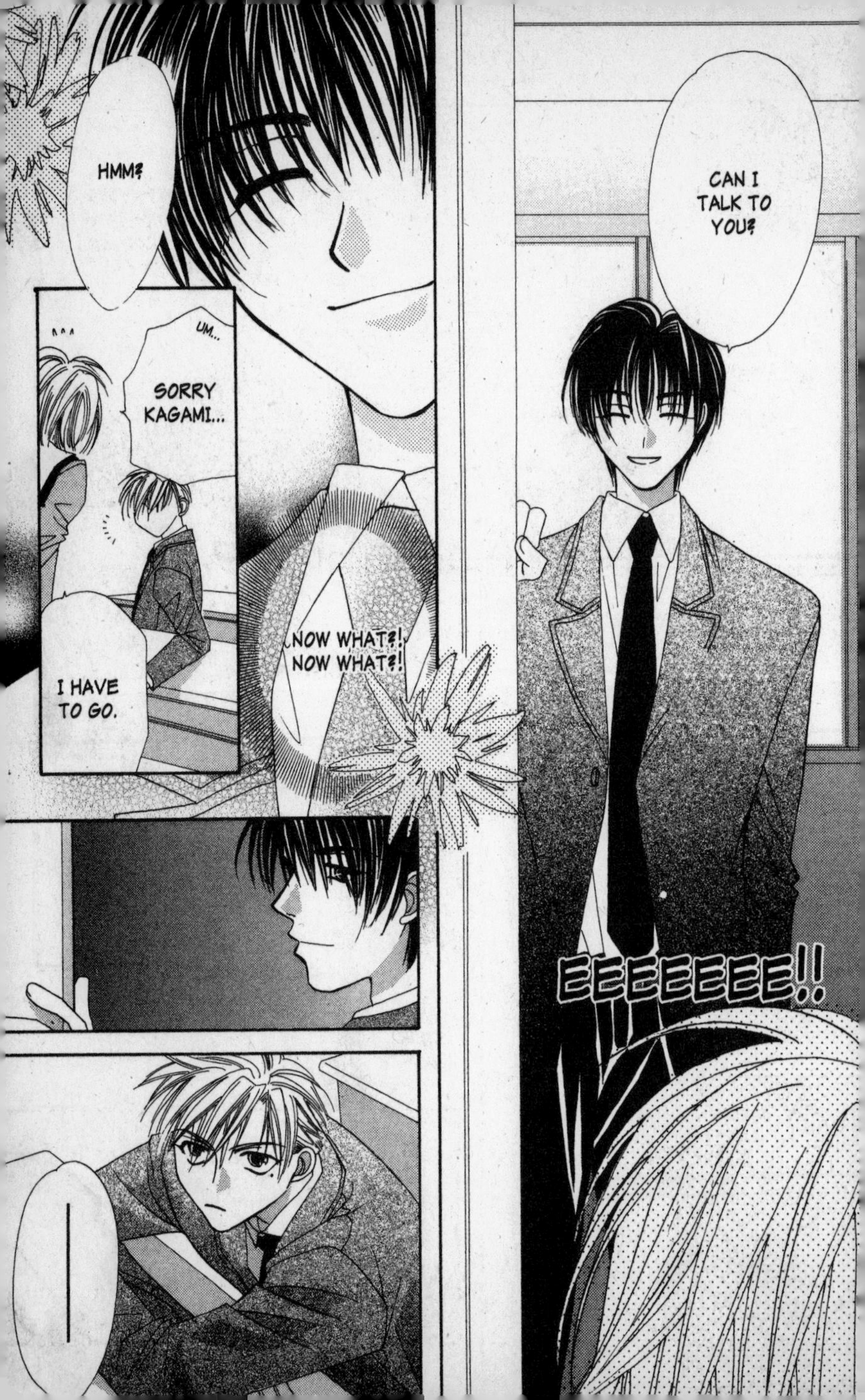
CAN I TALK TO YOU?
EEEEEEEE!!
HMM?
UM...
SORRY KAGAMI...
I HAVE TO GO.
NOW WHAT?! NOW WHAT?!
—

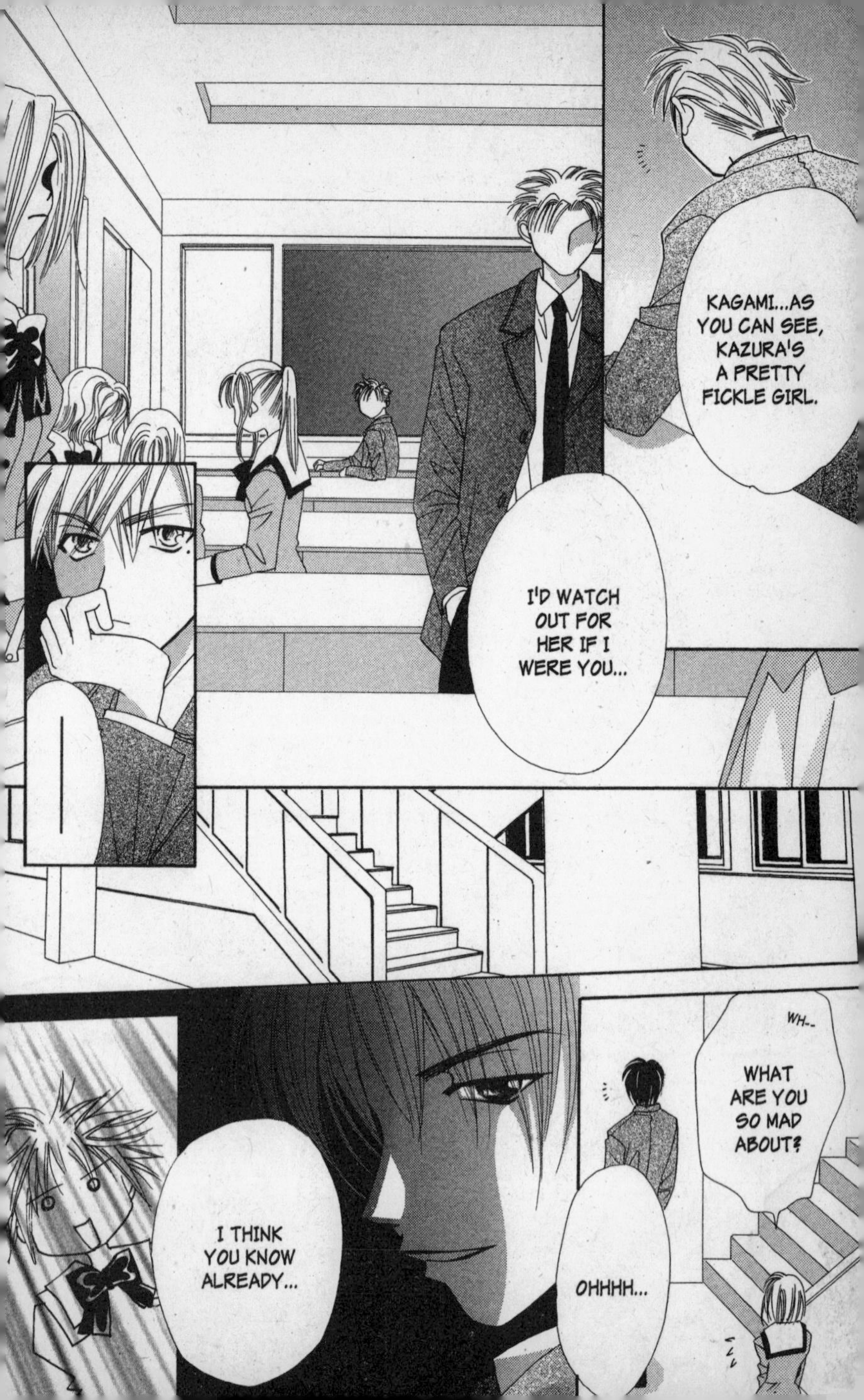
KAGAMI...AS YOU CAN SEE, KAZURA'S A PRETTY FICKLE GIRL.
I'D WATCH OUT FOR HER IF I WERE YOU...
WH--
WHAT ARE YOU SO MAD ABOUT?
OHHHH...
I THINK YOU KNOW ALREADY...

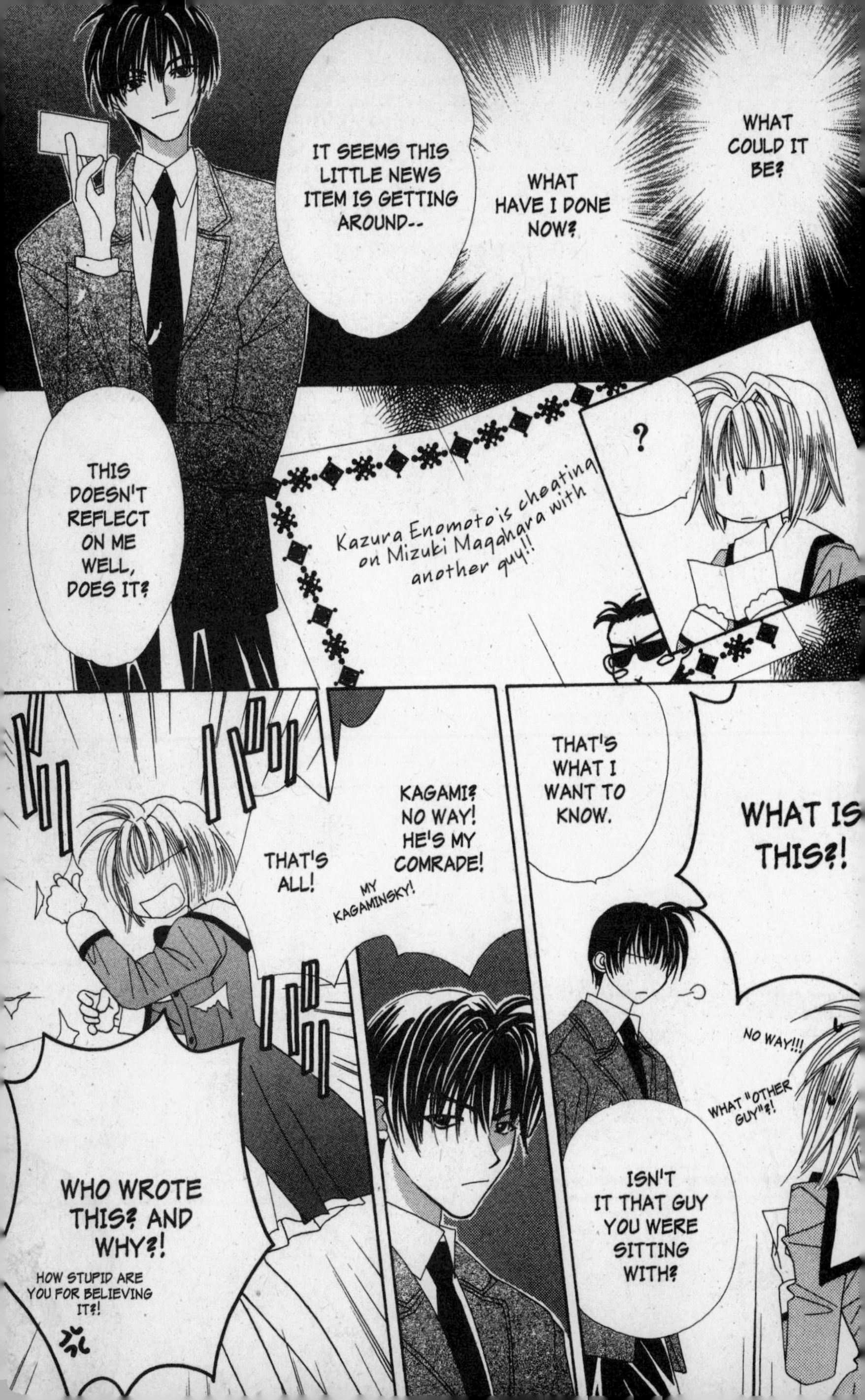
WHAT COULD IT BE?
WHAT HAVE I DONE NOW?
IT SEEMS THIS LITTLE NEWS ITEM IS GETTING AROUND--
THIS DOESN'T REFLECT ON ME WELL, DOES IT?
?
Kazura Enomoto is cheating on Mizuki Magahara with another guy!!
WHAT IS THIS?!
NO WAY!!!
WHAT "OTHER GUY"?!
THAT'S WHAT I WANT TO KNOW.
ISN'T IT THAT GUY YOU WERE SITTING WITH?
KAGAMI? NO WAY! HE'S MY COMRADE!
THAT'S ALL!
MY KAGAMINSKY!
WHO WROTE THIS? AND WHY?!
HOW STUPID ARE YOU FOR BELIEVING IT?!

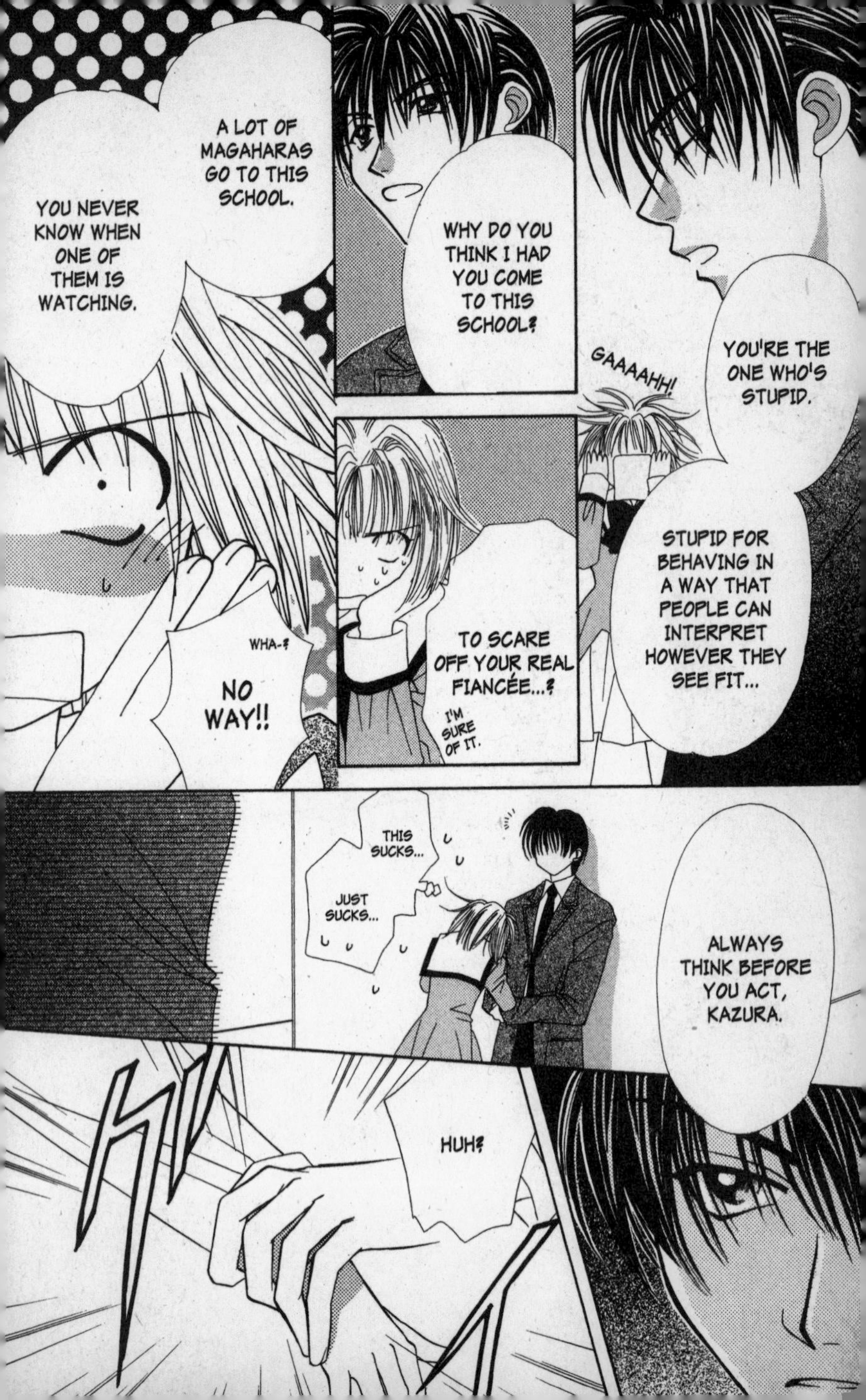
YOU'RE THE ONE WHO'S STUPID.
GAAAAAHH!
STUPID FOR BEHAVING IN A WAY THAT PEOPLE CAN INTERPRET HOWEVER THEY SEE FIT...
WHY DO YOU THINK I HAD YOU COME TO THIS SCHOOL?
TO SCARE OFF YOUR REAL FIANCÉE...?
I'M SURE OF IT.
A LOT OF MAGAHARAS GO TO THIS SCHOOL.
YOU NEVER KNOW WHEN ONE OF THEM IS WATCHING.
WHA-?
NO WAY!!
ALWAYS THINK BEFORE YOU ACT, KAZURA.
THIS SUCKS...
JUST SUCKS...
HUH?

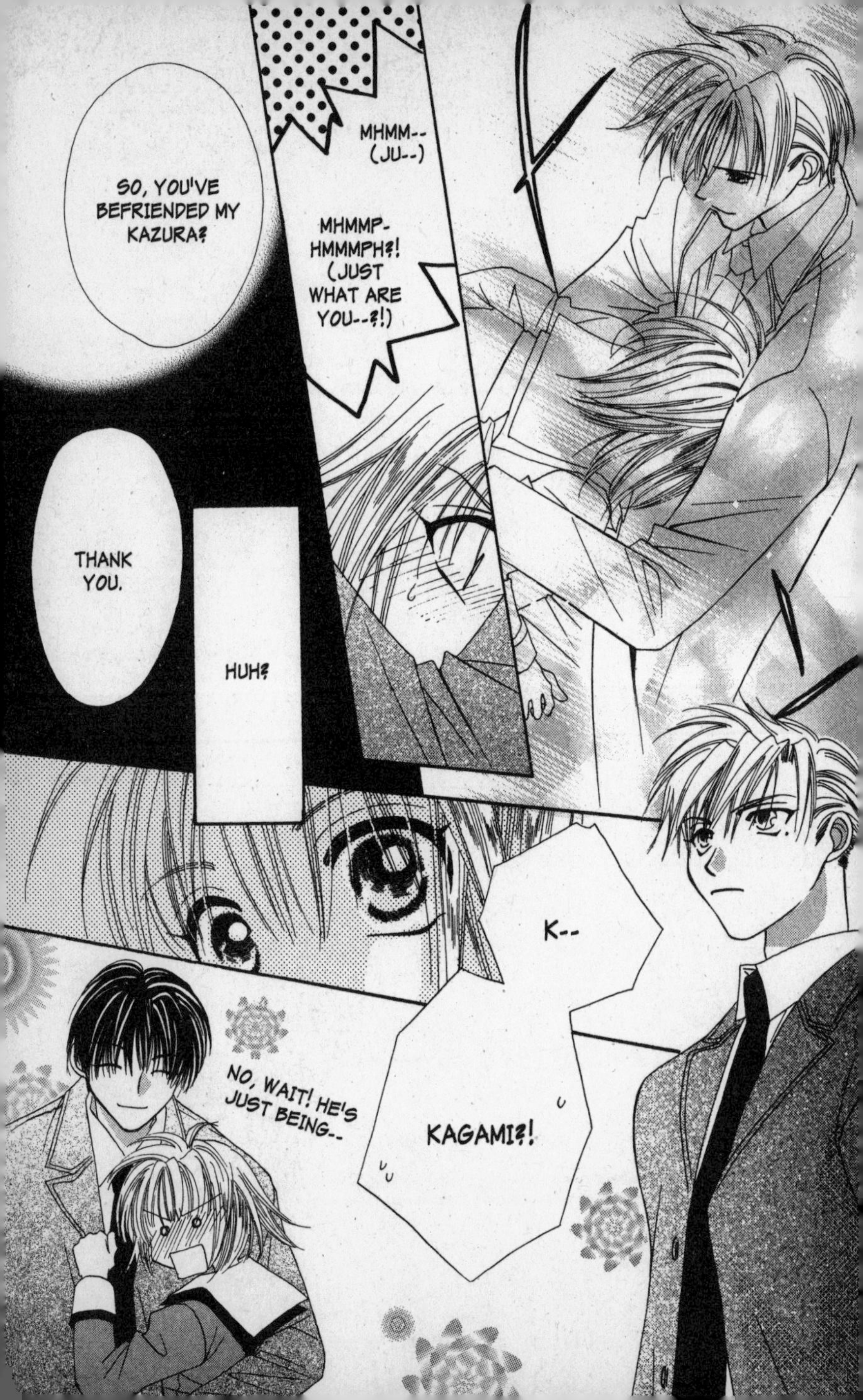
MHMM-- (JU--)
MHMMP-HMMMPH?! (JUST WHAT ARE YOU--?!)
SO, YOU'VE BEFRIENDED MY KAZURA?
THANK YOU.
HUH?
K--
KAGAMI?!
NO, WAIT! HE'S JUST BEING--

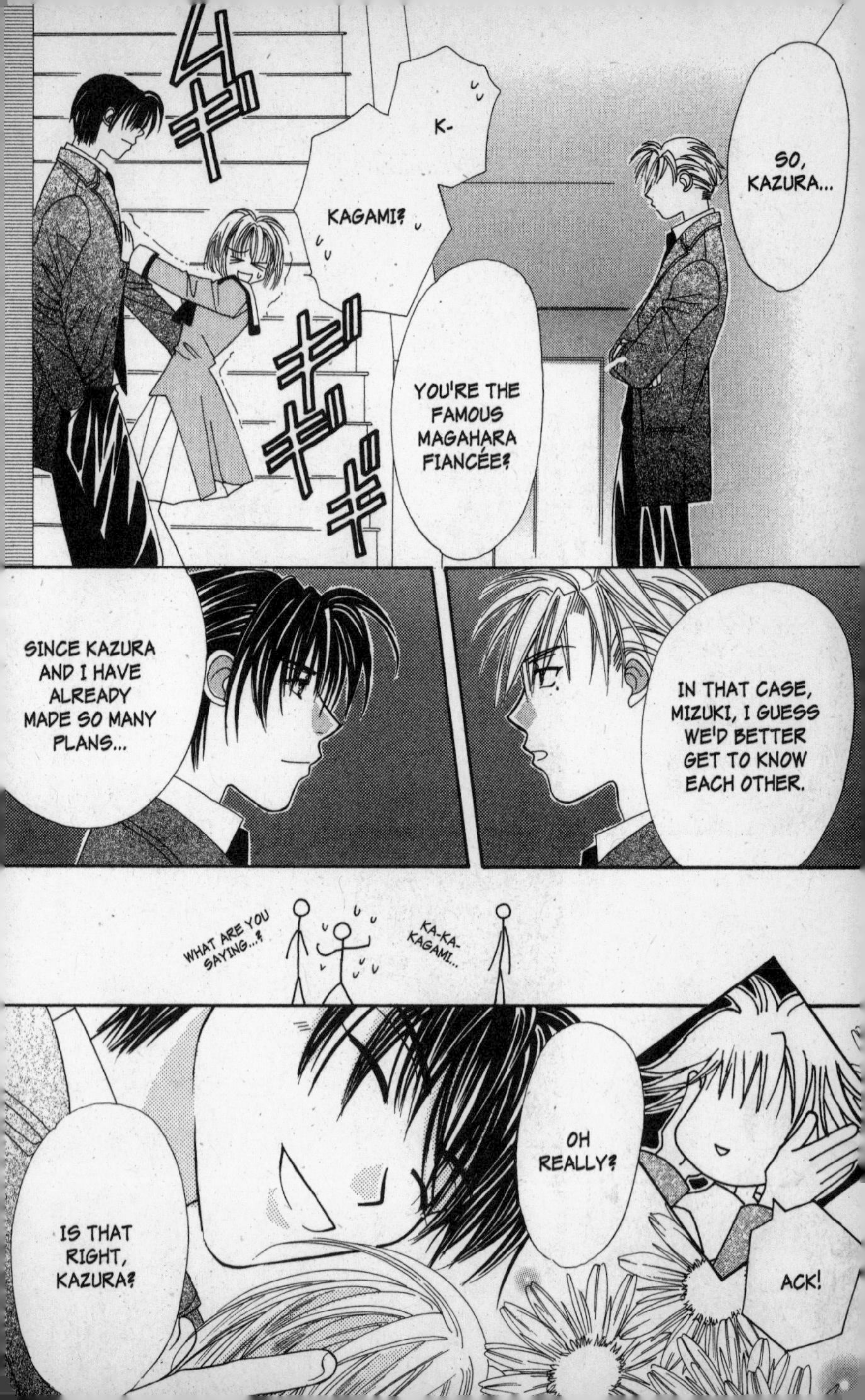
SO, KAZURA...
K-
KAGAMI?
YOU'RE THE FAMOUS MAGAHARA FIANCÉE?
IN THAT CASE, MIZUKI, I GUESS WE'D BETTER GET TO KNOW EACH OTHER.
SINCE KAZURA AND I HAVE ALREADY MADE SO MANY PLANS...
KA-KA-KAGAMI...
WHAT ARE YOU SAYING...?
ACK!
OH REALLY?
IS THAT RIGHT, KAZURA?

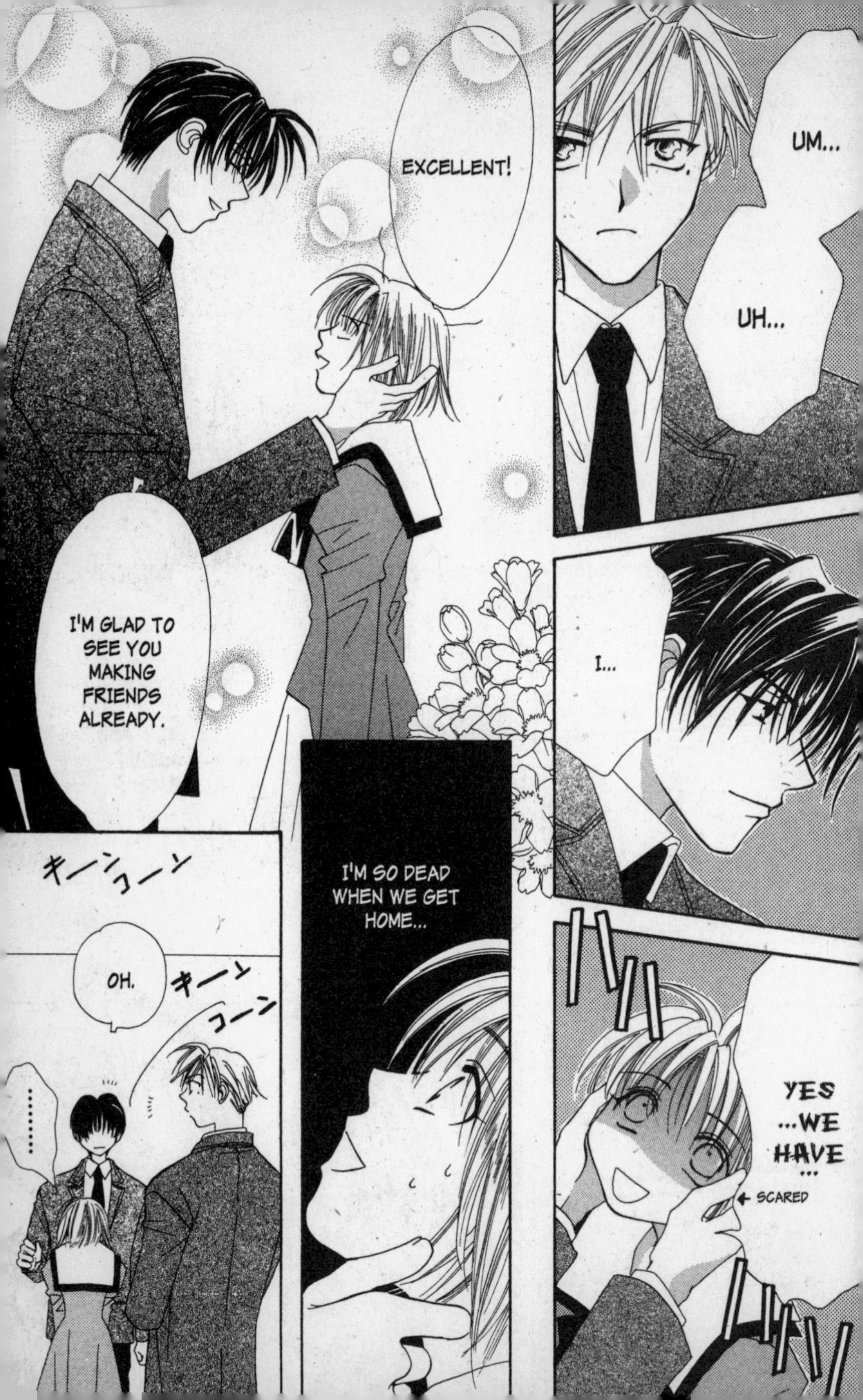
UM...
UH...
I...
YES ...WE HAVE ...
SCARED
EXCELLENT!
I'M GLAD TO SEE YOU MAKING FRIENDS ALREADY.
I'M SO DEAD WHEN WE GET HOME...
キーンコーン
OH.
キーンコーン
......

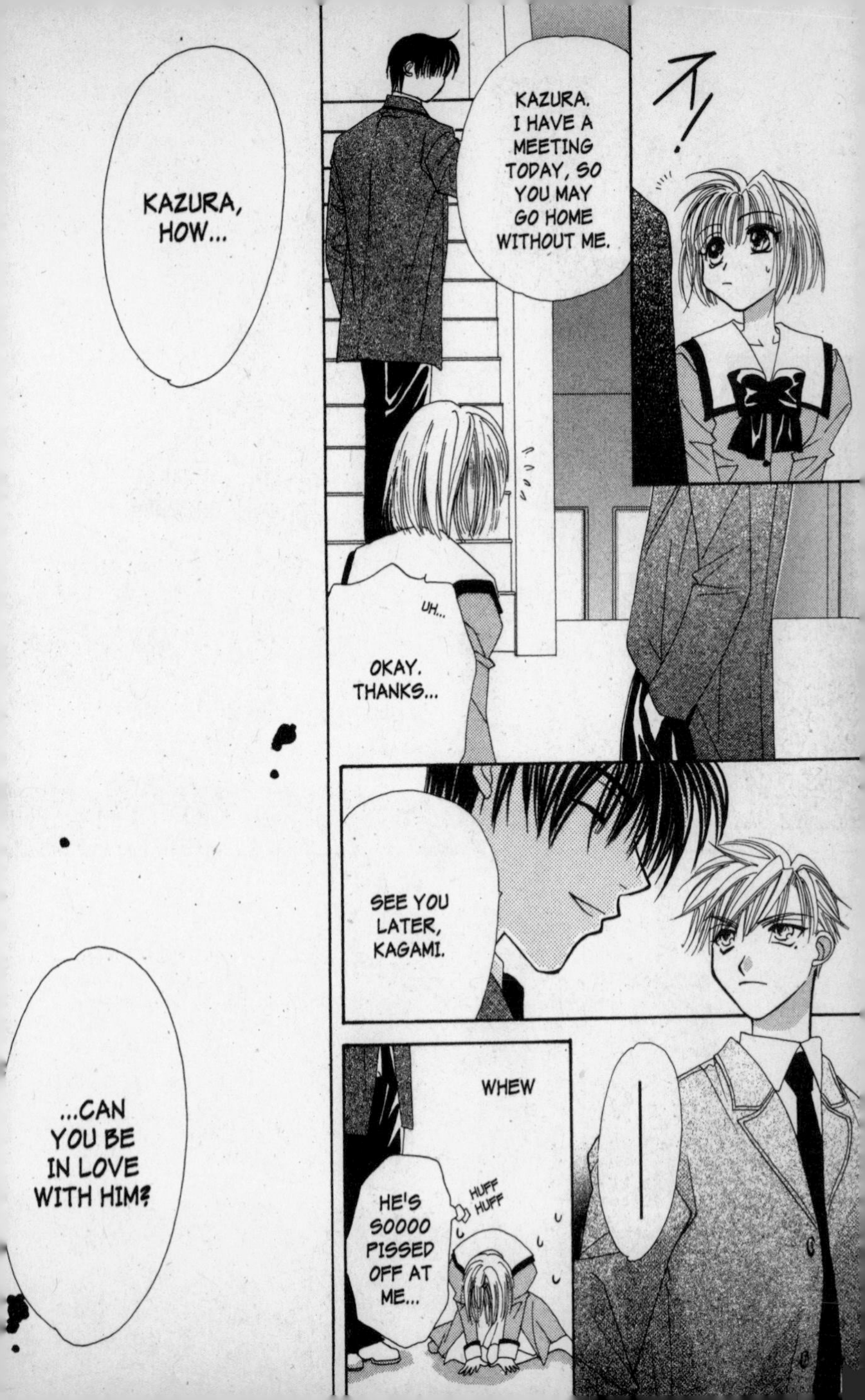
KAZURA. I HAVE A MEETING TODAY, SO YOU MAY GO HOME WITHOUT ME.
UH...
OKAY. THANKS...
SEE YOU LATER, KAGAMI.
WHEW
HE'S SOOOO PISSED OFF AT ME...
HUFF HUFF
KAZURA, HOW...
...CAN YOU BE IN LOVE WITH HIM?

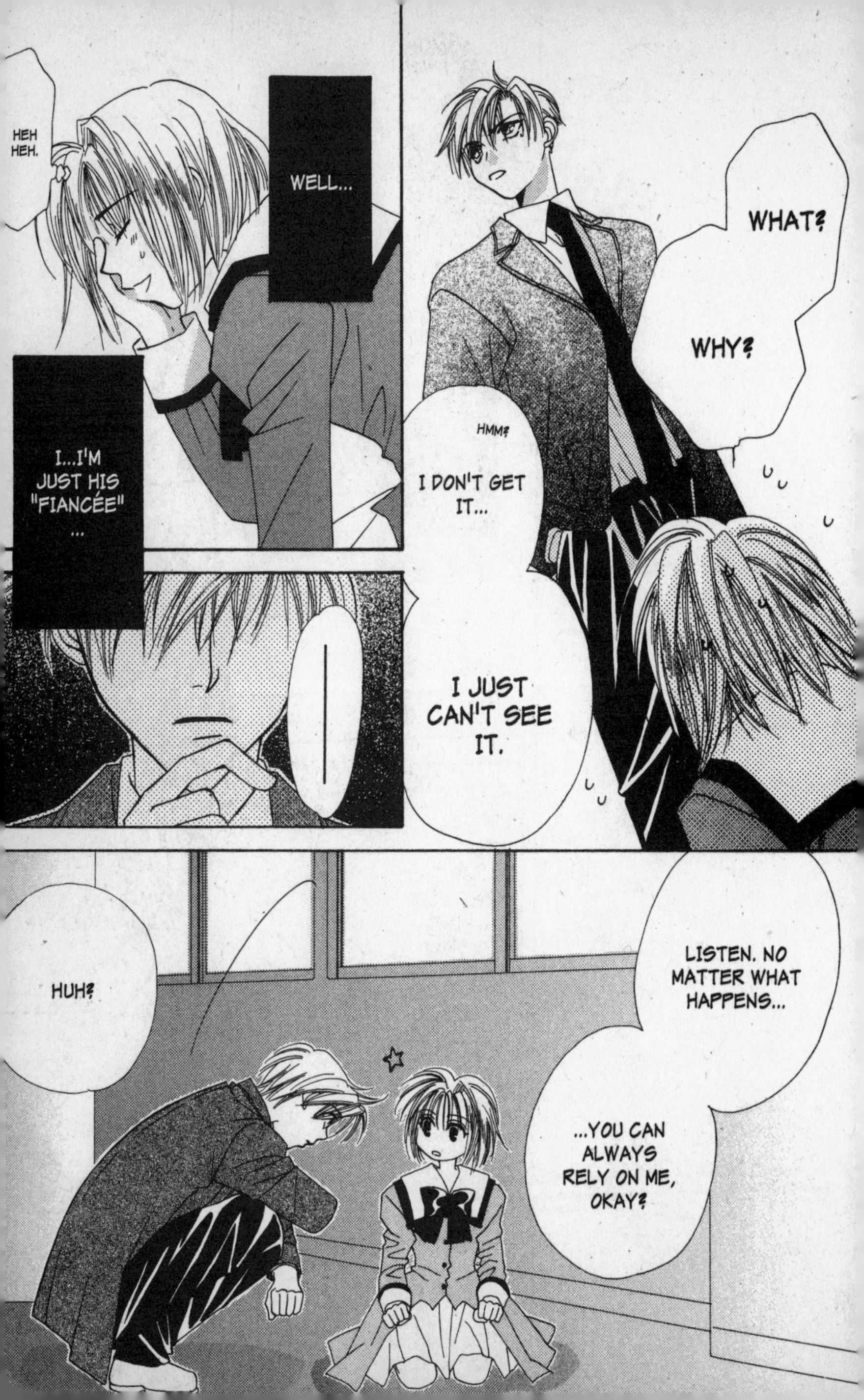
WHAT?
WHY?
HMM?
I DON'T GET IT...
I JUST CAN'T SEE IT.
WELL...
HEH HEH.
I...I'M JUST HIS "FIANCÉE" ...
LISTEN. NO MATTER WHAT HAPPENS...
...YOU CAN ALWAYS RELY ON ME, OKAY?
HUH?

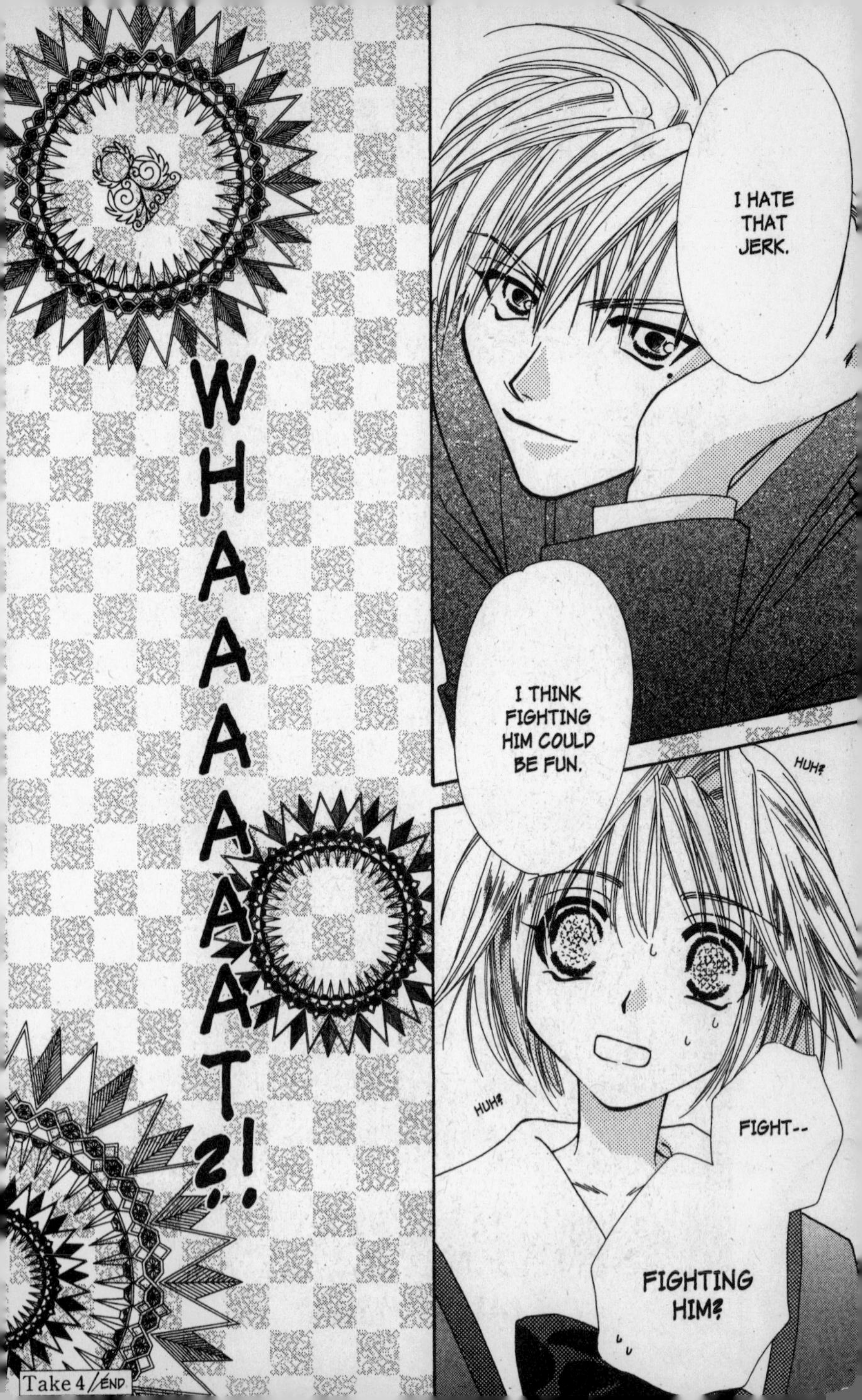
I HATE THAT JERK.
I THINK FIGHTING HIM COULD BE FUN.
HUH?
HUH?
FIGHT--
FIGHTING HIM?
WHAAAAAAAT?!
Take 4 / END

PLATINUM *garden*

COMING SOON!

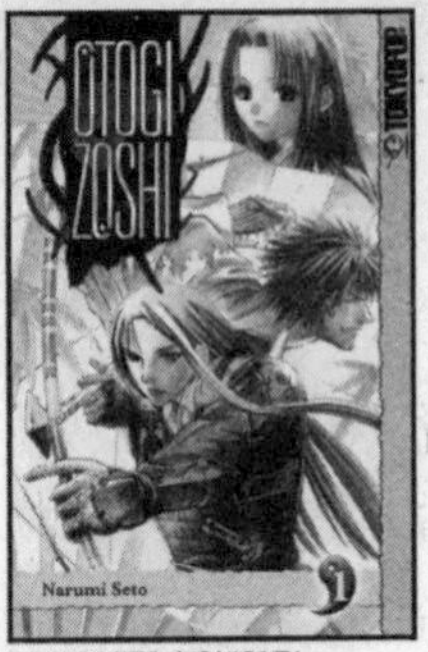
OTOGI ZOSHI
TOKYOPOP
Narumi Seto
1

OTOGI ZOSHI

BY NARUMI SETO

An all-out samurai battle to retrieve the Magatama, the legendary gem that is said to hold the power to save the world!

ACTION

T TEEN AGE 13+

Hot new prequel to the hit anime!

STRAWBERRY MARSHMALLOW

BY BARASUI

Cute girls do cute things...in *very* cute ways.

A sweet slice of delight that launched the delicious anime series!

COMEDY

T TEEN AGE 13+

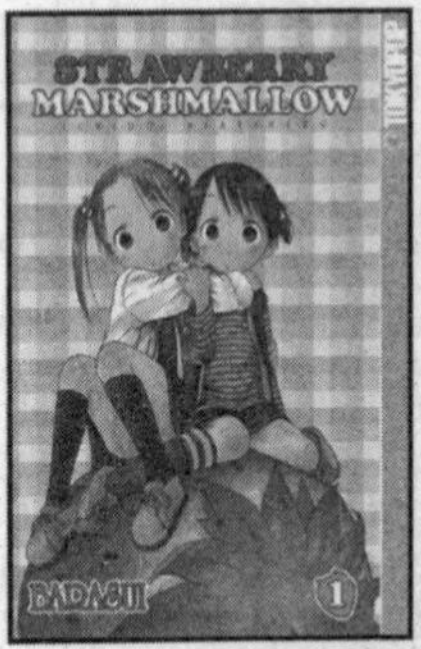
STRAWBERRY MARSHMALLOW
BARASUI
1

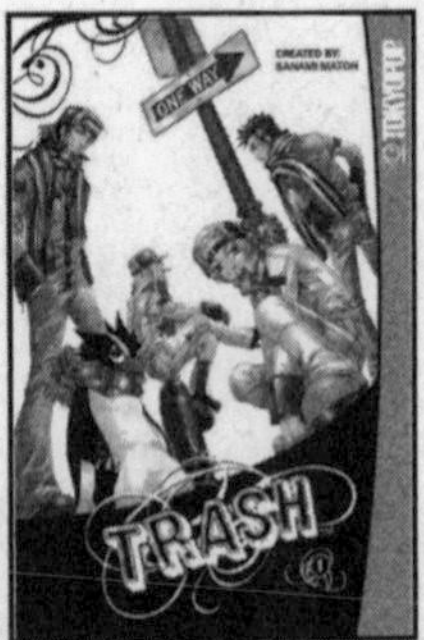
CREATED BY: SANAMI MATOH
ONE WAY
TOKYOPOP
TRASH

TRASH

BY SANAMI MATOH

When your uncle is the biggest mob boss in New York, it's hard to stay out of the family business!

COMEDY

OT OLDER TEEN AGE 16+

From the creator of the fan-favorite *Fake!*

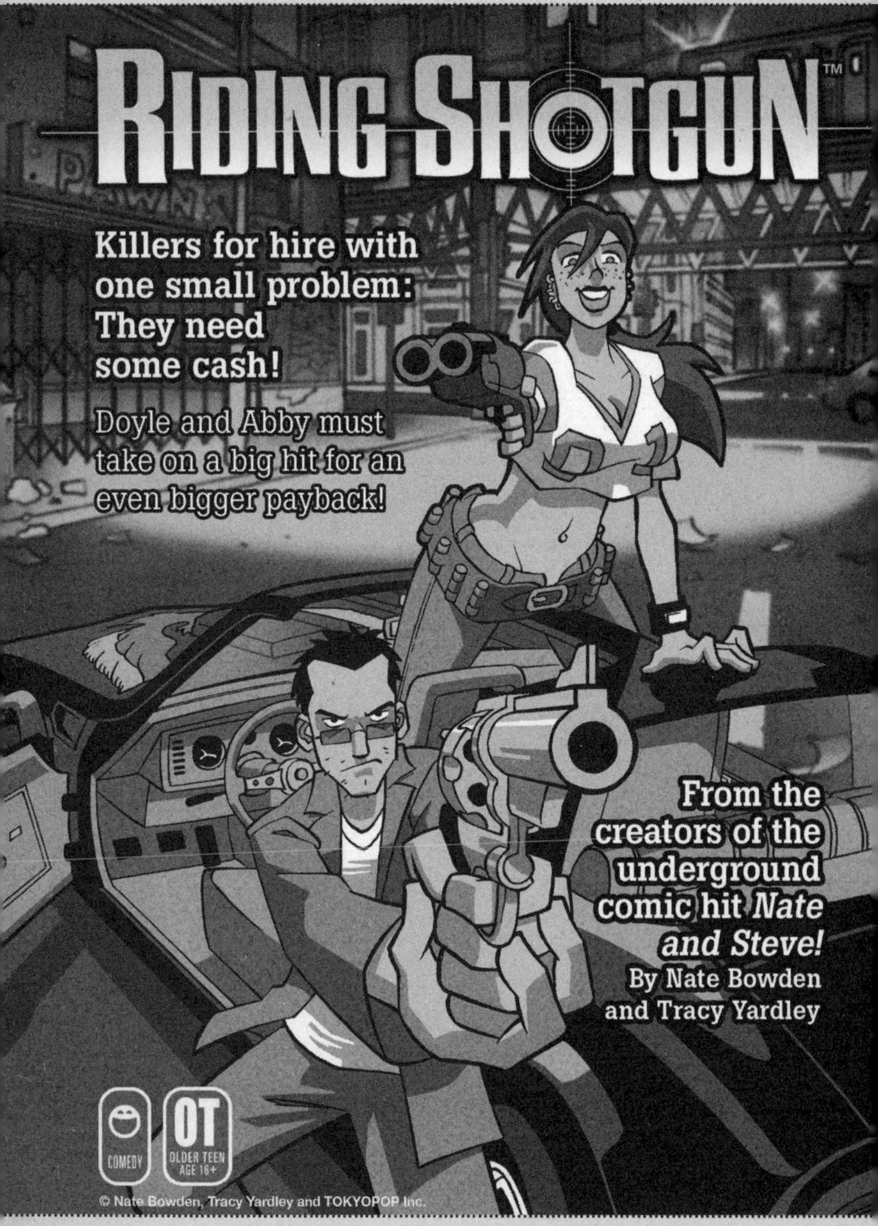
RIDING SHOTGUN™
Killers for hire with one small problem: They need some cash!
Doyle and Abby must take on a big hit for an even bigger payback!
From the creators of the underground comic hit *Nate and Steve!*
By Nate Bowden and Tracy Yardley
COMEDY
OT
OLDER TEEN AGE 16+
© Nate Bowden, Tracy Yardley and TOKYOPOP Inc.

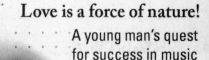

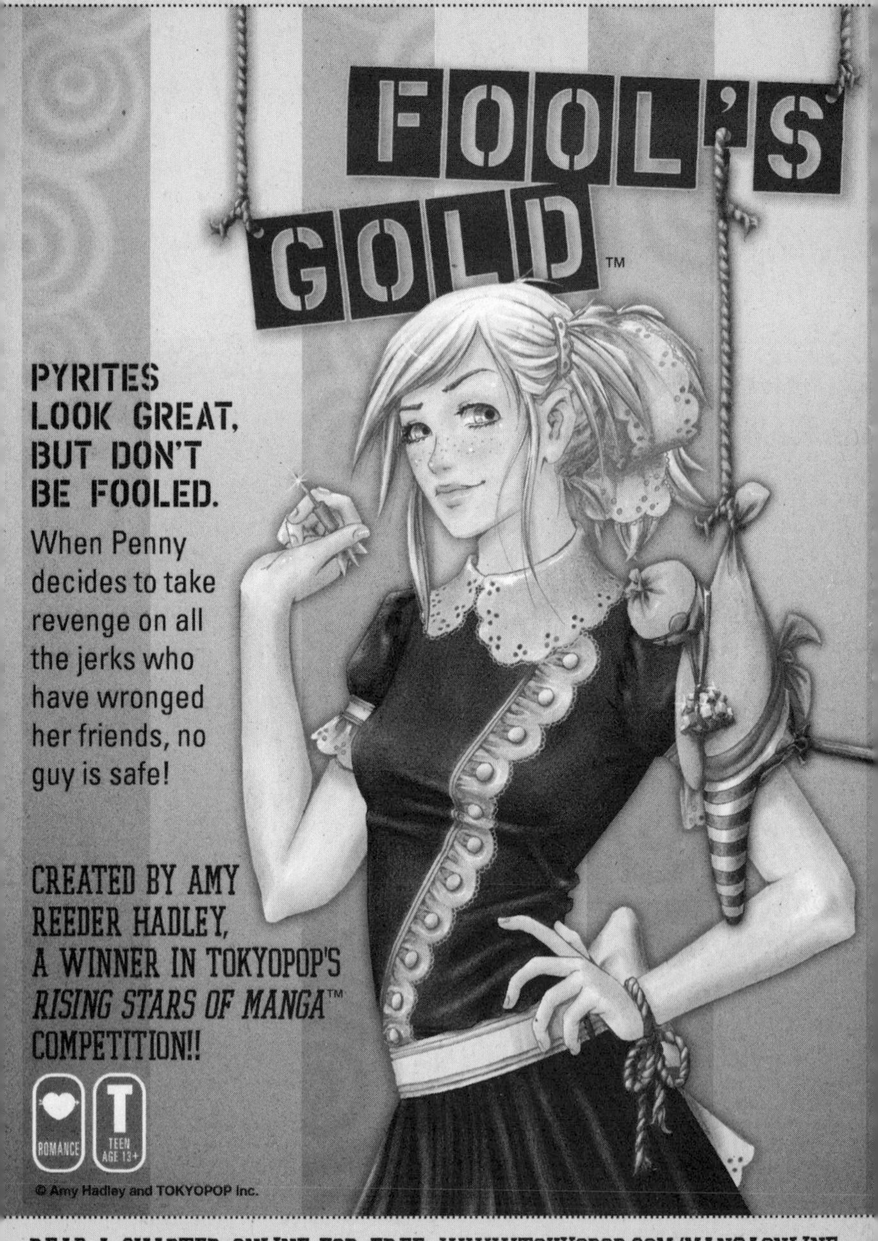
FOOL'S GOLD™
PYRITES LOOK GREAT, BUT DON'T BE FOOLED.
When Penny decides to take revenge on all the jerks who have wronged her friends, no guy is safe!
CREATED BY AMY REEDER HADLEY, A WINNER IN TOKYOPOP'S RISING STARS OF MANGA™ COMPETITION!!
ROMANCE
T
TEEN AGE 13+
© Amy Hadley and TOKYOPOP Inc.

TOKYOPOP SHOP

TOKYOPOP MANGA SUPPLEMENT

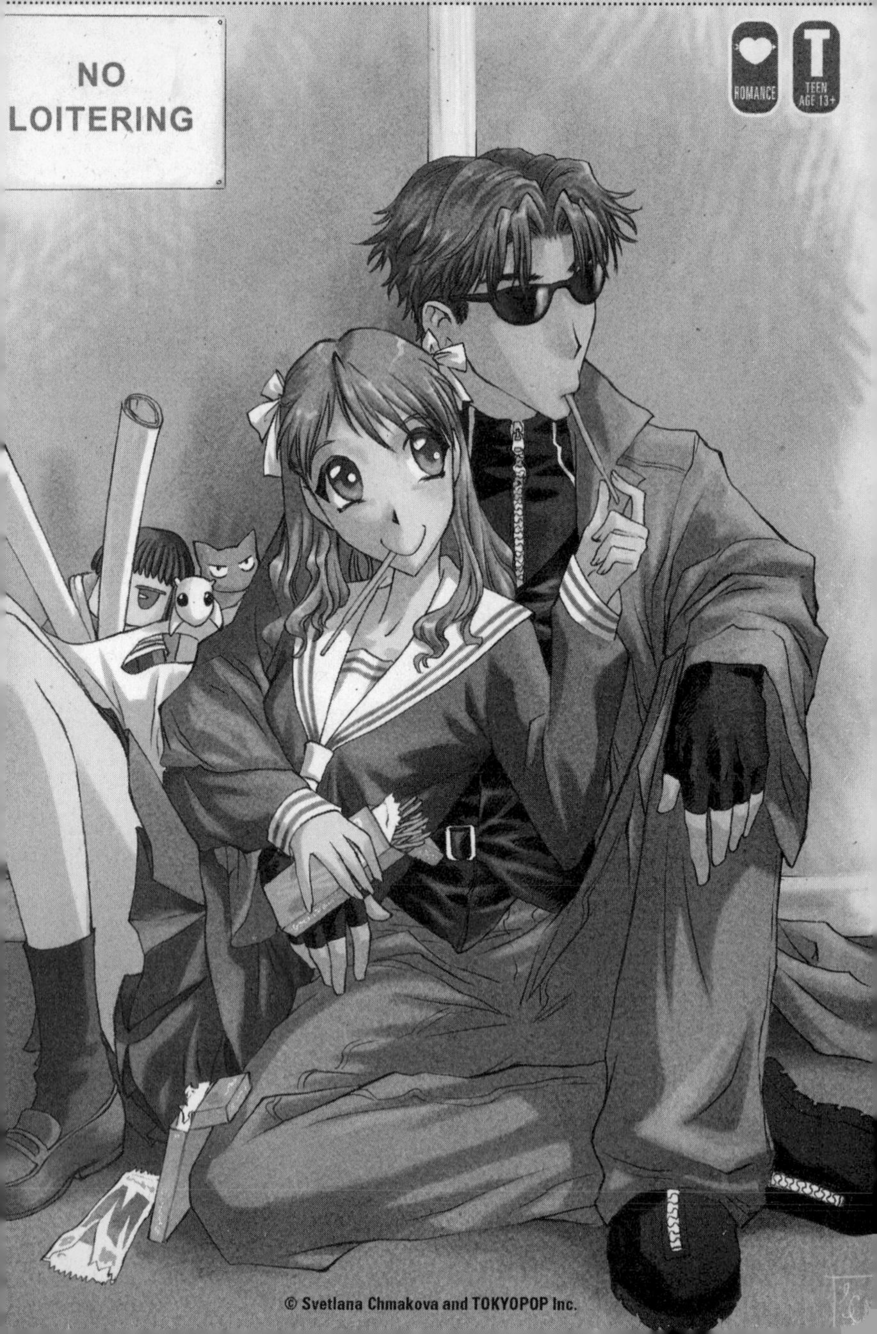
NO LOITERING
ROMANCE
T
TEEN AGE 13+

DRAMACON™

Sometimes even two's a crowd.

When Christie settles in the Artist Alley of her first-ever anime convention, she only sees it as an opportunity to promote the comic she has started with her boyfriend. But conventions are never what you expect, and soon a whirlwind of events sweeps Christie off her feet and changes her life. Who is the mysterious cosplayer who won't even take off his sunglasses indoors? What do you do when you fall in love with a guy who is going to be miles away from you in just a couple of days?

CREATED BY SVETLANA CHMAKOVA!

"YOU CAN'T AVOID FALLING UNDER ITS CHARM." -IGN.COM

READ AN ENTIRE CHAPTER ONLINE FOR FREE:
WWW.TOKYOPOP.COM/MANGAONLINE

STOP!

This is the back of the book.
You wouldn't want to spoil a great ending!

This book is printed "manga-style," in the authentic Japanese right-to-left format. Since none of the artwork has been flipped or altered, readers get to experience the story just as the creator intended. You've been asking for it, so TOKYOPOP® delivered: authentic, hot-off-the-press, and far more fun!

DIRECTIONS

If this is your first time reading manga-style, here's a quick guide to help you understand how it works.

It's easy... just start in the top right panel and follow the numbers. Have fun, and look for more 100% authentic manga from TOKYOPOP®!